Teaching Individuals with Physical and Multiple Disabilities

June L. Bigge

with Patrick A. O'Donnell

Both, San Francisco State University

Charles E. Merrill Publishing Company
A Bell & Howell Company
Columbus   Toronto   London   Sydney

Dedication

**To the memory of DICK OUTLAND
whose personal and professional
caring for and commitment to
special education enriched the
lives of many children and adults.**

Published by
Charles E. Merrill Publishing Company
A Bell & Howell Company
Columbus, Ohio 43216

*This book was set in Helvetica and Dill.
The production editor was Jan Hall.
The cover was prepared by Will Chenoweth.*

International Standard Book Number: 0–675–08527–6

Library of Congress Catalog Number: 76–53231

6   7   8   9—82   81   80

Printed in the United States of America

FOREWORD

Ideals and commitments have been combined with knowledge and experience of professional educators in the development of this publication designed essentially for teachers of children with physical and profound handicaps. June Bigge and her associates have prepared material which should be helpful to all teachers, supervisors, and teacher educators who are concerned with the education of *all* children and who recognize the need to be accountable to disabled children and their families.

Of particular interest to all educators is the clearly illustrated process of task analysis, a process essential in the education of children whose physical, mental, or emotional makeup may interfere in usual orderly development. Task analysis as an exercise or skill is not enough for the competent teacher. Thus, the authors have provided an overview of physical and accompanying disabilities with which educators need acquaintance if they are to work closely with professional colleagues in developing and carrying out appropriate individualized educational plans for each child.

Technology and methodology are giving us immense instructional power, but without intimate acquaintance with numerous disabled children and adults, their use can result in added frustration and failure. It is because of this varied experience that Dr. Bigge has assured her audience of acquaintance with the broad-base curriculum content required by the various individuals who make up the student population. The reader will find content accompanied by activities and tasks which are important for the developing child.

For the profoundly disabled youngster, the content includes management techniques as well as enriched life experience to be engineered for the student's active participation. Apparent to the reader are the emphases on improving the quality of life of each individual and the obvious respect for each child as a learner. Particularly noteworthy is the information and guidance offered to the teacher of the dying child, the one whose school presence often engenders fear and depression for those who do not understand.

This publication is steeped in reality. It is consistent in its message that effective teachers require knowledge and skill in determing educational needs and in developing programs for their students as integrated individuals. It is comprehensive in providing multitudinous instructional options for teachers working with children with mild or profound disability—with children functioning at infant or secondary school levels, with children in regular school classes or in protective therapeutic settings. The selection of these options in content and approach, however, demands that teachers obtain information, use available resources, and carefully analyze the tasks to be learned as well as the vehicles through which this learning will be facilitated. This publication reflects respect for its readers' desire to learn more about their students and to increase their effectiveness as teachers.

In the early 1970s, the U.S. Office of Education sponsored three provocative national conferences on the education of children with crippling and other health impairments to determine needs and make recommendations for improving instruction. Dr. Bigge and her associates have responded to her colleagues. They have considered the broadening needs of the population in a changing society; they are attempting to increase the competencies of teachers and other instructional personnel; and they are facilitating leadership development in building awareness of the options available to us and our students. This publication is an instrument through which those with physical disabilities can better be accommodated within the time and place of our lives—the social frame in which we all live.

F. Connor

PREFACE

This book is designed for teachers, consultants, supervisors, and others who teach and develop curriculum for individuals with physical and multiple disabilities. The introduction, p. 1, explains the intent and scope of this book. While much of the information presented should be helpful to parents, physicians, and others whose responsibilities intersect with those of the classroom teacher, the ideas, strategies, and materials are also appropriate for classroom use. Both pre-service students as well as experienced teachers should find this book helpful.

These ideas, techniques and resources are the outcome of June Bigge's experience in the classroom and training other teachers. She was primarily responsible for selection of content and contributors, for committing the plan to paper, authoring or co-authoring many of the chapters and for managing the myriad of tasks and responsibilities which are prerequisite to publication.

Patrick O'Donnell assisted authors in the preparation of their materials and prepared information for promotion and dissemination of the book.

Listed in the contents are individuals who made a major commitment to the book by contributing sections or entire chapters. Each spent numerous hours contributing their expertise in developing chapter design and content in accordance with the book's overall plan.

Contributing photographers are listed on the photograph credit page. Of particular assistance was Marvin Silverman. Ned Grove contributed the medical art in Chapter 2.

Over fifty other individuals have contributed in some way. Many have critiqued our ideas and made suggestions based upon their experience working with individuals with disabilities. Their assistance has expanded and enriched the scope and content of the book. We are pleased to have this opportunity to express our most sincere gratitude.

Specifically, we would like to thank the following colleagues who contributed to particular chapters of the book: 1, Gerald Wallace, Dee Tyack; 3, Nancy Howard; 4, Georgia Lee Abel, Jon Eisenson, Barbara Franklin, Philip Hatlen, Richard Holm, Eileen Jackson, Nikki Miller, Susan Mouchka, Arthurlene Towner, Betty

Wallsten, Berdell Wurzburger; **5,** Beatrice Wright, Sue Knight, Carla Thornton; **6,** Christopher Cadden, Katherine Croke, Maurice LeBlanc, Shirley McNaughton, Mary Ellen Rodda; **7,** Victor Alter, Mariam Lowrey, Carol Lee Rich; **8,** Norris Haring, Mary Falvey; **9,** Mary Frances Strathairn; **10,** Gerald Wallace, Christina Kusaba; **11,** Winifred Baker, Dorothy Clazie, Penny Silva Musante, Herbert Zettl; **12,** Charles Kokaska; **13,** William L. E. Dussault.

Many of the ideas incorporated in this work emerged from our involvement with graduate students at San Francisco State University. Many of these students are now teaching physically disabled persons or are now teaching in preservice teacher-training programs at colleges and universities throughout the country. Those who contributed specific ideas used in different sections of the book are Susan Aumann, Bobbie Brooks, Joyce Naftel Buell, Anne Corn, Ann Dowdle, Helen Manson, Ann Metlay, Peter Paulay, Sandra Rafferty, Mary Ellen Rodda, Linda Joseph Roessing, Barbara Sapienza, William Sciallo, Ruth Lee-Simon, Karen Wilbur, Dorothy Acton Williams, and Aileen Yacoub.

Students, staff, and administrators of these schools in California cooperated in arranging for photographs:

El Portal del Norte School, El Portal del Sol School, La Esperanza Development Center North, Crestmoor High School Program—San Mateo County Schools, San Mateo

Crestmoor High School—San Mateo Union High School District, San Mateo

Marindale School—Marin County Schools, San Rafael

Christina B. Cameron School—Richmond Unified School District, El Cerrito

Chandler Tripp School—Santa Clara County Schools, San Jose

Sleepy Hollow School—Orinda Unified School District, Orinda

The following individuals, although not in the above school programs, allowed us to photograph elements of their daily lives: Deborah, Charles, and Aimee Anderson; Christopher Cadden, Bonnie Cameron, Gary Heimeyer, Beverly Humphreys, Kim Kilburg, Norman Mach, and David Stoker.

Other individuals and organizations who made arrangements for special photographs are: Lawrence H. Weiss, ZYGO Industries, Inc., Portland, Oregon; John Crandall, COMM-AIDS, San Jose, California; Al and Marie Thiems, AMIGO, Inc., Bridgeport, Michigan; San Francisco Goodwill Industries; Hope Rehabilitation Services, San Jose, California; Spina Bifida Association of the East Bay.

The arduous task of completing the manuscript was made easier with the assistance of public school teacher Penny Silva Musante and university professor Barbara Sirvis, who provided consultation and technical assistance; research assistants who were helpful in tracking down materials and references for the manuscripts and in editing page proofs: Arlene Barbarotta, Mary Ellen Devine, Linda Warner, Denise Flaherty, Victoria Greenbach and Cheryl Hodgson; typists Colette Bailey, Glenda Deitch, Susan Johnston, and Joyce Jones; an administrative editor of the Merrill College Division, Tom Hutchinson, whose initial encouragement and continued support provided incentive for completion of this book; production editor, Jan Hall, who was largely responsible for helping us prepare the manuscript for publication; reviewers who were extremely helpful in reaction to early versions or portions of the manuscript: Knute Espeseth, Maria Bove, Gerald Wallace, Norris Haring, Beatrice Wright, Katherine Croke.

Finally, combined influence of the following individuals provided the point of view and experiences necessary for developing this book:

Ruth McKinnis Newman, who introduced a junior high school volunteer, June Bigge, to the excitement and challenge of working with children with disabilities.

Dr. Morris Bigge and *Ada June Bigge,* who supported this special interest by helping their daughter explore different specialties within the field of education, providing the opportunity to receive training, exchanging points of view on teaching and learning, editing sections of the manuscript, and sharing in many other ways.

Dr. Mabel Brenn Whitehead, a pioneer in the preparation of teachers of children with orthopedic handicaps, who helped us find ways to better teach children with physical disabilities.

Dr. Barbara Bateman, a forerunner in the advocacy of task analysis whose writing and courses influenced the task analysis focus of this book.

Professionals, parents, disabled persons, and others who have shared ideas that now contribute to the education and rehabilitation of individuals with physical disabilities.

We sincerely thank all who helped in this endeavor.

J. L. B.
P. A. O.

PHOTOGRAPH ACKNOWLEDGMENTS

Marvin L. Silverman: 40, 43, 52, 53, 58, 72, 89, 109, 112, 117, 118, 119, 120, 124, 125, 126, 129, 130, 131 top, 133, 141, 142, 143, 144, 148, 150, 155, 156, 162, 182 top and bottom, 183, 204, 211, 212, 230, 253, 255, 256, 264, 269.

Penny Silva Musante: 3, 4, 54, 144, 152, 157, 158 top, 221, 235, 250, 254.

John Stripeika: 15, 16, 151, 214, 253 bottom.

Jim Quarles: 133.

Don Schuman: 158 bottom.

J. Mark Rainez: 43 top and bottom, 154 left.

Steve Allen: 134.

American Printing House for the Blind, Louisville, Kentucky: 206.

Christina B. Cameron School, El Cerrito, California, La Esperanza Development Center Central, San Mateo, California: 208.

CONTENTS

Introduction

Whatever their potential for participating in the society in which they find themselves, we want to help children learn those skills and adaptive behaviors needed for self-sufficiency. Some of these children have physical disabilities which result from conditions such as Legg Perthes, cerebral palsy, muscular dystrophy, and spinal cord injury. The physical disabilities vary in the degree to which they affect each individual: children with Legg Perthes disease may be only temporarily inconvenienced, while some children with cerebral palsy may never be able to speak, walk, *or* use their hands. Some physically disabled children may have learning problems not unlike those experienced by some of their nonphysically disabled peers. Some may require program modifications to compensate for problems directly related to their physical limitations. This book is designed to guide readers in their efforts to help children and adults who have physical disabilities.

The variety of individuals helping children or young adults with physical disabilities may include any combination of the following: special education teachers, regular classroom teachers, parents, parent surrogates, relatives, medical doctors, therapists, child development center workers, hospital staff, preschool workers, psychologists, social workers, vocational counselors, and disabled persons themselves. While we refer to teachers, we are, in fact, providing direction, information, and suggestions for all persons who are responsible for the education and development of disabled children.

From the spectrum of ideas which could be suggested, we have selected those we consider to be fundamental and most crucial for persons with physical disabilities. We encourage readers to be selective in the use of material from this book, using what is appropriate for particular disabled individuals. Where material is not appropriate, we hope readers will use the final sections of each chapter, "References" and "Resources," as sources for additional assistance. Finally, we hope the ideas in this book will stimulate new and better ways for helping individual children.

Task analysis provides the basic framework for this book. The choice of content for most chapters and chapter components were derived as a result of the authors' use of the task analysis process. The chapters of this book divide content areas into tasks and subtasks that seem most relevant.

Content chapters focus on those activities and tasks which we assumed to be essential goals and objectives for disabled individuals. For purposes of organization, these activities and skills are described under chapter headings. The first chapter teaches several ways task analysis is used to help children. The next chapters provide background information and practical suggestions for teaching the physically disabled: conditions causing physical disability, motor development and deviations, other disabilities which may cause learning problems, severe communication problems, and psychological implications of physical disability. Chapters suggest goals and objectives which are crucial for children with physical disabilities. We conclude with guidelines for self-care, life experience programming, leisure use, working, and advocacy.

Chapter One teaches the process of task analysis. Data gathered through this process can be used to formulate and pursue instructional objectives. Task analysis used in this manner involves an inventory and analysis of each child's functioning. A brief explanation of methods for writing instructional objectives is provided. Sample analyses of cognitive, language, motor, self-help and other tasks are included. The use of task analysis enables professional and auxiliary personnel, and when possible, disabled individuals, to cooperate in assessing, planning, implementing, and evaluating instruction for individuals with physical disabilities.

Chapter Two provides an introduction to medical conditions which result in various physical disabilities. Dr. Grove provides that information which is most needed by classroom teachers. The content of the chapter is presented in a way that classroom teachers, both in special education and in regular classes, can develop sufficient general background to enable them to understand the various physical conditions. Etiology, treatment, and characteristics including the resulting functional problems, such as incoordination, weakness, and paralyses are described. References are included for those who wish to study the conditions in more depth.

In *Chapter Three* Kraemer and Bigge discuss general trends in motor development. Deviations, treatment, and training methods are described. The emphasis is upon suggesting ways teachers and therapists can help children build and maintain more normal postures and movement.

Chapter Four provides information needed to help those individuals who exhibit other disorders in addition to their predominant orthopedic or neurological disability. In addition to a physical disability usually resulting in some crippling condition, such individuals may exhibit hearing or vision acuity problems, combinations of these disorders, language and speech disabilities, or convulsive disorders. This chapter represents an attempt to suggest considerations and ideas for teaching individuals who have these accompanying disabilities.

Chapter Five includes discussion of the many varieties of psychosocial manifestations which often accompany physical disability. Information in this chapter will promote greater understanding of complex psychosocial variables and of ways to facilitate social and emotional development. The information should help teachers provide the climate and environment where physically handicapped individuals can become mature, independent, self-actualizing individuals. Other important areas of concern, such as death, dying, and family life education are also discussed in this chapter.

In *Chapter Six* there is an explanation of methods for teaching disabled individuals who, because of their disability, can neither talk nor write in order to be understood. Presented in detail are the needs of these individuals with severe communication problems and the many ways that communication between the disabled and nondisabled can be developed. Directions are included for teaching the basic fundamentals of communication, including knowing when and how to communicate concepts such as *yes/no*. A variety of alternatives are suggested for *yes/no* signals and other communication signs. Teachers are taught ways to involve nonvocal individuals in conversations so that their communications are not limited in content because of their inability to speak or write. The improvement of academic learning through more effective communication methods is explained and illustrated. Teachers are taught how to promote increase in amounts of student independence in doing school work by making adaptations in materials and processes for students who do not talk or write. Finally, teachers are introduced to samples of the various electronic communication devices.

In *Chapter Seven,* techniques and methods are presented which enable physically disabled individuals to function with maximum independence at home and in the community. Skills for self-care are explained in detail. Included in this chapter are ways that disabled individuals can be taught to increase their independence in eating, dressing, toileting, and managing a home. Stress is placed upon teaching those skills which will enable the person to live with some degree of independence, dignity, and satisfaction.

In *Chapter Eight,* Bradfield and Heifetz discuss diagnostic and assessment procedures for severely and profoundly handicapped individuals. A variety of training methods and procedures are explained in detail. Developmental "pinpoints," which provide the basis of a curriculum for the severely and profoundly handicapped, are discussed in the chapter.

In *Chapter Nine,* Howard and Bigge review research which indicates substantial failure of physically disabled individuals to adjust to various dimensions of their life situation. They outline some necessary components of an adequate program for teaching living skills to the physically handicapped. They describe how teachers can establish a "Life Experience Program." Sample lesson plans and listings of functional skills which will enable teachers to plan more carefully for instruction in this area are included.

In *Chapter Ten,* Compton and Bigge provide a brief description of common academic problems experienced by some physically disabled individuals. Suggestions for special instruction in reading, spelling, handwriting, and thinking skills are included. While this chapter does not present

a comprehensive approach to instruction in all academic areas, many of the basic principles and strategies can be applied appropriately in areas not discussed. In the sections on reading, spelling, and thinking, specific suggestions are given for those who cannot speak or write.

Chapter Eleven provides a brief discussion of the importance to physically disabled individuals of leisure-time activities. Included are examples of activities which can be introduced in school and continued after graduation. While the activities included do not exhaust the many possibilities for wise use of leisure time, they should indicate the *kinds* of activities which can be enjoyed both during the school years and in later life.

In *Chapter Twelve,* procedures for helping students prepare for present and future work activities are described. The authors stress the importance of certain skills and adaptive behaviors which contribute to successful accomplishment of any of a spectrum of work activities. Skills needed for accomplishment of daily chores, leisure activities, and paid jobs are included. Paramount among these skills and adaptive behaviors is the ability of the individual to compare personal skills and attitudes with those needed for different kinds of work activities. Also recognized is the fact that some severely involved persons may never work; suggestions are made for such persons.

Finally, *Chapter Thirteen* provides a delineation of ways that teachers and others can act to improve conditions for the physically and multiply handicapped. Suggestions for action involve problems such as architectural barriers, housing,

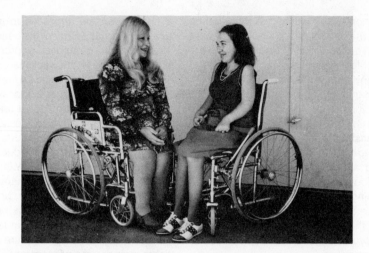

and transportation. When possible, suggestions are accompanied by addresses to which advocates may direct correspondence.

Summary

Since there is so much variance in the needs of individuals who have physical disabilities, there is no attempt in this book to group specific suggestions for use with groups of disabled persons in certain age ranges, for persons with similar mental capacities, or for persons with the same medical diagnosis. Rather, we have attempted to suggest tasks from which priorities might be chosen for children with physical disabilities. The following chapters will suggest processes for teaching these corresponding subtasks on a continuum from basic to complex. Whenever appropriate, suggestions for adaptations to accommodate specific disabilities are described.

We do attempt to stress the need for teaching activities which are most *functional* for each individual, considering the nature and severity of the disability, the age of the person, and the educational needs. Emphasis is upon functional problems regardless of their causes.

In many ways, the focus of this book is upon providing an individualized instructional program for each disabled person. In a sense, we do not suggest teaching "the physically and multiply disabled," even though we use this phrase because of its brevity. Rather, we suggest "teaching the individual who has a physical disability and perhaps one or more accompanying disabilities." Task, or component analysis, can influence decisions about what to teach—what should be selected from the seemingly infinite realm of what can be taught. If some individuals with disabilities are not able to learn as much as others, what kinds of things are most important for them to learn? Many disabled students can accomplish what is suggested in the book and *much more*. Whenever it becomes obvious that a child will be limited in ability to learn, teachers should identify and teach those skills and concepts which will be most functional in helping that child become as physically and mentally self-sufficient as possible.

Teachers should double their efforts to devise options to *maximally increase* the *amount* of learning and the *pace* of learning of each disabled individual with particular attention to those children who cannot talk intelligibly or cannot use their hands to do customary learning and practice activities. For all children with physical disabilities, we encourage individualized planning with the goal of implementing the overall program which best suits the unique needs and maximum abilities of each child.

TASK ANALYSIS

Teaching strategies with disabled children and adults reflect differences in basic theoretical assumptions about the influence of their disabilities, the nature of the learning process, and choice of teaching methods. Task analysis is a tool which can be used with the different theoretical approaches.

Task analysis is a process to guide your decisions about (a) what to teach next, (b) where students have difficulties when attempting but not completing tasks, (c) what steps are probably necessary to accomplish an entire task, (d) how adaptions can aid task accomplishments, and (e) what are some options for disabled persons for whom accomplishment of a particular task is not a feasible goal.

Within this framework, you assume that the reason a disabled person or any other person cannot accomplish a particular task is because of his inability to accomplish one or more sub-

parts of the task. Every task, simple or complex, can be broken down into as many components and subcomponents as necessary. In most cases, essential subskills can be identified and taught, thus allowing completion of larger tasks or problems. For some persons accomplishment of subskills must be adapted; for others, accomplishment is impossible and substitute goals need to be identified. In this chapter, we will briefly describe task analysis and teach its use through examples. Because most readers will want to relate the process of task analysis to the progress pupils make, we will provide a "mini course" on goals and objectives with emphasis upon evaluation. Finally, a sample case study will demonstrate one way to formulate, use, and evaluate objectives based upon the results of task analysis.

Potential Outcomes

If you can learn to isolate components of tasks you can complete the process of task analysis.

June Bigge, *Ed. D., is a professor of special education at San Francisco State University in San Francisco, California.*

Task parts need not always be written; they may be present only in your thinking. Most people use the skill to some degree without naming it as such.

Task analysis enables teachers to gather baseline data and keep records of student progress. It allows comparisons of accomplishments over periods of time. It enables decisions regarding acceptability of responses or performances as stated as *criteria* in instructional objectives and goals.

Teachers are often unsure of what students can do and what they know. Too often, we unknowingly cause students to repeat performances or learn materials which have already been learned. Needless to say, each unnecessary repetition wastes time and delays new learning. With task analysis, teachers can avoid establishing goals for already accomplished learning.

Task analysis also helps teachers analyze teaching-learning interactions. For example, you should determine if each lesson featured materials presented auditorily, visually or both. How much and what kinds of verbalizations were used? At what rate of speed were ideas or materials presented? How can a learner participate in problem solving using task analysis? What needed motor movements can a person voluntarily make? Did the child learn a particular kind of task faster when he was watching or listening? What other characteristics of the teaching-learning interaction seem to make a difference to this learner in this type of task?

Information provided by task analyses can be used to assist decision making about future goals (broad statements of general intent) and objectives (specific performances stated in measurable terms). *Immediate or short-term goals and objectives* may be derived from information about an individual's performance in relation to what can be learned in a few minutes, hours, or days. Choice of immediate objectives often depends upon information gained from task analysis. Following a task analysis, teachers of physically disabled children may need to make one or more of the following decisions:

1. Determine the next task.
2. Divide task into component parts.
3. Devise an alternative to the usual manner of performing the task.
4. Use special equipment or materials to facilitate task performance.
5. Select a different task for accomplishment.

Immediate goals and objectives become plans for immediate action. Often, they are part of more long-range goals and objectives. *Long-range goals and objectives* may be conceptualized as those skills most needed after an extended period of time: 6 weeks, 1 year, 4 years. According to Thompson and Altman, "The distinctive difference between a long range goal and a long range objective is the degree of specificity. . . . The area of concern (math, reading, physical skills, etc.) is the same but you will include more information in the long term objective, such as the present and expected level of performance" (1975, p. 1).

Long-range goals and objectives frequently evolve from the consolidation of information about present functioning of disabled individuals. They also are derived from information-supported hypotheses about which skills will be most needed in the future. *Categories of long-term goals and objectives may correspond with chapter headings in this book.* Content and subheadings of most chapters suggest goals and objectives for individuals with disabilities.

The Process

Process of Task Analysis

In task analysis you focus on subskills or components of defined tasks. Analyze tasks to be attempted and note which parts of the target task were demonstrated successfully by individuals and which were not. If all parts are demonstrated, the next step would be listing components of a future task one might attempt (see Figure 1-1).

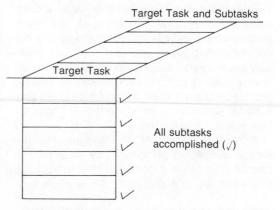

Target Task and Subtasks

Target Task

All subtasks accomplished (√)

Figure 1-1. Student attempts and completes all subtasks, resulting in determination of next target task and its subtasks.

If all components or parts of the original task were not demonstrated, those components not accomplished would be listed and targeted for future learning (see Figure 1–2).

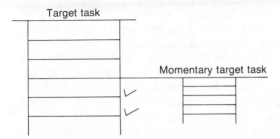

Target task

Momentary target task

Figure 1–2. Student attempts and does not complete all subtasks, so each unaccomplished subtask becomes the momentary target task having its own subtasks.

For those tasks not yet attempted, specify what the person needs to do in order to complete the entire task, noting each necessary step (see Figure 1–3).

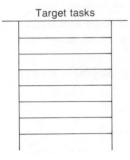

Target tasks

Figure 1–3. Summary of what a student must be able to do to accomplish an entire target task.

Decisions about which tasks are specified as target tasks are often arbitrary. Everything we learn to do is interrelated. It is likely that different persons will decide to start teaching at different points. As stated previously, problems can be divided into many components. Review these questions as you analyze a task:

1. What task or tasks should be learned next?
2. What parts of the target task are accomplished?

3. What parts of the target task are not accomplished?
4. What are all the probable steps necessary in order for a person to be able to accomplish the task of _____?
5. How should tasks be changed to accommodate persons with disabilities?
6. Under what conditions and to what degree are tasks accomplished?

Sample Uses

Ways of conducting and recording task analysis depend upon individual teachers and individual children. In this section we will demonstrate a few sample uses of task analysis, such as:

finding what comes next
defining results of unsuccessful trials
analyzing all components
screening performances
comparing skills of different persons
making guides for observations
studying recommended curriculum
teaching problem solving
analyzing tasks before teaching them
defining movements, or actions, for data collection
analyzing effects of disabilities
clarifying communication

Finding What Comes Next

Task analyses can be conducted after analyzing components of some published instruments. Standardized achievement tests, published diagnostic tests, and developmental scales are some examples of such instruments. These instruments may, when used in their entirety, yield information about student performances. Portions of them can also be used as guidelines for informal observations of children.

Standardized instruments and published diagnostic tests do not always pinpoint specific tasks an individual needs to learn or perform. Normative data do not always yield relevant information about the functioning of disabled individuals. Disability may affect the speed or sequence of a child's learning; therefore, normative data relating tasks to usual ages of development are not always useful. The manner and degree of the child's performances on specific items, however, provide the evaluator with information he can use for instruction. Descriptions of the usual sequences for performing different tasks can be very helpful if readers realize that some disabled individuals should not be forced to follow the sequence.

Lists of developmental milestones or pinpoints, with and without normative data, are helpful. They usually cover several areas of human development such as motor, language, and speech. A comprehensive list of developmental pinpoints is included in a reference in Chapter 8, "Education of the Severely and Profoundly Handicapped."

Defining Results of Unsuccessful Trials

Bigge (1970) provides a framework for observing, analyzing, and recording performances. Figure 1–4 shows a task analysis used by a classroom teacher as a tool to help Lisa, a first grade child with cerebral palsy. Lisa was able to function independently in school except that she was unable to open and close the classroom door. The teacher watched her as she tried to accomplish the task and then completed a task analysis based on the observation. Note in Figure 1–4 the precise definition of the task. Notice also the elimination of possible reasons why Lisa could not get through the door by noting what she *did* perform. Her teacher listed the components which were performed. What needs to be taught

is clearly indicated by the components that were not performed.

Analyzing All Components

One teacher helped a seven-year-old girl prepare to transfer from a special school to a regular school. The girl was incontinent (had no bladder control) because of *spina bifida*. The teacher and the girl knew the transition might be possible if the pupil could change her own diaper. Already the girl was able to close the door behind her, lower herself to the floor and propel herself to the cot carrying a diaper bag over one shoulder. A classroom attendant or parent had always completed the rest of the diaper-changing procedure. Now the child needed to learn to complete the task herself. The teacher first watched the classroom attendant complete the procedure. Next she and the child verbalized each step and worked out a routine to use. The following is a portion of the routine:

> Sit on a cot.
> Put crutches on floor.
> Take fresh diaper out of bag and place it on cot.
> Place bag near cot on floor.
> Raise legs to cot with hands.
> Turn and lie down with legs extended.
> Place diaper to left at level of buttocks.

Given the task of: *opening the classroom door and walking through it while using crutches*
the student *performed* these parts of the task:

1. walked to the door
2. stood in position to open door
3. released hand from crutch to reach for knob
4. reached door knob
5. grasped knob
6. turned knob
7. pulled door open
8. released door knob

but *did not perform* these parts of the task:

1. grasp the released crutch before the door closed
2. walk through the door
3. _____

Figure 1–4. Task analysis.

SOURCE. From *Systems of Precise Observations for Teachers* (printed guidelines, project S.P.O.T.) by June Bigge, 1970a, p. 20.

Roll to left.
Pull pants with elasticized waistband down.
Roll to right.
Pull other side down.
Lie on back.
Pull pants down further.
Unsnap used diaper.
Lower front of diaper.
Reach into bag for tissue.
Wipe self.
Place tissue between legs on soiled diaper.
Roll body to the left.
Pull diaper and plastic cover away with right hand.
Place on floor.
Lie on back.
Roll to right.
Pull fresh diaper and cover under buttocks with left hand.
Roll to left and straighten diaper, etc.

Screening Performances

In order to know where to begin instruction, it is helpful to find what a person already knows. This task can be accomplished quickly if you provide the child an opportunity to try at least one subskill which is representative of a group of subskills. Sometimes performance on a quick screening procedure or inventory provides a quick indication of learning needs or need for further screening.

Each arithmetic computation or operation (addition, multiplication, subtraction and division) has several different subskills. Looking at math computation from a task analysis viewpoint, one teacher selected representative problems and made an informal inventory (see Figure 1–5). Computations are divided into components or subskills based upon the four major operations. Within each operation are more finite components or subskills.

Addition

Simple facts

$$
\begin{array}{cccccc}
5 & 6 & 4 & 2 & 8 & 5 \\
+2 & +3 & +5 & +9 & +4 & +8
\end{array}
$$

$6 + 2 =$ $3 + 4 =$ $5 + 3 =$

Column addition

$$
\begin{array}{ccc}
4 & 3 & 7 \\
2 & 5 & 7 \\
+3 & 8 & 9 \\
 & +2 & +7
\end{array}
$$

No carrying

$$
\begin{array}{ccc}
24 & 50 & 47 \\
+43 & +2 & +300
\end{array}
$$

Carry from ones' place

$$
\begin{array}{ccc}
27 & 16 & 58 \\
+35 & +4 & +139
\end{array}
$$

Carrying from tens' place

$$
\begin{array}{ccc}
142 & 57 & 490 \\
+293 & +352 & +90
\end{array}
$$

Carrying from consecutive places

$$
\begin{array}{ccc}
273 & 316 & 4806 \\
+258 & +89 & +2998
\end{array}
$$

Carrying in alternate places

$$
\begin{array}{cc}
2582 & 87060 \\
+3908 & +38479
\end{array}
$$

Subtraction

Simple facts

$$
\begin{array}{ccc}
5 & 8 & 7 \\
-3 & -8 & -2
\end{array}
$$

$7 - 1 =$
$9 - 0 =$
$8 - 3 =$

No regrouping necessary

$$
\begin{array}{ccc}
47 & 89 & 302 \\
-26 & -40 & -102
\end{array}
$$

Regrouping in tens' and ones' places

$$
\begin{array}{cccc}
42 & 48 & 72 & 470 \\
-36 & -19 & -6 & -129
\end{array}
$$

Regrouping in hundreds' and tens' places

$$
\begin{array}{ccc}
473 & 500 & 7863 \\
-183 & -70 & -7793
\end{array}
$$

Figure 1–5. Locating operational difficulties with whole numbers.

Regrouping in consecutive places

526	800	9012
− 378	− 73	− 8236

Regrouping in alternate places

4238	60402
− 3919	− 15192

Multiplication

Simple facts

4	3	6	$9 \times 9 =$
×2	×3	×9	$4 \times 3 =$
			$5 \times 6 =$
			$7 \times 8 =$

No carrying

42	21	30
×2	×6	×3

Carrying from ones' to tens' place

46	58	209	705
×2	×3	×4	×7

Carrying from tens' to hundreds' place

150	371	3051
×5	×7	×9

Carrying in consecutive places

195	286	4857
×7	×9	×8

Carrying in alternate places

2519	6807
×3	×3

Multiplying by numbers ending in zero

43	267	487
×10	×50	×600

Multiplying by two- and three-place numbers

25	358	469
×12	×347	×408

Division—One-place Divisors

One-place divisors

2/8   6/54   4/24
$8 \div 1 =$ $9 \div 3 =$
$16 \div 8 =$ $6 \div 2 =$

Even division

3/96   2/180   4/2408

Uneven division—no remainders

4/72   3/174   5/3925

Uneven division—remainders

5/57   4/163   7/6934

Division—Two-place Divisors

Easy types

25/575   43/519   34/714

Complex types

92/3423   45/2393   56/8456

Estimation difficulties

37/15928   26/2376   18/13410

Zeroes in quotients

43/1720   97/4859   85/680439

Figure 1–5, cont.

SOURCE: Adapted in part from *The Diagnosis and Treatment of Learning Difficulties* by Leo John Brueckner and Guy L. Bond. New York: Appleton-Century-Crofts, 1955, pp. 274–275. Copyright 1955 by Prentice-Hall. Reprinted by permission.

Comparing Skills of Different Persons

Some teachers could use the Figure 1–6 format to find *patterns* in their students' skills. Weaknesses or errors can be tallied to provide a class profile, and those students with similar problems can be grouped for instruction.

Skills	Children's Names							Class Totals
	A	B	C	D	E	F	G	
1.								
2.								
3.								
4.								
5.								
6.								
7.								
8.								
9.								
10.								
11.								
12.								

Figure 1–6. Error analysis.

Making Guides for Observations

Observation keys can be used to direct attention toward certain elements to be observed. If the teacher provides space for check marks and a few descriptive words, these keys can simultaneously be used to describe present functioning. Observation keys can be dated and kept as descriptive data. (Refer to Figure 1–7, p. 12.)

Studying Recommended Curriculum

Some school districts and agencies publish curriculum guides with formats useful for task analysis. For instance, the Monterey County Office of Education has published a comprehensive curriculum for special education, *Roadmap to Effective Teaching* (1970). Figure 1–8 is a sample of this comprehensive curriculum book (p. 13).

Although mental ages are recorded after each task to indicate when most tasks are performed, they can be disregarded for disabled individuals including those over the age of 14. The right hand column can be designed to plot several successive trials of one child, can show a class profile, or show pre- and post tests on one or more children. In all cases, notation of the *date* of the trials is imperative.

Instructions for use of the previous chart suggest the coding system seen in Figure 1–9, p. 14. As each behavior is studied, it is described by use of this conventional code.

Teaching Problem Solving

A young woman whose disability resulted in paralysis of her legs (paraplegic) had a job offer. Since she had to provide her own transportation, her immediate goal became the task of getting herself and her wheelchair into and out of the car. The young woman considered specifications of cars. She bought a car with adequate clearance between the rear door and the front seat. She made sure the front door opened to at least a 60° angle, and that there was enough floor space behind the driver's seat for a wheelchair. She then

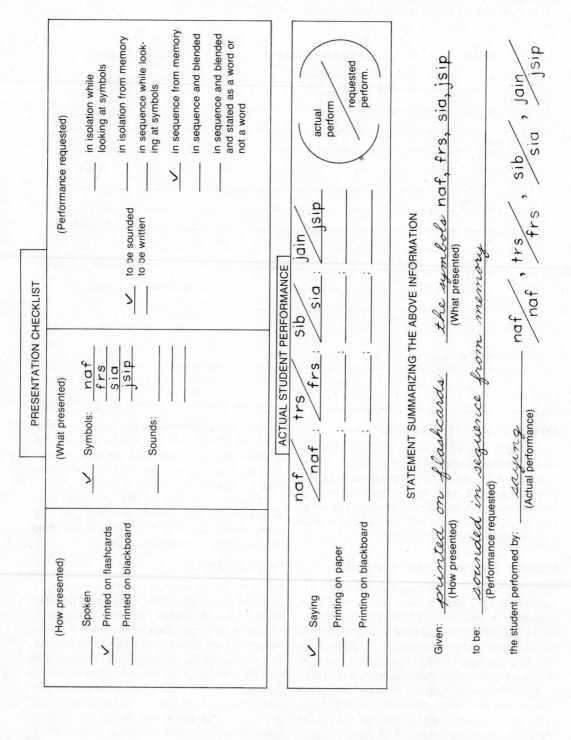

PRESENTATION CHECKLIST

(How presented)
— Spoken
✓ Printed on flashcards
— Printed on blackboard

(What presented)
✓ Symbols: naf frs sia jsip
— Sounds: ____

(Performance requested)
— in isolation while looking at symbols
— in isolation from memory
✓ to be sounded
— to be written
— in sequence while looking at symbols
✓ in sequence from memory
— in sequence and blended
— in sequence and blended and stated as a word or not a word

ACTUAL STUDENT PERFORMANCE

naf trs frs sib sia jain
naf ; frs ; sia ; jsip

actual perform / requested perform.

✓ Saying
— Printing on paper
— Printing on blackboard

STATEMENT SUMMARIZING THE ABOVE INFORMATION

Given: _printed on flashcards_ _the symbols naf, frs, sia, jsip_
(How presented) (What presented)

to be: _sounded in sequence from memory_
(Performance requested)

the student performed by: _saying_ naf , trs , sib , jain
(Actual performance)   frs , sia , jsip

12

Average Ages of Acquisition: Years–Months **Performance**

	Conversational	Date							
126	Acknowledges compliments/services with *thank you*. (4–0)								
127	Accompanies all requests with *please*. (4–0)								
128	Waits to be acknowledged before speaking. (4–0)								
129	Says *excuse me* when disruptive/to interrupt. (4–6)								
130	Pauses; allows other to speak. (6–0)								
131	Initiates or pursues appropriate conversation topics. (7–0)								
132	Politely concludes/accepts conclusion of conversation. (7–6)								
133	Makes introductions. (7–6)								
134	Models speech/tone after others in group. (8–0)								
135	Laughs at comments intended to be humorous. (8–6)								
136	Intentionally makes appropriately humorous remarks. (9–0)								
	Answering Telephone/Doorbell	Date							
137	Adjusts responses/actions to nature of call/caller. (7–6)								
	Personal Social Awareness	Date							
138	Refrains from unattractive actions in public. (5–6)								
139	Refrains from obvious staring/scrutiny of others. (6–0)								
140	Does not use a loud voice in public places. (6–0)								
141	Seeks privacy for grooming/toilet/clothing adjustments. (7–0)								
142	Maintains a posture which avoids immodest exposure. (8–0)								

Figure 1–7. Sample observation form for phonics and beginning reading.

SOURCE: From *Systems of Precise Observations for Teachers* (printed guidelines, project S.P.O.T.) by June Bigge, 1970a, p. 11.

Figure 1–8. Social emotional skills—social skills.

SOURCE: From *Roadmap to Effective Teaching* by the Monterey County Office of Education. Monterey, California: 1970a, Appendix, p. 9. Reprinted by permission.

Instructions to Accompany Figure 1–8

Following is a list of conventions used in marking this scale:

☒	Pupil performs successfully in a variety of situations when given free choice (5 out of 5 times).
☑ (diagonal)	Pupil may perform sporadically; practice needed to gain full success (3 out of 5 times).
⊟	Pupil does not perform; opportunity *has* been presented.
☐	Opportunity has not been presented; pupil may or may not perform task.

Figure 1–9. Marking system.

SOURCE: From *Roadmap to Effective Teaching* by the Monterey County Office of Education. Monterey, California: 1970a, p. 4. Reprinted by permission.

bought hand controls for the car. Then she had to devise a way to get herself and her wheelchair in and out without help from others. In her mind, she planned what tasks were necessary and how they could be negotiated. Once analyzed, the contemplated subtasks were "tried out." With some minor changes in her original plan, she found she could accomplish the following steps. (See pg. 15, left column.)

1. Take books out of book bag on chair.
2. Lock the wheelchair brakes.
3. Place left arm on car seat and right arm on the right wheelchair arm.
4. Push with arms to lift trunk and swing from wheelchair onto the bottom door frame.

But each time she collapsed the chair and tried to pull it into the car, the chair opened up again. After much experimentation and with the help of friends, she worked out a plan. They designed a clamp for the chair handles to prevent the reopening. Now she completed the task.

5. Collapse chair.
6. Push clamp down over second handle grip to keep the chair closed.
7. Turn the chair so the front wheels will go in first.
8. Pull front wheels over the bottom door frame and rest it there.
9. Use arms to lift body from door frame onto the car seat.
10. Use arms to lift legs inside car.

11. Slide to passenger side of car.
12. Push driver's seat back forward, reach over back of the driver's seat and pull chair into car behind driver's seat.
13. Slide back to driver's seat.
14. Fasten seat belt.
15. Drive using hand controls.

Analyzing Tasks Before Teaching Them

Teaching a 12 year old with muscular dystrophy to type is very complex. One teacher who was not very familiar with typing techniques had to analyze the steps for herself before she could teach the boy. Even though the boy was weak, he could be taught to do all the steps.

Defining Movements and Actions for Data Collection

Collection of performance data is often the purpose for conducting a task analysis. In Chapter 8 of this book, Bradfield and Heifetz define and illustrate *rate data, percent, duration, total length of activity* and *trials to criterion*.

Analyzing Effects of Disabilities

Page 17 lists several alternative ways for studying parts of a motor task and the influence of physical disability in attempting the task. The same techniques can be used to identify *all* probable important steps of a task. The techniques may help you anticipate points where assistance may be needed or where problems can be circumvented.

See steps 1–4 on p. 14.

See steps 5–15 on p. 14.

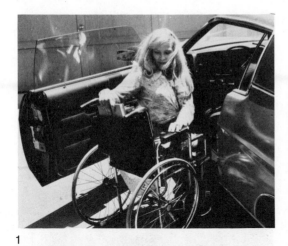

1

3

4

2

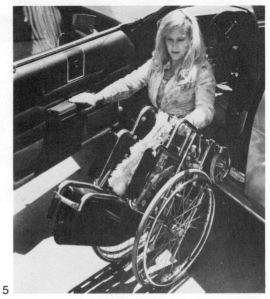

5

(cont.)

Continuation of steps 5–15, p. 14.

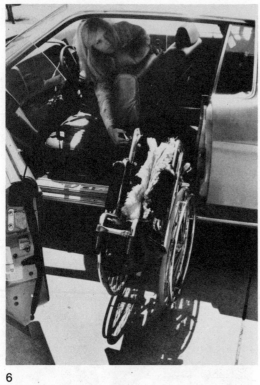

6

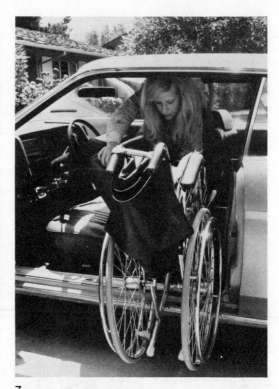

7

8

Critical Subtasks	**Supportive Prerequisites**
	Control volume
	Demonstrate understanding of concept *volume* or *loudness*
1. *Know how to operate recorder*	Differentiate difference in buttons: Demonstrate which button will make recorder play, which one will stop recorder, and which one will reverse the tape.
	Demonstrate understanding of concepts "stop," "play," and "reverse" or "rewind"
	Follow visual *or* oral instructions
2. *Keep arms out of way*	If necessary, secure arms to chair or body to prevent interference with stylus and prevent student from knocking over recorder.
3. *Sits in wheelchair & push buttons with stylus*	Maintain sitting balance in wheelchair
	Maintain head balance
	Move head horizontally to reach all buttons with head stylus
	Push with head to push buttons
	Extend head and release buttons
Assume use of head band & stylus. Outside assistance is needed in securing stylus on head.	
Where must the recorder be placed to prevent loss of balance when he leans forward to push buttons?	

Figure 1–10. Target task—Operating a tape recorder from a wheelchair to listen to tape and stop recorder at certain points. Severe flailing of arms and fingers, no speech; physically able to *hear* recorder.

One teacher chose to list *critical subtasks* or prerequisite skills for independent study before listing a further breakdown of *supportive prerequisite performances*. She was developing a plan to help a severely involved cerebral palsied child with athetoid movements. The child would thrash his arms and fingers and could not talk. Heretofore, the child required adult assistance in the classroom for almost every task. The teacher wished to develop a plan to help this student study independently for even a small portion of the day. Refer to Figure 1–10, a matching of supportive prerequisite skills with critical prerequisite skills for a plan she was testing.

Clarifying Communications

Task analysis assists in clarification of terminology and ideas. It can assist in clear descriptions of desired learner performances so that different teachers will have shared conceptions of goals and objectives.

Some instructional approaches rely upon the identification and remediation of *groupings* of pupil strengths and problems. Clusters or groups of problems are commonly classified under "umbrella terms" such as *visual perception, motor expression,* or *visual-motor integration*. These terms can be interpreted in many ways. Extensive elaboration may be necessary since *these terms are not precise descriptions of lesson characteristics and learner performances*. Some teachers may know the general area in which a problem falls, but cannot isolate the exact deficiency. For instance, a person with cerebral palsy may be described as having visual-motor problems. The diagnosis suggests corrective visual-motor activities. A teacher could engage in a wide range of traditional activities designed to remediate visual-motor problems as a group (i.e., tying the lace of a wooden shoe, stringing beads and tracing a geometric line drawing) and never help the child in functional skills which are top priority for him. Often, the most direct approach is to use task analysis for a *specific* task: *tie own shoes*. More precise observations may reveal that the child's problem in tying his shoes is remembering what to do next, maintaining body balance while using hands, holding the lace tip because of inadequate thumb-finger opposition, lack of previous instruction, lack of practice, or any combination of the above. From these more precise observations, remediation can be directed toward *specific* ways to help.

Once target objectives are agreed upon by all persons concerned, they can be implemented. Statements of objectives may be posted as references for all who work with the children. Notices and conferences can be used to solicit the parents' ideas and to gain their cooperation. Objectives known only by a few and filed in desk drawers are unlikely to be accomplished with efficiency.

A Basis for Goals and Objectives

The process of task analysis cannot be separated from the formulation of goals and objectives. One process leads naturally into the other. We have suggested the use of task analysis as one procedure for making commitments, in the form of public plans, to help each individual. From task analysis emerges broad goals and related objectives for learning.

Objectives, as used in this chapter, can be either instructional or behavioral. They differ from goals in that they include indications of how and to what degree they will be accomplished. Goals are commonly stated in less specific terms: i.e., *Joe will learn to read*.

Some *objectives* encompass tasks and subtasks which are quite extensive, requiring large blocks of time. Other objectives specify tasks for immediate accomplishment. Most objectives suggest time lines and standards for accomplishment or re-evaluation.

Guidelines for statements of objectives, developed by Mager (1975), can be found in *Preparing Instructional Objectives*. In this book he clarifies the definitions that are basic to guideline construction. He states that, in contrast to descriptions that tell about content and procedure, objectives describe an intended instructional outcome. Or, stated differently, objectives describe aims. Accordingly, an objective delineates a description of how a learner will be changed as a result of a teaching-learning process. Thus, it is a statement of the results of teaching and learning.

Construction of Objectives

Mager (1975) describes three characteristics of useful objectives:

Conditions. "Important conditions under which the performance is expected to occur" (p. 23). Task analysis helps us notice conditions which surround tasks: *what* (utensil, special equipment used); *where* (student desk, cafeteria, in conversations including several persons); *how* (what position of the body, substitution of what portion of the body for another); and *why* (purpose).

Performance. "What the learner is able to do" (p. 23). Task analysis helps us isolate movements or actions for data collection. To be effective, intended outcomes stated as instructional objectives must use explicit statements. The distinction between implicit and explicit statements, as clarified by DeCecco (1968), depends upon the selection of verbs. Verbs in implicit objectives include those subject to multiple interpretations, such as *understands, knows,* and *appreciates*. Explicitly stated objectives must include verbs like *name* and *differentiate*, which designate publicly observable acts.

Criterion. "The quality or level of performance that will be considered acceptable" (p. 23). Standards should be so precise that an affirmative answer can be given to the question, "Can another competent person select successful learners in terms of the objective so that you, the objective writer, agree with the selections?" (Mager, 1962, p. 12).

When establishing criterion, or standard, be sure the criterion chosen result in the most information possible. "Rate data," for instance, may not be as helpful with some disabled persons as "the ratio of times completed to times tried."

Basic Framework

Condition

Given, (*description of important conditions under which one expects the intended outcome to occur*)

Performance

Student will (*intended outcome expressed by a descriptive verb followed by a description of performance*)

Criterion

at least to the minimum requirements of (*standard; criterion*)

Sample Conditions, Performances, and Criteria

The following sample conditions, performances and criteria include some of those listed by Mager (1975).

Conditions

Given crutches,
Given a command, "Look!"
Given one-to-one instruction,
Given total physical assistance,
Given a pat on the tummy after every eye contact,
Given a list of
Given any reference of the learner's choice,
Given a matrix of intercorrelations
Given a properly functioning
With a one pound weight on each wrist and with a large Dixie cup shaped crayon tied to hand,
Without the aid of references
Without the aid of slide rule
Without the aid of tools
Without head support
Without physical assistance
Without verbal cues

Performances

bang head
talk out
roll
look
name

imitate
reply
write
recite
solve
construct
compare
differentiate
identify
describe
order
distinguish
contrast
ask
choose
perform
join
give examples
list
hold head in midline position and keep both arms in lap
describe in one paragraph
list and give evidence to support
write a position paper
reproduce in outline form
rebut using three lines of attack: (1) . . . (2) . . .(3) . . .
prepare a written analysis of any four of the five

Criteria

maintain
between   (5)   and   (7)
with no error
within a time limit of
at least
90% of
50% more than the pretest
up to
increase from 10 on November 5 *to* 15 by January 5
decrease from 8 per minute *to* 2 per minute by June 4
independently with at least 80% accuracy for 5 consecutive days

Sample Objectives

Condition: Given a 1″ by 1″ block placed on table; the command, "Block!"; and 10 trials
Performance: S. will pick up the block
Criterion: Independently with 80% accuracy of performance over 5 consecutive sessions.

Condition: Given no attention after temper tantrums

Performance: Greg will decrease the number of tantrums
Criterion: From an average of 10 a week to an average of 1 a week by February 28.

Condition: Given the task of moving onto a standing table without assistance
Performance: The student will stand behind the table, prop his crutches against the table, place his hands onto the edge of the table, lift body from floor onto platform of the standing table and insert the back support standard.
Criterion: The student will no longer be drilled on the task when he can perform this entire series of steps without assistance in less than one minute. He will be able to do all steps with no help by December 20.

Conditions: Given a first exposure to a list of words belonging to a word family, i.e., *at, cat, rat, bat;*
          Given teacher comment such as "What do you notice about these words?"
          Given directions to read these words and add more words
Performance: Carol will demonstrate recognition of patterns of family words by describing the pattern and using the pattern to read
Criterion: *All* listed *at* words and add at least four *at* words to the list.

Procedures if Standards or Criterion Are Not Achieved

If the standards have not been met, there are many alternatives. Some alternatives include redefinition of the task, choice of a different task and/or restatement of the criteria.

To avoid trapping all members of a group into meeting the same standards regardless of their individual differences, use phrases such as: three more than accomplished on the pretest, and half as many as were completed on a pretest. This approach to standards encourages those individuals who have a learning or motor problem that causes them to function at a lower rate than their classmates no matter how hard they try. Many times the students themselves are encouraged to set their own standards. Generally speaking, criteria should be stated so that agreement between any two persons can be reached.

Criterion-referenced evaluation is not the only way of arriving at achievement standards. However, students should feel they are being judged or are judging themselves in terms of improvement of their own performance, rather than being judged against some arbitrary set of standards. The phrase *at least* can always be used in an objective to suggest that the objective states only a *minimum* expectancy for learning and performance. There is always hope that students will learn more and exceed criteria.

A Case Study

The following is an informal example of a task analysis for the language development of an 8-year-old girl with mild cerebral palsy. We know language is a very complex set of behaviors, and a complete analysis of all aspects of her language would be extensive. But for this purpose, we are going to look at small aspects of linguistic behavior.

First, we transcribe a sample of the child's language taken from a tape recording. Second, analysis of errors and other patterns are noted beside the transcription. Third, patterns are summarized. Fourth, the child's performances are compared with normative data on nonhandicapped children. These data are used to identify appropriate objectives for her. The data indicate how the child's language compares with the language of others of similar age. Finally, instructional objectives and a teaching plan are included. The plan includes a method for publicizing the objective so others can assist with its attainment.

Transcription and Analysis of Language Sample

The following eleven sentences are a small portion of a language sample. When Fong played a table game with friends a portion of her recorded language sample included the following:

> OK. I'm gonna beat.
> Don't move it yet.
> No fair.
> You winning. (*are* missing)
> And Sloan winning. (verb error: *is* missing)
> I move your. (verb tense error: or, pronoun error in object noun phrase: I mov*ed* yours, or I moved your _____ .)
> She ever like that. (error unspecifiable because *like* could be either a preposition or a main verb in this section.)
> You winning. (verb error: *are* missing)

I winning. (verb error: *am* missing)
That stuck. (verb error: *is* missing)
She losing and me winning. (verb error: is missing; pronoun error)

Looking at a portion of the sample we see the following patterns:

Short simple sentences
Error patterns—verb errors:*is* and *are* are missing; pronoun errors.

Studying the literature we find that Fong's mean length of response (MLR) is more typical in length for a 2½- to 3-year-old child (Crystal, Fletcher, & Garman, 1976). It is becoming increasingly evident that in early stages of language acquisition, sentence length and complexity are closely related. Therefore, we decide to concentrate upon helping Fong increase length and complexity of her sentences. After children's sentences are about five words long, on the average (i.e., MLR or a mean sentence length of five words), length and complexity are no longer so interdependent (Brown, 1973). For a more detailed discussion of sentence length at different ages, as well as the order in which function words are acquired, refer to Tyack and Gottsleben, 1974.

Long-range Objective

Condition: Given daily group instruction in the Distar language program and given described classroom activities directed toward increasing sentence length and reducing error patterns observed in the language sample
Performance and criterion: Fong will increase the mean length of spoken sentences from the present 4.2 words to 5 words by May 1 (6 months). Data from a 56 sentence-language sample compiled during table games the week of May 1 will be compared with the initial 56 sentence-language sample.

Instructional Activities

1. Complete one Distar language lesson per day.
2. Stress verbs *is* and *are* in sentences used in Distar lessons.
3. Repeat sentence inserting *is* or *are* when reminded by a visual cue.
4. Incorporate other classroom activities to increase sentence length.
   a. Use pictures to develop sentences. The sentences can be increased in length by adding adjectives to describe the pictures more carefully.
   b. Play gossip (pass sentences by whispering to neighbor).
   c. Repeat short poems or rhymes. To make the game more competitive, points can be used for every word spoken in the correct order.
   d. Play store.
      1) The "customer" gives an order over the phone or in person from a real or imaginary list.
      2) The "grocer" has to remember it—may at first need to write down a cue such as the first letter to help him remember.
      3) The "grocer" gets out the real or imaginary items and repeats it back to the customer.
      4) The "customer" checks to see if he has everything. Playing restaurant can be played in much the same way.
   e. Model sentences of 5–6 words in length stressing adjectives, adverbs, pronouns and conjunctions.

Communication of the Objective

Posting the following chart (Figure 1–11) will help assure that different people working with Fong are consistent in their expectations.

	Mobility	Language	Self-Help
Fong	Board (deboard) school bus unassisted.	1. Remind her to include *is* and *are* in sentence by raising a pointer finger when she does not remember. 2. Model five-word sentences using descriptive words.	Throw into garbage food which has fallen on ground.

Figure 1–11. For consistency, make goals public.

Evaluation of Program

1. Complete the evaluation as stated in the objectives.
2. Make a record of the data.
3. Plan strategies if an objective was not met.
4. Plan strategies if objectives were met.
5. Collaborate with relevant persons on objectives and implementation.

 ### Summary

In this chapter, readers have been introduced to the process of task analysis. The samples demonstrate ways that a task can be divided into component parts and then recorded in useful ways. Several alternate methods for task analysis were included as examples.

References

Bateman, B. D. *The essentials of teaching.* San Rafael, Calif.: Dimensions, 1971.

Bateman, B. D. Three approaches to diagnosis and educational planning for children with learning disability. *Academic Therapy Quarterly,* 1967, 2 (4), 215–222.

Bateman, G., Lieurance, W., Manney, A., & Osburn, C. *Helping children think: Report of the implementation of a teaching strategy.* New York: Tri-University Project in Elementary Education at New York University, 1968. Sponsored by U.S. Office of Education (USOE).

Bigge, J. *Systems of precise observations for teachers.* Printed guidelines, project S.P.O.T. Bureau of Education for the Handicapped, USOE, 1970a.

Bigge, J. Systems of precise observation for teachers. In Frances Connor, Joan Wald, and Michael Cohen (Eds.), *Professional preparation for education of crippled children.* New York: Teachers College, Columbia University, 1970b. Sponsored by USOE.

Brown, R. *A first language.* Cambridge, Mass.: Howard University, 1973.

Brueckner, L. J., & Bond, G. L. *The diagnosis and treatment of learning difficulties.* New York: Appleton-Century-Crofts, 1955.

Crystal, D., Fletcher, P., & Garman, M. *The grammatical analyses of language disability: A procedure for assessment and remediation.* London: Edward Arnold, 1976.

Engelmann, S. *Preventing failure in the primary grades.* Chicago: Science Research Associates, 1969.

Jastak, J. F., & Jastak, S. R. *Wide Range Achievement Test* (WRAT). New York, N.Y.: Guidance Associates, 1965.

Lovitt, T. C., Kunzelmann, H. P., Nolen, P. A., & Hulten, W. J. The dimensions of classroom data. *Journal of Learning Disabilities,* 1968, *1* (12), 710–725.

Mager, R. *Preparing instructional objectives* (1st ed.). Belmont, Calif.: Fearon, 1962.

Mager, R. *Preparing instructional objectives* (ed.) Belmont, Calif.: Fearon, 1975.

Mager, R., & Pipe, P. *Analyzing performance problems.* Belmont, Calif.: Lear Sigler, 1970.

Monterey County Office of Education. *Roadmap to Effective Teaching.* Salinas, Calif.: Monterey County Office of Education, 1970.

Thompson, D., & Altman, M. *Writing long range and short range objectives: A programmed instructional sequence for people who hate to write behavioral objectives.* Grant 30135 PL 91–230, Title VI Part D. Olympia, Wash.: State Superintendent of Public Instruction, 1975.

Tyack, D. & Gottsleben, R. *Language sampling, analysis and training: A handbook for teachers and clinicians.* Palo Alto, Calif.: Consulting Psychologists Press, 1974.

Wallace, G., & Kauffman, J. M. *Teaching children with learning problems.* Columbus, Ohio: Charles E. Merrill, 1973.

Resources

Anderson, D., Hodson, G. D., & Jones, W. G. *Instructional programming for the handicapped student.* Springfield: Charles C Thomas, 1975.

Barnard, K. E., & Erickson, M. L. *Teaching children with developmental problems.* Saint Louis: C. V. Mosby, 1976.

Caplan, F. (Ed.). *The first twelve months of life.* New York: Grosset & Dunlap. 1971, 1972, 1973, 1975 printings.

Engelmann, S. *Conceptual learning.* San Rafael, Calif.: Dimensions, 1969.

Friedlander, B. Z., Sterritt, Graham M., & Kirk, Girvin E., (Eds.). *Exceptional infant: Assessment and intervention,* (Vol. 3). New York: Bruner/Mazel, 1975.

Hart, V. *Beginning with the handicapped.* Pittsburgh: University of Pittsburgh, 1974.

Sailor, W., & Mix, B. J. *The TARC assessment system.* Lawrence, Kansas: H & H Enterprises, 1975.

Struck, R. D., *Santa Cruz BCP observation booklet.* Special Education Management System Project Document Education for Handicapped Children Act (EHA) Title VI B Project #44–00000–0000–925; Elementary Secondary Education Act (ESEA) Title III Project # 1328, Santa Cruz, California: Santa Cruz County Office of Education, 1973.

2

CONDITIONS RESULTING IN PHYSICAL DISABILITIES

Teachers of children with physical disabilities share with physicians a concern for the total child. They are interested in the physical conditions affecting their pupils because knowledge of these conditions enables them to anticipate the child's ability to engage in physical activity. This information also helps them determine need for assistance and protection if required.

Information in this chapter is generalized and nontechnical. Many teachers will have more advanced knowledge of these conditions, or more specific information outlining the physical abilities of a particular child. Details about various treatments, precautions and special recommendations can be obtained from the child's physician. Knowledge of these conditions and observations of the individual child will aid task analysis.

Ned Murray Grove, *M.D., F.R.C.S. (C), F.A.C.S., is a consultant of orthopedic surgery for handicapped children at the El Portal del Norte School, San Mateo County, California. He also is a clinical assistant professor of surgery at Stanford.*

Introduction to Conditions Resulting in Physical Disabilities

Congenital abnormalities can be defined as defects present at birth. The incidence of all congenital defects is usually listed at 3%. However, if you include all birth abnormalities discovered within the first year of life, the rate is 6%. Birth defects are often multiple. The defect can be localized or generalized, mild or severe. A part or section of the body (e.g., a portion of a limb) can be absent, smaller than normal, abnormally formed, larger than normal, or formed in duplication. A joint may be absent (i.e., failed to develop) or dislocated (out of joint).

Some other conditions may or may not be present at birth (e.g., osteogenesis imperfecta and cerebral palsy). Other conditions known as acquired are not present at birth.

Arthrogryposis Multiplex

Arthrogryposis multiplex, a congenital condition, is characterized by stiffness and deformity of the limbs and trunk. The limb muscles are absent or much smaller and weaker than normal so that

23

there is little or no joint motion. The skin of the limbs is very tight and smooth. There can be many deformities involving the joints of the extremities (hip, knee, foot, hand, elbow, shoulder) or trunk (curvature). Treatment consists of physical therapy (stretching) and possible surgery. Bracing is often required.

Clubfoot (Talipes Equino-varus)

Clubfoot is a congenital deformity of the foot, hereditary in some cases. The condition is found in 2 per 1,000 live births and is more common in males than in females.

As shown in Figure 2–1, there are three components to a *clubfoot*. The forefoot, i.e., the front part of the foot, is turned "in" towards the midline (in relation to the back part of the foot). The heel is turned in toward the midline of the body, and the toes are pointing down—away from the body.

The deformities of clubfoot vary in degrees of severity. Some are easily corrected while others are difficult. Sometimes the condition can be corrected without surgery. Treatment may require the use of corrective manipulation, cast application, stretching exercises, a bar and brace, or corrective shoes. Many cases are severe and are very resistant to treatment. In addition, in cases treated and corrected, there is a great tendency toward recurrence. Surgery is often necessary; in younger children surgery of the soft tissues (joints and tendons) is carried out, while in older patients bone operations may be necessary.

Myelomeningocele (Spina Bifida)

Myelomeningocele is a condition present at birth. In this condition, there is a sac of improperly formed nervous tissue *bulging* through a deficit in the bone of the spine (spina bifida), usually in the region of the low back. The condition occurs in 2 in 1,000 births and may be more common in people of Celtic origin.

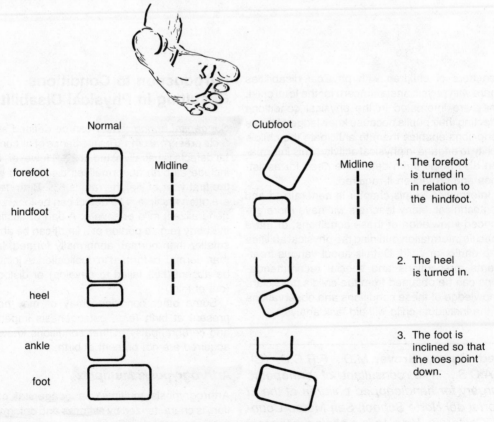

Figure 2–1. Three components to a clubfoot deformity.

There is decreased or absent sensation and partial or complete weakness of the lower extremities. There may be joint deformities. There is often loss of bladder and/or bowel control. There may be swelling and a hairy area of skin over the bulging sac. Patients will often have an associated condition of head enlargement known as *hydrocephalus*.

Some patients with myelomeningocele use a wheelchair. Some can take a few steps with braces and crutches under supervision. Others can ambulate independently with braces and crutches as required.

Treatment must be initiated at birth with repair of the bulging sac. The condition of hydrocephalus must be relieved by appropriate surgery. The child often receives physical therapy treatments for prevention of deformities and for gait training. Bracing is usually required to aid in support of the lower extremities and the trunk. Surgery is often necessary for release of contractures, tendon transfer, or correction of deformity. The loss of bladder control is often a problem requiring special maneuvers for emptying the bladder or surgery for diversion of the urinary stream.

Congenital Dislocation of the Hip

Congenital dislocation of the hip is a condition in which the hip joint of a newborn child is abnormally formed. A hip joint is a ball and socket joint; the ball is the round upper end (or head) of the long bone of the thigh (or femur), and the socket is the cup of the pelvis (or acetabulum). The joint is enclosed in a covering layer, the capsule. There are varying degrees of hip deformity in the newborn. The hip of a newborn child can be completely out of joint (dislocated), partially out of joint (subluxated) or merely unstable (*acetabular dysphasia*—meaning poor formation of the cup).

There is laxity (looseness) of the hip in 1 of 80 births. The condition of congenital dislocation of the hip is found in 1.5 per 1,000 live births. The condition is bilateral in over 50% of the cases. Females are affected 8 times as often as males. There appears to be a higher incidence in the populations in Italy, Israel, Japan, Great Britain, and Sweden and in their descendants in the northern states of the United States.

There is also a higher incidence in babies who are carried in positions with their legs together and the hips out straight (i.e., American Indians). There is a lower incidence in populations in which babies are kept with their legs wide apart and the hips flexed (a more stable position for the hips).

The examination of all newborn infants for evidence of hip instability is important. If a hip is dislocatable on testing, it should be treated. X-ray films confirm the diagnosis. If the diagnosis is made early, treatment consists of gentle reduction (replacement) and maintenance in the reduced position using any one of a number of splints or casts. The hip is maintained in the position of correction until the clinical and radiological findings are satisfactory and stability is assured.

If the child is 3 months–18 months of age when the diagnosis is made, surgery for release of tight tendons may be required prior to gentle reduction

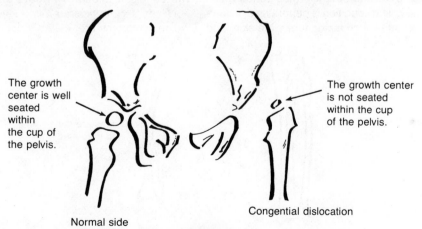

The growth center is well seated within the cup of the pelvis.

The growth center is not seated within the cup of the pelvis.

Congenital dislocation

Normal side

Figure 2–2. Comparison of normal hip and congenital dislocation of the hip.

of the dislocation. If the child is between 18 months–5 years of age when the diagnosis is made, it is likely that bone surgery (in which the pelvis is cut and the position of the cup, i.e., the acetabulum is corrected) will be required.

Amputations

Amputations means loss of limb or partial loss of a limb. They may be congenital or acquired. A congenital amputation is noted at birth. Any part of a limb may be absent. The stump usually has healthy, nontender skin covering. Therefore a prosthesis (i.e., an artificial limb) can be fitted without difficulty and the child can begin to wear the prosthesis at the earliest possible age.

Congenital constriction bands are thick bands of tough tissue running circumferentially "from the skin in" around a limb at any level. The condition may be mild, in which case simple release of the band is necessary. If the condition is severe, there may be "almost an amputation" of a portion of the limb. Surgery should then complete the amputation.

Acquired amputations is the term used for all other amputations, traumatic or surgical. Surgical amputation may be necessary for cases involving trauma, loss of blood supply, tumors, or long-standing, uncontrolled infection. A prosthesis should generally be fitted as soon as possible after the surgery.

Osteogenesis Imperfecta

In Osteogenesis imperfecta, known as brittle bones, there are improperly formed bones which break easily. The condition is generalized, involving other tissues such as the teeth, the skin, and the whites of the eyes. The disease is hereditary and may be congenital.

The congenital type of osteogenesis imperfecta is the most severe. There may be many fractures present at birth. Patients may die within the first few years of life. In the other type, known as the *latent type,* the condition first appears in childhood. The bones are fragile, the limbs are thin and may be deformed. If the patient lives to puberty, the condition may improve with a decrease in the tendency to sustain fractures.

Treatment consists of protection. Braces and crutches may be required. Surgery is often indicated to correct existing deformity and provide support. The most common operation is one in which the bone is cut and rethreaded over a rod.

Legg-Perthes Disease

Legg-Perthes disease is one of many names for a condition of unknown cause in which there is death of the tissue at the end of a growing bone due to loss of blood supply. The condition may involve one of many different bones. There is a different name for the same condition for each bone which may be involved. Figure 2–4 shows growth of bone. Children grow as bone length increases. There are growth centers at the ends of the long bones. Between the shaft and the growth centers there are growth lines where the actual growth takes place.

Most commonly, the condition involves the hip joint, and is then called *Legg-Perthes* disease. This condition involves the round upper end (or head) of the long bone of the thigh (the femur). The condition affects both boys and girls from 3–11 years. Both hips are often involved.

The symptoms are related to the hip joint and

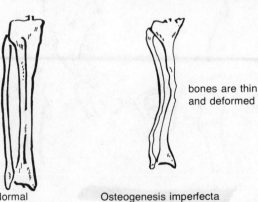

Normal   Osteogenesis imperfecta

bones are thin
and deformed

Figure 2–3. Changes in bones involved in osteogenesis imperfecta.

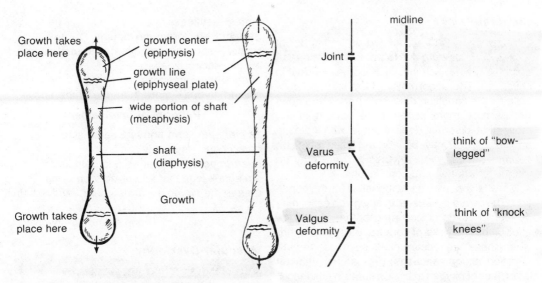

Figure 2–4. Figure 2–4a. Growing bone.   Figure 2–4b. Varus and valgus deformities.

the lower extremity. There is usually pain, an associated limp, and limitation of motion. The condition can be identified on x-ray films which are taken to confirm the diagnosis and to estimate the stage of the condition.

There are four stages which occur in sequence, as the condition runs its course: (*a*) death of tissue, (*b*) bone deposition (*c*) bone withdrawal, (*d*) bone healing and residual deformity.

The hip joint is protected throughout the treatment period. The child is usually placed in a position in which the lower extremities are spread wide apart and maintained in this position in a brace, splint, or cast. Weight bearing (walking with weight on the limb) is usually permitted. Occasionally, surgery is indicated. The younger the child at the time treatment is initiated, the better the chance of a good result.

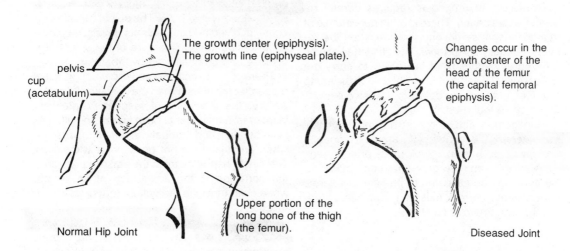

Figure 2–5. Normal hip joint and Legg-Perthes disease.

Cerebral Palsy

Cerebral palsy can be defined as a disorder of movement or posture due to a deficit or abnormality of the brain which initially becomes evident in childhood. The abnormality of the brain responsible for the condition does not change and does not become more severe. The pattern of the movement disorder does change with time. In addition, there may be abnormalities of sight, hearing, speech, and sensation. There may be mental retardation and convulsions.

Many factors may be responsible for the condition. The cause or causes, in any given case, may be factors acting or occurring before, during, or after birth. The risks of cerebral palsy are higher when there are occurrences such as prebirth infection, blood reactions, prematurity, difficult labor, lack of oxygen at birth, trauma in childhood, and postbirth infection.

The diagnosis of cerebral palsy implies that movement disorder is a prominent finding. The pattern of the movement or posture disorder may be primarily one of tightness, uncontrolled movements, tenseness, rigidity, grotesque posturing, incoordinated movements or rapid alternating movements. The patterns may be mixed, combining two or more patterns. The condition may involve the upper and lower extremities (arm and leg) on one side, the lower extremities only, or all the extremities (with the lower extremities, more involved, the upper extremities more involved, or one side more involved).

Evaluation of prognosis requires careful repeated examination. There is often persistence of infantile response beyond the age when the response usually disappears. The child may exhibit delayed development of the ability to carry out actions usually performed by children of the same age (i.e., grasping an object). Extensive evaluation may be indicated.

Management and treatment may require physical therapy, occupational therapy, speech therapy, and nursing. Medication, orthotic aids (appliances), and surgery may be indicated. Surgery may be indicated to prevent or release contractures, correct muscle imbalance or deformity, and improve function.

Terms

Types

spasticity—tightness
athetosis—uncontrolled movements

rigidity—stiffness
dystonia—distorted movement
tremor—spontaneous alternating movement
ataxia—incoordination
hypotonia—looseness
"mixed" types—more than one of the above

Patterns of involvement

hemiplegia—arm and leg, same side
paraplegia—legs only
quadriplegia—both arms and both legs
diplegia—legs more involved than arms
double hemiplegia—arms more involved than legs
—one side more involved

Muscular Dystrophy

Muscular dystrophy is a hereditary, familial condition in which there is progressive (increasing) weakness. The cause is unknown, and males are affected more frequently than females. The condition is usually transmitted by females who are not themselves affected.

The condition begins early in life and is usually diagnosed between 5–7 years of age. There are several forms. In the most common form, which is called *pseudo hypertrophic muscular dystrophy* (because it appears as though the muscles of the calf are bigger than normal), the *weakness* begins in the muscles of the shoulders and the hips spreading to involve all other voluntary muscles (muscles under the active control). There is gradual loss of respiratory function secondary to weakness and *scoliosis*. The spinal muscles become involved and the patients develop *scoliosis* (side-to-side lateral curvature of the spine). The disease can be confirmed by laboratory tests.

There is no specific treatment although active research continues. When the condition becomes severe, the incidence of respiratory infections increases. The patients have increasing difficulty in ambulation and gradually require crutches, and when ambulation is not possible, a wheelchair. The single happy event in the sad progression of the condition is the acquisition of an electric wheelchair in which the patient turns, spins, and races.

Physical therapy is utilized in attempts to prevent contractures. Surgery may be indicated to maintain ambulation by release of contractures (occasionally), and for correction of scoliosis. Patients often live until midteens or young adulthood and usually die of respiratory disease.

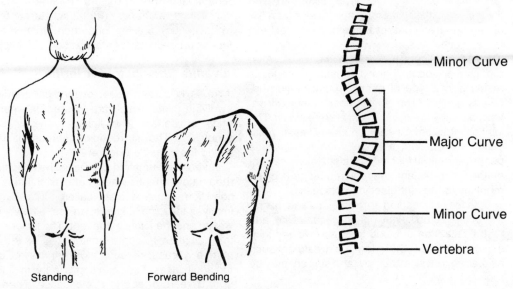

Figure 2–6. Scoliosis—lateral curvature of the spine.

Scoliosis

Scoliosis is the medical term for lateral (side-to-side) curvature of the spine. Some curves are caused by known conditions, such as birth abnormalities of the spine, and conditions involving weakness of muscles. Most curves are of unknown origin. It is now thought that many are due to genetic or familial causes. The condition is more common in girls.

The curve may involve any segment of the spine and be of any length. Some curves are mobile and tend to straighten on bending motion of the body. Other curves are rigid and will not straighten.

The curves are generally noticeable on observation of the patient's back. When the patient bends forward, the posterior aspect of the chest is more prominent on one side. X-ray films are essential, since degree of curvature is measured using the films.

There is no prevention of scoliosis. All children and adolescents should be examined at intervals. If a mild curve is diagnosed, close observation is indicated. The curve may progress (increase) and must, therefore, be re-evaluated at intervals. If the curve progresses from a mild to a moderate curve (or is significant when first noted), bracing may be used. The Milwaukee Brace is an effective device worn by many patients. If the curve progresses to a more severe stage, surgery may be indicated.

Terms

scoliosis—side-to-side (lateral) curvature of the spine
functional—flexible
    —tends to correct when patient bends
structural—rigid
    —does not tend to correct when patient bends
infantile—develops before 3 years of age
juvenile—develops between 3 years of age and puberty
adolescent—develops between puberty and maturity
adult—develops after maturity
apical vertebra (or *apex*)—the vertebra farthest from the midline of the patient
    —usually at or near the middle of the curve
idiopathic—due to no known cause
    —heredity is a probable factor
congenital—present at birth
    —usually due to an abnormality of a vertebra
neuromuscular—due to neurological or muscular diseases

Hemophilia

Hemophilia is an uncommon, hereditary disease characterized by increased tendency to bleeding due to a deficiency of one of the many factors which are required for proper blood clotting. The factor missing in the hemophiliac patients is called the *antihemophiliac factor.* There is less than 5% of the normal amounts of antihemophiliac factor in the hemophiliac.

Bleeding occurs primarily in the joints. After repeated episodes, there is damage to the joints resulting in a type of arthritis. Joint motion becomes limited. The joints most commonly involved are the knee, the ankle, and the elbow. The joint changes can be seen on x-ray films. Investigations reveal that a longer than normal time period is required for blood clotting. In one current method of treatment, the required factor is given regularly to prevent bleeding episodes.

Episodes of bleeding are treated by administration of the factor, splinting, application of ice, and rest. Evacuation of blood from an involved joint may be indicated. Other forms of treatment such as bracing, physical therapy, and surgery may be required.

Poliomyelitis

Poliomyelitis is a condition of viral origin, which involves those nerve cells which control muscular activity. There is a period of time between the exposure to the virus and the onset of symptoms. The initial severe symptoms are present for a period of approximately two months, the acute period. There is then a recovery period which lasts up to two years, during which some or all of the affected muscles recover some or all of their strength. Residual paralysis (weakness or complete loss of power of the affected muscles), if present, lasts indefinitely. The muscles of one or more limbs may be involved. If the trunk muscles are involved, spinal curvature (scoliosis) may develop.

Treatment is aimed at the prevention of deformities, the correction of deformities, improvement of muscle balance, function, appearance, and rehabilitation of the patient. Treatment may involve physical therapy (for muscle strength and re-education), bracing, or surgery (tendon transfers or procedures for stabilization of joints).

Juvenile Rheumatoid Arthritis

Arthritis is a term used for medical conditions involving joints, which are located between the ends of bones. The lining tissue is called *synovium.* The surrounding fibrous tissue is called the *capsule* (Figure 2–7).

Juvenile rheumatoid arthritis is the condition of rheumatoid arthritis when it affects children. The condition, which is often called *Still's disease,* involves the *joints*—knees, ankles, elbows, hips, wrists, and the joints of the foot. The incidence of the condition is approximately 5% of the total number of cases of rheumatoid arthritis, including the adult cases. The condition is found in children from 3 years of age to adolescence. There are twice as many female patients as male patients.

There are three types of *rheumatoid arthritis.* The first type affects less than 4 joints and occurs in younger patients, 30% of whom have eye involvement. In two to three years, 75% of the patients recover completely. The second type involves a generalized condition widespread throughout the body. There is usually fever, a rash, and signs of increased body response to inflammation. The outer cover of the heart is involved in 2% of the cases, and the kidneys may be involved. The third type involves more than 4 joints. The joints are swollen, red, tender, and restricted in motion. The joint of the spine, in the neck region, may be involved. The blood test for rheumatoid arthritis (which is usually negative in juvenile rheumatoid arthritis) may be positive.

A team approach to treatment is recommended. Physical therapy may be utilized to prevent or correct deformity; splints may be used,

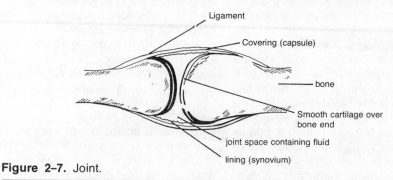

Ligament
Covering (capsule)
bone
Smooth cartilage over bone end
joint space containing fluid
lining (synovium)

Figure 2–7. Joint.

surgery may be indicated. Medical treatment, directed at the control of inflammation, is essential.

Spinal Cord Injury

Patients who have sustained trauma to the spinal cord may have permanent residual neurological deficit. If the injury has damaged the cord at the cervical level, there may be paralysis, weakness and sensory loss involving four extremities, and loss of bowel and bladder function. If the injury occurs at a lower level, the upper extremities will be spared; but there may be varying degrees of involvement of the lower extremities, and varying degrees of loss of bladder and bowel function.

Initially, the patient will be treated in an acute care hospital. Care is usually continued in a rehabilitation center where program of functional training will begin. When the condition is stabilized, the patient can usually be returned to school.

Intelligence is unimpaired. Psychological factors must be considered carefully as the patient is always aware of future social and vocational concerns.

There will be specialized care necessary for treatment of bowel and bladder functional loss. Orthoses (braces or splints) or specialized wheelchairs may be necessary. There is a great deal of research in the field of rehabilitation engineering. It is anticipated that new equipment will be devised for use by those who have sustained permanent spinal cord injuries.

Summary

Children who have the conditions of osteogenesis imperfecta or athetoid cerebral palsy may require protection against injury. Some children with any of a variety of conditions—cerebral palsy, muscular dystrophy, myelomeningocele, Legg-Perthes, scoliosis—may require bracing. Others may be confined to wheelchairs.

Although a considerable amount of energy expenditure is required, children who are orthopedically handicapped usually are eager to participate in classroom, playground, and community activities. Many will surprise us with their determination. Others (particular muscular dystrophy patients) will be daring in their use of "hotrod" electric wheelchairs. All will convey a sense of accomplishment which makes caring for them rewarding.

Resources

General

Bleck, E., & Nagel, D. A. (Eds.). *Physically handicapped children: A medical atlas for teachers*. New York: Grune & Stratton, 1975.

Local chapters of Foundations and Associations Serving Particular Disability Groups. (National address can be obtained from local chapters.)

Illingworth, R. S. *The child at school: A pediatrician's manual for teachers*. New York: Halstead, 1975.

Peterson, R. M., & Cleveland, J. O. *Medical problems in the classroom: An educator's guide*. Springfield, Ill.: Charles C Thomas, 1976.

Arthrogryposis

Lloyd-Roberts, G. C., & Lettin, A.W.F. Arthrogryposis multiplex congenita. *Journal of Bone and Joint Surgery*, 1970, *52B*, 494.

Brain Damage

Seidel, U. P., Chadwick, O.F.D., & Rutter, M. Psychological disorders in crippled children: A comparative study of children with and without brain damage. *Developmental Medicine and Child Neurology*, 1975, *17* (5), 563–573.

Cerebral Palsy

Alderman, M. (Ed.). Cerebral palsy: My baby is slow . . . *Patient Care*, 1972, *VI* (2), 21–43.

Bobath, K., & Bobath, B. Cerebral palsy. In Paul H. Pearson & Carol Ethun Williams (Eds.), *Physical therapy services in the developmental disabilities*. Springfield, Illinois: Charles C Thomas, 1972.

Christensen, E., & Melchior, J. C. *Cerebral palsy: A clinical and neuropathological study: Clinics in developmental medicine, no. 25*. Lavenham, Suffolk: Lavenham, 1967.

Cruickshank, W. (Ed.). *Cerebral palsy: A Developmental disability*. Syracuse, New York: Syracuse University, 1976.

Denhoff, E., & Robinault, I. P. *Cerebral palsy and related disorders: A developmental approach to dysfunction*. New York: McGraw-Hill, 1960.

Hoffer, M. M., Garrett, A., Koffman, M., Guilford, A., Noble, R., & Rodon, G. New concepts in orthotics for cerebral palsy. *Clinical Orthopedics*, 1974, *102*, 100–107.

Jones, M. Cerebral palsy. In R.M. Peterson and J.O. Cleveland (Eds.), *Medical problems in the classroom: An educator's guide*. Springfield, Ill.: Charles C Thomas, 1976.

Little, W. J. [On the influence of abnormal parturition, difficult labours, premature birth, and asphyxia neonatorum, on the mental and physical condition of the child, especially in relation to deformities.] *Obstet. Soc.*, 1862, *III*. (*Clinical Orthopedics and Related Research*, 1966, No. 46, pp. 7–22.)

Pearson, P. H., & Williams, C. E. *Physical therapy services in developmental disabilities*. Springfield, Ill.: Charles C Thomas, 1972.

Perlstein, M. A. Medical aspects of cerebral palsy: Incidence, etiology, pathogeneses. *American Journal of Occupational Therapy*, 1950, *IV* (2), 47–52.

Phelps, W. M. The treatment of the cerebral palsies. *Journal of Bone and Joint Surgery*, 1940, *XXII* (4), 1004–1012.

Phelps, W. Cerebral birth injuries: Their orthopaedic classification and subsequent treatment. *Clinical Orthopaedics and Related Research*, 1966, (47), July–August, 9–17. Reprint of paper read at the Section of Orthopaedic Surgery, New York Academy of Medicine, January 15, 1932.

Samilson, R. L. (Ed.). *Orthopedic aspects of cerebral palsy: Clinics in developmental medicine, nos. 52/53*. Philadelphia: Lippincott, 1975.

Scherzer, A. L. Early diagnosis, management, and treatment of cerebral palsy. *Rehabilitation Literature*, 1974, *35*, 194–199.

Wolf, J. M. (Ed.) *The results of treatment in cerebral palsy*. Springfield, Illinois: Charles C Thomas, 1969.

Ingram, T.T.S. *Pediatric aspects of cerebral palsy*. Edinburgh: E & S Livingstone, 1964.

Hemophilia

Salk, L., Hilgartner, M., & Granech, B. *The psychosocial impact of hemophilia on the patient and his family*. Social Science and Medicine, 1972, *6*, August, 491–505.

Pilling, D. *Child with a chronic medical problem*. New York: Humanities, 1973.

Legg-Perthes

Rosar, V. W. *Perthes and parents*. Springfield, Illinois: Charles C Thomas, 1963.

Limb Deficiencies

Aitken, G. T. (Ed.). *Symposium on the child with an acquired amputation*. Symposium presented at the meeting of the Committee on Prosthetics Research and Development, Toronto, 1970. Washington: National Academy of Sciences, 1972.

Muscular Dystrophy

Harris, S. E., & Cherry, D. B. Childhood progressive muscular dystrophy and the role of physical therapy. *Physical Therapy*, 1974, *54*, 4–12.

Moosa, A. Muscular dystrophy in childhood. *Developmental Medicine and Child Neurology*, 1974, *16*, 97–111.

Ziter, F. A., & Allsop, K. G. Comprehensive treatment of childhood muscular dystrophy. *Rocky Mountain Medical Journal*, 1975, *72* (8), 329–333.

Osteogenesis Imperfecta

Castells, S. New approaches to treatment of osteogenesis imperfecta. *Clinical Orthopedics and Related Research*, 1973, *93*, 239–249.

Shoenfeld, Y., Fried, A., & Ehrenfeld, N. E. Review of the literature with 29 cases presented. *American Journal of Diseases of Children*, 1975, *129* (6), 679–687.

Scoliosis

Odom, J. A., Brown, C. W., Jackson, R. R., Hahn, H. R., & Carle, T. V. Scoliosis in paraplegia. *Paraplegia*, 1973–1974, *11*, 290–294.

Roaf, R. *Scoliosis*. New York: Longman, 1967.

Rosenthal, R. K., Levine, D. B., & McCarver, C. L. The occurrence of scoliosis in cerebral palsy. *Developmental Medicine and Child Neurology*, 1974, *16*, 664–667.

Siegal, I. M. Scoliosis in muscular dystrophy. *Clinical Orthopedics and Related Research*, 1973, *93*, 235–238.

Spina Bifida/Myelomeningocele

American Academy of Orthopaedic Surgeons. *Symposium on Myelomeningocele*. Saint Louis: C. V. Mosby, 1972.

Beals, R. K. Myelomeningocele. *Western Journal of Medicine*, 1974, *121* (4), 321–322.

Bracklehurst, G. (Ed.). *Spina bifida for the clinician: Clinics in developmental medicine, no. 57*. Philadelphia: J. B. Lippincott, 1976.

Nergardh, A., Von Hedenberg, C., Hellstrom, B., & Ericsson, N. O. Convenience training of children with neurogenic bladder dysfunction. *Developmental Medicine and Child Neurology*, 1974, *16*, 47–52.

Pilling, D. *Child with spina bifida: Social, emotional, and educational adjustment*. New York: Humanities Press, 1973.

Specht, E., Goodner, E., Tanagho, E., Prince, B., Pevehouse, B., & Cohen, P., Myelomeningocele. *Western Journal of Medicine*, 1974, *121* (4) 281–304.

Spinal Cord Injury

Guttman, Sir Ludwig. *Spinal cord injuries: Comprehensive management and research*. (Vol. xiii, p. 694). Phil., Penn.: F. A. Davis, 1973.

3

MOTOR DEVELOPMENT, DEVIATIONS, AND PHYSICAL REHABILITATION

In a disabled child, movement and physical development are limited or prevented by abnormal reflexes and reactions, abnormal body tone, weakness or paralysis, absent body parts, or limited range of motion. In order to realize the physical potential of such a child, we need to understand the sequences of development and the efforts which might be taken to aid those people with disabilities. In this chapter, descriptions of normal motor development will help to determine what physical milestones a particular child has accomplished and what the child might need to accomplish. The chapter will also explain disabilities and provide simple suggestions for altering them and make the reader aware of necessary modifications of classroom activities. Finally, brief summaries of goals and approaches will aid in collaborative planning.

Karen A. Kraemer, *R.P.T., is the head therapist for physically handicapped children for the El Portal Therapy Unit. She is connected with the Crippled Children's Services of San Mateo County, California.*

June Bigge.

Normal Motor Development

Motion is defined as the act or process of moving. It is an essential part of one's everyday world. Movement can be accomplished through the integrated action of the nervous, muscular, and skeletal systems (nerves, muscles, and bones) of our bodies or through reflex action.

Two Major Types of Motion

Much of a newborn baby's motion is *reflex*. Reflexes are those set patterns of motion which occur in response to certain positional or sensory stimuli. *Voluntary motion* is carried out under conscious control through a coordinated effort of the nervous, muscular, and skeletal systems.

Role of Reflexes and Voluntary Motion in Normal Development

According to Fiorentino (1963, p. 5), "primitive reflexes are essential in normal development." They may be likened to conditioning exercises which prepare the body for more strenuous and complicated movements. However, at times the body has less need for these reflexes. As the body matures (particularly the nervous system) voluntary motion, along with complex postural reactions and equilibrium, becomes predominate, showing an integration of the nervous, muscular, and skeletal systems. If, due to damage to the nervous system, the primitive reflexes do not disappear, the development of voluntary motion proceeds abnormally.

Generalizations About Patterns of Normal Development

A study of normal patterns in motor development can be used as a guideline for exploring specific sequences of development in the disabled. O'Donnell (1969, p. 3) states that "there is general consensus that there are broad trends in motor development which appear to be relatively independent of environmental influence." A comparison of disabled individuals to "normal" or usual motor development can thus help teachers and therapists plan for the disabled.

One pattern, called the *cephalo-caudal pattern,* indicates that development proceeds from the head *(cephalo)* to the tail *(caudal).* In this process, head movements are among the first to be well controlled; following are the arms and then the legs.

The *proximal-distal pattern* indicates that development proceeds from the trunk *(proximal)* outward to the extremities *(distal).* Movements of the trunk and head are controlled to a large extent before movements of the hands or feet. Sitting is accomplished well before the child can use hands in any functional activity.

The *mass to specific* pattern describes the phenomena that undifferentiated movements involving the entire body precede more specific and refined movements. Babies turn over first with the entire body moving as a mass. Later, they turn by first rotating the shoulders and then the hip, or vice versa.

The *gross motor to fine motor pattern* indicates that development normally proceeds from the mastery of large muscle groups to the mastery of small muscles. The child learns to produce movements with the whole arm before isolating movement of the fingers. The child builds finer motor patterns upon a foundation of coordinated gross motor movements.

Finally, a *sequence* of motor development can be observed. Sequential development of motor patterns tends to be consistent among nondisabled individuals. An analysis of the sequences can be used as a reference upon which to base plans to help them.

Sequences of Motor Development

Bobath (1966, p. 1) says that "normal motor development proceeds in an orderly sequence of events." Yet each person achieves this development at an individual rate. Most babies acquire certain functions at specified stages. By checking these functions, frequently called *motor milestones,* one can determine whether physical development is proceeding at the normal rate and in the usual sequence. It must be remembered, however, substantial variation within stages may be "normal."

Persons working with disabled individuals are more often concerned with *sequence* rather than age of expected motor developments. Physically disabled children may not reach milestones as quickly as nondisabled children. Sequence and interdependence of normal milestones provide guidelines for analyzing present and potential functioning of disabled children.

Developmental sequences and age norms have been described by several authorities. Details of gross motor development, hand and eye development, and combinations of these accomplishments have been recorded (Gesell, 1940; Knoblach and Pasamanick, 1974; Illingworth, 1972). A brief outline of normal developmental patterns revealed in these studies is presented in Table 3–1.

Terms

Comprehension of these studies can be aided by knowledge of several terms.

Flexion—bending of the joints of the extremity (arm or leg), head or trunk. *Plantar* flexion is bending down (ankle); *dorsi* flexion is bending up (ankle).

Extension—straightening of the extremity, neck or trunk. *Hyperextension* is straightening beyond neutral.

Prone—the position in which the body is lying on a surface with the face side toward the surface.

Supine—the position in which the body is lying on a surface with the back toward the surface.

Adduction—movement of the extremities toward the midline of the body.

Table 3–1. Normal Developmental Patterns

	Gross Motor Development	**Hand-Eye Development**
Stage 1 (1–3 mo)	Lifts head in prone. Moves arms and legs in forceful manner from flexion toward extension. Begins to roll onto side.	Eyes begin to fix on objects. Fists hands. Grasps objects using grasp reflex. Brings objects to mouth.
Stage 2 (4–6 mo)	Lifts head and looks around. Rolls supine to prone. Holds head erect while sitting propped. Pushes self up on hands in prone and pulls toys toward self.	Turns head with eyes to look. Looks at objects coming into visual field and reaches for them with arms. Releases objects voluntarily. Fingers toys being held.
Stage 3 (7–9 mo)	Moves from prone to crawl and standing positions. Uses hands to pull to standing.	Handles and bangs large objects against supporting surface. Fixates on stationary objects. Tries to pick up small items but unable to do so. Slaps, rakes and scratches with hands.
Stage 4 (10–12 mo)	Spends most time vertical, not horizontal. Walks with widely spread feet.	Picks up beads with thumb and index finger. Explores objects with finger tips.
Stage 5 (13–24 mo)	Develops better balance. Begins climbing stairs, one foot leading. Sits self in chair.	Plays with blocks. Removes socks and shoes. Feeds self with spoon. Holds cup. Imitates a vertical stroke. Holds crayon with fingers.
Stage 6 (25–36 mo)	Runs. Jumps.	Turns pages of books carefully.
Stage 7 (37–48 mo)	Rides trike. Climbs stairs, reciprocally (foot over foot). Stands on one foot, 2 seconds. Hops.	Feeds self with fork. Cuts with scissors. Imitates circular and horizontal strokes. Copies circle.
Stage 8 (49–60 mo)	Skips. Swings arm with opposite leg when walking.	Holds a pencil in an adult manner. Copies a cross. Laces shoes (doesn't tie them).
Stage 9 (61–72 mo)	Descends stairs reciprocally. Walks balance board.	Establishes handedness. Copies square and triangle. Colors within lines.
Stage 10 (6–8 yr)	Improves quality or preciseness in execution of all gross motor skills.	Draws a straight line with ruler. Cuts food with knife.

Abduction—movement of the extremities away from the midline of the body.

Crawling—progression of the body across a surface, utilizing arms and legs alternately and reciprocally, with the abdomen remaining on the surface.

Creeping—similar to crawling, but with the abdomen not in contact with the supporting surface.

It should be pointed out that although all normal development proceeds in an orderly fashion, one child can achieve at a faster rate than another. An individual child may also accomplish gross motor skills at a faster rate than eye-hand tasks. This is of particular importance to remember when assessing the developmental levels of disabled youngsters.

Effects of Motor Disabilities

Abnormal or pathological reflexes and reactions, abnormal tone, incoordination, weakness and paralysis, absence of body parts, and limited range of motion interfere with motor function. They frequently alter the sequence, rate, and quality of motor development, which in turn negatively affects function.

We can help individuals best by recognizing and responding to *functional* problems. As mentioned in the previous chapter, the diagnosis of arthritis is described in terms of its resulting disability or presenting functional problem, the limited range of motion. Weakness and paralysis are consequences of polio which cause functional problems. If we study implications of weakness and paralysis, we can learn to help not only polio patients but also persons who have spina bifida and muscular dystrophy. With cerebral palsy, we respond to abnormal patterns of posture and movement.

Abnormal Reflexes and Reactions

Primitive reflexes are, as stated previously, essential in the development of normal postures and movements. Most of these reflexes, which have control centers in the spinal cord and brain, normally diminish or disappear as the nervous system matures. They are the basis for more complex patterns of equilibrium and balance which prepare the young infant for tasks such as walking. Some reflexes or reactions normally develop early and remain throughout life. These reflexes

are needed to maintain erect and functional postures. If, as in cerebral palsy, the central nervous system has been damaged or does not mature, the primitive reflexes do not appear or disappear at the expected times. They then are called *abnormal reflexes*. If they appear but persist past a usual time, or do not develop at all, it is common for physical therapists to attempt to inhibit or facilitate them as necessary. Other reflexes, which never appear in the normally developing infant but are frequently seen in the child with cerebral palsy, are called *pathologic*.

A brief description of a few of the major reflexes and reactions which affect motor development follows. Those conditions which provoke the reflex (or *stimuli*) are listed. Some should be facilitated because they have desired uses in infancy, and others are needed throughout life. Some, however, should be discouraged because they limit a child by interfering with motor development. Therefore it is essential to discuss *usability* and *limitations*. Note that the following discussion is very general; whenever possible, teachers should seek guidance from medical and therapy specialists. Some procedures intended to stimulate certain patterns or inhibit others may have undesirable side effects in a particular child.

Many good resources are available. Doris Sukiennicke (1971) has written generally descriptive material on reflexes; Peiper (1963) presents a detailed study; and Finnie (1975) describes and illustrates many practical procedures for inhibiting unwanted postural and movement patterns while facilitating the more normal patterns.

Rooting Reflex

Stimulus (that which incites the reflex): Touching or stroking the cheeks or lips.

Description: Movement of the head and mouth in the direction of the stimulus.

Useability: Aids the newborn in finding the mother's breast or a bottle.

Limitations: If it persists or is exaggerated, the rooting reflex may interfere with normal mouth closure and alignment necessary for proper feeding.

In the Classroom:

1. Avoid light touch around the mouth when presenting food to the child.
2. Avoid scraping off excess food with the spoon from the side of the child's mouth when feeding.

3. Consult the therapist for suggestions on desensitizing this reflex.

Moro Reflex

Stimuli: Shaking the child's head or dropping the child's head backwards when he is in a sitting or semi-reclining position.
Description: Extension and abduction of the arms, hyperextension of the head, extension and spreading of the fingers, and less detectable extensor tone in the legs.
Useability: None.
Limitations: Interferes with eye-hand coordination.
In the Classroom:

1. Provide adequate head and trunk support to make sure the child sits in good posture.
2. Seat the child with the knees tucked to the chest and with the head and arms forward *before* attempting to lift the child (Finnie, 1974).
3. Maintain the tucked position when lowering the child onto a chair or a trike.

Startle Reaction

Stimuli: Loud noise, bright light, or quick movement toward child's face.
Description: Rapid flexion of the extremities and fisting of the hands.
Useability: None.
Limitations: Interferes with sitting or standing balance; momentarily precludes hand activities.
In the Classroom:

1. Avoid loud noises. Prevent slamming doors by attaching friction or hydraulic devices which prevent the door from closing or opening quickly.
2. Move slowly toward the child or eliminate brisk movements of your hands as you approach the child's face.

Asymmetrical Tonic Neck Reflex

Stimulus: Rotation of the head to one side.
Description: Increased extensor tone of the extremities on the side of the body to which the head is turned; increased flexor tone of the extremities on the opposite side of the body (the fencing position). The response is more noticeable in the arms and frequently stronger to the right.
Useability: May assist in developing supporting tone in a baby.
Limitations: Inhibits eye-hand coordination, rolling, and feeding.

In the Classroom:

1. Present objects or activities on the side opposite that to which the head usually turns.
2. Face the child so that the stimulation is on the side opposite to the way the head usually faces in the abnormal reflex.
3. Feed from the side opposite to which the child usually looks.
4. Facilitate symmetry as the child is lying down.

Symmetrical Tonic Neck Reflex

Stimulus: Movement of the head in a downward and upward direction (flexion and extension of the neck).
Description: Extension of the upper extremities and flexion of the lower extremities as the head moves in an upward direction (neck extension); flexion of the upper extremities and extension of the lower extremities in response to a downward movement of the head (neck flexion).
Useability: Aids in developing supporting tone in a baby.
Limitations: Limits selective movements of the head as the arms and legs move in response to the motion of the head; prevents the hand-knee position and creeping because it restricts balance in this position; prevents functional ambulation.
In the Classroom:

1. Present activities at eye-level.

Tonic Labyrinthine Reflexes

Stimulus: Changes in the position of the total body, supine or prone.
Description: Increased flexor tone when the child is in the prone position (facedown); increased extensor tone when in the supine position (faceup).
Useability: Never seen in the normally developing infant.
Limitations: Prevents the child from lifting the head or turning over in either prone or supine; limits the ability to bring arms to the midline; inhibits crawling or creeping.
In the Classroom:

1. Avoid frequent or prolonged position in either supine or prone.
2. Provide adequate sitting support.
3. A prone board or wedge may be utilized for hand activities such as feeding.

Equilibrium Reactions

Stimulus: Tipping or shifting of the center of gravity of the body, in any position, prone, supine, sitting, quadruped, kneeling, or standing.

Description: Responses to maintain equilibrium or balance (not fully developed in child until about 7 years of age and continued throughout life).

Usability: Allows child to maintain assumed posture.

Limitations: None.

In the Classroom:

1. Facilitate the development of reactions through games such as see-saw (two children sit facing one another, hold hands, and rock backward and forward each attempting to tip the other over while maintaining sitting balance.

2. Encourage activity on a tiltboard or rocking board during recess or free-play periods.

Abnormal Body Tone

In order for a child to develop normally, the muscles of the body must have a certain amount of tone or tension. Too little tone is called *hypotonia;* too much tone is *hypertonia.* Either condition opposes normal motor development.

Hypotonia

A number of medical conditions result in hypotonia, including dystrophies, hypothyroidism, congenital heart disease, Down's syndrome or mongolism, certain types of cerebral palsy, spinal muscular atrophy, and myasthenia gravis. These conditions may be due to central nervous system disease, diseases of the neuromuscular system components, or primary muscle disease.

When hypotonia exists, delayed motor development is seen early in the infant. This delay is frequently noticed when the baby is not able to lift his head when in a prone position. Rolling comes slowly and the child may not be able to sit unsupported until much later than expected or, in some cases, not at all. The level to which the child will develop is usually indirectly proportional to the degree of hypotonia exhibited; that is, the very floppy infant has a poorer outlook for achieving independence in all functions of life than does the child with a lesser degree of hypotonia.

In the Classroom:

1. Young children who are unable to sit independently on a classroom chair may be placed in a car seat, propped in a tire, or on top of pillows on the floor.

2. Children with hypotonia may prefer to conserve energy through the use of electric typewriters and calculators. Typewriters may need to be placed in front of a child on the far and lowered side of a table so an individual can rest weak arms on the front and raised side. Wrists and hands then easily drop over the keys.

3. Armrests on ball bearing joints often allow hypotonic individuals to make more movements over wider ranges with less effort.

4. Sometimes it is helpful to provide armrests or trays on the wheelchair to place manipulative materials close to the body.

5. If a child gets progressively weaker, realize he may tire and get knocked down more easily. Provide rest periods, and modify or eliminate time qualifiers on tests, classroom assignments, and games.

6. Handle a child at the shoulders and arms. Use the child's arms and shoulders in order to encourage head control.

7. When lifting and carrying an hypotonic child, stabilize his hips firmly to allow him to extend his back and head.

8. Never lift alone when two or more people are needed.

Hypertonia

Some clinical conditions in which hypertonia is present include certain types of cerebral palsy and metabolic diseases in which there is hyperirritability of the muscles.

In hypertonic conditions, the time at which the delay in motor development is noticed is usually in direct proportion to the amount of excessive tone and the areas of the body which are involved. If there is minimal increased tone in only one (monoplegia) or both legs (paraplegia), the delay might not be apparent until the time at which the child should be walking. If there is a great deal of tone and all four extremities are involved (diplegia or quadriplegia) the abnormalities may be noted soon after birth. Rolling and all gross motor activities may be greatly delayed.

The child with spasticity, as in cerebral palsy, has permanent and strongly increased tone in parts or in all of the body. Delay in motor development is due to increased tone and abnormal reflexes, both of which restrict freedom of motion.

The severely spastic child has little or no fluctuation in the muscle tone. Movement in these children is extremely limited, except when aided. It is usually limited to the midrange, and the child's movements are small and labored. There is a great danger of deformities due to lack of movement and change in position. There is minimal initiation of voluntary movements, and reflexes are frequently seen. Equilibrium and protective reactions are often absent. Loud noises may startle the child.

Let us now consider the moderately spastic child. These children have normal to hypertonic response in muscle tone, depending on the stimuli. The child with moderate spasticity has a greater range of motion than the severely spastic child but still not a complete range. The amount of movement is indirectly proportional to the amount of spasticity. If the child is excessively stimulated, emotionally stressed, or overworked, he is less able to accomplish a task than if he were at ease. Deformities or contractions occur less frequently in such children than in the severely spastic. When they do occur, they are often due to abnormal reflex patterns. Learned skills are often performed in primitive fashion without selectivity or refinement in movement. The moderately spastic child may use some reflexes to facilitate some movements. The Moro reflex is often present.

The moderately spastic child is not quite as fearful as the severely spastic child. His apprehension when moving may inhibit his desire to participate actively. Hand use and speech problems may further discourage active interactions with his environment.

In the Classroom:

1. The hemiplegic child whose arm on one side tucks against his body (instead of swinging freely) may be encouraged to hold someone's hands with the more affected hand while walking. The thumb can be held out in proper position, the arm extended and swung in rhythm.
2. Clenched fists may be released by bending the child's hand down at the wrist.
3. Counteract simultaneous flexion of both legs when creeping by holding back the foot of one leg each time the opposite one is moved forward.
4. Encourage active participation by preceding activities and approaches with "Let's . . ." instead of "Do you want to. . . .?"
5. Prevent contractions and avoid patterns of flexion by encouraging the child to change positions while doing activities.
6. Counteract abnormal *flexion* by carrying the child so his back is straight, his arms are prevented from pulling down, and his legs are apart.
7. Before lifting extended child to a sitting position, "try rolling him onto his side where it will be found easier to bend his head and his shoulders forward and so to facilitate the bending of the hips" (Finnie, 1975, p. 144). See Figure 3–1, p. 40.

Effect of Incoordination on Motor Functioning

Athetosis and ataxia are the two major clinical conditions in which incoordination is apparent. These conditions result from some types of cerebral palsy, Friedrich's ataxia, and brain tumors.

Athetosis

Athetosis is characterized by slowing fluctuating muscular tone, writhing, purposeless involuntary movement, and diffuse postural tone. It is frequently mixed with spasticity, and occurs in choreoathetosis. In this condition the child has jerky motions which appear to be well coordinated but are actually involuntary. Pure athetosis is quite rare.

In some cases, delayed motor development in the child with athetosis may be noted early. In other cases, athetosis does not show until the child is three or four years old. In the very young, it is frequently seen as abnormal head movements. It will become more obvious at the point when the baby should begin to reach purposefully (6–9 months). Then it is easily recognized as the child begins to ambulate and/or becomes involved in desk activities and tries to hold his head still. Ambulation is achieved late; the degree of motor retardation is directly proportional to the severity of athetosis.

The athetoid child is hypermobile. He lacks control in midranges and has little or no selective movements. The child with the diagnosis of pure athetosis has muscle tone that fluctuates from no tone to normal. This child has no deformities because of the changing tone.

In the choreoathetotic child, tone fluctuates from hypotonic to normal and back to hypertonic. Deformities are rare because of changing tone. The choreoathetoid has large jerking movements, more proximally than distally. This child is often seen with his arms flying.

Spinal reflex patterns are often present in the child who exhibits both athetosis and spasticity.

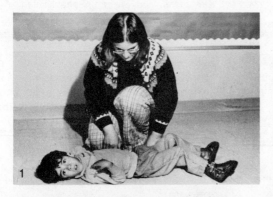

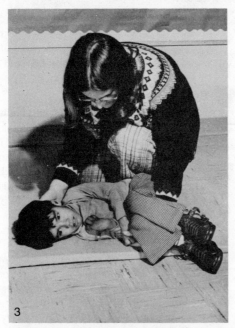

Figure 3–1. Steps toward picking up a usually extended child.

40

Protective and equilibrium reactions in the athetoid child are present, but sometimes exaggerated and unpredictable. Equilibrium reactions are very jerky in both the choreoathetoid and the pure athetoid.

In the Classroom:

1. To reduce unsteady and uncoordinated arm and hand movements, place your hand on the student's shoulders to provide support or stabilization.
2. To reduce a child's uncoordinated movements, position the child so that most of his body is supported, thus permitting him to concentrate on only one or two of his body parts, i.e., head, arm, or hand.
3. To increase the child's independence in movement, help the child devise ways to inhibit unnecessary movements (hold one flinging arm with the other while walking to avoid being thrown off balance by uncoordinated arm movements.)

Ataxia

Ataxia refers to incoordination of movement or a disturbance of balance. It may involve the trunk or may be limited to the extremities. It is characterized by a wide-based, staggering gait or incoordination when the index finger of an extended arm is brought toward the nose.

Ataxia can be mixed with spasticity, athethosis, or both. If a child has spasticity, the spasticity is usually more in the flexor than in the extensor pattern. Deformities are associated with the ataxic child because of the spasticity that may accompany the ataxia. His range of motion may be severely limited by his spasticity. Spinal and tonic reflex patterns are not present in the ataxic child. Righting reactions are highly developed, but the movements are very uncoordinated and may be exaggerated. Equilibrium reactions are again highly developed but are abnormally executed with incoordination.

Ataxia of the trunk is frequently not recognized until the child reaches the walking stage of development. Ambulation is usually quite delayed and external aids (canes or crutches) may be needed. Developmental delays are usually noted earlier if the ataxia involves the extremities. Lack of spatial orientation often affects development of refined motor movements and movement in space.

Weakness and/or Paralysis

Limitation or absence of movement may be brought about by severe weakness or paralysis. Conditions which cause weakness and/or paralysis include post-polio (poliomyelitis), spina bifida or myelomeningocele (congenital defect of the spine with damage to the nervous tissues), and spinal cord or peripheral nerve injuries.

Weakness

Weakness may result from atrophy of the muscles because of neural involvement. The nerve which innervates the muscle may be damaged by disease, as in the case of polio; by congenital deformity, in the case of spina bifida; or by trauma, in the case of spinal cord and peripheral nerve injuries. The factor which determines whether the result is weakness or paralysis is the degree and location of injury or disease. Depending on the cause and the degree of damage, regeneration of the nerve may be possible to some extent. However, even if regeneration does take place, some weakness usually results.

The level of development which the child will reach is dependent on when the insult to the nervous system occurs and how severe it is. In spina bifida, the level of motor functioning that the child will achieve depends on the extent and level of the defect and the amount and timing of treatment. Those factors discussed earlier in hypotonia which interfere with normal development are generally applicable to these conditions of weakness.

Paralysis

Paralysis may be partial or complete. If it is partial, function may be only mildly restricted and those statements attributed to weakness are applicable here. If paralysis is complete, as in high level spina bifida and complete spinal cord injury, there may be complete loss of power of motion *and sensation*. Paralysis may be flaccid (limp) or spastic, as in the case of some spinal cord injuries. The loss of sensation is a complicating factor when determining the effect of paralysis on motor development. Sensory nerves, in addition to motor nerves, are involved in this condition. Incontinence is often a result.

In the Classroom:

1. If a child is incontinent, encourage aides and parents to teach independence in diaper changing and proper use and care of other elimination apparatus.

2. If a child is paralyzed, watch for sores and other injuries a child may not feel. Encourage frequent changes of position.
3. If a child is weak or unable to make certain movements, complete the process of task analysis to find alternate ways to accomplish tasks.

Absent Body Parts

As discussed previously, absence of body parts (amputeeism) may be congenital or acquired. Parts of extremities may be involved or the entire arms or legs may be absent or lost.

In the discussion of normal developmental sequences, it can be seen that the extremities are very important tools. If these tools are absent, development will occur at a slower rate. Again, the degree of motor retardation of development is in direct proportion to the number of absent limbs and the degree of amputations. Interference with balance is the most significant factor affecting development.

In the case of the upper extremity amputee, the child may skip several developmental milestones, namely crawling and creeping, as he does not have his hand(s) or arm(s) to use as support. Upper extremity amputees will frequently walk at 7–9 months. Conversely, ambulation will be greatly delayed or impossible in the lower extremity amputee without external aids (prostheses or artificial limbs and canes or crutches).

Limited Range of Motion

Limited range of motion of the joints of the body may be seen in juvenile rheumatoid arthritis and a condition called arthrogryposis. In these conditions, the extremities, spine, and/or neck may not move to the degree that they do in the normal child. Limited motion may be due to swelling in the joints, abnormalities of the bones or soft tissue structures, or shortened or absent muscles and tendons.

Delays in development are frequently seen very early in the child with arthrogryposis. During infancy, contractures of the neck often restrict the beginning movements of the head in prone. Upper and lower extremity abnormalities may respectively restrict the use of the hands and ambulation, which can be significantly delayed or impossible.

Arthritis may be a temporary or a permanent debilitating disease. During those periods when the joints are inflamed, range of motion is greatly reduced. Depending on the timing of these periods, development may be affected. The degree of developmental delay in children with arthritis is in direct proportion to the severity of the disease and the number of joints involved.

Therapeutic Approaches

Basic to all of the treatment approaches is the concept of improving function of the individual. Treatment is directed at normalizing or bettering the patterns of motion to encourage maximum independence.

Systems of Therapy Used in the Treatment of Cerebral Palsied Individuals

During the past thirty years, a number of people have developed various systems of therapy based on neurophysiology. Gilette (1969) describes each of these approaches in depth. The most common therapeutic approach with the cerebral palsied patient is that developed by Bobath. Other systems have been developed by Phelps, Kabat-Knott, and Brunnstrom.

Bobath, a physical therapist, and her husband, a neurologist, collaborated in the development of a system of treatment in which abnormal reflexes are inhibited and normal patterns of motion and postural reactions are facilitated. It is called the Bobath approach or neurodevelopmental treatment. (In the previous section of this chapter we used principles of this method to suggest ways teachers can help motor performance of students.) Treatment principles from the neurodevelopmental point of view consist of reducing muscle tone, preventing abnormal responses, and facilitating movements using key points to guide the child along in his movements. Key points are usually points that are proximal or close to the trunk of the body.

Neurodevelopment principles include reflex-inhibiting patterns to reduce spasticity, tapping to increase tone, and working for sustained contractions and holding positions.

Approaches to Treatment of Other Physical Disabilities

Basic therapeutic approaches include maintenance or improvement of strength through resistive exercises, maintenance of normal range of motion and body alignment, and instruction in the use and care of prosthetic devices and/or crutches and canes. Again, developmental activities are incorporated into treatment.

Treatment for persons with limited range of motion depends upon the underlying cause of the limitation. Treatment may consist of relaxation techniques, heat, massage, or stretching exercises. Bracing or splinting may be employed.

Therapists and other specialists also have the major responsibility for choosing and designing adaptive and assistive equipment. They need information about vehicular travel, mobility, physical management, and selection and care of "hardware" such as braces.

Adaptive and Assistive Equipment

Several uses are illustrated here of adaptive and assistive equipment which have furthered independent accomplishments of children who have rather severe physical limitations. Finding ways these individuals can move from place to place (Figure 3–2) and change positions for working in the classroom (Figure 3–3) are two chal-

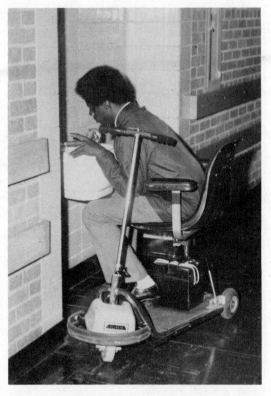

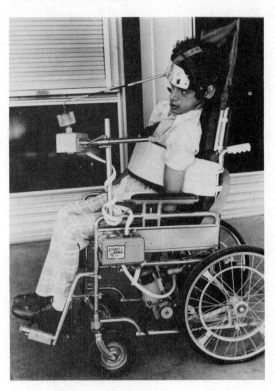

lenges facing teachers and therapists. Allow these illustrations to serve as a guide to your own explorations of possibilities. (Pp. 46–47.)

To aid therapists and teachers, Northall and Melichar (1975) have compiled a comprehensive information system on all kinds of adaptive and assistive equipment for persons with physical disabilities.

Summary

To assist the recording of present functioning of individuals and the recording of long-range predictions, we suggest as a guide Figure 3–4, the "Profile of Physical Capabilities." These data serve as guidelines for making present and future curricular and rehabilitation decisions, such as potentials for attending college, entering specific courses, enjoying specific leisure activities, caring for one's own needs, and being physically independent.

In this chapter, we have concentrated primarily upon immediate and short-range goals and corresponding objectives for improvement in motor functioning. All progress, of course, leads also to attainment of some long-range goals.

Name _____ Birthday _____ Date _____

Therapist _____
Therapist _____
Teacher _____
Teacher _____
Parent _____
Other _____

Code
Dates recorded in *pen*: Date of present performance.
Dates recorded in *pencil*: Predicted date of future accomplishment.

	Minimal	**Mild**	**Moderate**	**Severe**	**Comments**
VISION	( ) ( ) No trouble with vision; no glasses needed.	( ) ( ) Some correction needed; may wear glasses; not handicapped in seeing.	( ) ( ) Low vision: uses residual vision in most school tasks or uses special visual, auditory, and tactile aids.	( ) ( ) Almost blind; totally blind. Relies on tactile & auditory modalities for academic learning.	
HEARING	( ) ( ) No trouble with hearing.	( ) ( ) Some difficulty in hearing; may wear hearing aid satisfactorily.	( ) ( ) Quite handicapped in hearing: has difficulty when wearing hearing aid.	( ) ( ) Almost deaf; totally deaf.	
SPEECH	( ) ( ) Speech can be understood without difficulty by a stranger.	( ) ( ) Some difficulty in being understood by a stranger; able to get ideas across in speech.	( ) ( ) Speech hard for a stranger or immediate family to understand; hard to get ideas across in speech.	( ) ( ) Almost totally unable to communicate by speech; totally without speech.	
COMMUNICATION	( ) ( ) Able to get ideas across easily by speaking or by writing.	( ) ( ) Difficulty getting ideas across to strangers via speech or writing. Family can understand.	( ) ( ) Speech & writing not functional for getting ideas across. Depends upon gestures, communication board. Indicates "yes"-"no" to questions by listener.	( ) ( ) Responses are absent, inconsistent or too slow to be functional.	

	( ) ( )	( ) ( )	( ) ( )	( ) ( )
SITTING BALANCE	No difficulty in sitting unaided in a chair or at table.	Somewhat unsteady in sitting in a chair or at a table, but not handicapped in doing so.	Quite handicapped in sitting in a chair or at a table; needs a relaxation chair and tray.	Unable to maintain sitting balance unless fully supported.
ARM-HAND USE	No difficulty in using arms and hands for self-help activity.	Some difficulty in using arms and hands for self-help; slow and awkward.	May need special equipment to assist in performing daily living skills. Gross incoordination. Very slow. Unable to perform tasks quickly and unaided.	Unable to use hands to perform needed daily living skills, even with special equipment and assistance.
MOBILITY	No difficulty in walking. Normal or near normal gait.	Weight bearing. May have unsteady balance. Awkward, but able to get around. May use brace.	Weight bearing, but requires assistive device, i.e., cane, crutch, braces. Cannot walk without devices.	Either uses wheelchair, walks very precariously. Crawls, rolls or scoots. Completely dependent upon others.
INDEPENDENCE IN MOBILITY	No obstacle in traveling about the home or community.	Limited in traveling about the community. Needs assistance in boarding bus, in/out of cars.	Limited to home. Needs personal assistance for traveling in the community.	Confined to one place. Must be moved by another person.

Figure 3-4. Profile of physical capabilities.

SOURCE. Adapted from "A Survey of Degree of Physical Handicap" by Elias Katz, *Cerebral Palsy Review*, 1954, *XV*, 10–11. Copyright 1954 by Cerebral Palsy Review. Also from "Rating Scale of Physical Capabilities" in *Influences of Selected Variables upon Economic Adaptations of Orthopedically Handicapped and Other Health Impaired* by Winnie Bachmann, 1971, 175–176. (Doctoral dissertation, University of the Pacific, Stockton, California.) Both sources adapted and used by permission.

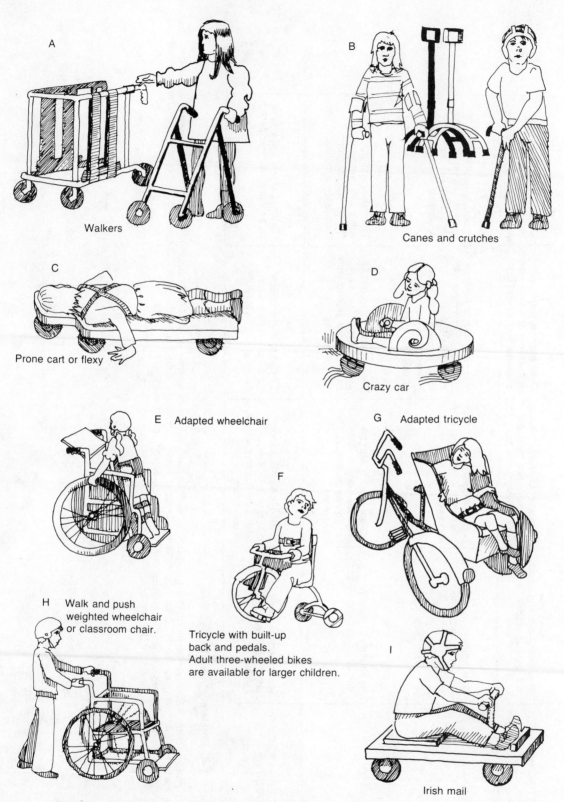

A Walkers

B Canes and crutches

C Prone cart or flexy

D Crazy car

E Adapted wheelchair

F Tricycle with built-up back and pedals. Adult three-wheeled bikes are available for larger children.

G Adapted tricycle

H Walk and push weighted wheelchair or classroom chair.

I Irish mail

Figure 3–2. Ways of moving from place to place.

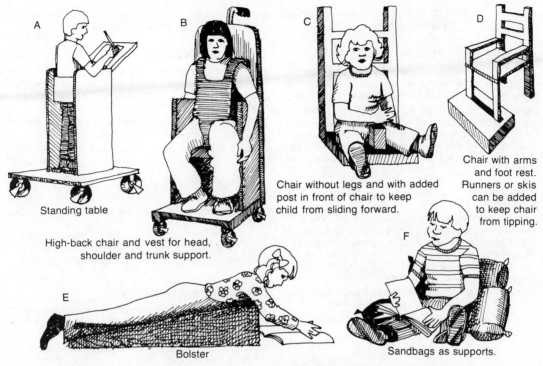

A   Standing table

High-back chair and vest for head, shoulder and trunk support.

Chair without legs and with added post in front of chair to keep child from sliding forward.

Chair with arms and foot rest. Runners or skis can be added to keep chair from tipping.

Bolster

Sandbags as supports.

Figure 3–3. Ways of positioning for working in the classroom.

Gathering all relevant data on an individual, teachers should attempt to collaborate with other specialists to plan implementation of immediate and short-range objectives and to predict long-range goals for motor functions and other physical capabilities.

References

Normal Motor Development

Bobath, K. *The motor deficit in patients with cerebral palsy.* Suffolk, England: William Heinemann, 1966.

Caplan, F. *The first twelve months of life.* Princeton, N. J.: Ed Com Systems, 1971.

Fiorentino, M. R. *Reflex testing methods for evaluating C.N.S. development.* Springfield: Charles C Thomas, 1963.

Gesell, A. L. *The first five years of life—A guide to the study of the preschool child.* New York: Harper & Brothers, 1940.

Gesell, A. L., & Francis, L., Llg. *The child from five to ten.* New York: Harper & Brothers, 1946.

Illingworth, R. S. *The development of the infant and young child: Normal and abnormal.* Baltimore, Md.: Williams & Wilkins, 1972.

Knobloch, H., & Pasamanick, B. *Gesell and Amatruda's developmental diagnosis: The evaluation and management of normal and abnormal neuropsychologic development in infancy and early childhood* (3rd ed.). Hagerstown, Md.: Harper & Row, 1974.

O'Donnell, P. A. *Motor and haptic learning.* San Rafael, Calif.: Dimensions, 1969.

Effects of Disability

Bigge, J. Some implications for classroom teaching of the Bobath approach to individual physical therapy (Master's thesis, San Francisco State College, 1960).

Bobath, K. The normal postural reflex mechanism and its deviation in children with cerebral palsy. *Physiotherapy,* 1971, *57,* 515–525.

Finnie, N. *Handling the young cerebral palsied child at home.* New York: E. P. Dutton, 1975.

Fiorentino, M. R. *Normal and abnormal development—The influences of primitive reflexes on motor development.* Springfield, Ill.: Charles C Thomas, 1972.

Peiper, A. *Cerebral function in infancy and childhood.* New York: Consultants Bureau, 1963.

Sukiennicki, D. A. Neuromotor development. In B. S. Banus (Ed.), *The developmental therapist: A prototype of the pediatric occupational therapist.* Thorofare, N. J.: Charles B. Slack, 1971.

Therapeutic Approaches

Bobath, B., & Karel, B. *Motor development in the different types of cerebral palsy.* London: William Heinemann, 1975.

Gilette, H. E. *Systems of therapy in cerebral palsy.* Springifeld, Ill.: Charles C Thomas, 1969.

Adaptive and Assistive Equipment

Bigge, J. *Systems of precise observations for teachers.* Film and printed guidelines. Bureau of Education for the Handicapped, U.S. Office of Education, 1970.

Northall, J. E., & Melichar, J. F. (Eds.) *Information system on adaptive and assistive equipment used in schools for physically handicapped children* (IS AARE). San Mateo, Calif.: United Cerebral Palsy Association of Portland, Oregon, Adaptive Systems, 1975.

Summary

Bachmann, W. H. Influence of selected variables upon economic adaptation of orthopedically handicapped and other health impaired. (Doctoral dissertation, University of the Pacific, 1971). Dissertation Abstracts International, 1971, *32* (5), 2510A. (University Microfilms No. 71—28079)

Delaware State Board of Education. *CADETS curriculum guides.* Dover, Del.: author, 1975.

Katz, E. A survey of degree of physical handicap. *Cerebral Palsy Review,* 1954, *XV,* 10–11.

Resources

Normal Motor Development

Association of Neurodevelopmental Treatment Therapists, *N.D.T. Newsletter.* Curative Workshop of Milwaukee, United Cerebral Palsy of Wisconsin, 10437 Watertown Plank Road, P. O. Box 7372, Milwaukee, Wisc. 53226.

Beter, T. R., & Cragin, W. E. *The mentally retarded child and his motor behavior.* Springfield, Ill.: Charles C Thomas, 1972.

Brazelton, T. B. *Infants and mothers: Differences in development.* New York: Dell, 1969.

Cratty, B. J. *Motor activities, motor ability, and the education of children.* Springfield, Ill.: Charles C Thomas, 1970.

Fraiberg, S. *The magic years: Understanding and handling the problems of early childhood.* New York: Charles Scribner's Sons, 1959.

Hackett, L. C. *A guide to movement exploration.* Palo Alto, Calif.: Peek, 1966.

Levy, J. *The baby exercise book: For the first fifteen months.* New York: Pantheon, 1973.

Stone, L. J., Smith, H. T., & Murphy, L. B. *The complete infant.* New York: Basic Books, 1973.

Effects of Disability

Bragg, J. H., Houser, C., & Schumaker, J. Behavior modification—Effects on reverse tailor sitting in children with cerebral palsy. *Physical Therapy,* 1975, *LV* (8), 860–868.

Cratty, B. J. *Developmental games for physically handicapped children.* Palo Alto, Calif.: Peek, 1969.

Geddes, D. *Physical activities for individuals with handicapping conditions.* St. Louis, Mo.: C. V. Mosley, 1974.

Haynes, U. *A developmental approach to casefinding.* (U.S. Public Health Service Publication No. 2017). Washington, D.C.: U.S. Government Printing Office, 1969.

Pearson, P., & Williams, C. (Eds.). *Physical therapy services in the developmental disabilities.* Springfield, Ill.: Charles C Thomas, 1972.

Therapeutic Approaches

American Journal of Occupational Therapy. Journal of American Occupational Therapy Association, 6 000 Executive Blvd, Rockville, Mo. 20852.

Bobath, K. & Bobath, B. The facilitation of normal postural reactions and movements in the treatment of cerebral palsy. *Physiotherapy,* 1964, *50,* 246–262.

Crickmay, M. C. Speech therapy and the Bobath approach to cerebral palsy. In Marie C. Crickmay, *The Bobath approach to cerebral palsy.* Springfield, Ill.: Charles C Thomas, 1966.

McDonald, E. T., & Chance, B., Jr. *Cerebral palsy.* Englewood Cliffs, N. J.: Prentice-Hall, 1964.

Physical Therapy. Journal of the American Physical Therapy Association, 1156 15th St. NW, Washington, D. C. 20005.

Scrutton, D., & Gilbertson, M. The physiotherapist's role in the treatment of cerebral palsy. In R. L. Samilson, *Orthopaedic aspects of cerebral palsy.* London: William Heinemann, 1975.

Swack, M. Therapeutic role of the teacher of physically handicapped child. *Exceptional children,* 1969, *35* (5), 371–374.

Summary

Capper Foundation for Crippled Children. *Begin at the beginning.* 1975, Early Education Project, 3500 West Tenth Street, Topeka, Kan., 66604. (Measurement techniques, physical and occupational therapy, speech pathology.)

4

ACCOMPANYING

DISABILITIES

● Physically disabled individuals also may have additional problems. This chapter briefly discusses some of these accompanying disabilities, including:

1. visual disabilities

2. auditory impairments

3. combination of visual and auditory disabilities

4. language and speech disorders

5. convulsive disorder

● Functional results of the disabilities should be used as a base for teaching. It is essential to obtain from a child's physician the information about the accompanying disability which might be helpful. The importance of medical evaluation when working with individuals who have identified or suspected accompanying disabilities cannot be overemphasized. Similarly, it is vital to seek assistance from educational and other specialists.

June Bigge.

Visual Disabilities

Physically disabled children, particularly those with cerebral palsy, frequently have severe visual problems. While in a few instances the children may be totally blind, in most cases they will have residual vision. Teachers are challenged to help the children to effectively use their remaining vision.

Teachers of physically disabled children who have a limited background in management of visual problems must realize what they do *not* know about helping children with visual disability. Such teachers will need the assistance of specialists in teaching the visually disabled. Specialists usually serve as itinerant teachers, resource specialists, and consultants.

Classifications of Visual Disability

Persons with visual disability can be described by the way they function in school. Visually disabled children either see with very limited vision and use that limited vision with adapted materials in print and audio form, or they may have almost no vision and require tactual and auditory learning materials.

According to Abel and Kellis, *"low vision* children are those children who because of visual disabilities, cannot handle easily and at the same rate the same educational materials and tasks that normally seeing children manage with facility" (1967, p. ii). They use their residual vision in most school tasks or use special visual, auditory, and tactile aids.

Those children commonly described as blind often have some useful vision. They just cannot "perform tasks which normally require gross vision without increased reliance on other senses" (Spivey and Colenbrander, 1976, p. 6). Therefore, rather than thinking of them as blind, we should think of them as children who have to rely heavily on the tactile and auditory modalities for academic learning. These children may or may not rely on braille for reading and writing.

Early Goals

Early goals for children with visual disabilities include communication, physical awareness of self and position in space, gross movement, reach, touch, grasp, exploration, posture, walking, orientation, and mobility.

Communication

Purposeful interaction with other persons, even if only very basic, is one milestone important to any child with a severe visual impairment. According to Fraiberg, Smith, and Adelson (1969):

> The response smile to the configuration of the human face, the selective smile for the face of the mother, the father and siblings, the discrimination of mother and stranger, the entire sequence of recognitory experience which leads to mental representation and evocative memory, are organized through visual experience. To a very large extent, eye to eye contact is the matrix of a signal system which evolves between mother and child. If the blind baby is cut off from this archaic language, so tragically, are the parents. (p. 122)

In order to counteract deficiencies caused by lack of eye to eye contact in initial communications, Fraiberg, Smith, and Adelson report how nonvisual experiences serve to bind the baby and her partner. Parents and others can use tactile and auditory stimulation to help a child find reason to interact with others and start to find meaning in her environment. Adults can cuddle, hold, and talk to an infant while feeding in order to make contact with others pleasurable. In this way, a child will want more, rather than less, of these kinds of contacts. As a baby becomes more content, she smiles and coos and turns her arms and legs in a way that indicates pleasure. *Finally*, interaction and a form of communication result from the adult's long and tedious hours of auditory and tactile soliloquy!

Consider now the consequences if a child not only has visual handicaps but also a motor problem like cerebral palsy. Unresponsive behaviors caused by physical disabilities do not encourage adult efforts to persist in providing auditory and tactile experiences. A child might have severe difficulty swallowing and eating due to sensorimotor disorders. The child may flail involuntarily in her mother's arms and accidentally knock the food off the spoon. Another child may be stiff and not be able to "relax" as the mother cuddles her. She may have a reflex to bite every time the mother puts the food in her mouth. Because of muscle problems in the face, these children may not be able to smile or make noise to indicate contentment.

Parents and others must learn to persist and treat these children as normally as possible. Adults must learn improved positions for holding and feeding, such as those suggested in Chapter 7, "Self-Care" and in *Handling the Young Cerebral Palsied Child at Home* by Nancy Finnie (1975). Adults strive to handle the babies with intimacy, talking to them as if they were among the most responsive of babies, i.e., "Open your hand and take the rattle. Hear the noise." These babies do not see well; their movements are abnormal; and they cannot gain sensory information in the normal way. Meaning must be conveyed through simultaneous guidance of physical movement with verbal descriptions of the movements, such as "Your arm is going into your coat sleeve." "Now your arm is relaxed. Good."

Physical Awareness of Self and Position in Space

Failure to develop body image, or *schema*, and a sense of position and movement in space accompanies visual disability. Limited vision or absence of vision prevents young children from relating to a reflection in a mirror or to the bodies of other persons. Movement limitations and irregularities further limit exploration of one's own body and subsequent development of body and schema.

Adaptive solutions can begin with a planned system of stroking. A terry cloth glove, silk scarf, fur mitt, or soft paint brush can be used. Each part of the body should be stroked gently and named. For example, stroke the arm while saying "Kathy's arm." Move to the opposite arm and repeat. Done frequently and to all parts of the body, this procedure will increase body awareness and nurture correct body image. The stroking routine also reduces tactile defensiveness. The gentle introduction of a child's hands to various prepared textures such as flour, sand, and corn meal can often be helpful.

Inner sense of one's own physical movement and position in space is called *proprioception*. Adequate proprioception helps us to maintain our balance in the upright walking position and to make successful directed physical movements. Intensify and increase this level of proprioceptive impulses in the child by attaching small weights such as bean bags or sandbags to various parts of the child's body. The added weights will cause investment of more effort in moving these parts, thus intensifying the sense of movement and increasing awareness of the weighted parts.

A child's sense of her relationship to space cannot be neglected. This sense, too, develops very early when auditory stimuli provide information regarding the direction and distance of persons or objects. Talk to the child from different parts of the room. Move her crib around in the bedroom and in the house. Feed her from different sides to let her experience differences in direction of movement. When she is old enough to throw objects, she can learn about up and down. Allow the child to throw or drop something. Pick it up, hand it back, and let her do it again. The child should have some idea of the space around her; it should have been defined for her in as many ways as possible, particularly through sound, touch, and movement in space.

Gross Movement

Gross movement tasks generally precede tasks requiring fine coordination. Gross movement tasks may be encouraged from early ages. If the floor is warm, place a child without clothes on a crib sheet on the floor. Let her move about freely, assisting when necessary. Rolling and other gross movements bring the entire muscular system into play. Put a child on her back and guide her into rolling; eventually move her into a crawl.[1] A toddler should be encouraged to move around the house to find toys with minimum assistance from bedroom to bathroom, from kitchen to living room, or in her own room. It is important that she be allowed this freedom even if she is disabled and must roll or scoot in the best patterns possible. Parents and other should try many different ways to encourage gross movement and thus promote a child's development.

At the preschool age various activities and toys can help develop further body control. Simple, guided gymnastics can be attempted as well as postural exercises. Swimming is an excellent activity, fostering movement exploration and body self-awareness while also developing some coordination. Heavy toys help to develop muscle strength; a child can push such objects across a given surface or space. Large beach balls, rocking boats, swings, teeter totters, and hobby horses are other toys which stimulate mobility and balance.

Reach, Touch and Grasp

Reaching, touching, and grasping are among first steps in exploration of materials and their qualities, characteristics, and uses. These explorative experiences provide the basis for cognitive development. Patterns of reach, touch, and grasp also help lay foundations for hand-eye coordination in youngsters with enough vision to distinguish form.

To assume that visually disabled children spontaneously and naturally develop good tactual skills is wrong. Use of tactual information often must be consciously and systemically taught. When a severely visually disabled child enters school, society's "touch taboos" have already been well-learned. Parents and teachers must work together to help the child learn to explore tactually and to use tactual information effectively.

Incentive for directional reaching can often be supplied by using sound cues. Sound cues may be used along with visual cues. For those children with sufficient vision, select objects or actions with high interest. Objects with vivid, solid, and contrasting colors are attractive to most visually disabled children. When visually disabled persons are not easily motivated, reinforcement techniques can help.[2]

Additional observations can help determine how to help physically disabled youngsters. Can the hand be extended to reach out? In cerebral palsy, it is often necessary to reduce some of the spasticity in the arms by tapping them or by moving them slowly so the arm can be extended. If the hand is clenched, a teacher must find a way that the child can approach an item with a more open hand. If a child can approach an item with an open hand but is unable to clench it, physical guidance of the child's fingers may help. If the problem lies in the fact that a child cannot judge distance or direction and plan appropriate movements, exercises for perceptual disorders may help. The child may be able to plan appropriate movement, but because of motor coordination problems, be incapable of precise movements of the arm to the location. It is important to analyze each child's attempts in order to determine how and when to help.

Exploration

A child with a visual handicap should be encouraged to reach out, explore, and feel. Because a partially sighted or blind child cannot always see "what is out there," she does not have the incentive to reach out and explore like children with normal vision. Items of interest should be placed nearby so she can take initiative to reach out, grab the item, and explore its features. Some items such as food may be put just beyond reach so she learns to reach farther and even move in order to get it. As with all children, memory of what they see, hear, and feel, as well as how they interpret what they see, hear, and feel, forms the basis of later perceptual and cognitive development.

Cerebral palsied children with severe visual problems do not see what there is to explore. In addition, they may not have the strength or coordination necessary to direct motion needed for exploration. It is important to guide the child physically into more normal movement patterns while encouraging exploration. (See Figure 4–1.)

Posture

Good posture is vitally important for a visually disabled individual. The child must be helped to develop sitting and walking postures. Encourage the child to hold her head erect while sitting, standing, and walking. Some children, however, may have to maintain unusual postures in order to use their residual vision more efficiently. Encourage the child to sit with her back against the chair with her feet flat on the floor. Often, visually disabled children exhibit unusual mannerisms such as rocking, rolling their heads, and flipping their hands. It has been theorized that some of these mannerisms are used by the blind child to determine where her body is in space. Rather than simply extinguishing all mannerisms, some should be looked upon as proprioceptive or "body in space" problems and treated accordingly.

Walking

If a child can walk, she should be taught techniques such as maintaining balance without spreading the feet too far apart. Free motion of the arms as part of the gait can be encouraged by actually swinging a child's arms during a walk. Reinforce the heel-toe technique of starting steps at the heel, rolling to the balls of the feet and ending on the toes. Finally, discourage her from

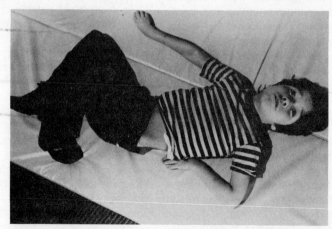

Figure 4–1. We must find how to help children learn even if they cannot see or move.

shuffling her feet. One may have to pick a child's feet up and put them down in order to give the feel of walking without shuffling.

●Orientation and Mobility

Individuals with visual disabilities and crippling conditions sometimes have serious mobility problems. To experience objects and persons a child first has to move to their locations. The concept of "confined space" allows the child to orient herself in a small space, to explore, and to gather information about people and items. One of the purposes of the *confined space playroom* described by Barrett, Hunt, and Jones (1967) is to help each child learn about body management in a confined space with different textures, levels, and places where the child can fall without getting hurt. Being put with others into a confined space, a child has opportunity of interacting with and touching other children. Young disabled students seldom get a chance to roll over each other, pull each other's hair, and feel each other's clothes like the children in Figure 4–2. These orientation and body management experiences are most important to the motorically disabled child and to the child with visual problems. Other opportunities for exploration should be found. If the child cannot get to different locations by herself, she should be assisted.

When normal postural positions and motor milestones are not reached at appropriate times, the disabled children should be guided physically to perform the prerequisite tasks. Children who are not pivoting, rolling, or turning over may be helped to perform these tasks. The baby who should be walking, but is not, should be guided to perform the prerequisite tasks of creeping and crawling.[3] Since she does not have a visual impression of normal motor activity, supply her with the kinesthetic experience. The child who is visually disabled and develops slowly should receive additional help from a physical therapist who can guide the progression of basic motor movements. Therapists can also show parents and teachers how to work on ambulation while discouraging or inhibiting unusual mannerisms and postures.

Therapy methods for cerebral palsied children have been used successfully to elicit desired righting reactions and to inhibit unwanted reflex behaviors in children who have accompanying visual problems. When these children begin to make movements such as walking, kicking, and jumping, one predictable motor problem will be balance. The teacher should plan activities which stimulate righting and balance reactions.

When these children enter school, they must be made to feel a part of the school community. They should develop a calm command of the physical plant in which they will spend most of the day. The teacher can assist by familiarizing the children with basic mobility techniques. They should be

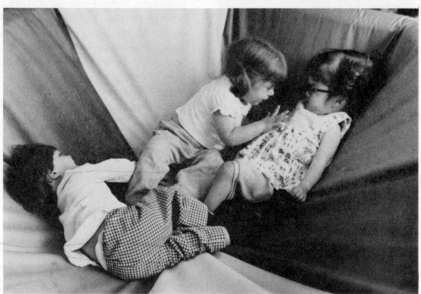

Figure 4–2. It's nice to be close!

taught to "trail," "square off," and "direction take." *Trailing* is the act of following along a surface with the back of the fingers. It helps to determine one's place in space, to locate a specific object, and to get a parallel line of travel. *Squaring off* is the act of aligning and positioning one's body in relation to a fixed object. It helps in establishing a line of direction and/or a definite position in the environment. Lastly, *direction taking* is the act of getting a line of direction from an object or sound. This process facilitates movement in a straight line to a desired location in the environment. If the child is adequately prepared in these three techniques and is familiarized with existing landmarks, her adjustment to school life will be easier (see Figure 4–3). For some orthopedically disabled students, these specific techniques may need adaptation to accommodate specific needs.

Figure 4–3. Ted maneuvers with little difficulty.

The visually impaired student should use one room in the school as a base for relating one location to another. For example, the student may note a drinking fountain outside of the classroom and count how many doorways must be passed before reaching the correct room. Familiarize the visually disabled person with the surrounding space and she will orient herself and gain confidence in mobility.

Principles for Working with Persons with Visual Disability

When interacting with persons with visual disability, remember the following principles:

1. *Expect progress.* Emphasize what the person *can* do. Avoid intensification of the handicap by noticing primarily what the individual cannot accomplish. Treat the individual as any non-disabled person by acknowledging strengths and conveying the message that she, also, has the opportunity to learn many new things.

2. *Encourage independence.* Visually disabled persons must be allowed to become as independent as possible. Far too often persons do not realize that they help visually disabled individuals too much. Sighted persons may feel momentarily uncomfortable when they see someone struggling to assemble something or to move toward a specific place. In order to relieve their own discomfort, they do not allow the disabled person to solve the problem. Similarly, visually disabled persons must be given responsibility for responding to situations independently. Disabled individuals need to learn to reassure others that they will be all right and probably will not get hurt while playing or while finding their way to specific places. Even normal children from time to time get hurt playing. It is important for disabled persons to explain firmly and graciously that help is not needed. If help is declined without causing embarrassment, the person may offer help in the future to some other disabled person who does need help.

3. *Use individual proficiencies.* Encourage the visually disabled to help others who are not as proficient in some areas. Care must be taken to allow disabled individuals to help other people and not be constant receivers of help.

4. *Encourage individual flexibility in finding directions and landmarks.* The visually disabled student should not routinely be given the seat closest to the door of the classroom. Teachers can encourage acquisition of orientation skills by placing students' desks in different locations

for short periods of time. In this way, the visually disabled child will approach objects within the room from a variety of directions. Variation in desk placement will also nurture development of cardinal directionality, i.e., *east, west, north, south* walls; *left, right* landmark locations; and *45°* and *90°* angularity turns. Variation in placement of desks applies also to children in wheelchairs or on crutches. Students need to learn to orient themselves to the environment from different perspectives. The visually disabled student needs to know the classroom well before proceeding to other areas within the school.

5. *Substitute for unseen visual cues*. Persons with severe visual disability are unable to interpret communication relayed by visual cues such as winking of the eye or raising of the eyebrow. Persons who interact with visually disabled persons must use cues which need not be seen to be interpreted. For instance, it is helpful to pat a child on the head to accompany a smile and to use voice intonations which reveal feelings ordinarily expressed with nonverbal cues. In the classroom, it is necessary for teachers to say aloud whatever they are writing on the blackboard and to describe what is being drawn. It is also important to make children aware what is going on around them so they, too, have options of responding, interacting, or learning.

6. *Use a variety of modalities*. Learning is enhanced for many children when they can utilize a variety of modalities. The use of smell, touch, and sound will help visually disabled persons learn. Often when an individual is exposed to different modalities, a certain channel can be identified as a particularly strong learning mode for certain kinds of tasks.

7. *Teach more acceptable behaviors*. Directly or indirectly disabled individuals should be taught that some of their actions or behaviors differ from what is usual. Because of these differences, disabled individuals may draw unwanted attention to themselves. Most of us learn acceptable behaviors by watching others. Severely visually disabled persons, however, cannot learn from visual clues. For example, a visually disabled individual may not be aware of her unusual walking pattern or her unusual manner of waving her hands. The child may not realize that the other children are sitting erect and participating while she is slouched with her elbows on her knees and her fists in her eyes. Visually disabled individuals must be taught how to manage themselves physically and how to interact in ways that minimize unusual attention and consequent negative attitudes toward their behaviors. The reduction of behaviors which look different or bizarre will facilitate acceptance of some disabled persons.

Concept and Language Development

There are numerous ways to facilitate concept and language development in visually disabled persons. Groves and Griffith (1969, pp. 1–26) discuss many of the following activities.[4]

Encourage as Much Visual Input as Possible

Individuals must be taught to use whatever vision they have. It is often difficult to determine how much of their vision children are using. One can encourage use of functional vision by infants by switching on a dim light in the room where the children are sleeping and then moving the light from time to time to stimulate the child. When children begin to reach, it is helpful to guide them to explore their own bodily features and objects in the immediate environment, such as the crib or a mobile. When visually disabled children begin touching and feeling, they should be provided with opportunities to experience different textures, surfaces, sizes, and sounds.

Verbalize What is Present and What is Happening

It is very important to explain to a visually disabled child what she is touching, what is happening, or how someone else is feeling. It is helpful, for instance, to name the item *sweater* and talk about putting an arm in a sweater as the child is helped to do the act. Describe different objects, activities, and expressed emotions and tell about people who are present.

Call attention to the many sounds around the house. This strategy will help the child learn what is happening around her and make her feel secure about her surroundings. The doorbell indicates that someone is at the door. The garbage disposal noise means that the garbage is being ground and one can feel vibration of the motor. Talk not only about items in the child's presence, but also about words for feelings and emotions.

"Oh, a crying child is feeling disappointment because she cannot go to her friend's house to play." "She is angry because she cannot unzip the zipper."

Develop Concepts by Using Actual Items within the Child's Environment

When attempting to develop concepts such as *big* or *little,* one must try to use examples within the child's experience. Be careful not to talk about *a little ball* and then give the child only one size ball to experience. Children may learn comparatives more quickly by experiencing examples of a concept and its opposite. It is also helpful to provide the child with several examples of a particular concept, and at least one example which does not fit the concept. Presenting "nonexamples" allows the child to eliminate certain attributes and concentrate on the common characteristics.

Concepts should be taught in ways that stimulate further awareness. For instance, the child could learn about *comparisons: big tree–little child,* and *big child–little toy.* Concepts can be taught when one talks to the child about the *color* of her clothes. *Action* concepts can be taught by having the child respond to language physically. For instance, if a favorite fairy tale mentions the action of spinning around and around, the child can be helped to sit on the floor and experience spinning.

Guide Verbalization into Conversation Patterns

It is important for the child to become involved in conversational patterns where there is content beyond simple questions and answers. Take the child to the closet and discuss with her what she would like to wear. Examine with her a flower growing in the yard. Many similar opportunities will present themselves.

Develop Ability to Think, Decide and Solve Problems

The ability to think, make one's own decisions, and solve problems are important skills to be developed by any individual. Children learning to talk should be given the opportunities to make decisions, such as choosing whether to go to the park or stay home. A somewhat older child might be able to choose the food for a bedtime snack. A preschool child can go to the store and choose a birthday gift for her best friend.

Provide Opportunities for Tactual Awareness and Manipulative Skills

Tactual awareness and manipulative skills are tools for concept development. These skills provide data from which the child learns to infer language equivalents. Children should be encouraged to search for details. For instance, ask them to manipulate two different stuffed animals and find differences in the shape of their ears and lengths of their tails. Children should learn relationships between models and actual things. More obvious models might be plastic apples representing actual apples and/or a model car representing an actual motor car.

Tactual awareness and manipulative skills are very important. They are vital for the development of sensory motor schemata and language. Visually disabled children should be encouraged to explore objects in their entirety rather than exploring them only with their fingers. Children should be encouraged to dispel fears of new and unusual tactual stimuli by handling and feeling a variety of objects with different textures. They can paint with their fingers, arms, elbows, and feet. They can hold live caterpillars or houseflies and can play on hilly, grassy surfaces. Once children have developed some tactual awareness and manipulative skills, they can apply these skills to everyday activities. Some may try carpentry, while others may be encouraged to assemble a peanut butter and jelly sandwich.

Concepts developed should not be limited to those found at home and in school. Disabled individuals should be encouraged to explore new environments and develop the concepts and language which accompany those environments. Children with crippling conditions may need physical assistance in order to explore their world. The world of these children may be small because of lack of mobility; with an additional handicap such as a severe visual loss, concepts of the world beyond may be even more limited. However even the most severely disabled child may be helped to stand on roller skates and roll along in order to feel and "know" the concept of roller skating.

Reception of Information

Chalkboards, Large Charts, and Flannel Boards

Chalkboards, large charts, and flannel boards are helpful tools for persons with visual disabilities.

Any one of these portable items can be used to illustrate nursery rhymes, stories, alphabet letters, or numbers. By trying a variety of colors, the best color contrast for each individual can be identified.

Discs and Tapes

Discs and tapes may be useful for visually disabled students with a slow reading rate. These aids are particularly useful for individuals who are able to see only a portion of the whole word.

Talking Books are recordings provided for legally blind and physically disabled persons. Recordings range from children's books to full length novels, including many textbooks used from elementary school through college. Applications for recordings are available through:

The American Printing House for the Blind
1839 Frankfort Avenue
Louisville, Ky 40206

Library of Congress
Division for the Blind and Physically Handicapped
Washington, D.C. 20540

Applications must be accompanied by a signature of a medical doctor stating the need and the qualifications of the individual. Once an individual has been accepted for the services, she will be given a choice of the format in which she wishes to receive her recorded materials. She will receive the appropriate machine on which to play the materials and she will receive catalogs of all recordings in the disc and tape libraries. An individual with motor coordination or weakness problems may request different switch styles such as chin switches and switches under foot pedals.

Many groups provide specific books. In California, the prisoners at Vacaville, a California State Correctional Institute, make tapes to order. Sources of volunteer recording services can be obtained through local State Departments of Education.

While audio materials may not always adequately replace printed matter, they can be used in conjunction with other modes for receiving information. It is therefore important to encourage young children to learn how to order and use these audio aids.

Compressed Speech

Compressed speech is a process for "shortening the time required for speech" (Connor, 1974,

p. 81). In tapes with compressed speech, a figurative "snipping away" and resplicing of tape produces speech which remains intelligible. These tapes require significantly less time for listening.

Reader

Blind persons often need to gain information immediately and call upon a friend to read or employ someone to do reading for them. Funds for reader services for the blind and severely disabled are available from state departments of vocational rehabilitation. It is hoped that these same sources or other similar sources can be used by those physically disabled individuals who cannot read but who can understand what is read to them.

Magnetic Card Readers

Cards for magnetic card readers can be used as flash cards. When these cards are inserted in the machines, they simultaneously show the word in large print and produce the word audibly. For variations, the large print word may be seen first, read, and then heard in audio form as verification.

It is important to note that different brands of the magnetic tape readers have varying features. The Language Master [5] is set up so that the card slides across the top of the machine, whereas on the Audio Flash card machine [6] (shown in Figure 4–4), the card remains stationary on the machine. Stability of the card may be a desirable feature for visually disabled children who find it easier to focus upon or tactually explore braille or objects on the cards.

Objects can be glued to the cards and words can be brailled on the cards in place of printed words. Audio cues or directions can be recorded on the cards. In response to directions to find a "big ball," the child can attempt to select a big ball from a box of objects and place it into a second box. Activities on these machines need not be limited to simple directions.

Optacon

The Optacon is a compact, portable reading aid which gives blind and/or deaf-blind people independent and immediate access to the world of print. Using advanced electronics, the Optacon converts the image of a printed letter into a vibrating tactile form that a blind person can feel with one finger. Different type styles and languages can be read with the Optacon because it reproduces exactly what is printed. The usual step of tape or braille transcription is

Figure 4–4. Braille words can be put on the cards so visually disabled children can *read and hear* or *read and record*.

thus eliminated, providing Optacon users with a new degree of independence and privacy. (Telesensory Systems Brochure R17608A, June 1976)

The implications of technological development such as the Optacon [7] are exciting for the visually disabled. Due to its cost, however, its use is now limited.

Closed-Circuit Television

Closed-circuit T.V. is becoming a useful tool for the partially sighted. With television, printed material can be projected on a television screen enabling quick and comfortable reading.

Print

Print size must be considered when selecting reading materials for each individual. As a general principle, use the smallest print which the child can read comfortably. If the child is struggling, she should be encouraged to move the page closer or use larger print. Generally, it is not necessary to worry about any eye damage caused when persons read (Faye, 1970; Fonda, 1970). Attention, however, must be given to adequate lighting, glare prevention, and other conditions which facilitate reading.

For young children, the print in books used by their peers may be satisfactory. Books for young children are usually printed in large type (twelve to eighteen point).

To illustrate:

Nine point. (This textbook.)

Twelve point.

Eighteen point.

It is wise to select children's books carefully, asking the following questions:

1. Which type size does the visually disabled child choose for herself?
2. Is the print clear, bold, and large enough for the child to read comfortably?
3. Is there adequate spacing between the lines, words and letters?
4. Are the margins suitable? Is the paper of good quality without a glossy finish?
5. Is there maximum contrast between background and print?
6. Are the illustrations clear?

Magnification

Some children may need low vision optical aids and can be referred to a low vision clinic for services. The clinic will assess children's visual functioning, provide recommendations for maximum visual efficiency, and, when appropriate, prescribe specific optical aids. Low vision clinics will also provide follow-up services for children, parents, and teachers.

Peer Readers

Peers can provide visually disabled children with printed and graphic information. The visually disabled child can ask a classmate to place carbon paper between two sheets of paper and make a copy of class notes. Carbon copies of broad assignments can be given to the resource teacher to translate into braille. Peers are also very helpful for description and interpretation of what is seen in movies, pictures, or on the playground.

Signs, Markers and Other Visual Cues in the Environment

As children gain reading skills, they should be encouraged to use signs, markers, and other environmental clues for information. To find an exit, the child need not read each of the four letters in the word. The location, shape and size of exit signs are reliable clues. The child does not need to be able to read letters on the doors of the restroom; *men* is a three-letter word, while *women* is a five-letter word.

Children should learn more about use of their vision. They should be aware of the many patterns in our physical world. For example, local supermarkets offer innumerable patterns. Hard rolls are near the bread, while hand soap is near the laundry detergent. The checkout stands are near the exits.

Even normally sighted people need not read each word to get the meaning of a sentence or word. So it is with the person with low vision. They may recognize one or two letters or parts of letters, but not necessarily all of the letters in the word. They may recognize patterns or Gestalts of the word. For instance, if the person desires beef broth, she may recognize the pattern of beef, by the *b* in the beginning and an *f* at the end by the ascenders that extend about the body of the word on the label. Children with limited vision should be encouraged to find such techniques for making maximum use of their vision.

Expression of Information

Handwriting

If the child can accomplish writing tasks, she should be taught to write in a standard size. Children in regular classes will find it an advantage to write the same size as their peers. Writing extra large letters is more difficult because the muscles of the eye must move more across the page, but writing small will not cause any damage to the eyes.

Signature guides or cards on the paper give blind children a line to follow when writing their names. Using Wilhold glue, a teacher can outline with thin threads the guides and boundaries. These threads will dry and become transparent.[8] Simple drawings or shapes can also be outlined in this manner so that children can color within the slightly raised, textured lines.

Typewriting

Typewriters with standard and large print are available to visually disabled children for expression of their ideas. Because of difficulties in writing, many visually disabled children are taught touch typewriting at an early age. It is an *essential* communication tool for blind and low vision children.

Braille

Some blind children use braille as their primary avenue for reading. They may prefer to use braille as an alternative method for writing. Braille is a system of touch reading using a cell of six dots: three high and two wide. From this, 63 different characters can be formed by placing dots in specific positions within the cell. With braille, children can read a variety of material since there is a literary code, a mathematics and science code, and a music code.

Braille is written by using a small braille slate or braille writer. With a stylus, individuals write from right to left by punching into the paper. In order to read braille, the page must be turned over and read from left to right. A braille writer is often chosen for school work even though it is larger than the slate. With a braille writer, dots in each cell are embossed simultaneously, making writing faster and more efficient. Use of braille equipment may be limited for individuals with little or no hand control. Lack of motor control or of sensation in the fingers may make braille reading and/or writing unfeasible. The one-handed brailler may fit the needs of some individuals.

Learning Self-Help Skills

A child with severe visual problems does not have the opportunity to notice others demonstrating self-help skills (Fraiberg, Smith, & Adelson, 1969). The visually disabled child does not have opportunity to recognize series of activities or events leading to results. In the case of feeding, the severely visually disabled child does not see the events involved when people feed themselves. It is often necessary to have an adult guide them through the steps while discussing each step briefly. This strategy is particularly important for children who also have motor coordination or weakness problems. To encourage self-feeding, it is helpful to put well-liked food pieces in a similar place on the tray.

Self-help skills establish a child's confidence in her own abilities. Self-help skills are tasks for which she can assume responsiblity.

Questions to Improve Instruction

1. Does the child have sufficient sensation in her fingers to feel the object being discussed, or does she need to explore it more globally with her arms, body, and perhaps face?
2. Does the child have sensation in her fingers sufficient for "feeling" differences in whatever materials she explores?
3. Can she see color?
4. Can she see light and dark?
5. Will the child be able to use print as a mode of communication? In reading? In writing?
6. Will a child with poorly coordinated hands be able to use braille?
7. Does the child need to be informed when furniture has been rearranged?
8. Did the child have an opportunity to explore the classroom, restroom, and playground prior to the first day of class?
9. Does the child function best when the classroom is kept orderly—chair in place, toys on floor in only one portion of the room?
10. Has the child been evaluated for mobility instruction?
11. Can the child discriminate between unacceptable and acceptable patterns of eating?
12. How can the child be helped to utilize auditory cues?
13. How can the child be helped to utilize tactile-kinesthetic cues?
14. Through what other modalities can a blind child learn?
15. What adaptations in lessons must be made to enhance the teaching-learning situation for the visually disabled child?
16. Does the child have a peripheral-field defect and consequently need preferential seating?

17. Do extraneous head movements interfere with the child's ability to focus upon a book or blackboard?

Remember, the important factor in working with children with visual disability is how well they use the vision they have. Helping the child to do this is one of our most important responsibilities.

Teaching the Hearing Impaired *

A *handicap* can be defined as any condition which causes increased dependency; *deafness* is a handicap which increases dependency in communication; and *cerebral palsy* is a handicap which increases dependency in movement. Cerebral palsy combined with deafness more than doubles the effect of each handicap alone because traditional methods of minimizing the effects of one handicap are often blocked by the second. For example, a deaf child can't speak, sign, or finger spell if cerebral palsy prevents her from controlling her fine muscular coordination. People involved in the nurture and education of a child with a dual handicap must define their priorities in terms of which dependencies can be reduced, which must be accepted, and which might be increased.

Because a hearing handicap interferes with the capacity to acquire language without conscious effort, the priorities of those working with hearing-impaired individuals must be centered on language acquisition and use.

Motor and hearing handicaps cannot be treated as separate entities. Since problems relating to motor disabilities are discussed elsewhere in this book, the contents of this section include a description of hearing impairment, a rationale for early intervention, a description of methods used to detect hearing loss, a description of hearing aids, suggestions for educating the hearing impaired, and further sources of information.

Hearing Impairment

Degree of hearing loss is determined by measuring an individual's response to varying intensities (loudness) of sound at specified levels of pitch. Those measurements are recorded on an audiogram in terms of *decibels* (loudness) and *frequency* (pitch).

---

* This section was written by Mariam T. Allen, who is a teacher in the San Mateo County Classes for the Deaf, San Mateo, California.

A conductive hearing loss, which originates in the outer or middle ear, is quite mild and rarely exceeds a level of 50 decibels (dB) (Ling, 1975). A conductive loss prevents sound from reaching the inner ear, or *cochlea*. It can often be corrected. A 40–50 dB loss affects the scanning and background functions of hearing. It may make conversation difficult if there is a noisy background, if distance separates the speaker and listener, or if soft tones of voice are used. Amplification may be needed if surgical remediation is not possible. A loss of this type could slow a child's progress in school and yet go undetected.

A sensorineural hearing loss originates in the cochlea and/or the auditory nerve. It may range from a mild to an almost total loss. It usually cannot be remediated since cochlear implants today are still highly experimental. Mild loss can result in reduced speech discrimination and retarded language development, while almost total loss can prevent acquisition of language and communication by normal means (Ling, 1975).

Individuals with hearing impairments vary in their ability to use residual hearing, so classification according to decibel loss alone may be misleading. In general, factors which will affect the social, educational, and linguistic development of a hearing impaired individual can include:

1. the age at which the loss occurred (prenatal or postnatal)
2. the type of loss (conductive or sensorineural)
3. the age at which the loss was discovered
4. the cause of the loss (maternal rubella, heredity, birth problems, disease after birth)
5. the amount of loss at each frequency

Early Intervention

Most authorities agree that a hearing-impaired infant should experience a social and linguistic environment similar in many ways to that of her hearing counterpart if the effects of her hearing loss are to be minimized. For this to happen, several conditions should be met:

1. The hearing loss must be detected.
2. Appropriate amplification should be provided.
3. The parents should be supported and trained.
4. The infant should be exposed to meaningful verbal and nonverbal communication.
5. The infant should be encouraged to progress through the developmental stages of language learning.

Detection of Loss

Hearing loss can be detected by giving routine screening tests to the newborn, observing an infant's behavior, and checking infants in the high-risk category.

Now no single endorsed method of mass screening is available for hearing, but two tests, the *Arousal Test* and the *Crib-o-gram,* are being used. In each test, the infant's movement in response to sound is detected and measured.

High-risk infants are those babies with a history of hereditary hearing loss, those whose mothers had some predisposing condition such as rubella during pregnancy, and those infants who evidence problems during delivery or shortly after birth. Parents who are aware of the expected sequence of listening behavior in infants and who observe and compare their own infant's listening behavior to the expected sequence can detect deviations which may indicate a hearing loss. The following chart shows examples of expected behavior:

Age	Expected Behavior
Birth–3 mo	Startled by sudden sounds
	Quieted by mother's voice
	Makes murmured sounds other than crying
3–6 mo	Searches for sounds with eyes
	Turns in direction of sound
	Increases in awareness of less intense sounds
	Increases vocalization

Age	Expected Behavior
6–12 mo	Increases in ability to locate sounds
	Puts sounds together to form rudimentary words
12–24 mo	Shows understanding of words by appropriate behavior
	Imitates and matches rhythm and inflection of spoken phrases
	Uses at least 20 words
	Follows simple commands

Amplification

If a loss is suspected, the infant should be referred to a physician, a pediatrician, or an ear, nose, and throat specialist (ENT) who will either test the infant's hearing or will work closely with an audiologist who will perform a hearing evaluation. They will provide diagnostic information about the degree of loss and will recommend specific amplification and follow-up care.

Hearing aids are small, personalized units which amplify sound. There are a number of different styles.

The traditional body-type aid consists of a small pocket-worn unit (containing the microphone, amplifier, volume control, and battery). The unit is connected to the ear by a cord, at the end of which is the loudspeaker (usually referred to as the 'button' or 'receiver'). The ear-level type hooks around the top and back of the ear and contains all the basic components . . . in a single shell. The eye glass type is similar to the ear-level type, but is built into the temple portion of a pair of eyeglasses. The all-in-the-ear type is a subminiature aid which fits directly into the . . . hollow portion of the outer ear. All these aids require some form of ear mold and none of them is invisible to the observer. (Israel, 1975, p. 22)

Hearing aids can be worn in one ear or both. The aids can be designed to meet each user's need. It is easier to design an aid for individuals who know what sound means than for an infant who has never heard meaningful sound. The infant does not know what to expect and cannot tell the audiologist which aid helps the most. The choice of aid, then, depends on cooperation between the audiologist, parents, and teachers. Each can evaluate an infant's response to a particular hearing aid. A hearing aid is only an instrument which brings in amplified sound; however, since meaning to sound is learned, a child who has been fitted with a hearing aid may not show immediate changes in listening skills.

Auditory training units are designed for use in classrooms where group and individual amplification is needed. Many of the systems are designed so that children are able to hear the teacher's voice at a level slightly above general classroom sounds. Some auditory training units are used by themselves; others are combined with the child's own hearing aid.

The age of the child being fitted and the type and extent of her disabilities will affect the final prescription of a hearing aid.

After the aid has been fitted, parents and teachers can help in the following ways:

1. Listen to the aid daily, at the same volume setting, to compare the quantity and quality of sound being delivered.
2. Replace batteries when the quality and quantity of sound changes.
3. When replacing batteries be sure that the positive end of the battery matches the positive end of the battery compartment in the aid. Each is designated with a "+" sign.
4. Handle batteries by grasping the center rounded portion, not the ends. Oil from the fingertips on the ends of batteries shortens battery life.
5. Handle aids with care to avoid dropping.
6. Detach the ear mold from the aid and observe it to be sure it is clean and free from

wax. Wash the mold with warm, soapy water. Use a pipe cleaner to clean the canal. Dry the mold thoroughly.

7. Observe the cord and/or tube to check for breaks or twists.
8. Make aid inspection and daily fitting a pleasant, brief procedure that is taken for granted.
9. Make listening important. (Talk about things which interest the child.)
10. Have the aid and the child's hearing checked at routine intervals as prescribed by the audiologist. Some hearing aid dealers provide a free, routine checking service for their customers.
11. Be aware of the effect of noisy environments. A hearing aid amplifies all sounds equally. Noise near a child, such as pencil tapping or paper shuffling, may prevent her from hearing a speaker several feet away. Loud playground noises or continuous loud sound can damage hearing. Find out how each hearing aid is designed to handle unusually loud sounds.

Early Training and Development

Following normal linguistic development, an infant is able to cry at birth. A short time later, she babbles and then plays with these babbled sounds as she hears her own voice. Soon she is able to use her sounds to respond to the speech of others. Then she imitates the intonation and rhythm patterns of the speech she hears. Eventually, this essential prelinguistic activity is transformed as the child fits syllables and words into the intonational and rhythmic track which she has already mastered. The child learns to attach meaning to the words she hears and uses them to satisfy her needs and organize her world. A hearing infant and a hearing-impaired infant both cry and babble. The hearing-impaired infant, *if not encouraged,* will gradually stop babbling and will become retarded in developing a linguistically patterned way of organizing her concepts.

Parents are the major sources of early linguistic encouragement. They often need support in handling their emotional response to the discovery of their child's handicap and training in how to maintain the essential flow of verbal and nonverbal communication (Connor, 1976). There are about a hundred infant programs throughout the United States where combinations of teachers, audiologists, psychologists, and psychiatrists are available to support and train hearing-impaired infants and their parents. The following is a summary of ways to help hearing-impaired infants and children.

1. Remember that the affective relationship between parent and child may be more important in developing language than the method of teaching. (Connor, 1976)
2. Convey acceptance, love, and warmth verbally and nonverbally.
3. Look at the child when communicating and maintain eye contact.
4. Speak to or use total communication with the child using a natural voice, rhythm, and inflection.
5. Imitate the sounds the child produces and wait for a response.
6. Use phrases, sentences, and single words in normal patterns.
7. Position the child to face the speaker at eye level.
8. At other times hold the child so that her head rests against the speaker's chest as she is rocked or held (sound is conducted by bone as well as air).
9. Make nonsense sounds and play peek-a-boo.
10. Play singing games such as pat-a-cake.
11. Sing songs like "Rock-a-Bye Baby" and "Baa, Baa, Black Sheep."
12. Read nursery rhymes aloud.
13. Help the child notice environmental sounds by calling attention to the ringing of a phone or doorbell.
14. Help the child locate the direction from which sounds originate.
15. Give the child toys which make noise.
16. Become sensitive to natural, informal situations in which meaningful language can be used.
17. Use meaningful, short sentences about things the child can see, touch, taste, smell, and/or understand.
18. Vary pitch and phrasing patterns. (*Look* at that black kitty! Did *you* see that black kitty?)
19. Carefully associate spoken and signed words with the things for which the word stands. Use the word many times in varying contexts.
20. Read aloud (with or without signs) with the child facing you. Give the child an opportunity to look at the pictures and then at you. She can't watch both at the same time.

21. Also read aloud with the child's head resting against your chest and the book in the child's lap. Your finger should follow along under the words being read.
22. When using a picture book, give the child names for specific items and information about the item. "That's a cat." "A cat says, 'meow'." "Cats drink milk."
23. When the child is familiar with the picture book, ask "Where's the cat?" or "What does the cat say?" or "Point to the cat."
24. Encourage the child to respond when she hears her name by turning her head, answering, and by coming when called.
25. Expect the child to respond to directions, such as "Please bring me your shoes."
26. Encourage the child to ask for things she wants instead of anticipating her needs.
27. Provide a variety of experiences around which meaningful language can be developed.
28. Expose the child to situations where she can see, smell, taste, feel, and move.
29. Make communication fun and essential.
30. Be aware that language does not just evolve naturally with a hearing-impaired child. It takes extra time, thought, attention, and many hours of input.
31. Be sure to give the child a chance to "listen" and then to respond. Communication is a give-and-take process.

Communication Systems

A number of communication systems can be used. These vary from a strictly oral approach to one using coded symbol blocks. The choice of method will depend on the nature and extent of the child's handicap.

A Signed Approach

The signed approach involves teaching a child to understand language and to express thoughts by using any of several signing systems. The American Sign Language (ASL or Ameslan) is a language system which is based on concepts. It has a grammatical structure and symbol system different from that of English. Other sign systems such as Siglish, The Manual English System, Signing Exact English, Linguistics of Visual English, and Seeing Essential English are based on either the concept of Ameslan with variations which move the system closer to standard English

or on word order and elements of English which follow standard grammatical relations.

Fingerspelling is a system for spelling words as they are spoken, using hand configurations for letters of the alphabet. It can be combined with signs or used exclusively. In the Rochester Method, fingerspelling is used with speech.

A Tactile Approach

The tactile approach involves teaching a child to communicate by pointing to and watching others point to blocks or boards on which special symbols or letters are depicted. One could also teach communication using the Lorm system of spelling words into a "readers" hand by touch and movement (Carmel, 1975).

An Oral Approach

The oral approach involves teaching a child to understand and speak using residual hearing, speech reading, and vocal mechanisms. Residual hearing is that remaining hearing which can be amplified. Speech reading is the process of understanding a speaker by associating meaning with facial movements, especially those of the lips. The oral approach employs the use of rhythmic and correctly spoken patterned sounds, words, phrases, and sentences.

A Cued Speech Approach

The cued speech approach involves teaching a child to understand speech and to speak using eight hand positions in four areas on the face to supplement speech. The positions are used to make the elements of spoken language more visible.

A Total Communication Approach

The total communication approach involves teaching a child to understand and speak language by using speech reading, residual hearing, vocal mechanisms, fingerspelling, and sign language which duplicate rhythmic spoken patterns.

Social Development

Myklebust (1966b) indicates that as a hearing-impaired child grows older she may be less socially mature than her hearing peers. Myklebust feels that a program for social development should start at an early age by first meeting a hearing-impaired child's psychological needs. Many feel that a program for social development should include the following:

1. The child needs to know she's loved and valued. Many of the softly spoken words of affection never reach her ears. Use nonverbal means of showing affection. (Yelling, "I love you" hardly does the job.)
2. The child needs structure and limits.
    a. Use pictures to illustrate simple routines.
    b. Use role playing to show her important rules.
    c. Prepare for sudden changes in routine.
    d. Have consistent routines and rules.
    e. "No" must mean "no." A hearing disability is no excuse for disregarding the rights of others nor is it an invitation to unlimited self indulgence.
    f. Make sure the child understands what is forbidden.
3. The child needs to be included in the activities of others. She can learn social skills by imitation and example.
4. The child needs to learn to care for herself and be independent. Give her opportunities to do things on her own whenever possible.
5. The child needs to learn to solve problems to satisfy herself and not just to please others. (Some children don't know whether they are right or wrong unless someone smiles or frowns.) The child eventually needs to develop internal standards that are reality tested.
6. The child needs to use her strengths and feel satisfaction in achievement.
7. The child needs to be exposed to problems which have a variety of solutions.

Perceptual Development

A hearing-impaired child needs opportunities for perceptual development. Perception is "a process of organizing and interpreting sensory data by combining them with past experience" (*New Westminister District,* p. 32, 1973). Part of the learning process, it occurs at a point on a continuum between sensing and thinking. It is possible to present sensory stimuli, or to have them occur naturally, in such a way that a child begins to see a pattern of similarities and differences. She uses this pattern to classify things and to group them on the basis of her discoveries. As she does this, she is developing the thinking skills, knowledge, and attitudes toward learning which she will use throughout her life.

The following are examples of ways to present stimuli for perceptual development:

1. Give the child several sizes and shapes of colored paper. Ask her to sort them into piles. When she has finished, give her the vocabulary she needs to explain her groupings. For example, "You put all the red pieces together"; "You put all the circles together." Eventually, after many experiences with input, the child will tell you the reasons for her grouping.
2. Ask the child to classify things on the basis of taste (sweet, sour, salty), or odor (smoky, fragrant, spicy) or texture (rough, smooth, soft).
3. Ask the child to match a sound she has just heard with the object making the sound (drum, bell, voice).
4. Ask the child to point to a picture of the object making the tape-recorded sound she has just heard (siren and fire engine, ringing and telephone). Arrange several pictures in front of the child. Ask her to point to the appropriate picture after she has heard the related sound.
5. Play singing games which allow the child to move, see, and hear, such as "Ring Around The Rosy," "The Farmer In The Dell," "Roly Poly," and "Clickity, Clickity Clack" (Allen, 1974; Sweeney and Wharram, 1973).
6. Give the child a simple, rhythmic movement pattern to follow (swaying, swinging arms, clapping). Add simple, vocalized sound to accompany the movement.

Each task should lay a foundation for the next task, and the ability to perform a task at one level should be incorporated into the next level. Teaching isolated facts in subject areas without helping a child to discover the interrelationships and progression of learning will overwhelm her with bits of partially absorbed, rapidly forgotten information.

Early Education

When a hearing-impaired child enters preschool, she begins formal training devoted to enhancing her communication skills and broadening her experiential background. Parents and teachers continue to focus on helping the child develop a broad language base through natural, everyday situations, as well as more structured situations.

The use of singing games that faithfully duplicate the inflection, rhythm, and word order of English is especially appropriate in preschool. Singing games give a child the opportunity to practice listening, watching, signing, and speaking in a situation where she needs to understand and to be understood in order to play the game.

Playing the games gives the child practice in visual, auditory, and motor coordination as she relates her movements to what she sees and hears. It gives her an opportunity to solve problems and make discoveries in the areas of movement, linguistics, and social development. The musical game appears to have special application in teaching the multihandicapped, since each child can function within the limits of her handicap and yet participate on a meaningful level at all ages from preschool through the elementary grades (Allen, 1974).

Preschoolers can be taught to count, but an understanding of numbers is something they must develop out of their own experience. "Number is a logical concept built up from the fusion of two prenumber ideas—classification and seriation (arranging in order)" (Sharp, 1969, p. 23). Classification and seriation undergird learning language, including reading.

A preschooler's day can be filled with things to classify, arrange, tear, cut, color, paint, construct, and explore bodily. She needs time to discover, solve problems, compare, infer, and time to put all of this into meaningful language. Collections of rocks, buttons, bark, shells, nails, screws, plastic tokens, and seeds are invaluable for sorting, classifying, and arranging.

Just as infant training provides a foundation for preschool, then preschool provides a foundation for kindergarten and the elementary grades. A hearing-impaired child brings a level of perceptual, cognitive, and social development along with her background of experiences and concepts to the subject matter areas taught in day school, residential school, or regular, mainstreamed classes.

In teaching the child of elementary school age, parental support is just as valuable as it was in the preschool years. There are many things more easily taught at home: family relationships (sister, brother, husband, wife), household items, addresses and phone numbers, manners, the language of household tasks, daily activities, and the preparation of food. Parents can provide rich experiences for teachers to use as background for vocabulary development. As a teacher, you can acquaint parents with school activities so that the language involved can be practiced at home.

Teachers who have not had training in teaching the deaf have asked, "How can I tell how deaf a child is and what does that mean to me as her teacher?" Suggestions for these questions follow:

1. Check with the child's parents, previous teachers, and audiologist to see how she functions in each situation.
2. Devise a quick test like the items following to see how the child functions:
   a. Call the child by name from across the room to see if she turns around. If she does not, try b and c.
   b. Call the child by name when she is nearby with her back turned.
   c. Call the child by name when she is nearby and looking directly at the speaker.
3. Perform the test when the child has her hearing aids on and when she has them off. The child who can hear her name called and turns around from across the room will usually have more intelligible speech, less difficulty acquiring linguistic skills, and will need less help in acquiring language-based learning than the child who can only recognize her name when she is called from a few feet away.

Teaching materials and textbooks that are produced for regular classes constitute the bulk of what is available for teachers of hearing-impaired children. Materials based on tape-recorded lessons, the use of listening skills, and phonics are harder to adapt for use with the hearing impaired than materials based on a visual, manipulative, experiential approach. Suggested resources are

1. Language-experience approach. The child dictates her story to her teacher who helps her correct the language. The child copies her corrected story; when she has learned and illustrated it, she teaches it to her classmates (Lee & Allen, 1963). For example, a child points to her shoes and says, "Red." Her story might be "I like my red shoes," or "I have some new red shoes." As the child develops, the stories she tells should expand into phrases, sentences, and paragraphs.
2. Education through music approach. Play a singing game. Draw a map of the game and write the words to the song on the map in appropriate places. As the child retraces her map with her finger, she sings and "reads" the words she has written (Allen, 1974).
3. High interest-low vocabulary materials available through major publishing houses.
4. Menus, recipes, directions for games, comics, *T.V. Guide,* newspapers, safety signs,

common public directions, and labels are all sources of material which help a child realize why learning to read is important.

5. Curricula for teaching English as a second language or for teaching language disadvantaged children.

6. Curricula developed by day-school and residential programs for the hearing impaired.

7. Mathematics and science materials based on concrete experience, discovery, and manipulation (Barrata-Lorton, 1972).

8. Teaching machines and programmed materials
   a. Programmed instruction in language, reading, thinking skills, and perceptual skills are available through Project Life.[9]
   b. A computerized information retrieval system of reading materials suited to the needs of the hearing impaired is available at the University of Nebraska-Lincoln, Specialized Office For The Deaf and Hard of Hearing, Lincoln, Nebraska.

9. Films and filmstrips, video tape, and television:
   a. Educational and recreational captioned films are available through Captioned Films for the Deaf [10] and the National Association for the Deaf.[11]
   b. Joyce Motion Picture Co.[12]
   c. Commercial and educational television stations provide instruction in lipreading and sign language. Some newscasts are captioned and others are signed by the newscasters.

10. Telephone communication assistance devices. Telecommunication devices such as *Phonetype, M.C.M.,* and the *TV Phone* enable persons with hearing impairment to use the telephone. The devices are designed for "those who, even with amplification and training, cannot either sufficiently hear, or discriminate, a voice on a telephone" (Ward, 1974, p.3). Obtain information from:
    Teletypewriters for the Deaf
    Box 28332
    Washington, D.C. 20005

11. Communication boards. A communication board consists of blocks or a flat surface on which the alphabet, numbers, common words, or other symbol systems are printed or illustrated. The "speaker" points to the symbols in sequence, using her finger or a pointer mounted on her head, chin, or mouth.

12. Resource centers. Teacher-prepared materials and suggestions are available for distribution through centralized locations.

13. Notebooks. Those who are unable to write can use a notebook filled with commonly needed questions and statements that are classified under appropriate headings similar to foreign language phrase books for travelers. The user can point to the phrases she needs, such as "How much is that?" or "Where are the restrooms?" The notebook needs to be prepared individually for the user so that she can learn to recognize the words and phrases she requires.

In addition to resources for materials, the following should be taken into consideration in a classroom composed entirely or partially of hearing-impaired children:

1. Reduce the noise level of the room (acoustic tile carpets and drapes help).

2. When a child uses infantile patterns of speech, rephrase what she has said so she hears and sees the accepted pattern.

3. Give the child the vocabulary she needs to express herself but be sure that the vocabulary matches what the child has in mind. Use pictures and actions to check meanings.

4. Help the child to attend to all of what is being said. A hearing-impaired child will often watch until she catches a word she knows and then jump to a conclusion. Her conclusion may or may not be correct.

5. Expect a response which indicates understanding. Many deaf children will smile pleasantly at the speaker while not understanding a thing she has said.

6. Talk with the child about things that interest her. Use short simple sentences and a natural rhythmic voice quality.

7. Seat the child so she can see the speaker.

8. Use an overhead projector and face the class when speaking.

9. Keep papers away from in front of your face.

10. Speak, then show materials, or vice versa.

11. Remember that nonverbal clues are an important part of communication. A physical handicap may alter the flow of nonverbal clues or heighten the use of them. In each case the communication process will be affected.

Depending upon the aptitude and achievements of the hearing-impaired child, she may stay in special day- or residential-school classes, spend part of her time in a regular class, or spend the entire day in a regular class with help from tutors, speech therapists, and other specialists.

The child who has multiple handicaps will need specialized guidance to help her accept her limitations and develop independence. Close cooperation with school counselors and curriculum specialists who can acquaint teachers with vocational guidance and practical living skills is necessary even in elementary grades. If a child has a limited academic potential, she needs to start learning practical living skills through a modified curriculum at an early age.

Junior High and Beyond

As the hearing-disabled person grows older she needs special help in managing social situations. Much of social grace is linguistic. Hearing-impaired young people sometimes fail to see the relationship between their behavior and the responses of others. As they grow older they are sometimes excluded socially and experience great loneliness. Many of the problems they encounter will be due to their hearing handicap, but some problems will be due to their age and circumstances. They will need help in understanding that some problems are inherent in the situation and have nothing to do with deafness.

At the junior high and high school levels, it is often painful to be different from others. The hearing-impaired person may object to wearing a hearing aid because it is a visible indication of her difference. Long hair, which hides a small hearing aid, is sometimes a solution to this problem.

At this stage, there is no longer one class and one teacher to which the student can relate. She must move from class to class and situation to situation. Each may present different problems. Teachers and students need to become acquainted with the needs of the hearing impaired outlined earlier in this chapter.

Seating in classrooms and the manner in which the teacher presents material become particularly important. The teacher who paces back and forth in front of the class, looking at the floor as she delivers a lecture, makes it impossible for a hearing-disabled individual to follow what is being said. In a class where much of the material is presented in lecture form, some provision can be made for the hearing-impaired student (ask another student to share her notes or to use carbon copies of them). In group discussions, provisions for helping the hearing-impaired student follow the conversation can also be made (speakers can raise their hands).

Vocational guidance and acquaintance with hearing-impaired adults who share ideas about career opportunities and challenges of adulthood are particularly important. Hearing-impaired children need to meet older hearing-impaired youths and adults. Some children might think that their hearing disability will just disappear at age 21 because they never see a hearing-impaired adult either in real life or mentioned in their reading material.

Vocational guidance and career education should include a realistic appraisal of an individual's limitations and strengths and a wide exposure to opportunities in trades, professions, and sheltered workshops. The hearing-impaired young adult should know how to use resources such as the vocational rehabilitation state agency, employment agencies (especially those for the deaf), the classified section of a newspaper, the local library, and books such as *The Dictionary of Occupational Titles*. Training both in filling out application forms and in job interview techniques are also important.

Information about the possibilities for continuing education and community resources should be made available to the hearing impaired. Regional occupational training centers provide educational opportunities for the high school student. Community colleges, public and private colleges and universities, Gallaudet College, and Rochester Institute of Technology provide higher education for the high school graduate. Organizations in many communities sponsor social, cultural, religious, recreational, and educational opportunities for the hearing impaired of all ages.

A hearing handicap is more than a major inconvenience, but given the care and attention required, it need not doom its owner to a life of isolated frustration.

To summarize, we quote Nietzsche in conversation with Frankl. Nietzsche said, "He who has a 'why' to live for can bear almost any 'how' "(Frankl, 1968, p. 164). If educators, parents, and friends can expose the hearing-impaired, cerebral palsied individual to some structured cognitive processes, to communication skills, and to shared life experiences, that individual will be able to construct his own "why" to cope with almost any "how."

Combination of Visual and Auditory Disabilities

This section deals with children who have a combination of auditory and visual impairments— and physical disability. They are called multihandi- capped, or *deaf and blind*, or *deaf-blind*, despite the fact that a majority of these children have some hearing and vision they can learn to use.

Such a multiple disability requires extraordinary input for the child to experience stimuli. Some compensation can be provided by aids such as glasses, magnification, hearing aids, and amplifiers. Still, particular approaches must be considered to meet the intense demands of such a disabled person. The combinations of dis- abilities presents complex problems in areas such as communication, motor, language, concept de- velopment, and self-help.

Characteristics

Many characteristics of these children are identi- cal or similar to characteristics of children dis- cussed in earlier sections of the chapter. Readers will gain even more ideas from Chapter 8. Let's consider other characteristics common in deaf- blind children: unresponsiveness and resistance to human relationships, undifferentiated and stress crying, physical defensiveness and com- munication problems. The infant with severe vi- sion and hearing difficulties often exists with minimum human interaction because adults do not know how to handle unresponsive children. The infant may seem contented or discontented in an undifferentiated sense, without any relation to mothering. A deaf-blind infant who requires more than average stimulation may actually elicit less stimulation. She can be deprived of the stimula- tion essential for physical and emotional growth. She does not cue nor reinforce handling. Interven- tion should involve a regular program of stimula- tion and the development of active interaction with the infant.

Active rejection of the mother and other human contact is sometimes present. A child often dis- courages handling and other stimulation neces- sary for development. A mother may see a direct causal relationship between her mothering be- havior and discomfort in her infant. Intervention must stress calm and assured handling regard- less of the objections of the infant. Persons han- dling such children must be reassured that the infant can learn to tolerate and later enjoy physical contact.[13]

Undifferentiated and Stress Crying

Undifferentiated and stress crying, accompanied by hypertonicity, are characteristics often exhib- ited in deaf-blind children. The mother or another adult may interpret undifferentiated crying as an indication of a need which demands satisfaction. In reality, it may not be a cue cry and might continue independent of any attempt at help or relief. The deaf-blind infant can have a devastat- ing effect on family life unless intervention brings the problem into proportion. The mother may be unsuccessful in developing a schedule for the infant. She may be continously involved in abor- tive attempts to appease while other aspects of her life erode. Fatigue and physical deterioration may affect the mother. If her attempts at mother- ing are frustrated over a sustained period of time, a process of alienation may begin. Intervention must include restoration of some degree of bal- ance in the family life. The mother must be helped to develop greater tolerance for the crying. She must be supported in her mothering activites until the time when the infant can benefit from them.

Physical Defensiveness

Tactile stimulation results from bodily contact in the infant's daily routine. Stroking, patting, and rocking are all instinctive methods of tactile stimu- lation. However, problems arise when an infant responds defensively to touch. One must ap- proach the infant with finesse. Varying degrees of physical closeness can be presented. For exam- ple, the mother may begin by lying the baby on a pillow. The parent can lie down two or three feet away from the infant and remain motionless with- out touching for a period of time. When she has tried this strategy on several occasions, the threat posed to the infant by human intervention should diminish. The mother can then progress nearer to the infant and later introduce stroking and talking. Eventually, the infant can be cradled in the arms. Parents must be urged to continue handling with a firm but gentle touch. With familiarity and consis- tency, anxiety associated with a particular routine will be reduced. Extinction of physical defensive- ness is a major advance toward educability.

Deaf-blind infants cannot be allowed to thwart tactile stimulation. The alleviation of tactile defen- siveness is critical for the implementation of a program of physical therapy. The process therapy is dependent upon the child's acceptance of human touch and manipulation. Therapy is very much facilitated by a child's neutral or positive disposition. Therapy is hampered by undifferentiated crying and the accompanying hypertension. Without a planned program of intervention, the deaf-blind infant may successfully prevent the development of significant human relationships and discourage activities which promote her growth.

Communication Difficulties

Communication, of course, is a primary problem for such children. Communications must deal with human contact and interaction since it is in this way that the children will receive most information. To process meaningful input the child must first develop awareness, recognition, and association of sensory cues. Eventually, some basic systems of communication can be developed.

Often, multihandicapped infants appear content without physical contact. The infant neither cues nor reinforces handling. Therefore daily routines should include a regular program of stimulation and attempts to establish at least primitive forms of communication. Much information in the previous sections of this chapter pertains also to deaf-blind children. Communication problems, of course, are intensified when children have a combination of vision and hearing deficits. Expression of language is a major difficulty. Some deaf-blind children may never learn basic signs and gestures. Others may learn at least to indicate if they are hungry, thirsty, physically uncomfortable, or have to be taken to the toilet. Even when children could learn to use signs and gestures, physical disability may restrict their ability to use them. Many children will be able to understand language better than they express ideas. A small portion of these children learn to communicate through speech in addition to basic gestures and signs. Those children with considerable hearing may learn oral language; those with functional sight may learn written language.

Concept and Language Development

Teachers should understand that these children usually have some vision and hearing which they can be taught to use. Miller (1972) suggests a series of necessary steps that are directed at the use of residual hearing by the child. They are

Develop an awareness of sound
Recognize sounds of the environment
Make the sounds meaningful
Develop communication with and for the child
(p. 21)

Awareness of sound can be encouraged when picking the baby up or putting her down. During play with the infant, more sounds can be presented. After responses to sound are obtained, the child needs to investigate the sounds of her environment. Sounds must be associated with activities such as eating, taking a bath, or going for a ride in a car. Sounds should not startle or frighten a child; ways to help the infant associate environmental sounds with pleasure should be explored. The mother could slam a door and then walk into the room and pick the infant up. An adult and child could drop a toy on a hard surface so as to make a noise.

Not only should a child's early experiences with sound be loud and frequent, but these experiences must also be meaningful. Meaningful information is learned more rapidly and retained more easily. "The parent and teacher should talk in the child's ear at this stage. Singing, talking, laughing, cooing, babbling and calling the child's name can be fun" (Miller, 1972, p. 22). Physical activities and the manipulation of materials within the environment will help the child experience visual sizes and shapes. The child's hand can be placed so she feels her face, lips, chin, chest, or the top of her head. Parents and teachers can say "Up you go" while lifting a child.

Once a child reaches school age, cognitive development may be delayed unless a language system is developing. Bisno (1972) lists six hierarchical language objectives for preschool- and school-age multihandicapped, deaf-blind children:

1. awareness of sound, seeking out sources
2. awareness of visual stimuli, seeking out sources
3. discrimination of both auditory and visual stimuli
4. attaching meaningfulness to auditory and visual stimuli
5. following directions, oral and/or sign language
6. expressive signing or oral speech (p. 71)

Basic to these language objectives is the philosophy of total communication, combining sign and word with the use and coordination of the residual senses.

Once means of input and output are established, conceptual tasks can be presented to the child through these channels. Compensatory devices and special equipment that magnify visual and auditory stimuli can and should be used.

Learning to Communicate

To develop a systems of communication, Miller further states:

> The child needs to be observed to determine whether he has developed any symbols, any babbling, (or) any reactions to sounds that can be used to help structure his world. One wants to discover the natural signs, gestures, or vocalizations that the child has in order to help him to begin to express his ideas as they relate to his needs. (1972, p. 22)

A child with severe vision and hearing loss may need to be taught gestures by physical guidance. Behavior modification techniques can also be used to develop gestures, speech, or other communication signals. Speech sounds or gestures become meaningful when the child uses them to manipulate her environment. While she may not understand language, it should be used when you try to relate to her because it gives her an opportunity to associate language and experience with "an attitude within . . . [her] environment" (Miller, 1972, p. 25).

Learning Self-Help Skills

Before a child can be helped to learn self-help skills, there must be acceptance of human touch. Once the child has accepted touch, a program of motor learning and motor planning can begin.

When normal postural positions are not reached at appropriate times, the infant should be passively manipulated into these postures and movement patterns. A baby who is not pivoting, rolling or turning over must be pivoted, rolled over, or turned over. A baby who should be crawling but who is not must be manipulated in a crawl. Since these children do not have a visual impression of normal motor activity, they must be supplied with the kinesthetic experience of normalcy.

The methods described by Bobath and Bobath (1972) and Finnie (1975) for cerebral palsied children have been successfully used to elicit righting reactions and to inhibit unwanted reflex behaviors of infants with visual problems. When these children begin to walk, they will experience balance problems. One should begin early to plan activities which stimulate the vestibular (balance) system and elicit righting reactions.

Fine motor activities must be established. By rubbing the child's hands and moving her fingers in all directions, one provides some general stimulation for grasping. Then the child should be given

soft materials for squeezing. Gradually, the objects should be varied in size, shape, and consistency (e.g., beanbags, balls). To encourage the child to reach and grasp, one can put objects on the child's lap, shoulder, or wherever she must reach to remove it. Constant massaging, fingerplay, and object-finding will further help her to learn the use of her hands. Guide the child's hand by holding it. As a task is attempted, move support away from the hand to the wrist. Gradually allow the child to take over more control of her movements.

Give attention to exercises such as jumping, tumbling, kicking, and swaying. Establish maximum mobility. The child needs to know her physical environment before she can "let herself go." Because of her sensory limitations, she must be provided with conditions of absolute safety. When the child is "confident that danger arising from mobility is controlled" (Schlesinger, 1972, p. 14) she will take part in these activities more eagerly.

Tactile, kinesthetic, and proprioceptive feedback are the primary sensory channels for motor stimulation. She must be taught to use her physical capabilities for self-help skills. Tasks must be presented step-by-step. Teachers should proceed first, giving total assistance on each step, then partial assistance, verbal cue, and finally giving no assistance. For example, to teach eating, start by letting her feel the food. Next, guide her hand full of food to her mouth. When she is sure of this routine, offer only partial assistance, saying "Eat, Sara." Finally, reduce the amount of help and teach her to eat upon verbal cue. Eventually, she should learn to handle a spoon. Finally, she needs to learn acceptable eating behaviors.

Toilet training should be a set and frequent routine. A signal should be established so the child will know what behavior is expected. The adult should be supportive, gentle, and patient. In time, the child will associate the reinforcement with the appropriate behavior.

The disabled child with a crippling condition who is also visually and/or auditorally impaired must be the recipient of extraordinary time and effort. This section has suggested a few ways in which the special needs might be met.

Language and Speech Disorders

Children with physical disabilities, particularly the cerebral palsied, frequently have language and speech disorders. However, because of the breadth and complexity of the information about language and speech development, we choose to list references which will help you with your concerns about this topic. The topic is also interwoven throughout this book. Using information from local language and speech specialists, from the references, and from the following parts of the book, readers can apply task analysis processes to determine accomplishments and deficiencies in the language and speech of certain individuals.

Chapter	*Concerns*
Chapter One, "Task Analysis"	Milestones of language and speech development.
Chapter Four, "Accompanying Disabilities"	Special language and speech considerations for individuals with accompanying disabilities such as visual disability and hearing impairment.
Chapter Six, "Severe Communication Problems"	Prerequisite skills and knowledge for using communication systems other than talking or writing; a demonstration of alternatives.
Chapter Eight, "Education of the Severely and Profoundly Handicapped"	Use of behavioral analyses and behavior management to elicit wanted speech and language.
Chapter Seven, "Self-Care"	Relationships to feeding, training, and prespeech.

Figure 4–5. The speech therapist demonstrates to the teacher and the parents so all can help the child.

Instruction

Once problems are detected and defined, some problems can be treated primarily by speech and language specialists. Others can be reduced through the efforts of several persons. Teachers, parents, and therapists need to collaborate in their efforts to observe a child's performances and provide activities and language models appropriate to the level and nature of the child's performances. In addition, they can encourage growth into the next successive steps and stages as suggested by research reports and as described in the references. (See Figure 4–5.)

Convulsive Disorders

Some students with physical disabilities also have convulsive disorders and are subject to seizures. It is possible to control convulsive disorders with medication.

If you work with students who have occasional seizures, become aware of the nature of seizures so that you can assist with the management of the student if a seizure occurs. Common types of seizures are grand mal, petit mal, and psychomotor.[14]

Grand mal seizures are distinguished by violent shaking of the entire body accompanied by temporary loss of consciousness. They usually last about 2–5 minutes. They may occur as often as one or more times a day, or as infrequently as once a year or more.

Petit mal seizures result in a simple staring spell (often mistaken for daydreaming). They usually last less than a minute (often only several seconds) and may occur repeatedly in one hour.

Psychomotor seizures result in inappropriate or purposeless behavior with subsequent amnesia regarding the episode. They usually last 2–5 minutes and may occur weekly, monthly, or annually.

Everyone associated with the seizure-prone child must be aware of some basic considerations. Generally, treat the child who has seizures as you would any other child—avoid pampering the child for fear she will have a seizure; do not let her manipulate others; do not fear or pity her. Encourage normal physical and mental activity during the school day. This strategy has the beneficial effect of reducing seizures. The child may have a seizure at any time, so keep common sense safety rules in mind. Make sure the child avoids playing in high places, using power tools without close supervision, and swimming without an observer. Some children will have no restrictions. A child's physician, however, can tell you if any are needed. Realize that the seizure itself does not hurt but falling might. Some children know they are going to have a seizure just before it happens. They should be encouraged to tell, or in the case of nonvocal children, signal someone when they get this "aura" so safety precautions may be taken. Occasionally, a child will be awake during the seizure, while others are unconscious. Some children remember what happened and others will not be able to recall anything about it. Always stay with the child during the seizure; talk softly and stroke her as she returns to normal. It is often frightening and confusing for a child to find herself in a different place than she last remembered.

Check with the physician for effects of drugs the child may be taking. Drugs used to control seizures often have noticeable side effects: swelling of the gums, difficulty in paying attention, drowsiness. (Epilepsy Foundation of America)

First Aid for Grand Mal Epilepsy [15]

1. Remain calm. Students will assume the same emotional reaction as their teacher. The seizure is painless to the child.
2. Do not try to restrain the child. There is nothing you can do to stop a seizure once it has begun. It must run its course.
3. Clear the area so that she does not injure herself on hard or sharp objects. Try not to interfere with her movements in any way. Turn her on her side to prevent choking.
4. Do not force anything between her teeth. If her mouth is already open, you might place a soft object like a handkerchief between her side teeth.
5. It isn't generally necessary to call a doctor unless the attack is followed almost immediately by another major seizure, or if the seizure lasts more than about 10 minutes.
6. When the seizure is over, let the child rest if she wants to.
7. The child's parents and physician should be informed of the seizure.
8. Turn the incident into a learning experience for the entire class. Explain what a seizure is, that it is not contagious, and that it is nothing to be afraid of. Teach understanding for the child—not pity—so that her classmates will continue to accept her as "one of the gang." (Epilepsy Foundation of America)

Summary

Many children with physical disabilities have multiple disabilities which complicate their education. In every case educational plans need to include the cooperation of many professionals in order to insure the maximum development of the child.

Notes

1. These and other gross motor activities are described in Bobath and Bobath (1975), and in Finnie (1975).

2. For more information on reinforcement theory, behavior modification, and behavior management, refer to Chapter Eight, "Education of the Severely and Profoundly Handicapped," references and resources sections.

3. Some blind babies do not learn to crawl and creep before they walk.

4. Material in this section adapted from *Guiding the Development of the Young Visually Handicapped* by Doris Groves and Carolyn Griffith, 1969, pp. 1–26. Adapted by permission.

5. Language Master is available from Bell & Howell, 7100 McCormick Rd., Chicago, Ill. 60645.

6. "Audio Flash" is from Electronic Futures, Inc., a division of KMS Industries, 57 Dodge Ave., North Haven, Conn. 06473.

7. Available from Telesensory Systems, 1889 Page Mill Road, Palo Alto, Calif. 94304.

8. See section on handwriting in Chapter Eight.

9. Project Life, Instructional Industries, Inc., Executive Park, Ballston Lake, New York 12019.

10. Captioned Films for the Deaf, Media Services and Captioned Films Branch, Bureau of Education for the Handicapped, ROB Building, 7th and D St., Washington, D.C. 20202.

11. National Association for the Deaf, 814 Thayer Ave., Silver Spring, Md. 20910.

12. Joyce Motion Picture Company, 8613 Yolanda, PO Box 458, Northridge, Calif. 91324.

13. Refer to Chapter Eight for other suggestions to reduce a child's resistance to handling.

14. Information on the three common types of seizures is adapted from public information brochures distributed by the Epilepsy Foundation of America; by permission.

15. First aid information is adapted from brochures distributed by the Epilepsy Foundation of America; by permission.

References

Comprehensive

Bransford, L. A., Baca, L., & Lane, K. (Eds.). Cultural diversity and the exceptional child. *Proceedings of an institute and conference of the Council for Exceptional Children,* Las Vegas, August 1973. Reston, Virginia: Council for Exceptional Children, 1973.

Brazelton, T. B. *Infants and mothers.* New York: Dell, 1969.

Cruickshank, W. M. (Ed.). *Cerebral palsy: A developmental disability.* Syracuse, N. Y.: Syracuse University, 1976.

Cruickshank, W. *Education of exceptional children and youth.* Englewood Cliffs, N.J.: Prentice-Hall, 1967.

Denhoff, E., & Robinault, I. P. *Cerebral palsy and related disorders: A developmental approach to dysfunction.* New York: McGraw-Hill, 1960.

Dunne, L. N. (Ed.). *Exceptional children in the schools: Special education in transition.* New York: Holt, Rinehart & Winston, 1973.

Haring, N. *Behavior of exceptional children.* Columbus, Ohio: Charles E. Merrill, 1974.

Gearheart, B. R., & Weishahn, M. W. *The handicapped child in the regular classroom.* St. Louis: C.V. Mosby, 1976.

Gain, K. (Ed.). *Planning programs and activities for infants and toddlers: A bibliography.* Chapel Hill, N. C.: University of North Carolina Technical Assistance Development Systems, 1975.

Lambie, D. I., Bond, J. T., & Weikart, D. P. *Home teaching with mothers and infants.* Ypsilanti, Mich.: High Scope Educational Research Foundation, 1974.

Visual Disabilities

Abel, G. L. (Ed.). Developing behavioral objectives and curriculum guidelines to meet the special education needs of visually handicapped students. *Proceedings of the Special Study Institute.* Palo Alto, Calif.: California State Department of Education, 1971.

Abel, G. L., & Kellis, T. (Eds.). Optical rehabilitation and the education of low vision children and youth. *San Francisco State College Summer Institute Report.* August, 1967.

Abel, G. L., & Hatlen, P. J. *The regular classroom teacher and the visually impaired child.* Unpublished report, California State University, San Francisco, June, 1973.

Association for Education of the Visually Handicapped. Selected papers. *Proceedings of the 52nd Biennial Conference.* San Francisco, Calif., June, 1974.

Barraga, N. C. Development of communication skills in visually handicapped. In Developing behavioral objectives and curriculum guidelines to meet the special educational needs of visually handicapped students. *Proceedings of the Special Study Institute,* Palo Alto, Calif. Sacramento, Calif.: California State Department of Education, 1973, pp. 53-66.

Barraga, N. C. *Visual handicaps and learning: A developmental approach.* Belmont, Calif.: Wadsworth, 1976.

Barrett, M. L., Hunt, V. V., & Jones, M. H. Behavioral growth of cerebral palsied children from group experience in a confined space. *Developmental Medicine and Child Neurology,* 1967, *9* (1), 50–58.

Connor, A. Compressed speech, listening skills, and handicapped students. *Proceedings of the 52nd Biennial Conference of the Association for Education of the Visually Handicapped*. San Francisco, Calif. June, 1974.

Cratty, B. J. *Movement and spatial awareness in blind children and youth*. Springfield, Ill.: Charles C Thomas, 1971.

Faye, E. E. *The low vision patient*. New York: Grune and Stratton, 1970.

Finnie, N. *Handling the young cerebral palsied child at home* (2nd ed.). New York: E.P. Dutton, 1975.

Fonda, G. *The management of the patient with sub normal vision* (2nd ed.). St. Louis, Mo.: C. V. Mosby, 1970.

Fraiberg, S. Parallel and divergent patterns in blind and sighted infants. *The Psychoanalytical Study of the Child*, 1968, *23*, 264–300.

Fraiberg, S., Smith, M., & Adelson, E. An educational program for blind infants. *The Journal of Special Education*, 1969, *3* (2) 121–139.

Groves, D. & Griffith, C. *Guiding the development of the young visually handicapped—A selected list of activities*. Columbus, Ohio: State School for the Blind, 1969.

Rex, E. J. (Ed.). Methods and procedures for training low vision skills. *Proceedings of the Special Study Institute*. Normal, Ill.: Illinois State University, Department of Special Education, 1971.

Scott, R. *The making of a blind man*. New York: Russell Sage Foundation, 1969.

Spivey, B. E. & Colenbrander, August. Classification of visual performance: Tentative definition. San Francisco, Calif.: Pacific Medical Center, January 1976. (Available from the Committee on Terminology, American Academy of Ophthalmology and Otolaryngology, and Committee on Information, International Council of Ophthalmology, Pacific Medical Center, P.O. Box 7999, San Francisco, Calif. 94120.)

Telesensory Systems, Inc. Brochure R 17608A, June 1976. (Available from 1889 Page Mill Rd., Palo Alto, Calif. 94304.)

Hearing Impaired

Allen, M. T. *Dance of language*. Portola Valley, Calif.: Richards Institute, 1974.

Barrata-Lorton, M. *Workjobs*. Menlo Park, Calif.: Addison-Wesley, 1972.

Barrata-Lorton, M. *Mathematics their way*. Menlo Park, Calif.: Addison-Wesley, 1976.

Carmel, S. J. *International hand alphabet charts*. Rockville, Md.: Studio Printing, 1975.

Connor, L. E. New directions in infant programs for the deaf. *The Volta Review*, 1976, *78*, 8–14.

Davis, H. & Silverman, H. R. *Hearing and deafness*. New York: Holt, Rinehart & Winston, 1970.

Frankl, V. E. *Man's search for meaning*. New York: Washington Square, 1968.

Franklin, B. The effect of combining low and high frequency passbands on consonant recognition in hearing-impaired. *Journal of Speech and Hearing Research*, 1975, *18* (4), 719–727.

Gallaudet Today. Communication. Washington, D.C.: Gallaudet College, Winter 1974/75.

Grammatico, L. F., & Miller, S. D. Curriculum for the preschool deaf child. *The Volta Review*, 1974, *76* (5), 281–289.

Grammatico, L. F. The development of listening skills. *The Volta Review*, 1975, 77 (5), 303–308.

Israel, R. H. The hearing aid. *The Volta Review*, 1975, 77 (1), 21–26.

Jerger, J. *Modern developments in audiology*. New York: Academic, 1973.

Lee, D. M., & Allen, R. V. *Learning to read through experience*. New York: Appleton-Century-Crofts, 1963.

Ling, D. Recent developments affecting the education of hearing-impaired children. *Public Health Reviews*, 1975, *IV* (2), 117–152.

Masland, M. W. Speech language and hearing checklist. *The Volta Review*, 1970, *70* (1), 40–42.

Meadow, K. P. The deaf subculture. *Hearing and Speech Action*, 1975, *43*, 16–18.

Menyuk, P. *The acquisition and development of language*. Englewood Cliffs, N.J.: Prentice-Hall, 1971.

Myklebust, H. *The psychology of deafness*. New York: Grune and Stratton, 1966a.

Myklebust, H. *Your deaf child*. Springfield, Ill.: Charles C Thomas, 1966b.

New Westminister School District #40. *Perceptual Training*. Vancouver: Author, n.d.

Northcutt, W. (Ed.). *Curriculum guide: Hearing-impaired children—Birth to three years and their parents*. Washington, D.C.: The Alexander Graham Bell Association for the Deaf, 1972.

Pollack, D. *Educational audiology for the limited hearing infant*. Springfield, Ill.: Charles C Thomas, 1970.

Schlesinger, H., & Meadow, K. P. *Sound and sign*. Berkeley, Calif.: University of California, 1972.

Sharp, E. Thinking is child's play. New York: Avon, 1969.

Sweeney, F., & Wharram, Margaret. *Experience games through music*. Portola Valley, Calif., Richards Institute, 1973.

Urban, B. Identification and management of the hearing-impaired. *The Volta Review*, 1975, 77 (1), 10–20.

U.S. Government Printing Office. *Dictionary of occupational titles*. Washington, D.C.: Bureau of Employment Security Manpower Administration, U.S. Dept. of Labor.

Ward, P. Telephone communication for deaf people: USA, Canada, and England. *Hearing*, Sept. 1974, pp. 3–4.

Combination of Visual and Auditory Disabilities

Bisno, A. The application of Piaget model to a sequential development task curriculum for deaf-blind. In W. A.

Blea (Ed.) *Proceedings of the National Symposium for the Deaf-Blind*. Pacific Grove, Calif.: California State Department of Education, July 1972.

Bobath, K., & Bobath, Berta. Cerebral palsy. In Paul Pearson & Carol Williams (Eds.), *Physical therapy services in the developmental disabilities*. Springfield, Ill.: Charles C Thomas, 1972.

Finnie, N. *Handling the young cerebral palsied child at home* (2nd ed.). New York: E. P. Dutton, 1975.

Miller, J. The use of hearing by the deaf-blind. In W. A. Blea (Ed.), *Proceedings of the National Symposium for the Deaf-Blind*. Conference of the Southwest Regional Deaf/Blind Center. Pacific Grove, Calif.: California State Department of Education, July 1972.

Mouchka, S. A. The deaf-blind infant: A rationale for and approach to early intervention. *Proceedings of the International Conference on the Education of Deaf-Blind Children,* 1971. Howe Press. Paper presented at the Perkins School for the Blind, Watertown, Mass.

Schlesinger, H. S. Out of isolation and despair. In W. A. Blea (Ed.), *Proceedings of the National Symposium for the Deaf-Blind*. Conference of the Southwest Regional Deaf/Blind Center. Pacific Grove, Calif.: California State Department of Education, July 1972.

Sherrick, C. E. (Ed.) 1980 is now. *Proceedings of the Conference on the Future of Deaf-Blind Children*. Conference of the Southwest Regional Deaf/Blind Center. Los Angeles, Calif.: John Tracy Clinic, 1974.

Language and Speech Disorders

Cazden, C. B. *Child language and education*. New York: Holt, Rinehart and Winston, 1972.

Irwin, J., & Michael M. (Eds.). *Principles of childhood language disabilities*. New York: Appleton-Century-Crofts, 1972.

Mussen, P., Henry, C., Janeway, J., & Kagan, J. *Development and personality* (3rd ed.). New York: Harper and Row, 1974.

Schiefelbusch, R. L., & Lloyd, L. L. (Eds.). *Language perspectives—Acquisition, retardation, and intervention*. College Park, Md.: University Park, 1974.

Speech

Eisenson, J. *Is your child's speech normal?* Reading, Ma.: Addison-Wesley, 1976.

Eisenson, J. & Ogilvie, M. (Eds.). *Speech correction in the schools* (4th ed.). New York: Macmillan, 1977.

Travis, L. E. (Ed.). *Handbook of speech pathology and audiology*. New York: Appleton-Century-Crofts, 1971.

Van Riper, C. *Speech correction, principles, and methods* (5th ed.). Englewood Cliffs, N. J. Prentice-Hall, 1972.

Language and Speech

Cerebral Palsy

Crickmay, M. C. *Speech therapy and the Bobath approach to cerebral palsy*. Springfield, Ill.: Charles C Thomas, 1975.

Darley, F. L., Aronson, Arnold E., & Brown, Joe E. *Motor speech disorders*. Philadelphia: W. B. Saunders, 1975.

Denhoff, E., & Robinault, I. *Cerebral palsy and related disorders*. New York: McGraw-Hill, 1960.

Haeusserman, E. *Developmental potential of preschool children*. New York: Grune and Stratton, 1958.

Irwin, O. *Communication variables of cerebral palsied and mentally retarded*. Springfield, Ill.: Charles C Thomas, 1972.

Jones, M. Habilitative management of communicative disorders in young children. In D. B. Tower (Ed.), *Nervous system vol. III: Human communication and its disorders*. New York: Raven, 1975.

Lencione, R. M. The development of communication skills. In William M. Cruickshank (Ed.), *Cerebral palsy: A developmental disability*. Syracuse, N. Y.: Syracuse University, 1976.

Mecham, M. J., & Berko, F. G. *Speech therapy in cerebral palsy*. Springfield, Ill.: Charles C Thomas, 1960.

McDonald, E., & Chance, B. *Cerebral palsy*. Englewood Cliffs, N. J.: Prentice-Hall, 1964.

Mueller, H. Speech. In Nancy Finnie, *Handling the young cerebral palsied child*. New York: E. P. Dutton, 1975.

Mysak, E. D. Cerebral palsy speech syndromes. In L. E. Travis (Ed.), *Handbook of speech pathology and audiology*. New York: Appleton-Century-Crofts, 1971.

Mysak, E. D. Cerebral palsy speech habilitation. In Lee Edward Travis (Ed.), *Handbook of speech pathology and audiology*. New York: Appleton-Century-Crofts, 1971.

Westlake, H., & Rutherford, D. *Speech therapy for the cerebral palsied*. Chicago: National Society for Crippled Children and Adults, 1961.

Epilepsy

Epilepsy Foundation of America. (Brochures available from 1828 L St. N.W., Washington, D.C. 20036.)

Resources

Visual Disability

Barraga, N. C. (Ed.). *Teacher's guide for development of visual learning abilities and utilization of low vision*. Louisville, Ky.: American Printing House for the Blind, 1970.

Bateman, B. D. Reading and psycholinguistic processes of partially seeing children. *Research Bulletin* of the American Foundation for the Blind, 1965, (8), pp. 29–44.

Drouillard, R. C. *Games with a purpose: A collection of orientation and mobility games*. Lansing, Michigan: Michigan State, n. d.

Lowenfeld, B. *The visually handicapped child in school*. New York: John Day , 1973.

Lowenfeld, B., Abel, G. L., & Hatlen, P. H. *Blind children learn to read*. Springfield, Ill.: Charles C Thomas, 1969.

Raynor, S., & Drouillard, R. C. *Get a wiggle on: A guide for helping visually impaired children grow*. Mason, Mich.: Ingham Intermediate School District, 1975. (Available from 2630 West Howell Road, Mason, Mich. 48854.)

Spivey, B. F., & Colenbrander, A. *International nomenclature of ophthalmology*. San Francisco, Calif.: Pacific Medical Center, forthcoming.

Spivey, B. F., & Colenbrander, A. *International nomenclature of ophthalmology*. San Francisco, Calif.: Pacific Medical Center, forthcoming.

Stocker, C. S. *Listening for the visually impaired: A teaching manual*. Springfield, Ill.: Charles C Thomas, 1973.

Hearing Impaired

Alexander Graham Bell Association for the Deaf, 3417 Volta Place N.W., Washington, D.C. 20007.

American Annals of the Deaf, 1974, *119*, (2), program and service directory.

Calvert, D. R., & Silverman, R. S. *Speech and deafness*. Washington, D.C.: Alexander Graham Bell Association for the Deaf, 1975.

Fant, L. J. *Ameslan: An introduction to the American sign language*. Silver Springs, Md.: National Association of the Deaf, 1972.

Fellendorf, G. W. Bibliograph on deafness. Washington, D.C.: A. G. Association, supplement 1966–1972. (Available from 3417 Volta Place, N.W., Washington, D.C. 20007.)

Furth, H. *Deafness and Learning: A psycho-social approach*. Belmont, Calif.: Wadsworth, 1973.

Grammattee, A. *Deaf persons in professional employment*. Springfield, Ill.: Charles C Thomas, 1968.

John Tracy Clinic, The. *Tracy Clinic correspondence lessons for parents of deaf children*. (Available from 806 West Adams Blvd., Los Angeles, Calif. 90007.)

National Association for the Deaf. 814 Thayer Ave., Silver Spring, Md. 20910. General resource for parents and teachers; emphasizes total communication.

Specialized Office for the Deaf and Hard of Hearing. A computerized data bank of resources for deaf education. Barkley Memorial Center, Room 318, University of Nebraska, Lincoln, Neb. 68583.

The Endeavor. International Association of Parents of the Deaf. (Journal available from 814 Thayer Ave., Silver Spring, Md. 20910.)

The Exceptional Parent. Boston, Mass.: Psychology Education Corporation. Guidelines for parents of children with disabilities.

The Volta Review. Alexander Graham Bell Association. (Journal available from 3417 Volta Place, N.W., Washington, D.C. 20007).

Combination of Visual and Auditory Disabilities

Blea, W. (Ed.). *Proceedings of the National Symposium for Deaf-Blind*. Pacific Grove, Calif.: California State Dept. of Education, July 7–10, 1972.

Jones, T. W. Jr. (Ed.). *Manual for language development: A handbook of strategies for teaching children whose communicative skills range from nonresponsiveness to use of academic language*. Bronx, N.Y.: Mid-Atlantic-North and Caribbean Regional Center for Services to Deaf-Blind Children, January 1975.

Walker, J., Tucker, J., Lauro, C., & Mirro, L. *Individualizing services to deaf-blind and other multiply handicapped children: State of the art: 1975*. Austin, Texas: Texas Regional Resource Center, 1975.

Language & Speech

Bowlby, J. *Attachment and loss* (Vol. I, Attachment). New York: Basic Books, 1969.

Brown, R. *A first language*. Cambridge: Harvard University, 1973.

Hunt, J. McVicker. *Intelligence and experience*. New York: Ronald, 1961.

Bereiter, C., & Englemann, S. *Teaching disadvantaged children in preschool*. Englewood Cliffs, N.J.: Prentice-Hall, 1966.

Bricker, D., Dennison, Laura, & Bricker, W. *Constructive interaction: Adaption approach to language training*. Monographs of the Mailmen Center for Child Development, 1975, (1). MCCD Monograph Series No. 1. Miami: Mailman Center for Child Development. Univ. of Miami, 1975.

Bricker, W. A systematic approach to language training. In R. L. Schiefelbush (Ed.), *Language of the mentally retarded*. Baltimore: University Park, 1972.

Jones, M. A new look at toddlers. *Twelfth Annual Distinguished Lectural Series in Special Education and Rehabilitation*. Los Angeles, Calif.: School of Education, University of Southern California, 1974. (Available from the U.S.C. bookstore.)

Jones, M. Habilitative management of communicative disorders in young children. In D. B. Towes (Ed.), *The Nervous System* (Vol. 3, Human communication and its disorders). New York: Raven, 1975.

Kent, L. *Language acquisition program for the severely retarded*. Champaign, Ill.: Research, 1974.

Mahler, M., Pine, F., & Bergmar, A. *The psychological birth of the human infant: Symbiosis and individuation*. New York: Basic Books, 1975.

Menyuk, P. *The acquisition and development of language*. Englewood Cliffs, N.J.: Prentice Hall, 1971.

The National Institute for Rehabilitation Engineering (NIRE).*Electronic Speech Aids*. [Brochure] Pomptom Labes, N.J.: January 31, 1976.

Piaget, J. *The origins of intelligence in children*. New York: International Universities Press, 1952. (Originally published, W. W. Norton & Co., New York, 1963.)

Schiefelbusch, R. L., & Lloyd, L. L. *Language perspectives—Acquisition, retardation, and language intervention*. Baltimore: University Park Press, 1974.

Tyack, D., & Gottsleben, R. *Language sampling, analysis and training*. Palo Alto, Calif.: Consulting Psychologists, 1974.

Uzgiris, I., & Hunt, J. McVicker. *Assessment in infancy: Ordinal scales of psychological development*. Urbana: University of Illinois, 1975.

White, B. L. *Human infants*. Englewood Cliffs, N.J.: Prentice Hall, 1971.

Epilepsy

Castle, G. F., Fishman, L. S. Seizures. *Pediatric Clinics of North America,* 1973, *20*, 819–835.

Epilepsy Foundation of America, 1828 L. Street, N.W., Washington, D.C., Suite 406, 20036.

Lagos, J. *Seizures, epilepsy and your child*. New York: Harper & Row, 1974.

Wright, G. (Ed.). *Epilepsy rehabilitation*. Boston: Little, Brown and Company, 1975.

Psychosocial Aspects of Physical Disability

Beyond the basic physical needs of the disabled, psychosocial variables play a prominent role in adjustment to physical disability. Factors of social interaction and socialization have a significant impact on the physically disabled. This chapter will focus on some of those problems which the physically disabled may encounter as deterrents to adjustment.

Gross generalizations about social interaction patterns as related to specific disabilities are not possible. The trend has been to assume that the greater the physical disability, the more involved will be the related psychological problems. However, in actuality, there is no specific set of psychological characteristics associated with the nature and extent of disability. The comments which follow in this chapter are of a general na-

Barbara Sirvis, *Ed.D., is an assistant professor of special education at the University of Washington, Seattle, Washington.*

Josephine L. Carpignano *is a school psychologist for the San Francisco Unified School District, San Francisco, California.*

June Bigge.

ture. All physically disabled persons have needs to relate to others and to their environment. The goal in analysis of potential barriers is to anticipate in order to avoid problems and/or aid in their solution through understanding.

It is helpful from the beginning to establish the difference between *disability* and *handicap*. Though used interchangeably, the two words differ in their application to the physically disabled population. A disability is measurable and constant from person to person. The loss of a finger limits the use of the hand for all people. In comparison, a handicap is a condition brought about by some disability. Because of past experience and expectations, a disability may have a damaging effect on a person's life. A violinist who loses a finger might well be handicapped, but a truck driver experiencing the same disability might find little difficulty in adjustment, and therefore is not handicapped.

Only the one who is handicapped by a disability can give an accurate picture of the nature of the handicapping condition. In this chapter, the authors attempt to define relationships between disabilities and psychosocial problems encountered in conjunction with resulting physical limitations. Problems associated with ego development, stress, family life education, and death are discussed. While this text is hardly an exhaustive treatment of the problems, a range of important psychosocial phenomena will be explored.

Psychological Implications

Psychological Manifestations of a Physical Disability

In a discussion about the psychological impact of disability, Levine (1959) states:

Blanket generalizations about the disabled, as convenient as they may be, are apt to be in error by virtue of their oversimplifications. . . . The extent of the impact experienced by each individual is related to the significance which the disability possesses for him. This in turn will depend on the pattern of events in his life that have contributed to the values he holds, the way he perceives himself in relation to the rest of the world, and the form which his reactions to stress take. (p. 1)

Almost 20 years ago there was already the clear recognition that psychological problems found among those with physical disability were unique to the individual. The problems represented the person's own adaptive dysfunction rather than being related solely to the disability. Though attitudes are changing, there still exists, even in this enlightened decade, a number of preconceived notions about physical disabilities. Many of these misconceptions are unrealistic and discriminatory. The person with a disability needs to consider this discrimination as one more "fact" with which he must come to terms.

In addition to the potential psychological problems imposed by a disability or handicap, psychological problems may be caused indirectly or directly by attitudinal and architectural barriers created by a society in which the disabled person must function as a "minority." Like a member of any other minority group, a person with a physical disability must face a number of prejudicial and stereotypical responses from others. He must overcome depreciatory attitudes and a number of social barriers in order to live the kind of life enjoyed by the "majority."

It is because of this "minority" status that many psychological problems arise for the physically disabled. The fact that a disabled person may be different in appearance, behavior, or habits often suggests to others (and eventually to the person himself) that there is something deviant or deficient about him. If the disabled person can be perceived as "a person with a disability" rather than as "a disabled person," there will be greater emphasis placed on the person than on the disability.

Growing up in a family with fixed attitudes toward disability, and living in a society which treats persons with disability as a disfavored minority, the person with a disabling condition is faced with preconceived distorted perceptions of his state. In their discussion of "disability as a special psychological problem," Neff and Weiss (1965) mention several psychological considerations unique to the condition of physical disability.

1. There must be a distinction made between the consequences of a congenital impairment (or one that occurs in very early childhood), and one which happens after the individual has become an adolescent or adult. In the one case, there are issues of influence on the developmental process. At a later time in life, the onset of disability means a disruption of what was already established as a life style with firmly set personal and interpersonal patterns.
2. If the disability or injury occurs sometime after birth and entails dismemberment or paralysis, then a sense of loss becomes an important issue to consider. Loss of part of one's body or loss of the function of part of the body often entails deep feelings of grief and despair.
3. The disabled person is typically seen by others as being different, and he generally perceives himself as different. This in turn assigns the disabled person a unique social status. (p. 789)

We interpret the "unique social status" of the disabled to be parallel to what occurs with other minority groups, including the disadvantages of discrimination and prejudice which accompany that status.

Other psychological considerations mentioned by Neff and Weiss (1965) include special problems with psychological testing, techniques and objectives of psychotherapy, and issues related to rehabilitation. Whatever role (parent, family member, friend, teacher) others play in relation to the person with a physical disability, there should be greater emphasis placed on assets than on liabilities.

Basic Psychological Needs of the Physically Disabled

Psychological needs of the physically disabled are identical to those of their nondisabled peers. Maslow (1954) designates five basic groups of needs:

1. *physiological or survival needs*—air, water, food, shelter, sleep
2. *safety needs*—security, stability, protection, and freedom from fear
3. *belongingness and love needs*—affection, affiliation, and sexual relatedness
4. *esteem needs*—adequacy, mastery, competence, or *self-esteem;* recognition, appreciation, and status, or *esteem from others*
5. *self-actualization needs*—to become everything that one is capable of becoming

After the basic survival and safety needs are met, then the belongingness and esteem needs emerge and develop. Hunger for affectionate relationships with people, a real place in the peer group or family, and the desire to gain self-esteem and the respect of others are strong drives in all of us. Frustration of these needs may cause the individual to feel keenly the pangs of self-rejection and isolation.

For the disabled, fulfillment of needs to belong and to be esteemed may be directly influenced by the nature and extent of the specific disability. Patterns such as amount of self-direction, level of self-concept, and ability to interact in reciprocal relationships with others are related to fulfillment of these needs. These patterns are directly related to the amount of control one has over the functions of one's own body and over the environment in which one lives. To the degree that this control is impaired (locomotion, communication, educational, and vocational skills), and to the extent that the person continues to be concerned with safety and survival needs, developmental delay is a predictable consequence. However, if the individual has alternative ways to control and influence the environment, and if support and encouragement are available from parents, teachers, and others, there is every reason to

expect that a healthy personality will develop. With compensatory experiences, striving for belonging, self-esteem, and other basic psychological needs can be fulfilled. Striving for self-actualization will result after basic needs are met.

Some special problems occur when the development of disabled and nondisabled children are compared. Certain physical skills are generally expected to develop at specific ages (feeding, walking, toilet training, language) and are strongly related to development of personal independence. Frequently, the normal developmental time frame for physical skills does not apply to physically disabled children; however, we must not confuse rate of physical development with psychological and social skills development. We may contaminate our perceptions by expecting children who function physically at younger levels to also behave less maturely. It is essential that we recognize that, because of the child's unique physical disability, the "normal" avenues for developing psychological and social maturity may be blocked. A four year old who cannot feed or dress himself because of a physical handicap may not be similarly delayed in personality development; and, since he is necessarily more physically dependent, other opportunities for independence and self-direction must be made available. Although it may be more convenient for parents and teachers to "translate" the poor speech of an older child with severe articulation problems, it is usually wiser to encourage the youngster to develop greater clarity or use initiative to find other ways to convey messages. Allowing the child maximum independence and encouraging him to use his capabilities will provide the strongest foundation upon which to build a healthy personality.

Psychological Reactions to Physical Disability

We need to feel "in common" with others. Physically disabled persons often see this need as unattainable because of their physical "difference."

Some common adverse reactions to physical difference as a result of disability are listed by Jourard (1958):

1. *Denial* or refusal to acknowledge that the disability exists or that it imposes any limitations whatsoever.

2. *Resignation* or "giving up"—seeing the situation as hopeless and refusing to help oneself or be helped.
3. *Regarding oneself as the victim* of injustice perpetrated by others and punishing the "others" by hostility or withdrawal.
4. *Showing arrogance and rebellion,* rejecting help or empathy, making aggressive demands, and remaining aloof.
5. *Viewing the disability as a punishment* for real or imagined infractions of family or societal rules.
6. *Becoming dependent and demanding* because remaining helpless seems the only way to assure attention, affection, and care. (pp. 140–143)

Among the major psychological problems encountered by the physically disabled person are unresolved feelings of dependency and inadequate ways of dealing with necessary physical dependence. Development of an excessive psychological dependence on those upon whom they rely for physical assistance may interfere with the process of developing a healthy independence and sense of self-sufficiency, thereby preventing adequate growth of self-esteem.

Recognition of actual physical limitations, understanding the nature of the disability, and maximum use of independent skills are major psychological tasks for every disabled person. Superficial recognition of a disability may often mask subconscious self-rejection, inner contempt and anger towards dependencies, and/or unrealistic expectations which deny the existence of the condition or use it as an exploitation of others.

To avoid these maladaptive patterns, the young physically disabled child needs adults who accept the disability as a limitation but who also refuse to allow it to become punishment or an excuse. Those who learn healthy, adaptive attitudes at an early age are more likely to have the necessary skills to meet conflicts and stresses with confidence and self-assurance.

Sources of Stress on the Physically Disabled

Although it is difficult to identify adjustment problems specifically related to the physically disabled, it is possible to examine the sources from which stress might originate. As a result of stress

source identification, it is also possible to anticipate some potential areas of adjustment difficulty. Reynell (1973) developed a hypothetical model in an attempt to illustrate the possible sources of stress on cerebral palsied children placed in a special school. The model was designed to show how patterns and intensities of stress vary in the lives of children at different ages.

Jane Scandary adapted and expanded the basic model designed by Reynell (1973) to make it more applicable to several different populations of physically disabled persons.[1] The Reynell model suggests the following major sources of stress:

1. parental reactions to a child's handicap and/or parental concerns for the future
2. hospitalization, medical care, treatment, and/or general health care
3. limitations of activity, internally or externally generated
4. social limitations and difficulties in social relationships
5. dependence on others
6. educational or employment demands
7. self-awareness and realization of handicap (Reynell, 1973, p. 145)

This model outlines major difficulties commonly confronted by the handicapped as they progress from infancy through adulthood. It also suggests that the pattern may be similar among individuals with different handicapping conditions. However, the schema is a basic pattern which can be applied generally. It is hypothetical and permits and facilitates discussion, analysis, and planning.

Figure 5–1 illustrates these sources of stress by age groupings. Intensity of stress is designated by size of the stress source block, i.e., the larger the block, the greater the possible stress.

The diagram illustrates (beginning at far left) that the major source of stress for the child from birth through infancy is the parental reaction to the child's handicap. This reaction may be expressed in varied feelings and behaviors by the parents, including guilt, fear, shock, anger, grief, and bewilderment. In addition, stress in the child may be caused by early hospitalization, separation from parents for medical treatment, and limitation of physical activity which in turn limits experience and hampers individual development.

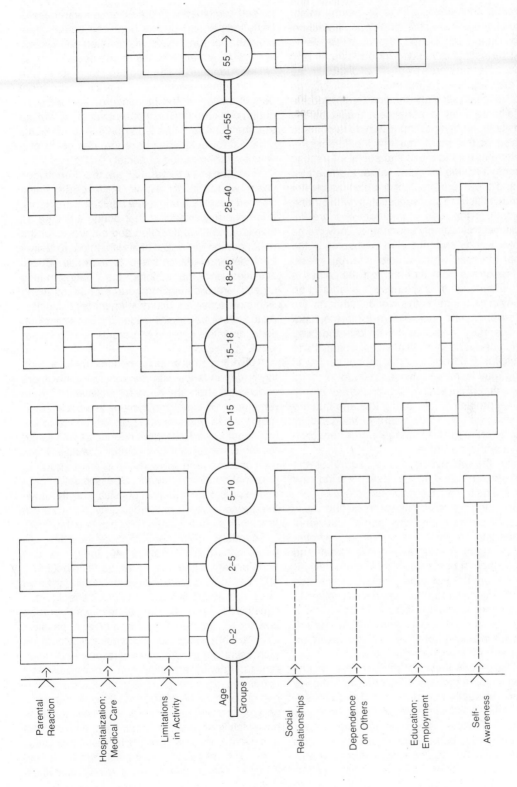

Figure 5–1. Sources of stress. SOURCE: From an adaptation of "Children with Physical Handicaps" by Joan Reynell. In *Stresses in Children* edited by Ved P. Varma. London: University of London, 1973, p. 145. Reprinted by permission.

Age Groups: 0–2, 2–5, 5–10, 10–15, 15–18, 18–25, 25–40, 40–55, 55 →

Parental Reaction

Hospitalization; Medical Care

Limitations in Activity

Social Relationships

Dependence on Others

Education; Employment

Self-Awareness

Parental concerns continue to be the major source of stress during the toddler and preschool period. During this period, the child begins to exhibit the instinctual need for independence, and if this need is hampered by physical disability, the child may experience frustration, hostility, and anger. Hospitalization and medical treatment continue to be traumatic experiences, and limitations of activity again hamper individual development. It is also at this point that the toddler or preschooler attempts to move into social interaction situations. It is time for group rather than parallel play, and the overprotected disabled youngster may find it difficult to play successfully with others.

Children at the early elementary age are delightfully but frustratingly egocentric. They create their own worlds and thus eliminate some of the external stresses which create internal stress. They feel stress from parents, but the stress is lessened because their attention is scattered on so many new things in the world. Although the child is dependent upon others for some functions, Scandary feels that the child is too busy exploring his world to allow physical limitations to be stressful. Entrance into the school setting at this age may increase tensions related to social relationships. Educational demands may create additional problems. It is during this age that the child becomes more fully aware of his disability and the difference in body image. Some impact on self-concept is inevitable.

During the pubescent years, some of the former stresses tend to be less pressing and others intensify. Social relationships, peer acceptance, and friendship seem to be the basic sources of stress during this age. Educational demands and concerns are not yet overwhelming, while the increasing awareness of self and the realization of one's disability is extremely intensified. Parental concerns continue to exist, but the child's concerns tend to have been resolved to some degree. Medical treatment is becoming a part of his lifestyle and is generally accepted. Limitations in activity continue to cause frustration as his need for independence grows.

Adolescence is the most difficult time for any growing child, regardless of whether or not he is disabled. All reactions are intensified and stress is a very difficult problem with which adolescents must deal. Social relationships and peer acceptance are major sources of stress as are the anxieties and worries about education and employment opportunities. The adolescent's search for self combined with the ultimate awareness of limitations posed by the handicap create great pressure for the physically disabled adolescent. Medical treatment focuses on the need for physical independence. The need to move about with and like others of the same age creates a great deal of anxiety. Parental concerns also increase during this time because parents begin to realize that their child's future is in doubt in terms of his potential for achievement of the stereotype of a "positive contribution of society."

The ages of 17 through 25 are the "in-between years" with some of the major anxieties remaining from adolescence and a few additional problems. It is generally expected that during this time an individual will find direction and emphasis for the major portion of the rest of his life. Intense desires for independence continue to increase. Social activities and interactions, the "dating-mating urges," are a continuing source of stress along with the worries about employment opportunities. As the individual begins to identify his own inclinations, anxieties created by parents recede somewhat.

A disabled adult does not become more accepting of dependence with maturity but rather more concerned about the need for assistance for the remainder of life. Employment anxieties are a major stress because they directly relate to the individual's need for independence as well as the feeling of responsibility for self and family. Social relationships tend to focus on a small group of personal and family friends. Stress is still experienced due to limitations in physical activity. However, reconciliation to the disability, if not acceptance of it, hopefully takes place during this time.

Scandary (1975) notes that, as the physically handicapped adult reaches 40, they, too, can hopefully agree with the old adage, "Life begins at 40." The trials and tribulations of learning to know one's self and to live with one's self should have diminished; however, the handicapped person now is at an age when health and physical strength may show signs of weakening, causing increasing stress. Activity limitations and resultant frustrations are similar to those previously experienced. Understandably, the fears and worries of being dependent upon others continues to be a major source of concern. Social relationships have stabilized, and the demands for employment and a stable income continue to create anxieties.

As the physically disabled approach the "Golden Years," they face increasing difficulties.

Physical limitations may be increasing and may create further concern about dependence on others and need for physical care. The need for physical assistance is a continuing problem for the disabled as they age.

Goals and Attitudes Which Nurture Healthy Psychological Adjustment

Accurate appraisal of what is achievable is an important goal for the successful integration of any personality. It has primary significance for the physically disabled. There are at least three separate dimensions to this task:

1. Arrive at acceptance of limitations.
2. Make an accurate appraisal of strengths and abilities.
3. Apply concerted effort toward what is achievable.

The first two dimensions require objective judgment, and the third requires drive to achieve self-actualization. Taking risks and trying out new ways of solving problems are important avenues for exploration in making decisions around all three tasks. To know what limitations there are, what strengths and abilities exist, and to determine what is achievable requires repeated trials and continuous re-evaluation.

Underlying the drive for self-actualization are attitudes about the self:

1. Conception of the self which includes both positive and negative dimensions of reality, rather than fantasies of helplessness or omnipotence.
2. Firm feelings of adequacy and confidence based on actual ability to function in personal, social, educational, and vocational areas.
3. Attitudes of independence and self-direction.

There cannot be too much emphasis placed on the need for recognition of assets and liabilities and on the necessity for confident assurance that one can influence one's environment. In a study by Jones (1974) of 102 disabled students between the ages of 6 and 16 years, higher academic achievement and better interpersonal relationships were found among those who felt that control resided within themselves rather than in the external environment. Most significant, in terms of the discussion here, was that neither lack of mobility nor extent of physical dependence was related to achievement or social adjustment. Only the degree of *psychological* dependence was related to these variables. Thus, the nature and extent of physical disability may not be as significant for adjustment as are psychological attitudes and self-perceptions.

Helping the Physically Disabled Achieve Psychological Adjustment

In discussing the physically handicapped child in relation to his family, Ross (1964) makes several suggestions which can be helpful to parents and teachers.

1. *Accept the disability*. Acknowledge limitations it imposes while providing recognition for skills and abilities that the child possesses.
2. *Set and maintain expectations for performance and accomplishment*. Avoid comparisons with other children and set standards according to individual potential. Expecting more than a child can accomplish may result in frustration and a sense of failure and inadequacy. Expecting too little often leads to overdependence and feelings of helplessness and resignation.
3. *Support and encourage the child's attempts at independence*. The physically disabled are likely to remain dependent on others longer than the nondisabled. Therefore, the greater the number of independent activities they can perform, the less handicapping the disabilities will be for them.
4. *Provide a variety of experiences in the child's areas of strength*. While helping the child to develop his capabilities in areas where he is disabled, the parent or teacher should also encourage achievement in areas of strength.
5. *Provide appropriate discipline*. The disabled child must have reasonable limits set which are consistently enforced. (pp. 123–138)

Ross notes that parents often either expect more than the child can accomplish or overprotect the child because of low expectations. Ideally, parents and teachers of the physically disabled child will learn that, because their child requires more physical assistance than most, doing for the child things he *can* accomplish is not necessary or adaptive. Overly high expectations with resulting failures also will not help him overcome dependency. Acknowledgment of limitations and expectations that the child can develop areas of potential will nurture psychological health and the development of a positive self-concept.

Special attention should be given to adult attitudes and behaviors related to "achievable goals" for children with disabilities. It is all too easy, for example, to encourage a youngster with cerebral palsy to continue his talk about becoming a baseball hero, an airplane pilot, or a ballet dancer and dismiss these expressed plans as transient "childhood fantasies." It is, however, much kinder to guide children at an early age to distinguish fantasy from reality, and to help them make judgments about how their particular limitations may affect their plans for the future. Individuals with physical and multiple disabilities often require considerable guidance in making judgments about achievable goals.

Conversely, it is even more important to identify and support the *real* capabilities and exceptionalities which many disabled children have. Encouragement and support in full development of skills is essential to productive living as well as self-esteem. Good role models may be found in those who have been successful in achievable pursuits and who may have physical handicaps. Attention may also be directed to the "achievable" qualities in role models who are not disabled, and emphasis should be placed on those qualities which can also be achieved by the young admirer. For example, if a football player is admired by a 10-year-old boy with cerebral palsy, the child should be guided to focus on the qualities of fair play, shrewd planning on the field, and/or showing team spirit rather than focusing *solely* on the ability to run fast or kick the ball well.

Self-Awareness and Self-Concept

"Self-Concept" and How It Develops

Self-concept is one's perception of oneself as a physical, emotional, intellectual, and social person. It is our idea of who we are and how we relate to others and to the environment in which we live. The idea includes body image, emotional experience, social and moral values, and other aspects of our life experience. Perceptions of abilities and disabilities are integrated in the self-image. Every individual has limitations in some area and to

some degree. We are, each and every one, retarded or disabled in some facet of our lives. The relevant question is *which aspect* and *to what degree*.

Personal growth is the product of the way we view our limitations and strengths and of the methods we use to form integrated self-perceptions. Great distortions in self-concept often result from exclusion of information about ourselves or in alteration of information of which we disapprove and are unwilling to accept as part of our concept of ourselves.

Self-concept is learned. It is learned from parents and others who make statements about us as we grow to adulthood (and these need not be only verbal statements). It is learned as well from those who serve as identification models (people we admire and try to imitate). Self-concept is also learned from our own observations about ourselves as we behave with others and compare ourselves with our peers. A *positive self-concept* implies that an image acceptable to us has developed. Conversely, a *negative self-concept* indicates that there has developed a dislike for the person we believe ourselves to be.

One of the most important components of self-concept is body image. This image is the mental picture we have of our physical appearance in combination with internal and surface sensations and the orientation of our body in space. The body is the focus of an individual's identity. Its limits define a boundary that, despite developmental and accidental changes, separates him from his environment. For the physically disabled person, the body image is often the most difficult to integrate positively with the self-concept because it is this specific aspect of the person which is limited and which is responsible for the observable difference from others. Recent studies (Flatley, 1973; Goldberg, 1974) indicate that the greater the "visibility" of the handicapping condition, the greater the effect on social adjustment and self-concept.

Joel (1975) places an adequate self-concept at the top of his priority list for individuals disabled by cerebral palsy. "[The person with cerebral palsy] . . . must have a deep and abiding faith in his own value as a person and be fully aware of . . . [himself]" (pp. 18–19). In infancy and early childhood, touching, holding, cuddling, and stroking by significant others in the child's environment are the first steps in acquiring a positive self-concept. Acceptance, comfort, and security are conveyed through these very early sensory communications. They tell the infant he is wanted and loved and is therefore a valued and worthwhile person.

Self-Awareness and Self-Concept Development: Early Stages

There are a variety of indicators of emerging self-awareness which are basic to the development of self-concept, including the following:

1. Infant responds positively to being held and spoken to by parent.
2. Infant actively seeks contact with others, indicates own needs by crying, reaching out, turning away, etc.
3. Infant recognizes parent and self as separate individuals.
4. Infant regards self in mirror and shows recognition.
5. Child responds to own name and identifies self by first name.
6. Child recognizes others in family by name.
7. Child is aware of and can locate various body parts.
8. Child recognizes objects as belonging to himself and others.
9. Child shows appropriate emotions in response to various situations.
10. Child is able to tell his full name, age, and sex.
11. Child can entertain himself with toys or other objects.
12. Child can play cooperatively with other children.
13. Child can work with adults imitatively and cooperatively.
14. Child can associate various articles of clothing with appropriate body parts.
15. Child can name major feeling states in relation to himself (happy, sad, angry, afraid).

In later stages, self-concept is more closely related to values applied to the self through a variety of experiences in the physical environment and in relationships with peers and adults.

For the young physically disabled child, restricted ability to explore the environment and barriers to "normal" relationship goals may present difficulties in self-acceptance. Body image becomes a crucial factor when the disabled youngster begins to compare himself with age mates who are not disabled. Warm acceptance

must be available at times when the positive self-concept is being challenged. Problems of physical appearance and limitations on movement should not be ignored or denied, but strengths and abilities must be stressed at these times.

Self-Concept When the Disabled Child Goes to School

Adequate self-concept is as important to academic learning as it is to emotional well-being and adjustment. Attitudes toward achievement and academic excellence rely heavily on whether the child has learned that his efforts will meet with some measure of success, whether he can compare favorably with others, and if it is possible for him to experience pleasure in new experiences. For the school age child, involvement in school-related tasks is a crucial experience. It is essential that needless frustration and failure be avoided. It is equally essential that the child be challenged to achieve his fullest potential.

In helping the disabled child learn new skills, teachers and parents should be cognizant of the following suggestions made by Wallace and Kauffman (1973):

1. Use all available sources of information about the child so that the task to be learned can begin at the current success level.
2. Define what the expectations are in terms of performance of specific tasks. Make directions clear.
3. Expect the best response possible according to the child's ability. Build on strengths and competencies.
4. Pinpoint problems and present appropriate learning tasks to remediate the problem.
5. Provide the learner with feedback, giving support and encouragement without excessive or undue sympathy for failures.
6. Present a structure for behavior and adhere firmly to the limits.
7. Observe progress and acknowledge to the child the success of his efforts. Keep a record to show where growth has occurred. (pp. 96–99)

Several recent studies are cited by Lambert, Wilcox, and Gleason (1974, pp. 179–180) in which primary factors influencing school achievement were determined to be (a) the evaluation of one's own ability in relation to others and (b) the sense of control over one's environment. In one study cited, the investigator concluded that achievement was significantly affected in an adverse direction by the following:

1. High expectation for failure by the learner.
2. Negative reactions towards adults who expect too much, or positive reactions towards adults in expectation of approval (i.e., dependency on the evaluation of others).
3. Distrust of one's own solutions to problems.

What can be seen here is the relationship between poor academic achievement and negative or inadequate self-concept. In all studies cited by Lambert and her colleagues (1974), there were significant correlations between self-concept and academic achievement.

In assessing attitudes of self-concept in relation to the school setting, the following questions [2] may be asked of the child:

1. How smart do you think you are in comparison with others in your class? (One of the smartest, average, one of the lowest.)
2. Do you sometimes feel it's just too hard for you to learn reading or arithmetic?
3. Do you think you would learn better in school if the teacher did not go so fast?
4. Do you think that good luck is more important than hard work for good grades in school?
5. Do you feel that every time you try to get ahead, something or somebody gets in your way or stops you?
6. Do you believe that people like you don't have much of a chance to do well in life? (Coleman, Campbell, Hobson, McPartland, Mood, Weinfeld, & York, 1966, Appendix I)

Analysis of responses to these questions may aid in identification of students whose poor achievement is related to negative self-concept.

Special Problems with Self-Concept

When adolescence is approached, attitudes toward personal, social, sexual, vocational, and marital aspects of living are altered, and plans for the future need to be modified by more mature considerations. With the onset of adolescence, multiple changes occur which may require changes in previous adaptations. Freeman (1970) lists a number of areas in which problems of adjustment may arise:

1. There may be a change in physical condition.
2. The fantasy of someday being "cured" must be abandoned.
3. Peers become acutely aware of differences at this age, so that the disabled young person may feel even more "left out" than before.
4. The disability may prevent participation in certain activities which provide others with social status and feelings of competence.
5. Sexual maturation brings with it problems of impulse expression.
6. Changing schools or leaving school may be traumatic since the problems of new people and a new environment must be met. (pp. 64–70)

In addition to the many special needs of non-disabled adolescents, meeting the unique needs of physically disabled adolescents requires added attention. Special needs of the disabled adolescent, according to Freeman (1970), include

1. *The need for privacy:* Developing sexual maturation and ensuing interest and curiosity, along with need for exploration of self and experimentation with others, requires a greater amount of privacy than before.
2. *The need for participation:* Continuing to treat the adolescent as a child by excluding him from discussions and decisions which affect him and his future is an insult to his independent strivings and tends to foster dependency and sometimes regression at this age.
3. *The need for confidence:* One needs to stress assets and abilities of the adolescent while helping him to set realistic goals for the future.
4. *The need for knowledge:* An understanding of the disability and some of its personal, social and vocational implications should be provided at this time.
5. *The need for support:* Support and encouragement from adults are needed to facilitate risk-taking behavior, involvement with new experiences, and the assumption of greater responsibility.

Behaviors Indicating Difficulties

Rappaport (1964) reports five characteristics which indicate difficulties with self-concept:

1. *Lack of tolerance for frustration,* evidenced in emotional outbursts, when used as a way

Figure 5–2. The "Futures Now" group raps about their individual futures and personal concerns about their present situations.

of controlling the environment, suggests that efforts to protect a weakened self-concept are being made.

2. *Flight from challenge* and avoidance of risk suggests a need to limit activities to those which are assured of success. Excessive fear of failure is at the root of this behavior.

3. *Overcompensation* or exaggerated investment of energy in one particular area of strength may be a means of denying a deep seated sense of inadequacy.

4. *Control and manipulation of others* may result from an inadequate sense of mastery, inadequate control over self, or inability to achieve goals by one's own efforts.

5. *Power struggle* or negativism may indicate an attempt to stave off a sensed impending loss of identity. (p. 42)

The appearance of one or more of these characteristics in the physically disabled child, adolescent, or adult should be cause for concern and attention.

Strengthening Self-Concept

Awareness of one's unique disability, the limitations it imposes on one's life and aspirations, and possession of feelings of confidence and assurance regarding one's intrinsic value should be the personal goal for every handicapped person. Since visibly disabled people are often seen as "different" or "strange" by the uninformed, they are sometimes the object of scorn and dis-

crimination. Because they frequently are the recipients of pity or maudlin sympathy, their self-concepts need to be especially stable and resilient.

Since self-concept begins to develop early, it is important for parents, teachers, and others in the child's environment to be aware of its significance and provide experiences which nurture its growth. The following are suggestions gleaned from various sources, including Joel, 1975; Killilea, 1952; Ross, 1964; and Wright, 1960. The following may be helpful for parents and teachers:

1. In infancy and early childhood, the disabled child needs frequent physical contact with a warm, loving adult who fully accepts and cares deeply for the child.

2. A warm, positive, reassuring attitude on the part of the child's family will help develop feelings of safety and security and allow development toward a sense of adequacy and independence.

3. In early years, the child will perceive his disability in the same way as his parents. Through the process of identification, he internalizes their view of him and develops that concept of himself. If they see him as helpless, he will adopt that view; if they see him as worthwhile and able, he will assimilate that perspective of himself.

4. Encourage the child to become acquainted with his own body. He must learn to know what "feels good" and should become familiar with words that describe emotional states.

Full awareness and acceptance of sensing and feeling states is essential for a healthy self-concept.

5. Support and encourage all attempts at participation in new experiences. Develop habits of exploration and investigation. Well-developed curiosity and a sense of safety evolve out of successful risk-taking behaviors and contribute to positive self-concept.

6. Allow autonomy, independence, and self-reliance to grow. Give the child time to play alone; allow him to take as much responsibility for self-care as he can manage. Provide many opportunities for him to engage in making decisions.

7. Allow the disabled child to experience frustration. High frustration tolerance is important in meeting the challenges to be encountered throughout life. If the disabled child is over-protected and prevented from experiencing some degree of frustration and failure, he is deprived of opportunity to learn coping skills. He needs to develop the concept of himself as a person who can fail without losing self-esteem.

8. Talk with the disabled child about his disability. Encourage him to express his feelings about it, his disappointment with the limitations it imposes, and his hopes for the future. Let him experience hope and despair, confidence and doubt, pride and shame. He needs experience with the full range of human feelings.

9. Encourage the child to have his own thoughts, feelings, and attitudes. The experience of autonomy and independence which grow with the freedom to express one's views is invaluable to the developing self-concept.

10. Encourage consideration for the rights and feelings of others. Respect for others is a reflection of respect for self. The child must learn this respect through imitation, identification and practice.

11. Set reasonable limits on behavior and formulate appropriate expectations for achievement, allowing some measure of success but promoting growth to the next level. Success does not mean a "perfect" performance, but a task completed to the best of the child's ability.

12. Discuss the universality of shortcomings and handicaps. The disabled child should learn that he is not unique in having a disability. Rather, he is a unique person who happens to have a particular handicap.

13. Provide identification models. The disabled person needs such models from the ranks of other disabled individuals. These may be older handicapped children in school who are successful, public or personal heroes.

14. Provide opportunities to share problems. Children profit from opportunities to share and to discuss real problems with people such as the following:
    a. A sympathetic adult who is able to acknowledge the child's feelings and allow emotions to be ventilated.
    b. A friend, disabled or nondisabled, who is close to the child's age.
    c. Peers who have similar disabilities and parallel experiences.
    d. Identification figures of the same sex who have similar disabilities and who are independent, self-accepting, and self-sufficient.

15. Help the verbal child label his experiences. Language supplies a method for controlling the external environment and impulses from within. Naming feelings and describing events will provide perspective and will allow him to have a measure of objective distance from which to observe and to evaluate.

Family Life Education

Family life education can help physically disabled children, adolescents, and adults develop better self-images and improve the quality of their lives.

Physically disabled learners have the same drives, needs, wants, and desires as their nondisabled peers. Because of disability and confinements, some physically disabled do not have the opportunity to interact with their peers, both disabled and nondisabled, and thus may not learn the sexual nuances of our society. This lack of opportunity limits their experience in situations such as being held comfortably in a mother's arms to eat, "playing doctor," "telling it all" behind the barn, reading the graffiti in public restrooms, and being physically able to masturbate. Understanding also may be hampered by intellectual ability. Many learners may have reading problems and, therefore, not have an opportunity to gain any knowledge of sex from books or magazines. Others may be unable to retain what is told or read. Still other adolescents have been sheltered by parents and others. Because of this lack of socialization outside of school, and because they are often treated as children well into adulthood, some physically disabled persons get incorrect information or no information at all about social and sexual development. Their lack of understanding is evident to sensitive teachers. Parents, teachers, counselors, and therapists need to be better informed so they can help disabled persons develop an awareness of and positive feelings toward their sexuality.

Helpful Persons

Disabled persons and their parents, teachers, and counselors must establish an atmosphere of mutual trust and openness since disabled youngsters can begin to examine their sexuality best when a comfortable atmosphere is created. The attitude of the student is nurtured by the approach and guidance of the adult. Teachers need to be aware of their own discomforts in dealing with both sexuality and disability. This awareness is necessary so they do not impose their own values on students. If a guide or relative is frank, open, honest, and factual, children will feel more free to listen and to talk. Sex information is best provided in discussions, not lectures. Nondisabled adults cannot possibly know the outlook of disabled persons unless the disabled are allowed to express their feelings. The acceptance of expressed impressions, feelings, and opinions, including those sometimes contrary to the teacher, will facilitate the development of a willingness to share on the part of the students. They will begin to explore their self-image as well as their sexual potential and limitations.

Material Resources

A variety of resources* for family life education, including printed and media resources, are available to those who work with the disabled. These materials are very helpful for those who want to undertake this important and ongoing educational process.

Some local agencies may have resources developed for use with the able-bodied which can be useful in a curriculum for family life education for the disabled. Local Planned Parenthood Associa-

---

* See sections at the end of this chapter for references and helpful materials.

tions offer library materials, workshops for interested teachers, class visits, birth control and venereal disease information, and multimedia materials. Some local chapters of United Cerebral Palsy Association offer rap sessions and other programs for the disabled. A few local medical centers offer courses in human sexuality for professionals, as well as counseling for disabled people. Often universities have groups of disabled students interested in discussing sexuality and social development with other disabled students. If there is no university nearby, a member of the community may be able to act as a resource person. The support and involvement of parents should aid in facilitation of the independence and confidence needed by the disabled students. Public school curriculum guides on home and family life are often available.

Features of Family Life Classes

Response to a Need

The teacher should plan a program in family life and sexuality with the needs and interests of the specific participating individuals in mind. The teacher should be aware that these needs are both physiological and social.

> . . . sex education is more a social than an intellectual concern and is best accomplished as part of an approach treating all aspects of human development. It is based upon the further conviction that sex education should be a gradual, continuous and spontaneous process rather than a rigidly prescribed unit or series of units from a science or health manual, and that it should be introduced when the children indicate that they are ready, not when a curriculum guide indicates that they should be ready. (Uslander, 1974, p. 35)

Young children most often indicate their sex-related needs and interests by asking about a mother who is going to have a baby or by asking about differences in the anatomy of boys and girls. These questions may come as the result of experiences such as the birth of pets, trips to the zoo where they see animals mate, and television programs. Advice and information for young children should be given as their curiosity and resultant questions warrant it.

Teachers must be aware that if older disabled and able-bodied students enrolled in regular family life classes have not had sex education curricula at earlier ages, they may feel uncomfortable talking about sex. Therefore disabled students may not be sufficiently confident to ask questions which relate to their particular disabilities, and, further, they may be unable to articulate their own needs and drives.

Since physically disabled persons are often over-protected and do not have the necessary information to help them make decisions which affect their sexual lives, they may often fret over questions such as: Is masturbation normal? Will my handicap be transmitted to my offspring? Will I be appealing to a mate? Will I be sexually satisfied and be able to satisfy a mate? A retarded adult may ask, Can I have babies? A woman with spina bifida might particularly want to know, Can I conceive and give birth? Questions such as these deserve answers.

Built upon Input from Several Sources

There is a large number of resource personnel available to assist teachers with family life education. Teachers, parents, administrators, program planners, school psychologists, school nurses, social workers, state departments of rehabilitation personnel and clients, other interested persons, and students themselves can serve as resource personnel.

Use of Appropriate Instructors

Some personal factors must be considered in selecting a teacher for a family life education class. It is essential that the teacher feel comfortable with the subject matter. The teacher should be nonjudgmental, have the ability to listen, know available resources, be familiar with the subject matter, and recognize the special needs of students.

The ideal classroom situation in which to present sex education would be one where services of a team of professionals—two or three people from different disciplines—are available to share skills and resources. Teams having at least one male and one female member may make students feel more at ease. The inclusion of a person who has a disability may help to convey the message that people with disabilities are sexual beings like anyone else. The team must feel at ease with each other as well as with the students. They must be willing to express their own feelings frankly and honestly. The discussions should be held at a time of day when there is a minimum of classroom interruptions.

Rapport between learners and teachers is crucial when sex education is the topic. Adults and children must have developed an atmosphere of openness, honesty, respect, and trust. Group discussions concerning attitudes toward physical handicaps, feelings toward parents and peers, relationships between teachers and students, and concepts of their own bodies must precede discussions of sex. The students must feel accepted as complete, important individuals.

The "I know it all" student, often a group leader, may make the development of open discussion difficult. Allow the student to tell the group all he knows or question him about the "facts of life." It is most important not to degrade the student. Let him discover for himself that he might not know it all. Get him on the team; he may later help establish the atmosphere necessary.

Normalcy is an important dimension in all discussions of sex. Physically handicapped adolescents may have developed the fear that they are not "normal" in their sexual drives due to their lack of social contact and communication with their peers. Open discussion of sexual feelings and drives and assurance that they are normal does much to develop a receptive environment and helps the disabled person realize his thoughts and drives are not different. Open discussion also provides an opportunity for the disabled to raise concerns specifically related to the issue of the significance of their own disability with respect to sexual function and acceptability.

Involvement of Parents

It is very important to meet with the parents of disabled students to allow them to deal constructively with their fears and anxieties. Often parents of handicapped students are themselves handicapped with regard to the sexuality of their children. Ideally, many parents are growing at the same time as their children. Perhaps parents can meet one evening a week during the time the teacher is meeting with their children. In this way, communication may develop where previously there may have been none.

Program Content

Robert Perske (1973) discusses the importance of a continuum of family life education from early ages. He states that "sexual development begins at birth and continues until the day we die" (p. 37). He contends that all human beings have their sexual development coded deep within their personalities, saying that the "continuum stretches through child-bearing, child-rearing, separation from children and even the declining years" (pp. 36–37). Perske suggests the continuum might include:

Being held close in a mother's arms and being fed.
Being tickled and bounced on father's knee.
Being hugged and shoved around by brothers and sisters.
Feeling the relief of giving up body wastes at the right time in the right place.
Having curiosity about all the parts of one's own body.
Running, playing and wrestling with friends in the neighborhood.
Girls making fun of boys, and boys teasing girls.
Having a best pal and always wanting to be with him.
Awakening to find strange feelings in one's own private parts and discovering the exciting feelings one's own hands can produce.
Daring to go on a date.
Having a steady.
Feeling a strange attraction for one another and feeling fearful and guilty because of it.
Touching.
Wanting each other.
Deciding to have intercourse or to keep distance.
Deciding to break up or stay together.
Discussing what real love is.
Talking about marriage.
Making plans.
Breaking it off.
Making plans.
The ceremony or agreements toward an emotional partnership without a ceremony. (pp. 36–37)

Family life education is not a short course, but rather is a lifelong course which begins at birth. Parental figures play the major role in sex education when children are young. Hopefully, they will continue to help children and young adults learn about family life and sex. Sometimes parents and school personnel may collaborate in the sex education course. Sometimes parents may request that their children receive sex education in school as early as elementary school. Arlene Uslander (1974) describes such a program based on the belief that:

Our children learn at an early age that subjects such as childbirth, sexual reproduction, menstruation and the physical differences between male and female are not taboo, to be discussed only on the playground or in the washroom. They learn that they can talk about such topics openly and honestly, without fear of being censored or ridiculed. (p. 35)

Children need to feel free to ask questions and to participate in discussion. They need to realize their questions will not be met with embarrassment and avoidance.

Uslander (1974) directs program suggestions to classroom teachers in regular elementary schools. These suggestions are equally helpful to teachers of disabled children who do not attend regular classes. She lists and explains guidelines for answering questions, choosing not to answer some questions, and leading sex education discussions with children of all ages. She also lists and suggests answers for the questions most asked by children of different age groupings. Her article "Everything You Always Wanted to Know About Sex Education," and other printed resources are very helpful to those teachers who are interested in sex education for physically disabled students of elementary-school age.

Useful secondary level program suggestions are described by Sapienza and Thornton (1974). A slightly adapted outline of their curriculum, *Secondary School Family Life Curriculum for the Physically Disabled,* is included as a reference to readers on p. 94.

Clearance for Implementation

Not all school districts or schools will allow family life education. Many will not allow teaching of information on venereal disease or contraception. Not all parents will give permission for their children to participate in sex education programs. Permission from the school district, principal, and each child's parents is mandatory and can be gained most easily by personal contact. Parental permission is most readily attained by conferring individually with each set of parents. Many parents are relieved to know that someone else is going to help teach their child. After parental permission is obtained, the team should present the content and films to be used in the course to the parents and principal.

Benefits

Continuous programming in sex education can

broaden the students' knowledge and experiences and help the students become more accepting of their drives, needs, wants, and desires. The program will help them to understand that they are normal, acceptable, presentable, important human beings. Well-taught sex education classes can improve the image that physically handicapped adolescents may have of themselves. Improved self-image should influence the rest of their living.

Secondary School Family Life Curriculum
for the Physically Disabled*

I. *Possible Processes in Curriculum Development and Implementation*
   A. Introduce program
      1. Overview of class
      2. Student ideas for class content
         a. Anonymous questions from each class member placed in question box
      3. Student/teacher goals
   B. Invite selected visitors and consultants
      1. Invite participation with various "well adjusted" disabled people—persons with cerebral palsy, spina bifida, or spinal cord injury—to discuss their sexuality and adjustments to physical inconveniences
      2. Invite consultation and visits from local medical doctors and other local persons specializing in educational programing in human sexuality and the disabled
   C. Use selected films and tapes
      1. *Don't Tell the Cripples About Sex*
      2. *Like Other People*
      3. *Stigma I & II*
   D. Encourage parental involvement
      1. Provide opportunity for simultaneous growth of parents and students
      2. Recognize fears, needs, anxieties of parents
         a. Rap sessions
      3. Share materials
      4. Encourage input
      5. Obtain approval for course material
      6. Encourage parents to preview films
      7. Facilitate communication among parents, students, and school personnel
   E. Encourage student social experiences
      1. Join one social organization of choice as part of assignment
      2. Bring a friend to class for rap session
      3. Plan and attend a social function to culminate class
   F. Evaluate—Teacher & Student
II. *Possible Topics*
   A. Separation or individuation
      1. Becoming an individual
         a. How dependent were you 5 years ago?
         b. Project how independent you'll be 2 years from now
      2. Independence
         a. What is independence?
         b. What are some of the responsibilities that go along with it?
         c. Fears and anxieties?
         d. Kinds of things that make you dependent?
         e. How do you break down dependencies?
         f. Why strive for independence?

---

*Adapted from Barbara Sapienza and Carla Thornton, "Curriculum for Advanced Family Life for the Physically Disabled." Used by permission.

1) Advantages
2) Disadvantages
3) Reality of independence
4) Recognition of independence

g. Does becoming an adult also mean becoming independent?
h. Does independence mean isolation?
i. Are new contracts negotiable?
j. Are new relationships necessary to replace the old ones you are leaving?
k. What are the finances of being independent?
    a. Rent, food, utilities, health care, etc.
    b. Bank accounts
    c. Budgets
    d. Accessible apartments
    e. Part-time jobs
l. What does the state owe people who are disabled?
m. Is anyone ever totally independent?
    a. Interdependence

B. Conflict*
1. How do you deal with conflicts?
2. Kinds of conflict
    a. Moral
    b. Emotional
    c. Financial
    d. Parental acceptance
    e. Independent travel
    f. Dating
    g. Racial
    h. Dress, hair
    i. Authority
    j. Self-imposed conflict
3. Why these conflicts?
4. Does everyone experience conflict?
5. How could it become less of a problem?
6. How could it be averted?
7. Should it be averted?

C. Rights and responsibilities of disabled students*
1. Adaptive equipment
    a. Electric wheelchairs
    b. Autos with adaptive equipment
    c. Grievance process
    d. Architectural barriers
        1) Rights of the disabled to have access and safety in public buildings

D. The capacity for tenderness toward others
1. Adolescent period—"normal" progression
    a. Strong friendships between members of the same sex develop
    b. Beginnings of relations with opposite sex
    c. Some adolescents learn about each other's bodies, thoughts, emotions, sexual responses, social rules, and customs of behavior
        1) Intense curiosity
        2) Avid pursuit of sexual information

---

*This discussion on conflict can be supplemented with passages from literature which display conflict.
*Stigma I & II will supplement this discussion.

        3) Sex-oriented conversations
        4) Double meanings
        5) Daydreaming and fantasies
        6) Masturbation
        7) Body contact games
        8) Playful roughhousing
        9) Experimenting

2. Importance of friendships
   a. Sharing feelings
   b. Caring and being cared for
   c. Having someone with whom to laugh and cry
   d. Ego gratification
3. Why is it sometimes difficult to engage in friendships?
   a. Opening-up—expressing oneself
   b. Accepting others
   c. Desire
   d. Opportunity or lack of it
   e. Aggressiveness
   f. Friend-enemy relations
   g. Feelings of being different
   h. Using differences so that they become advantages
   i. Dealing with questions concerning handicaps
      a. Accepting oneself
      b. Assertiveness
4. How many friends do we need?
5. How do we display affection?
   a. Affectionate behaviors (slides depicting various affectionate behavior)
      1) Holding hands
      2) Smiling
      3) Touching
      4) Kissing
      5) Crying
6. Culture dictates acceptable and unacceptable behavior.
   a. Two people of the same sex walking arm in arm—acceptable or unacceptable?
   b. How do other cultures deal with affectionate behaviors?
7. Boy-Girl relationships
   a. Dating
   b. Love—What is love?
      1) Infant-mother
      2) Maternal
      3) Paternal
      4) Peer-mate love
      5) Heterosexual love
   c. Intimacy
   d. Marriage
   e. Living together
   f. Marrying a disabled person—Does this mean marrying a disability?
   g. Communication
   h. Getting to know one another
   i. Breaking up
   j. Grieving

E. Competency and Achievement

    1. What is success?
       a. Feeling good about what you do
       b. Doing something well as measured by self and others
       c. Grades
       d. Athletic ability
       e. Friends
       f. Relationships
    2. Future plans and goals
       a. Do current achievements influence future plans?
       b. Fantasies for the future
       c. Self-expectations
          1) Jobs
          2) Marriage—partnership
          3) Possibility for career and marriage for women as well as men
          4) Do expectations change?
          5) Do we need time to re-examine our goals?
          6) Goal rigidity—Does it have a place?
    3. Roles
       a. What is a "good" mother?
       b. What is a "good" father?
       c. What is a "good" partner in a relationship?
       d. What is a man?
       e. What is a woman?
       f. Should a woman work if she is a mother?
       g. Are women inferior?
       h. Should a woman have equal rights in a relationship?
       i. Should a man have full responsibility in financing a household?
       j. Does a woman need to have a baby to feel fulfilled?
F. Are all thoughts normal?
G. Are all behaviors normal? Legal?
    1. Masturbation—mutual masturbation?
    2. Homosexuality—heterosexuality—bisexuality?
    3. Oral-genital sex?
    4. Anal sex?
    5. Child exploration and discovery (playing doctor)?
H. Sexual morality codes
    1. Different codes for different people?
    2. Society's code?
I. Sexual myths
    1. Penis size
    2. "Simultaneous orgasm"
    3. "Masturbation causes blindness."
    4. "Marriage is the ultimate expression of sexuality."
J. Adapting to physical inconveniences
    1. Mechanical adaptations
    2. Adaptations to catheters and ileostomies
    3. Options to intercourse
       1. Masturbation
       2. Oral-genital sex
       3. Massage
    4. Other areas of sensitivity
       1. What feels good? Face? Lips? Nose? Ears?
K. Venereal Disease Information with Pretest & Follow-up

          1. Signs
          2. Symptoms
          3. Treatment
          4. Prevention
  L. Methods of birth control
          1. Special considerations for the disabled
             a. Circulatory problems and the pill
             b. Problems with insertion with use of diaphragm, foam, and jellies
          2. Role-playing situations
             a. How do I obtain pills?
             b. I'm pregnant, where do I go? What do I do?
             c. I'd like to buy some condoms
  M. Pregnancy
          1. Specific considerations
             a. Scoliosis—labor and delivery
             b. Spina bifida
                1) Feeling in genitals
                2) Fertility
                3) Labor and delivery
                4) Normalcy of child
             c. Polio
                1) Contractions during labor
             d. Congenital heart disease
             e. Muscular dystrophy
             f. Cerebral palsy
             g. Genetic counseling
             h. Teenage pregnancies
                1) High incidence of premature babies
             i. Prevention of birth defects
          2. Prenatal care
             a. Critical first three months
             b. Diet, rest, exercise, medical and dental care
             c. X rays?
             d. Drugs?
             e. Smoking?
          3. Medical examination for women
             a. Pap test
             b. Pregnancy test
             c. Speculum
             d. Stirrups
             e. self-examination for breast cancer
          4. Overpopulation and its implications
          5. Planned parenthood and the spacing of children
          6. Abortion
          7. Adoption
          8. Child-rearing practices and responsibilities
  N. Critical issues
          1. Abortion
          2. Birth control
             a. Who should take the responsibility?
          3. Incest
          4. Prejudice
          5. Prisons

    a. Situational homosexuality
    b. Possible solutions to forced homosexuality
 6. Rights of the disabled
 7. Available resources
    a. Counseling
    b. Sex therapy
    c. Agencies
    d. Funds

Terminal Illness: Psychological Implications

Altogether it is difficult to imagine any way in which one could prepare a child for death, either that of a fellow patient or his own. For the children themselves, death has little meaning apart from the idea of being away or gone. For the adults who have to watch it, the death of a young child remains an event against nature, an experience which many find beyond acceptance (Bergmann, 1965, p. 78).

Death is a reality of life. Physically disabled children encounter death more frequently than their nondisabled peers, but they unfortunately have little or no preparation for, or understanding of, it. It is an unknown made more frightening by the fact that adults will not discuss it. Adults try to protect children from knowledge about death. They often rationalize that death is too difficult for children to understand or too painful for children to confront. Therefore, adults spare themselves the discomfort of talking about a subject which they, too, find difficult and painful.

People used to be born at home and die at home. Children witnessed the birth, and often the death, of infant siblings. The extended family living under one roof also brought children in contact with the death of elderly relatives. Certainly, death was not welcome, but also it was not the unknown taboo it is considered today. Modern medical technology now has removed dying from the home and placed the event in hospitals, thus sheltering children from these direct experiences.

"Death is a problem, or, perhaps, a mystery which every child faces individually. It is a mystery to which each human must find his own interpretive answer" (Carr, 1973, p. 701). Parents and professionals have a responsibility to physically disabled children, especially those with terminal illnesses, to help them develop an understanding of death as part of the natural cycle of life.

Children's Concepts of Death

The literature indicates some disagreement on the developmental stages of a child's knowledge and understanding of death. However, in general, most people cite the work of Nagy (1948) in which she outlined three basic stages in children's thoughts about death:

1. Up to age 5—The young child does not recognize death as final but rather as a form of separation or departure of a human love object. It is a separation anxiety much like that felt when children are left with the babysitter for the first time, not really sure that their parents will return. The child realizes the limiting nature of death but still considers the dead to be "living" in another environment in which they are aware of happenings on earth.
2. 5 to 9 years—The child tends to personify death as a distinctive, invisible personality, e.g., "the boogieman." The important shift in thinking is toward a concept of the finality of death, but personal death is still seen as avoidable. Children cannot understand that death may, and will indeed, happen to them.
3. 9 to 10 years (and presumably thereafter)—The child begins to understand both the finality and the inevitability of death as well as the universality that no one is exempt. In addition, the child realizes that not just the old die.

The consensus seems to be that age 10 is generally the earliest possible point at which a youngster may truly understand the full impact of death. Many feel that adolescence is really the point at which the concept of death becomes reality, after the "need for detachment" from parental figures is met and as adolescents struggle with independence and autonomy in control of their lives. Before death can be understood, the child must first have an understanding of change, destruction, and disappearance as related to a concept of self-constancy. Death may be seen as a threat to the possibility that the adolescent will ever become that self he values and toward which he is moving (Kastenbaum and Aisenberg, 1972).

Psychological Stages Encountered by the Terminally Ill

Kübler-Ross has done some of the most extensive work with terminal patients. In her book, *On Death and Dying* (1969), she emphasizes the need for family and professionals to understand a patient's communication, needs, fears, and fantasies. In her experiences, patients dealt with openly and frankly were better able to cope with the imminence of death. Denial of reality at a time when the dying person is ready to talk leaves him with feelings of desertion, isolation, and loneliness. Kübler-Ross (1969) outlines five stages in the dying person's attitudes toward impending death:

1. *Denial*—The patient totally rejects the reality, or even the remote possiblity, that he will die soon. In this stage parents often travel from doctor to doctor, seeking a "miracle cure" for their child.
2. *Anger*—This stage is indicative of the first real step toward acceptance and marks the end of the difficult period of denial. It is characterized by the question "Why me?" Rage and resentment are most often ventilated against healthy people who represent those things which the dying person will lose.
3. *Bargaining*—The patient promises something in exchange for prolongation of life. The promise often follows a religious vein, e.g., "If You (God) give me one more year to live, I will attend church or synagogue regularly." Such compromise marks the beginning of the dying person's recognition of his limited time.
4. *Depression*—When the person can no longer deny his illness, is forced to undergo more surgery or hospitalization, and/or becomes thinner and weaker, he can no longer deny the inevitable nature and course of his illness. Depression may be preparatory for the total loss of everything and everyone he loves. The dying person should be allowed to express this grief and mourning, encouraging completion of this stage more quickly and easily.
5. *Acceptance*—If the person has had enough time and help in adjusting, he may reach a stage where he is neither depressed nor angry about his fate. Granted, he is not joyfully happy; but the struggle is over, and reality is accepted. In this stage, the dying person begins to separate from interpersonal relationships and may prefer the company of only one loved one. The fear, bitterness, anguish, and concern about unfinished business are gone. Comfort consists of having someone there who is quietly reassuring.

Although these stages may be more difficult to distinguish in terminally ill children, the stages are basically the same for all age groups. It should be noted that parents and professionals also usually go through these stages, often at a rate different than the children. Parents and professionals must be aware of the way children may choose to communicate these feelings in order to be most helpful and supportive.

Ways Terminally Ill Children Communicate

Children tend to pick one or two significant adults with whom to communicate. Kübler-Ross (1974) notes that parents often are not the "chosen ones" because children have a sense of their parents' grief. They may choose to avoid causing them to grieve more than necessary. Thus, they may not choose to discuss the depth and breadth of their feelings with their parents. They may well choose a teacher, classroom aide, or therapist as their confidante.

Kübler-Ross (1974) outlines the ways in which youngsters may communicate their feelings about death and dying:

1. *"Plain English"*—This approach is by far the easiest to understand and the easiest to respond to because children talk openly and freely. These children probably seek to get as much as they can from life, coping with their impending death and its reality as a part of life. However, just because they seem to cope so well, they should not be denied the right to talk about aspects which may bother them, to get answers, and to feel support.

Most youngsters are not completely open in their communication and use some form of symbolic language which is more difficult to respond to and assess.

2. *Symbolic Nonverbal*—This type of communication is especially prevalent among younger

children who do not have sufficient mastery of verbal skills to express their feelings adequately. Their best outlet for expression may be found in paper and crayons. Art projects provide an outlet for expression, and subsequent sharing of drawings provides an opportunity for insight and help.

3. *Symbolic Verbal*—Sometimes it is necessary to look for real concerns and questions beneath children's words. A seemingly simple question may have deeper significance. Thus, it may be necessary to look for underlying implications while being cautious not to read too much into conversations. It is not necessary to perseverate on the subject of death. It is only necessary to face its reality.

The essence of these "languages" is their expression of the dying person's feelings and needs in a way which is comfortable for the dying person. The challenge is to listen and to hear when a request for help, support, and/or comfort is expressed.

Parental Reactions to Terminal Illness

Parents generally react to the knowledge that their child has a fatal disease with feelings of guilt, anger, bewilderment, and sorrow; a state of acute crisis may follow. Overwhelming anxiety may make it difficult for the parent to attend to discussions about the disease, impair their judgment, and/or limit their active participation in the care of the child. Worrisome and demanding behavior may appear as a result of negative feelings, or even lack of simple information. In turn, blame may be projected on the child, spouse, or physician. Some parents may "shop" for a new physician whom they feel has a "magical cure" or who will tell them what they want to hear. Still others will avoid discussion of the illness as if it were nonexistent (Green, 1967).

Parents often report feelings of helplessness. Their involvement in the care of their child can reduce this feeling. Proper counseling can also help to alleviate some of this feeling. Parents should be given adequate information but should be allowed room for continued hope as a "buffer" against the crushing impact of the knowledge that their child will die before he has had ample opportunity to fulfill his and their dreams for his life (Lourie, 1963).

Parents need to feel pain, to adjust, and to deal with reality. Most importantly, they need to know that professional support services are available from a number of sources if needed. Parents need time to become more realistic in their behavior towards their child. They may need assistance in avoiding the tendency to become overprotective. Overprotection, in the form of hiding the truth and/or doing everything for the child with nothing required in return, can be most detrimental to the child's development of a healthy attitude and outlook.

"Anticipatory grief" reactions can be both helpful and harmful for parents as they grieve and mourn the potential loss of their child. If parents and loved ones complete the anticipatory grief process long before the death of the child, the child may be forced to face the loneliness and fear which imply the total reality of death. Having reached a stage of acceptance, parents may not feel the compulsive urge to be with the child, having essentially "buried him alive." Parents often do not realize that they act this way and should avoid leaving children alone, even after their anticipatory mourning is complete. Sometimes they may even wish the child would die and may covertly communicate this feeling (Friedman, Chodoff, Mason, & Hamburg, 1963).

Role of the Professional with the Terminally III

The crisis or conflict of the dying child often presents a conflict situation for the professional who works with dying children and their families. The role of the professional is complicated by the difficult task of contemplating death. The role is complex, requiring the professional to deal directly with the dying child as well as with the family, classmates, and peers. Before the professional can assume responsibility for the development of a supportive, often intimate relationship with the dying child, examination of personal feelings is essential. There is a need for relief from feelings of fear and helplessness as the professional finds personal meaning in the experience of dying and understanding death.

Educators should be encouraged to deal directly with children. Death should never be made a taboo subject, although the subject may not be a central focus in any classroom or teaching setting. In general, children should be encouraged to realize the appropriateness of feelings. When they are able to experience feelings of sadness, anxiety, and anger and realize that these are natural feelings, they can begin to deal with feelings related to death (McDonald, 1963). When death is discussed, it should be done with realistic terminology rather than with euphemisms or extractions such as "He is with the angels," "She went to Heaven," or "He has gone to sleep" (Galen, 1972).

Pattison (1967) suggests some guidelines for a supportive assistance role which would be helpful to the dying person. He notes a need for sharing the responsibility of the crisis so the person has help in dealing with the impact of anxiety. He emphasizes the need for human contact to be continuously available. Assistance is necessary to help the dying person in the separation from and grief over the losses of family, body image, and self-control. The dying person must be further helped in maintaining communication and meaningful relationships with those who will be lost. Most importantly, the dying person needs support and encouragement.

Best (1974) surveyed teachers of terminally ill children. He notes that many teachers are totally insensitive to the reality that some of their students may die. One of the teachers interviewed made a universally applicable comment with regard to dying children and teacher-human responses: "Find a place and a space to cry." Best emphasized the need to be realistic, open, and honest about feelings and responses related to the dying child.

Essentially, professionals need to cope with their own feelings and develop their own concept of and attitude toward death. Only then will they be able to provide the dying child or adolescent with the necessary supportive environment.

Help them [children and adolescents] to face fear and show them that through strength and sharing we can overcome even the fear of dying, then they will be better prepared to face any kind of crisis . . . including the ultimate reality, death.(Kübler-Ross, 1972, p. 32)

Suggested Strategies and Attitudes

The most important step for the teacher is to acknowledge the reality of death and the fact that some children may die. The following are some suggested strategies and attitudes which may be helpful for parents and/or professionals who work with terminally ill children:

1. Treat all children the same. If children with cerebral palsy are disciplined, so should those with terminal illnesses be disciplined.

2. Try to be objective in goal setting, building towards attainable goals.

3. Assist in maintaining their mental health. Be available, not only to those who are dying, but to those who will remain after the death of a classmate.

4. Develop an understanding of Kubler-Ross's stages and how children and parents and professionals may progress through them. Recognize that all may not progress at the same pace, and leave room for individual differences in methods of coping.

5. For teachers, define your role as an educator, remembering that your role and responsibility are to teach. Included in that role is a responsibility as a human being to meet the personal needs of students. However, your primary role remains that of a teacher.

6. Respond to and accept your own feelings of anxiety, anger, guilt, and sorrow, and share these, when appropriate, with children.

7. Recognize your role as a catalyst for hope, but do not let yourself become foolishly optimistic.

8. Prepare yourself to answer the child's questions. Questions such as "Am I going to die?" need to be answered carefully—but honestly—in response to the individual needs of the asker.

9. Prepare yourself to deal with the behavior of youngsters who cannot act out physically and thus may verbally rebel against the world.

10. Take time to establish good rapport with professionals in medicine and mental health; they are valuable resources.

11. Lastly, deal with yourself.

Summary

The most important thing that people can do to help the physically disabled adjust is to provide opportunities for the development of their abilities, talents, and interests. Activities should be adjusted to the child's level of ability so that the child can experience sufficient success to insure motivation and development. Concurrently, activities should be provided which prepare the child to risk disappointment in working toward a challenging objective. Risk-taking is important because it requires learning to handle disappointment and frustration as well as satisfaction when efforts are successful.

The physically disabled need to be encouraged to express their *real* feelings, including anger at those with whom they are working. Without recognition of honest feelings, there can be no acceptance of their disability and their human needs. In addition, they need to learn acceptance of constructive criticism, and to be able to meet frustration and disappointment without a fatal blow to their ego. They should learn to analyze criticism and/or unsuccessful experiences so that such experiences may be turned into learning experiences; the knowledge gained can then be applied to later situations which may be similar. They need to evaluate each experience and use all of the available information for some future activity.

Essentially, it has been the focus of this chapter to examine some psychosocial implications of physical disability. Parents and professionals must understand and remember that physical disability does not necessarily imply a massive psychological problem. The most important realization is that the disabled person shares with all people the need to feel important, to have a sense of self that is positive, and to share with those around them what they have to offer. A disabled person has a sincere need to feel accepted and valued as a participant in society. They have resources and strengths which can be an asset to those around them if they are appropriately tapped.

Notes

1. This information was incorporated into a 35 mm slide and tape presentation for teachers of physically disabled children designed by Jane Scandary, a Special Education Teacher Consultant. Ingham Intermediate School District in Mason, Michigan.

2. Questions adapted from Coleman, Campbell, Hobson, McPartland, Mood, Weinfeld, and York, Equality for Educational Opportunity, Washington, D.C., U.S. Office of Education 1966—as reproduced in Appendix I of Lambert (1974).

References

Psychological Implications; Self-Concept

Bleck, E. E., & Nagel, D. A. (Eds.). *Physically handicapped children: A medical atlas for teachers.* New York: Grune & Stratton, 1975.

Coleman, J. S., Campbell, E. Q., Hobson, C. J., McPartland, J., Mood, A. M., Weinfeld, F. D., & York, R. L. Equality of educational opportunity. In Lambert, N.,

Wilcox, M. R., Gleason, W. P. (Eds.),*The educationally retarded child* (Appendix I). Adapted. Washington, D.C.: U.S. Office of Education, 1966.

Flatley, J. M. The relationship of selected characteristics of physical disability to self concepts of the physically disabled. *Dissertation Abstracts International,* 1973, *33*, 5582A–5583A. Order no. 73-7434, 90 pp.

Freeman, R. Psychiatric problems in adolescents with cerebral palsy. *Developmental Medicine and Child Neurology,* 1970, *12*, 64–70.

Goldberg, R. T. Adjustment of children with invisible and visible handicaps. *Journal of Counseling Psychology,* 1974, *21*, 428–32.

Joel, G. S. *So your child has cerebral palsy.* Albuquerque: University of New Mexico, 1975.

Jones, R. L. Correlates of orthopedically disabled children's school achievement and interpersonal relationships. *Exceptional Children,* 1974, *41*, 191–192.

Jourard, S. M. *Personal adjustment.* New York: Macmillan, 1958.

Killilea, M. *Karen.* New York: Dell, 1952.

Lambert, N. M., Wilcox, Margaret R., and Gleason, W. Preston. *The educationally retarded child.* New York: Grune & Stratton, 1974.

Levine, L. S. *The impact of disability.* An address presented to the Oklahoma Rehabilitation Association Convention, Oklahoma City, Oklahoma, October 1959.

Maslow, A. H. *Motivation and personality.* New York: Harper and Bros., 1954.

Neff, W. S., & Weiss, Samuel A. Psychological aspects of disability. In B. B. Wolberg (Ed.), *Handbook of clinical psychology.* New York: McGraw-Hill, 1965.

Rappaport, S. R. (Ed.). *Childhood aphasia and brain damage: A definition.* Naberth, Pa.: Livingston, 1964.

Reynell, J. Children with physical handicaps. In Ved P. Varma (Ed.), *Stresses in children.* London: University of London, 1973.

Ross, A. O. *The exceptional child in the family.* New York: Grune & Stratton, 1964.

Scandary, E. J. *Aspects of life adjustment for the physically handicapped.* A slide/tape production, 1975. (Available from the Ingham Intermediate School District, Mason, Michigan.)

Wallace, G., & Kauffman, J. M. *Teaching children with learning problems.* Columbus, Ohio: Charles E. Merrill, 1973.

Wright, B. A. *Physical disability—A psychological approach.* New York, Harper & Row, 1960.

Family Life Education

de la Cruz, F. F., & La Veck, G. D. (Eds.). *Human sexuality and the mentally retarded.* New York: Bruner/Bezel, 1973.

Gore, G. V. A selected bibliographic listing of articles, texts, pamphlets, and films for the parent-teacher-other professionals. Xerox outline, 1975. (Available from the Department of Elementary and Special Education, Michigan State University, Lansing, Michigan.)

Perske, R. Sexual development. *The Exceptional Parent,* 1974, *4* (1), 36–39. (Originally published in Perske, R. *New directions for parents.* Nashville: Abingdon, 1973.)

Preston, H. *How to teach your children about sex.* Chatsworth, Calif.: Books for Better Living, 1974.

Sapienza, B., & Thornton, C. Curriculum for advanced family life for the physically disabled. Outline for students, 1974 (Available at McAteer High School, San Francisco United School District, San Francisco, Calif.)

Uslander, A. S. Everything you always wanted to know about sex education. *Learning,* 1974, *3* (2), 34–41.

Psychological Implications: Terminal Illness

Bergmann, T. *Children in the hospital.* New York: International Universities, 1965.

Best, G. Teachers talk about the terminally ill child. Paper presented at the Council for Exceptional Children Convention, New York, April 1974.

Carr, R. L. Death as presented in children's books. *Elementary English,* 1973, *L* (5), 701–705.

Friedman, S. B., Chodoff, P., Mason, J. W., and Hamburg, D. A. Behavioral observations on parents anticipating the death of a child. *Pediatrics,* 1963, XXXII (4), 610–625.

Galen, H. A matter of life and death. *Young Children,* 1972, *27,* 351–356.

Green, M. Care of the child with a long-term, life-threatening illness: Some principles of management. *Pediatrics,* 1967, XXXIX (3), 441–445.

Kastenbaum, R., & Aisenberg, R. *The psychology of death.* New York: Springer, 1972.

Kübler-Ross, E. *On death and dying.* New York: Macmillan, 1969.

Kübler-Ross, E. Facing up to death. *Today's Education,* 1972, LXI (1), 30–32.

Kübler-Ross, E. Children and death. Paper presented at a conference sponsored by the National Institute for the Psychotherapies, New York, May 1974.

Lourie, R. S. The pediatrician and the handling of terminal illness. *Pediatrics,* 1963, XXXII (4), Part I, 477–479.

McDonald, M. Helping children to understand death: An experience with death in a nursery school. *The Journal of Nursery Education,* 1963, XIX (1), 19–25.

Nagy, M. H. The child's theories concerning death. *Journal of Genetic Psychology,* 1948, LXXIII (2), 3–27.

Pattison, E. M. The experience of dying. *American Journal of Psychotherapy,* 1967, *21,* 32–43.

Resources

Psychological Implications; Self-Concept

Barker, R. G., & Wright, B. A. The social psychology of adjustment to physical disability. In James F. Garrett (Ed.), *Psychological aspects of physical disability.* Washington, D.C.: Office of Vocational Rehabilitation, 1952, pp. 18–32.

Barker, R., Wright, B. A., and Gonick, M. R. *Adjustment to physical handicap & illness: A survey of the social psychology of physique and disability.* Social Science Research Council Bulletin #55, 1946. (Available from 230 Oak Park Ave., New York, N. Y.)

Buscaglia, L. *The disabled and their parents: A counseling challenge.* Thorofare, N. J.: Charles B. Slack, 1975.

Cruickshank, W. M., & Johnson, G. O. (Eds.). *Education of exceptional children and youth.* Englewood Cliffs, N. J.: Prentice-Hall, 1975.

Dembo, T., Ladiew, G., & Wright, B. A. Adjustment to misfortune: A study in social and emotional relationships between injured and noninjured people. Final Report to the Office of the Surgeon General, 1948, MS.

McDaniel, James W. *Physical disability and human behavior* (2nd ed.). New York: Pergamon Press, 1976.

Social Security Administration, *Emotional problems associated with handicapping conditions in children.* Washington, D.C.: Children's Bureau Publication No. 336, 1952.

White, R. K., Wright, B. A., & Dembo, T. Studies of adjustment to visible injuries: Evaluation of curiosity in the injured. *Journal of Abnormal and Social Psychology,* 1948, *43,* 13–28.

Family Life Education

Books for Young Children

Lerrigo, M. O. *A doctor talks to 9–12 year olds.* Chicago: Budlong, 1967.

Mayle, P. *Where did I come from?* Secaucus, New Jersey: Lyle Stuart, 1973.
This book, with its creative illustrations, is written to help adults answer the questions that children ask. Suggested reading for liberal-minded parents, teachers, and counselors.

Meilach, D. A. *A doctor talks to 5–8 year old.* Chicago: Budlong, 1965.
This book helps to answer children's questions about reproduction, birth, and growth among people and animals.

Widerberg, S. *The kids own XYZ of love and sex.* New York: Stein and Day, 1972.
This book is basically a question-answer book for children 7 years old and older that attempts to answer directly and simply the questions that kids raise.

Books for Adolescents

Arms, S. *A season to be born.* New York: Harper and Row, 1973.
This book is a tender story, told by a pregnant woman and photographed by her husband. Through pictures, the readers are able to identify with this couple and share their love and hope for the new child. It helps answer the questions, "What is it like to be pregnant? How does it feel? What is labor like?"

Gordon, S. *Facts about sex: A basic guide.* New York: John Day, 1969.

Gordon, S. *V.D. claptrap. Ten heavy facts about sex. Drug youse—A survivor's handbook. Protect yourself from becoming an unwanted parent. The eater's digest.* Syracuse, New York: Ed-U Press, 1973.
These publications are a series of comics to which teenagers are able to relate.

Hansen, S., & Jensen, J. *The little red schoolbook.* New York: Pocket Books, 1971.
Addressed to students who want the truth about things that matter—and to parents and teachers who don't think they know all the answers. Discussion includes, among other subjects, masturbation, wet dreams, menstruation, child molesters, impotence, homosexuality, and abortion.

Mayle, P. *What's happening to me.* Seacaucus, N.J.: Lyle Stuart, 1975.

Books and Articles for Teachers and Counselors

Buscaglia, L. *The disabled and their parents: A counseling challenge.* Thorofare, N. J.: Charles B. Slack, 1975. (Available from 6900 Grove Rd., Thorofare, N. J. 08086.)

Geiger, R., & Knight, S. The sexuality of people with cerebral palsy. *Medical Aspects of Human Sexuality,* March 1975, pp. 72–79.

Goldstein, H. *The social learning curriculum.* Columbus, Ohio: Charles E. Merrill, 1974.

Gordon, S. *Facts about sex.* New York: John Day, 1969. (Available also from ED-U Press.)
A clear, sensible paperback for youngsters (good for parents and teachers, too). Limited mainly to the physical facts of sex presented in a frank, straightforward manner.

Gordon, S. *Living fully: A guide for young people with a handicap, their parents, their teachers, and professionals.* New York: John Day, 1975. (Available from 257 Park Ave., South, New York, N.Y. 10010 for $8.95.)

Gordon, S. Okay, let's tell it like it is (Instead of just making it look good). *Journal of Special Education,* 1971, *5* (4), 379–381.

Gordon, S. *The sexual adolescent, Communicating with teenagers about sex.* North Scituate, Massachusetts: Duxbury, 1973.

Hall, J. E. Sexuality and the mentally retarded. In R. Green (Ed.), *Human sexuality: A medical student's text.* Baltimore: Williams and Wilkins, 1975.

Handman, H., & Brennan, P. *The sex handbook: Information and help for minors.* New York: G.P. Putnam's Sons, 1974.

Johnson, W. R. Sex education and the mentally retarded. *Journal of Sex Research,* 1969, *5* (3), 179–183.

Johnson, W. *Sex education and counseling of special groups: The mentally and physically handicapped, ill and elderly.* Springfield, Ill.: Charles C Thomas, 1975. (Available from 327 East Lawrence Ave., Springfield, Ill.)

Kempton, W., Bass, M., & Gordon, S. *Love, sex and birth control for the mentally retarded: A guide for parents.* Philadelphia: Planned Parenthood Association of Southeastern Pennsylvania, 1971. (Available from 1402 Spruce Street, Philadelphia, Pa. 19102.)

Kempton, W. *Sex education for persons with disabilities that hinder learning: A teacher's guide.* North Scituate, Mass.: Duxbury, 1975.

Kimberly-Clark Corporation. *How to tell the retarded girl about menstruation,* 1964. (Available from Life Cycle Center, Neenah, Wisconsin 54956.)

Kirkendall, L. A., & Gaborne, R. F. *Teacher's question and answer book on sex education.* New London, Conn.: Croft Educational Services, 1969.
Specific, helpful, includes curriculum outline based on growth and development concept: preschool to 12th grade.

Livingston, V., & Knapp, M. *Human sexuality: A portfolio for the mentally retarded.* Seattle: Planned Parenthood, 1975.

Neff, J. *Behavioral objectives and learning activities in human sexuality for the visually handicapped.* New York: American Foundation for the Blind, 1976.

Reich, M. L., & Harshman, H. W. Sex education for handicapped children: Reality or repression? *Journal of Special Education,* 1971, *5,* 373–377.

Richardson, S. People with cerebral palsy talk for themselves. *Developmental Medicine and Child Neurology,* 1972, (14), pp. 524–535.

Schultz, E. D., & Williams, S. R. *Family life and sex education: Curriculum and instruction.* New York: Harcourt, Brace, Jovanovich, 1969.

Sex Knowledge Inventory, The Form X. Revised, 1967. (Available from Family Life Publications, Box 427, Saluda, N.C. 28773.)
Includes an 80-question inventory of sex knowledge and attitudes as a basis for counseling and teaching on a broad range of topics (from anatomical knowledge of menstruation, childbirth, masturbation to attitudes, superstitions, and misinformation). Useful with or without the actual survey as a manual for leading discussion. Recommended for 17–24 year olds.

Social competency inventory. (Available from Family Life Publications, Box 427, Saluda, N.C. 28773.)
A checklist used by professional personnel to estimate social competence of handicapped, mentally retarded, or senile adults.

Multimedia Resources

Use of multimedia resources are limited to specific groups. For further information write to Multi-Media Resource Center, 1525 Franklin, San Francisco, Calif. 94108. Information also available from Perennial Education, P. O. Box 236, 1825 Willowroad, Worthfield, Ill. 60093.

A three-letter word for love. 27-minute color film. (Available from: Texture Films, 1600 Broadway, New York, N. Y. 10019.)

Inner-city youngsters discussing sex and a play within a play of a young girl persuaded to have sex by a young man who fails to come through when he learns she is pregnant.

About sex. Film. (Available from: Texture Films, 1600 Broadway, New York, N. Y. 10019).
A discussion by inner-city youth with a leader followed by some facts to allay their fears.

Don't tell the cripples about sex. Film. (Available from the Multi-Media Resource Center.)
A rap session involving adult cerebral palsied individuals. They discuss their sexuality and need for sexual expression. It helps to dispel some of society's myths regarding the sexual potential and desires of the cerebral palsied.

How babies are made. Colored slides of paper sculpture. (Also available in book form from Time-Life Books. For slides, contact General Learning Corp., 3 East 54th Street, N. Y. 10022.)
Appropriate for first grade. Can be used in a viewer by parent or child.

Just what can you do? Film. (Available from the Multi-Media Center.)
A rap session. Spinal cord injured people and their mates discuss the attitudes and myths surrounding the question of sexuality and the spinal cord injured person.

Like other people. Film. (Local offices of Planned Parenthood lend this film to interested groups.)
Produced by the English Spastic Society. This film is appropriate for parents, teachers, counselors, as well as adolescents. It depicts the lives of two severely involved people with cerebral palsy living in a residential home in England.

Mimi. Film. (Available from Billy Budd Films, 235 E. 57th St., New York, N. Y. 10022.)
Autobiographical documentary of a woman with spina bifida, in which she discusses stigma, socialization, love, and marriage.

Stigma I & II. Tape. "What It Is Like to be Disabled" and "The Physically Disabled and the World." (Available from the Center for Independent Living, 2539 Telegraph Ave., Berkeley, Calif. 94704.)
Young adults discuss what it is like to be disabled.

Sources of Pamphlets, Films, Consultants, and Bibliographies

American Alliance for Health, Physical Education, and Recreation
Health Education Division
1201 16th St., N.W.
Washington, D. C. 20036

American Medical Association
Dept. of Health Education
535 N. Dearborn St.
Chicago, Ill. 60610

American School Health Association
Executive Secretary
515 East Main St.
Kent, Ohio 44240

American Social Health Association
Executive Director
1740 Broadway
New York, N. Y. 10019

Center for Independent Living
2539 Telegraph Avenue
Berkeley, Calif. 94704

Child Study Association
9 E. 89th St.
New York, N. Y. 10028

Ed-U Press (Institute for Family Research and Education, Syracuse University)
760 Ostrom Avenue
Syracuse, N. Y. 13210

Family Life Publications
Box 427
Saluda, N. C. 28773
(Has more than 100 publications available on sex/marriage counseling)

University of California
School of Medicine
Human Sexuality Program
Special Education and Counselling Project
350 Parnassus #700
San Francisco, Calif. 94143

Mental Health Association of San Francisco
(Sex education for the mentally retarded.)
655 Van Ness
San Francisco, Calif. 94102

Multi-Media Resource Center
1523 Franklin Street
San Francisco, Calif. 94109
(Source of films through Film Catalogue, Bibliography of Sex Education Books, Bookstore and seminars through the National Sex Forum)

Planned Parenthood—World Population
810 7th Ave.
New York, N. Y. 10019

SIECUS (Sex Information and Education Council of the United States)
1855 Broadway
New York, N. Y. 10023

Psychological Implications: Terminal Illness

Feifel, H. (Ed.). *The meaning of death*. New York: McGraw-Hill, 1959.

Grollman, E. A. *Explaining death to children*. Boston: Beacon, 1967.

Grollman, E. A. (Ed.). *Concerning death: A practical guide for the living*. Boston: Beacon, 1974.

Kavanaugh, R. E. *Facing death*. Baltimore: Penguin, 1972.

Kübler-Ross, E. *On death and dying*. New York: Macmillan, 1969.

Kübler-Ross, E. *Questions and answers on death and dying*. New York: Collier, 1974.

Kübler-Ross, E. *Death–The final stage of growth*. Englewood Cliffs, N. J.: Prentice-Hall, 1975.

Neale, R. E. *The art of dying*. New York: Harper and Row, 1971.

Wolf, A.W.M. *Helping your child to understand death*. New York: Child Study Association of America, 1958.

6

SEVERE COMMUNICATION PROBLEMS

Individuals who are unable to acquire intelligible speech or legible writing skills must be provided with alternative communication systems for expression. These nonvocal* individuals have thoughts and desires which need to be expressed. When the individual cannot produce speech or handwriting, we must look for alternatives. We must also consider what prerequisite skills and knowledge are necessary to enable physically handicapped people to use alternate communication systems.

Use of Yes, No, and *I Don't Know*

If a verbally disabled individual has no system for communication, it is imperative that we develop with her the ability to use the responses *yes, no,* and *I don't know*. To accomplish this, you must analyze the child's attempts at communication to determine the nature of the problem. Perhaps

---

* "Nonvocal" individuals may be able to vocalize but not articulate and phonate so they can be understood.

June Bigge.

motor difficulties limit or prevent use of discernible signals to specify *yes* or *no* responses. The individual may not grasp the basic concept of responding *yes* and *no*. The problem may not be with the individual at all but rather with unclear questions.

Signals to Relay Messages

In order for a child to use a *yes-no* response, she must be able to make at least one movement that is distinctive from all other movements. Furthermore, she must be able to make this movement on command so that, when she wishes to signify *yes,* she can consistently use the *yes* movement. Absence of that movement can mean *no*. Generally, it is better for the child to make two distinctive movements, one movement to signify *yes* and the other to signify *no*. Should the individual learn to use a third response option, *I don't know,* it will be necessary for her to use some reliable movement for that message. For many children, a drop of the head is an easy movement that relays to the receiver this third concept.

Some of the more common signals used to relay these messages are given with the head. A glance upwards means *yes*; a glance to the side means *no*; a drop of the head means *I don't know*. Another system of signals might involve only movement of the eyes in different directions. Individuals like the child in Figure 6–1, below, might look at a smiling face or the word *yes* printed on the right arm of their wheelchairs and a frowning face or the word *no* on the left. They may be able to shrug their shoulders for the signal *I don't know*. This type of communication system can always go with them wherever they use a wheelchair.

Sometimes signals are worked out for individuals to use only in particular situations. For instance, *yes* may be written on the left side of a lap tray and *no* on the right. The student could use these signals only when her lap tray was on her wheelchair. Likewise, a teacher may write *yes* on one side of the blackboard and *no* on another. To respond, the student would look in the direction of her answer. Other less portable *yes-no* communication systems are machines that light up and reveal the word *yes* when activated by touch and electric buzzers which the child hits with her head, once for *yes* and twice for *no*.

Assessment of Independent Motor Actions

Observing the movements of a child in an unstructured situation is one way to identify which

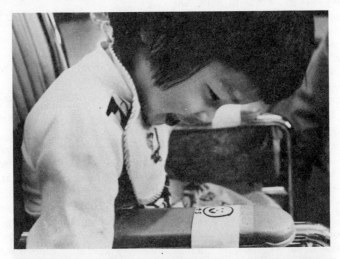

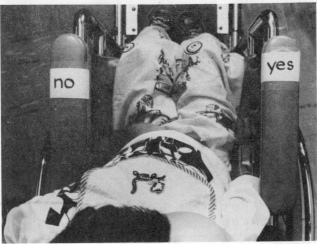

Figure 6–1. Chosen signals must be easily recognizable by others.

movements the child controls. Many times handicapped individuals use certain movements consistently to signify basic communications. For instance, one child may always look at the clock when hungry. Watching her use this signal and others would reveal her ability to make voluntary movements. Communication requires utilization and production of movements over which the individual has voluntary control.

Structured assessment can be planned so that the child is encouraged to use her hands or feet. While assessing voluntary use of more obvious parts of the body, less obvious controlled movements can be noted. The child may not be able to move her head in a consistent manner but may be able to move her eyes or eyebrows on command. Likewise, she may not be able to move her whole leg or foot, but may be able to press her thigh against a chair seat to activate a switch.

Sometimes the use of behavior modification techniques are helpful for assessing ability to repeat movements upon command. A game of Simon Says can be useful for younger children who enjoy game-like situations. For the more mature, participation in problem solving may help determine what works best.

Once a reliable system for indicating *yes, no* and *I don't know* has been established, it is imperative that the system be known by everyone who interacts with the individual. A descriptive or illustrative badge, wrist band, sign, or poster can accompany the child. These instructions prevent confusion which may occur when others attempt to communicate with the person. (See Figure 6–2.)

Teaching the Meaning and Use of Yes and No

The use of the concepts *yes* and *no* at appropriate times is one of the most important skills the child can acquire. These responses provide a basic communication system. The child need only be able to make at least two distinguishable and opposing movements in order to begin to communicate.

The child must be able to use the signals at the correct times. It is necessary for her to recognize occasions when she should use the signal *no*. Later, it is important to know when to use the signal *I don't know*. The *yes* and *no* concepts and related signals can be taught by using another "normal" child or adult as a model. The model

Figure 6–2. A child can wear instructions around his neck.

would use the signals that had been selected for use by the disabled individual. In the presence of the disabled child, the model would respond with the signal for *yes* when offered something desired such as ice cream or a favorite snack.

The teacher might start by asking the model, "Do you want ice cream?" and the model signals *yes*. Next, the teacher repeats the question to the child. If the proper signal is not used by the child, the teacher passes the child by and returns to the model. It is important to be consistent and to allow the person time to respond. In passing up the handicapped child, the teacher may feel uneasy. However, the child may never learn if given the reward without being required to use the signal. While this procedure may seem harsh, failing to learn the concept is ultimately more punishing to the child.

If, after several trials, the person does not seem to "get the idea," an intermediate step can be introduced. More than one model can be used. Offer the ice cream to one model at a time and encourage the models to exaggerate the motor response for *yes*. Praise them for using the *yes* signal by saying, "Good, you showed me you want ice cream by looking up." Again, give the disabled person a turn with the ice cream in view.

Provide only minimal physical guidance or other clues to help the child make the appropriate signal, praise her for making the signal, and then give her the long-awaited ice cream. Repeat the entire sequence using first the models, then the child. With each repetition, provide less physical assistance. Repeat the process over several days if necessary. Other foods known to be liked by the child may also be used.

Some children can learn the concepts yes/no by being encouraged to communicate everyday needs and desires. If a child is asked, "Do you want to go outside?" or "Do you want this toy?", she must use the appropriate signal, preferably with the least possible help. Absence of the appropriate signal, or presence of a wrong signal, should result consistently in undesired consequences. The child must realize that the presence or absence of certain signals causes consistent actions on the part of others.

Teachers can select solutions in which both yes and no are possible and appropriate. In each case the instructor should know what is appropriate for a particular child. If, for instance, a teacher (and child) know the child's mother is coming today, the teacher could ask "Is your mom coming today?"

If a child does not learn the concepts yes and no simultaneously, then first establish the use of yes in many situations. After the signal for yes is established, use similar procedures for teaching the no signal. The models and child can be presented with questions to which a definite no is anticipated. For instance, she might learn to signal no when disliked food is offered. From observation of others and through trial and error, a disabled individual will learn to use the concepts yes, no, and, eventually, I don't know.

Keys for Releasing Communications

To communicate with individuals with unintelligible speech, certain verbal techniques are available. These techniques might be considered "keys" for releasing communications "locked" inside. They not only help make conversation possible, but they also increase precision. Often, people assume what the disabled person is trying to say and respond accordingly. If the assumptions are wrong, the disabled person may be left very frustrated. Because these individuals are accustomed to this error, they may hide their frustration with smiles. Sometimes, a teacher feels a bit nervous and rushes through a conversation, allowing the disabled person only time to respond yes or no to salutatory and superficial questions. The teacher may be both asking and answering her own questions.

Needless to say, frustration is a perplexing part of the lives of children who have a great deal to say but cannot talk or be understood. Frustration is present, too, when teachers try to communicate with nonoral persons but do not know how. The following are some "keys" for helping nonvocal individuals release communications:

1. Find and use signals for yes, no, and I don't know, sometimes, and maybe.
2. Find what other signals a person uses.
3. Provide opportunity for initiative in communication.
4. Ask questions one at a time.
5. Avoid giving clues.
6. Accept only clear signals.
7. Allow time for expression of ideas.
8. Narrow the options of what the individuals may be communicating.
9. Continue conversations until expressed messages, ideas, feelings, or attitudes are clarified (for as long as the discussions seem important).
10. Talk "up to" not "down to" disabled individuals.
11. Recognize deadlocks.
12. Teach others what works.

Find and Use Pre-established Signals

As described previously, either motor signals or abbreviated verbal signals must be substituted by some children for verbal responses such as yes and no. Sometimes, signals used by children are obvious to the observer. For example, a nodding of the head may mean yes; another nodding of the head may mean no; and a dropping of the head may mean I don't know. Or the signals might be verbalization of the vowel sound in yes and the verbalization of the vowel sound in no as two distinct responses. On the other hand, if a person's pre-established system is not obvious, one might ask for a demonstration of the signals. "Please show me how you say yes." "Please show me how you say no." Once these signals have been demonstrated, find out if the disabled person has signals for I don't know, sometimes, and maybe.

Observe Other Signals Used

A nonoral speaker, no matter how severe her physical disability, can use signs and signals. To start a conversation, she probably looks toward an object and makes some sound. The object is a clue to the subject for the conversation. She probably has been taught ways to indicate *yes* and *no*. If she reads to any degree, she may indicate letters or words on a communication board or with finger-spelling. Each nonoral speaker has a personal set of symbols which have evolved over time and through need. These symbols are limited by the number of distinct movements the child can make. Because they are limited in number, some may have gained several meanings. These meanings should be explored with the disabled child.

Let us take one individual as an example. Chris, an 18-year-old boy, was severly involved with athetoid cerebral palsy. He was unable to control movements of his hands, legs, or trunk but was able to use head and eye movements for communication. Over the years, Chris had developed signals which he used to communicate with parents, family, and friends. He looked at his teacher's forehead to say *think some more,* or *search your memory*. If he lowered his gaze to the teacher's eyes, it meant *please read my mind*. He looked at his lap to refer to himself, to something he owned, to something he wanted, or to a relative. He looked at his hand to ask for it to be moved, but he also used that signal to indicate that he was going to get a school ring. Chris looked at the clock to speak of time. That behavior meant a specific hour, the duration of something, the next anticipated event, or a time span of days, weeks, or months. Chris's most frequently used symbol was to look up. (See Figure 6–3, right.) He looked up to say *please pull me up, I don't know,* or *I'm still thinking about it*. He looked up to say *some place other than here*. He also looked up to say that an anesthetic made him feel high, to talk about an airplane flight, to say someone had died, or to refer to God.

Chris's signals were not known to all who worked with him. Some thought he wanted to be pulled up each time he looked up, not being aware of eight other possible meanings. Teachers may inadvertently limit the number of signs that children can use successfully. We must recognize repetitive movements and explore with an individual the possible multiple meanings for each communicative signal.

Figure 6–3. Chris depends on this signal to communicate many different ideas.

Provide Opportunity for Initiative

Conversations may be initiated by greeting a nonvocal person and trying to evoke a smile or greeting from her. With young children, it is sometimes helpful to hold both hands of the child in a friendly fashion so that she cannot turn away. Sometimes it is helpful to shake the child's hand to gain her attention.

A disabled child may initiate a conversation by making some very purposive noises and movements to attract attention. One should immediately respond by asking, "Do you want to talk with me?"

Regardless of who initiates a conversation, it is important to maintain eye contact. It is helpful to bend to the level of a very small child or a child in a wheelchair to be at eye level. If chairs are available, they often provide all parties a feeling of psychological comfort. The conversation is not taking place "on the run." At times, of course, there will be no chairs available, and it will not be appropriate to bend to the level of the child. In this case, the fact that one party is sitting and the other standing should not be permitted to deter the conversation.

Ask Questions One at a Time

You can encourage communication by structuring decision-making situations for the disabled child. Hold up two toys so the child is confronted with a choice. Hold one toy toward the child and then the other. Ask, "Do you want this . . . or this?" It is best, of course, to start with only two alternatives.

If the child does not understand the choices, first explain the alternatives, then give her a chance to respond to one option at a time. Ask, "Do you want a drink of water or milk?" Then repeat each question separately: "Do you want water?" "Do you want milk?" The same process would be used to find out if a person wanted to stay inside or go outside.

For some, more basic questions are necessary. "(Do you want) Ice cream?" "(Do you want your) Coat?" are simple one-word queries to which children can learn to respond affirmatively or negatively. Ask only one question at a time. At first, ask only simple questions. Wait and give the child a chance to think of an appropriate reply to make the movement that signifies that reply.

Avoid Giving Clues

You must take precautions not to "give away" the correct answers in school work. Changes in voice inflections for the correct choice, unusual pauses over the correct item, and other gestures made unconsciously by teachers provide clues for the child. Students are deprived of the opportunities to learn from making mistakes. One child never did learn to read but his teacher honestly reported he answered correctly the comprehension questions she asked on his third grade readers. She was totally unaware she was giving him clues to answers.

Accept Only Clear Signals

Sometimes students are uncertain of answers. They have learned to give unclear signals, knowing that when teachers want them to succeed and they sometimes interpret unclear responses as being correct. This problem can be reduced by encouraging students to be honest and use the signal for *I don't know*.

Allow Time for Expression of Ideas

Time must be permitted for individuals either to make the necessary motor movements to relay their communications or to think which motor movement would most appropriately relay a communication. The motor response itself may be very slow for some children, particularly those with cerebral palsy or severe motor weakness. Individuals also need time to think of an answer, a way to respond, or a way to initiate an idea. They may need time to think of ways to change the direction of conversation to more nearly approximate their original intent. At times, a person may be trying to direct the conversation with her answers and may need more time to decide how to communicate the most accurate answer. When asked if students in the class like the teacher, the individual could give an immediate *yes*. She would not, however, be answering so much in terms of truth as in terms of expediency. The other option could be to let the inquirer know that *most* all the children in the class like the teacher.

When a disabled person is talking about feelings or opinions, she needs to have more time to determine her answer. This need is easy to understand when we realize she has only limited response capability and little potential for shades of gray. Often you may ask a question and the child may think about possible answers. In the meantime, you may conclude that the child did not understand and either rephrase the question or ask another one. Now, the disabled person cannot decide whether to answer the first or the second question. Meanwhile, you probably have asked yet a third. The child fails to respond to three questions in a row and the conversation seems somewhat confused. Here, you can help the child redirect the conversation by asking, "Do you need a chance to think? Would you like to go back or do you want to try something new?"

Narrow the Options

Sometimes it is obvious that a child is trying to tell or ask something. Yet, there are innumerable possibilities for content. How, then, does one expedite the matter of finding which of the possibilities an individual is trying to communicate? We suggest narrowing the options by finding a classification or category. Ask, "Is it about home? School? Or someplace else, or none of these?" Then repeat each of the categorical topics as we have suggested earlier to allow the person to indicate which of the options best describe her communication. For very young children, it is most helpful to start with the basic questions: "Is it about home? Is it about school?" The majority of communications will be centered around one of these two places. Perhaps the person is not even thinking of a place, so you could have expedited matters even further by first asking: "Are you thinking of *telling* something? Or *asking* something?" Once you have decided that, then it is helpful to find out, "Do you want to talk about somebody, someplace, some things or feelings, or none of these?" Further helpful questions include information about a time frame. "Is it something that has already happened, is happening, or will happen?" "Is it about the past? The present? The future?"

Continue Conversations Until Messages Are Clarified

You can make conversation quite satisfying to a nonvocal speaker by:

1. keeping in mind the range of what may be communicated
2. checking each impression with the "speaker" and cooperatively refining the impressions
3. encouraging the expression of feelings, opinions, and original ideas
4. allowing the speaker to choose whether to continue to pursue a communication which has reached a barrier

The range of what a nonvocal individual can communicate is often determined by the teacher or another partner in communication. It is relatively easy for a person to tell about something that happened or to answer specific *yes–no* questions. It is harder, however, for her to say that there is one more detail; that something happens to her constantly; to express her opinion about something; to tell how she feels as a result of it; or to tell about a better way to do something. The expressions of such generalizations, feelings, opinions, and ideas depend greatly upon the initiative and flexibility of a teacher. You can encourage expression by asking: "Is there more? What do you think about that? How does that make you feel? Do you have some ideas about how you can change that?"

Questioning is only the beginning. Next, you must paraphrase the *yes* or *no* you receive in answer to one of your questions. You must try to reflect what the *yes* might represent. Expression of opinions, feelings, and ideas is made difficult for the nonvocal speakers by the fact that they must depend upon others to guess, interpret,

reflect, or "restate" what they would like to say. If nonvocal persons are not sure of their feelings or thoughts, then you must help to clarify the thoughts and feelings as well as helping express them. This uncertainty may mean a disabled individual will want to return to a previously rejected statement. A teacher in a difficult situation involving feelings or opinions should try to remember to ask the child if she would like to return to something. A child may let you know she wants to go back either by repeating the signal that she used earlier in the conversation or by dropping out entirely. Those signals are frequently misunderstood as "let's drop this subject."

The following conversation shows why persistence and *clarification* are vital.[1] The teacher (T) has established that the student (S) is speaking of a new wheelchair that he is getting and that he is worried about it.

T: Is that right?

S: Yes.

T: Is there more to it?

S: Yes.

T: Do you want to talk about why you're worried?

S: Yes.

T: You're worried that it won't be ready on time?

S: No.

T: Are you worried it won't work?

S: Yes.

T: You won't be able to run it?

S: No.

T: Wait! Do you think you'll have trouble making it run?

S: No.

T: Steering it?

S: No.

T: Stopping it?

S: No.

T: So it doesn't have anything to do with getting from place to place. Is that right?

S: Yes.

T: Oh. But you *are* worried that it won't work?

S: Yes.

T: Let's see . . . what "works" on a wheelchair?

S: (looks at lap)

T: Your seating?

S: Yes.

T: Do you think you'll be uncomfortable?

S: Yes–no.

T: Wait, Did you say *yes* and *no*?

S: Yes.

T: Um, did you just say *yes*?

S: No.

T: You're worried about the seating.

S: Yes.

T: About whether you'll be comfortable?

S: Yes.

T: Is it that sometimes it will be uncomfortable?

S: No.

T: Always?

S: No.

T: Do you think it will ever be uncomfortable?

S: Yes.

T: A specific time?

S: Yes.

T: One or several times each day?

S: No.

T: Do you mean after you've had your chair for awhile?

S: Yes.

T: A week?

S: No.

T: Several weeks?

S: No.

T: Months?

S: Yes. (looks at body)

T: Are you worried about growing?

S: Yes.

T: You've been getting taller, haven't you?

S: Yes.

T: Let me see if I understand your concern. You're afraid that, after you've had your chair a couple of months, you will start outgrowing it and you'll be uncomfortable. Is that right?

S: Yes.

T: Is there more?

S: Yes. (with emotion)

T: You seem agitated.

S: Yes.

T: Do you think you'll have to *stay* uncomfortable?

S: Yes.

T: Do you mean that you're afraid they won't modify it in case you grow?

S: Yes.

T: Is that exactly it?

S: Yes.

T: That's what you want people to know you've thought about.

In the next part of the conversation, the teacher assisted the student in developing ideas on what questions to ask and how to communicate his concern to the people who were designing his new wheelchair. The reader should notice how many times in this short conversation the teacher had to repeat and clarify what she thought the student was saying in order to avoid distorting the message.

●Obviously feelings are difficult for a cerebral palsied nonvocal individual to express. A child may have a relatively small repertoire of facial expressions. Feelings of anger, hurt, anxiety, or eagerness are difficult to communicate and may be mistaken for each other. As such, you should check the impressions you gain before pursuing the reasons for a child's feelings. Anger, disappointment, and hurt are difficult feelings with which to deal. The speaker needs the opportunity to put them into words and to have them accepted without criticism and with understanding. "Is that *exactly* what you feel, or can I say it better?" "Am I close?" Paraphrasing the feelings of another individual to the child's satisfaction will probably be the hardest task for a teacher, but the effort to do so will yield insight into the speaker.

The limits of what a child can say are almost entirely determined by you. It is a great temptation to ask the child only fact-level *yes* and *no* questions. But a nonvocal speaker has ideas, feelings, and reactions to share with those who will listen. Some of her ideas are only partially formulated. Her feelings and reactions may not be completely understood, even by herself. This statement may be true for any of us, but the confusion presents added problems to the nonvocal child, who must decide if her thoughts match those reflected by her teacher. It is the teacher's task, then, to clarify, stating notions of the messages received and then asking questions, such as "Am I close?", "Is there more to it than that?", "Do you want to change part of what I said?", "Is this too specific or too general?", and repeatedly, "Is that *exactly* right?"

Talk "Up To" Not "Down To"

When communicating with an individual who is

limited to *yes–no* answers, talk to her at her own level. It is tempting to talk down to a person who can only respond with *yes–no* answers, but you should attempt to stimulate the student's intellect, not to bore her. Finding out a person's needs, feelings, interests, family relations, and problems in such a way as to help solve problems is a very important skill. Each student, in her own way, has much to say, but is limited in ways to say it.

We can "put down" nonvocal children by ignoring them. Adults often feel they do not have time to stop and work out the problems involved in communications. They may not realize that the disabled child has something to say. Some people erroneously assume that a child without intelligible speech is equally without intelligence. To be sure, these children could relate innumerable instances in which they have been treated as mentally retarded or infantile. It is not unusual to see adults stand next to nonvocal children and ask another person if they are mentally retarded.

If we remember our early attempts at conversation with severely disabled children, we should be able to also remember that we, too, needed reminders to direct our conversations in an upward manner. We must also help others for whom such communication is a new experience. Too often, disabled children find themselves answering questions over and over again on the same topics and at the same level. Often, the child, regardless of her age, repeatedly answers questions about her family, her brothers and sisters, her school, how she likes school, and her pets. How dull this must be to be denied opportunity for variety and depth in conversations! For many disabled children, their disability has indeed become a severe handicap to them because they cannot learn about the world around them through verbal interactions with others. Compare how often you talk about yourself in conversations with nondisabled persons and how often you tell about yourself to disabled persons. We bombard disabled children with simple questions about themselves. Seldom do we give these children an opportunity to gain information about us or about other people.

You may feel uncomfortable because you are unable to find a way to achieve immediate understanding. You may not want to embarrass or humiliate the child by talking at higher levels than can be understood. However, you must realize that, regardless of the child's age, you would be doing her a favor by allowing her to try to reach higher to understand.

Ask questions such as, "If you could manipulate reality in any way you wanted, what would you do or be?" "Does it make you sad that you probably never will be a _____?" "Does it give you pleasure to think about _____?"

Recognize Deadlocks

In conversations with nonvocal children, barriers are frequently encountered. For example, the child may wish to say something you are not reflecting; or perhaps you don't change tracks to get to the information. Sometimes, the child may realize that a block has been reached over an unimportant topic and would rather drop the subject than waste time. You can help the speaker by saying, "I'm really stuck. Do you want to go on trying?" Be certain the child does not feel pressured into changing topics. Sometimes a teacher or others simply cannot decipher what a nonvocal person is trying to say. Both parties may feel highly frustrated (See Figure 6–4, p. 117). It is important to persist if the child indicates it is important to do so.

If you must terminate a conversation before you and the child are satisfied, keep the communication open by saying, "I have to leave, but I'll think about it. You think too, and maybe you'll find another way of telling me."

There are several mistakes that lead to deadlocks. We can learn to recognize and correct unwillingly erected barriers. The most frequent mistake is reaching premature conclusions without clarifying what was "heard." A cerebral palsied boy told about a party at school, the refreshments, activities, and people invited. The teacher checked all the details and said, "You must have enjoyed that."

C: No.

T: You didn't?

C: No.

T: But you told me all about it. Did something bad happen?

C: No.

T: But you didn't enjoy it.

C: No.

T: Well you did go, didn't you?

C: No.

Figure 6–4. "Yes, it's frustrating for both of us, but let's keep trying."

T; You didn't! Why not? Were you somewhere else?

C: No.

T: Were you ill?

C: No.

T: I don't get it then.

The problem was the child was attempting to tell about a party that his class had planned, *but which hadn't yet taken place*. The assumption by the teacher was that the party was a past event.

Erroneous assumptions about meaning often involve the child's attitudes, reactions, feelings, or opinions; interpretations of signals that may have multiple meanings; distinctions between events which have *occurred* and those which are *anticipated*. The best method for identifying erroneous assumptions which block conversation is by checking information phrase-by-phrase with the speaker. (For example: "We're talking about a party?" "Yes." "At school?" "Yes." "That your class had?" "No.") If this strategy fails, ask, "Am I missing something? Is it about someone? Some place? A time? A thing? A feeling?" Erroneous assumptions may not always leave the child dissatisfied, but they always leave the teacher with false information. "Is that exactly right?" is again the important question.

If you try to ask questions that the child does not wish to answer, a barrier is created. These questions might concern feelings, personal concerns, events the child is not ready to discuss, or topics that draw conversation away from where the speaker wishes to go. The nonvocal child has no way to say, "I don't want to talk about that right now," or to head the conversation in another direction. Ask, "Do you feel like going into this?"

A barrier may be created when the child wants to talk about a topic which makes you uncomfortable. Perhaps you can suggest someone else with whom she can discuss her concern, remembering that the number of people with whom she can talk is limited and that conversation is necessary for her to develop her own ideas. Perhaps you could serve as facilitator until persons unfamiliar with the child learn to communicate with her.

Teach Others What Works

We should provide opportunities for nonoral persons to expand their conversations to new people and outside of school. Signs and signals must be taught to others so that consistent procedures are used. Parents must teach babysitters, family friends, relatives, neighborhood children, and favorite restaurant persons. Teachers must teach schoolmates, classroom aides, and regular classroom teachers.

Uses of Communication Boards

Once a nonvocal individual can use the responses *yes, no,* and *I don't know* in communication with others, he has an outlet for his thoughts and ideas. There is, however, a severe limitation on the range of thoughts and ideas that can be expressed to others by answering questions with *yes, no,* or *I don't know*. It is helpful if additional methods, such as communication boards and similar systems, can be used.

Communication Boards

Communication boards are often called *conversation boards*. They are charts of pictures, symbols, words, letters of the alphabet, and numbers to which nonvocal persons point to relay their thoughts. *Yes, no,* and *I don't know* are usually the first ideas placed on a board. They are placed in opposite corners so as to reduce confusion over which of the responses is being expressed.

Features

Basic information can be displayed in many different ways. Usually, it is placed under a plastic sheet and supported by a stiff cardboard or desk top. It may be portable for use on a lap, table, or wheelchair tray. The basic information may be painted or attached to the top of the wheelchair tray, the top of a stand-up table, or the top of a worktable.

Portable communication boards can be designed so different sheets can be inserted depending on the kind of information desired at a particular time. For instance, a sheet depicting pictures of the various choices of play activities could be inserted just before a young child goes out to the playground. He can place his fist on a picture, or in some other manner indicate his choice of activity during the recess period. (See Figure 6–5, below.) The sheet can be changed before lunch so the child can communicate whether he wishes milk or juice.

The size and shape of the board and the location of information depend upon the specific needs of each child. The individual should be pretested to determine which movements or gestures can be used to indicate the information to be conveyed. It is necessary to note desirable spacing between items so that the child's uncoordinated movements relay one response and one response only. It is also necessary to determine optimum size for pictures or print in order to accommodate a person's problems with visual disability or problems trying to see with excessive head movement. Again, some factors that must be considered when constructing a communication board are length and direction of the child's reach, distance between information, accommodations for the child's motor inaccuracies, desired content, and size of print.

In addition to flat, portable communication boards, there are also other styles. An individual may carry information by topics on stiff sheets of paper in three-ring notebooks of various sizes. A cerebral palsied person with very poor hand control may carry a large notebook. A cerebral palsied person with no speech but fine hand movements may carry a pocket-sized notebook

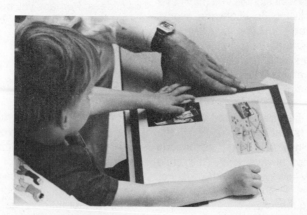

Figure 6–5. Given choices of block play, painting, and "something else," Chris chooses painting.

with categories of words to which he can point. With a book of words and phrases, an individual can move in the community and communicate thoughts to persons such as store clerks and bank tellers. The young man in Figure 6–6, below, carries his communications in an expanding plastic photo holder.

Figure 6–6. With letters, phrases, and other options for communications in different sections of a plastic photo holder, Ron communicates to strangers.

Content

If a person is just learning the use of a communication board, it is most helpful to start with essentials such as words or pictures which indicate hunger or need for the bathroom. Additional information is added as the child is able to use it. If the child is studying vowel sounds, vowels can be added to the board and used to practice lessons. It is helpful to add letters in the order that is used on a typewriter so that later a child can easily add the typewriter as another tool of communication.

Additional words or pictures can be placed around the outer edges of the board. Each board is designed according to each person's needs. On the board used by Peter (see Figure 6–7, p. 120) words are grouped from left to right: nouns, pronouns; verbs; and descriptors. Phrases needed most often are written beside the alphabet letters.

Pointing

Means of pointing to communication boards vary. Some disabled individuals are able to point with some part of a finger or hand. Others use the entire fist.

For an individual unable to control a single finger for pointing, it is possible to attach a plastic splint to the clenched fist with an extending appendage. This plastic stem, which extends beyond the clenched fist, can be used as a pointer.

Use of the hand for pointing may be limited and unsatisfactory for some severely disabled individuals. Some other means are needed for pointing. Wands and various other apparatus attached to the hands or in the mouth are often used for this purpose.

A wand, usually a wooden or metal dowel approximately 5″–8″ long, is attached to the forehead part of a helmet and extends from the forehead or from in front of the mouth (see Figure 6–8, p. 121).

There are many attachments and varieties of dowels used for pointers. Some attachments are permanent in that only one dowel at one angle may be used. Other attachments allow insertion of different lengths and angles of dowels for different purposes. A communication-board pointer or typewriter-stick dowel may be longer and have a slight curve, whereas a page-turner dowel may be short and straight.

Direct focus headlights (like those used by dentists and doctors [3]) often substitute for pointers. They can be worn on the head and adjusted to throw a small, brilliant light on different elements of a communication board (see Figure 6–9, p. 121)

Your Responsibility

To facilitate communication between you and an individual using a communication board, a few key procedures should be used. The listener names the picture or the letter as the disabled person points. As soon as the listener knows the word being spelled, he should say that word. It is

Figure 6–7. Peter uses his communication board to tell jokes, debate, and interact with classmates in different high school classes.

not always necessary to make the individual spell the entire word; anticipating the word spelled by the individual makes the conversation move much more rapidly.

Systems for Those Who Cannot Read or Spell

Some people help severely/profoundly disabled persons learn to understand language and express themselves by using simple or modified

sign language.[4] Some (Schlesinger, 1975) propose that sign language may be a useful adjunct in the treatment of nondeaf cerebral palsied children. In addition to introducing very basic communication to individuals, signing might be used simultaneously with unintelligible speech. When making a decision about the advisability of teaching signing, consider this question: Does the person have the dexterity to sign at the level of communication which matches her communication potential?

Another system of symbols used as a substitute or supplement for spoken language has been devised for use by severely handicapped persons who have no speech. The symbol communication system is based upon Blissymbolics, a visual symbol system [5] created between 1942–1949 by an Austrian chemical engineer, Charles K. Bliss (1965). It was his intent to use the symbols as a medium for international communication. In 1971, an interdisciplinary team at the Ontario Crippled Children's Centre, Toronto, Canada, recognized the potential of Blissymbolics as an alternative form of communication for nonspeaking, physically handicapped persons (Ontario Crippled Children's Centre, 1974). From the hundreds of symbols in the original system, symbols were selected and arranged into 3 vocabulary levels. By progressing through these levels, the nonspeaking, prereading person is able to greatly expand communication potential. The unique and consistent organization of the symbols enables her to convey many aspects of human experience.

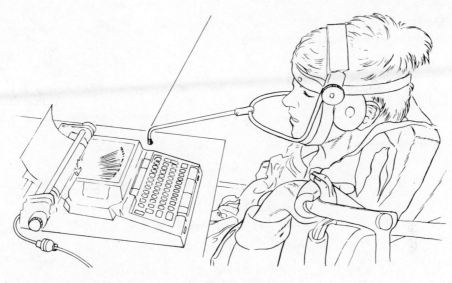

Figure 6–8. Head-mounted wand designed by a teacher.[2]

Figure 6–9. The sharp light beam can be seen in a lighted room.

Questions can be formulated; feelings can be expressed; assertions can be made. The symbols deal with abstract concepts as well as the concrete objects in the person's environment. The symbols are arranged in displays of 100, 200, and 400 symbols. These displays fit on a wheelchair tray. For the severely involved person, electronic symbol displays of 200 and 512 symbols have been developed. Interfaces, such as joysticks, control the lighting of the symbols. A selected word synonym always appears below each symbol to allow communication with persons who are not familiar with the symbol system (Ontario Crippled Children's Centre, 1975). See p. 122.

Each symbol is composed of visual elements which relate to meaning, sometimes directly through pictorial representation; sometimes indirectly by representing an idea related to the meaning; sometimes arbitrarily. Utilizing a basic core vocabulary of symbols, the symbol user can combine and recombine symbol parts to arrive at an unlimited number of meanings. Interpretation of the precise meaning of a symbol is dependent upon the context in which it is used. Thus, each symbol is capable not only of forming new meanings through being combined with other symbols, but it is also capable of a range of translations depending upon the situation in which it is used. The symbol for *food* would be translated as *breakfast* if it appeared in the symbol sentence: "In the morning, before I go to school, I eat my *breakfast*." The same symbol would be translated as *supper* or *dinner* if it appeared in the symbol sentence: "We always wait for Dad to come home from work to have our *dinner*." The symbol *food* can also be combined with the symbol *outside* to mean *picnic*, and with the symbol *little* to mean *snack*.

As well as serving as a means of communication, the symbol system provides a medium which facilitates creative thinking, inductive processing, and concept clarification. By combining several

Blissymbols—

Sometimes look like the things they represent:

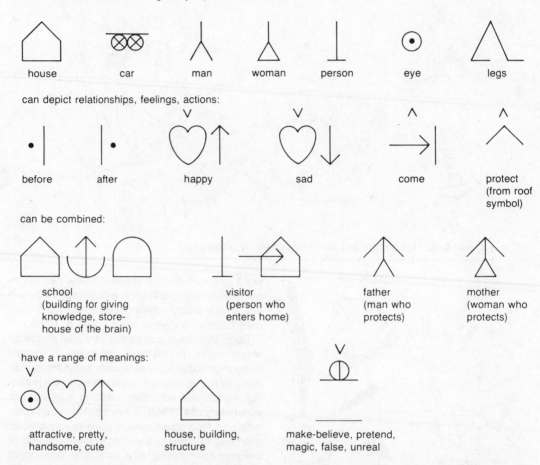

| house | car | man | woman | person | eye | legs |

can depict relationships, feelings, actions:

| before | after | happy | sad | come | protect (from roof symbol) |

can be combined:

| school (building for giving knowledge, store-house of the brain) | visitor (person who enters home) | father (man who protects) | mother (woman who protects) |

have a range of meanings:

| attractive, pretty, handsome, cute | house, building, structure | make-believe, pretend, magic, false, unreal |

symbols, the young child can "create" new symbols; for example: *witch*— "make-believe woman who flies in the sky"; *robot*— "part person, part machine"; *traffic*— "a gathering of cars"; *toothbrush*— "a tool which makes your teeth clean." The person combines meaning elements in order to represent a new meaning.

Those who teach children symbol communication find that utilization of the symbols can also support the reading and language programs by providing children many opportunities to process visual symbolic information and by extending the child's language experiences. It provides the opportunity for students to learn to build sentences even though they cannot yet read, spell, or write. Some teachers may feel that for some nonvocal students who read and spell, use of Blissymbolics is more efficient than the use of communication boards limited to words and letters.

In order to facilitate symbol instruction in the many settings to which it is spreading, the Blissymbolics Communication Foundation (BCF) has been established to standardize symbols as they appear in vocabularies and to produce and disseminate symbol materials. Mr. Bliss has given the BCF a world-wide license on his copyright and is serving as consultant to the Foundation.

Systems for Those Who Cannot Use Pointers

Some students with no functional speech also are unable to point in any manner. You must substitute some skill in place of pointing. Several devices have been developed to solve this problem.

Format and Needed Signals

A variation of the communication board is based upon the use of a tic-tac-toe format.[6] By using a chart with three lines of horizontal cells and three rows of vertical cells (such as used in the tic-tac-toe game) (see Figure 6–10), a nonvocal individual can use nine cells to communicate nine things. Once this task is learned, students can learn to communicate with choices in multiples of 9.

Figure 6–10. A tic-tac-toe format gives nine choices.

First, we must help children find voluntary and distinguishable movements of the head and eyes to indicate each of the nine positions of the tic-tac-toe format. The student could look up for the top row, open his mouth for the middle, and look down for the bottom row. After indicating the row, an individual could then indicate a square or *position* on that row which is occupied by the item of information he wishes to relay. A glance to one side means the square on that side of the row; a glance to the other side means the square on that side of the row; and, opening the mouth means the middle square. One distinct movement would indicate the row; another movement, the position.

Some individuals may be able to take a "short cut" and combine movements: looking up and over to the right for the top right square, straight across to the right for the middle right square, and down and to the right for the bottom right square. (Refer again to Figure 6–10.) Patterns of movements look like this:

⌐→ for cell "May I try."

⌐↓ for cell "Out of wheelchair, please."

→ for cell "trike"

(open mouth) for cell "more" (such as more lunch, more drink, more trike)

Still another variation of the above signals may be as follows: The upper square or space on the top row and to the right of the disabled individual may be indicated by a diagonal glance upward and over the individual's right shoulder. Likewise, the square on the left and on the bottom may be indicated by a glance down over the left shoulder. Patterns of movements look like this:

↗ for cell "May I try."

↙ for cell "Out of wheelchair"

→ for cell "trike"

(open mouth) for cell "more"

In teaching this system, an individual is first shown just one tic-tac-toe format. For young children, pictures of familiar objects or pictures representing choices for the children may be put into the nine respective positions of the grid. If a person can spell or use letters to give phonic clues, letters are placed in the cells.

Once an individual has mastered a system for indicating a particular square of the nine squares with head and/or eye movements, he is ready to increase the options for communication to a minimum of 54 positions (*two* rows of three boxes) or 81 positions (*three* rows of three boxes). (See Figure 6–11.)

An individual is then asked first to locate which tic-tac-toe grid, or which box contains the information he wishes to relay. Using one of the nine signals established, he may indicate the middle box on the bottom row (Box 8), which in itself has nine possibilities. Second, he is asked which position in that box contains the piece of information to be communicated. He is once again using one of the same sets of nine signals to designate one particular cell. *It is imperative* that instructions be included somewhere (perhaps in place of one of the boxes) to assist those persons who do not know how to use the system or ask the appropriate questions.

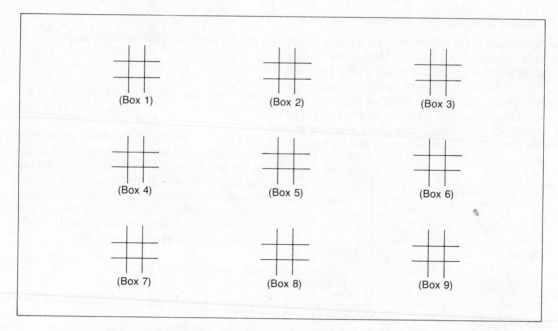

Figure 6–11. A tic-tac-toe format on a placard gives 81 choices.

For convenience to the "receiver," a grid system can be used where the receiver of the message does not have to be directly beside or looking over the shoulder of the sender to see the chart. Rather, a permanent grid can be placed on *both sides* of a placard or, as in Figure 6–12, on both sides of a folded sheet to tagboard. The content of the grid can be written *in reverse* on the back of the board for the convenience of the receiver. It is necessary to reverse the order of the symbols so that when the sender looks toward the information on his upper right, the receiver will have the same information on the position of the board to which the student is looking. The receiver can now face the sender—a much more natural way to communicate.

In the following figures 6–12 to 6–16, Chris is sending a short message to *you,* the reader. Notice he uses two rows of three boxes, or 54 positions. See what he has to say. The first figure, 6–12, is how one side of the board appears to Chris.

You are facing Chris. Figure 6–13, p. 125, is how the situation looks to you. You ask, "What box?" He answers by giving these two signals.

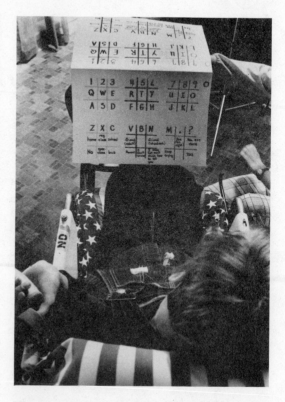

Figure 6–12.

The communication board showing:

9	8	7		6	5	4		3	2	1
O	I	U		Y	T	R		E	W	Q
L	K	J		H	G	F		D	S	A

?	.	M	N	B	V	C	X	Z
You are close	You are right!		friend (student)	Miss Joy	friend (adult)	school	reg class	home
Yes		Keep trying	I know but can't think how to tell	I don't know	Parents	bus	spec class	No

Figure 6–13.

Now that you know he is referring to the box that includes:

6	5	4
Y	T	R
H	G	F

You ask, "What position?" He answers:

9	8	7		6	5	4		3	2	1
O	I	U		Y	T	R		E	W	Q
L	K	J		H	G	F		D	S	A

?	.	M	N	B	V	C	X	Z
You are close	You are right!		friend (student)	Miss Joy	friend (adult)	school	reg class	home
Yes		Keep trying	I know but can't think how to tell	I don't know	Parents	bus	spec class	No

Figure 6–14.

Now you know the first letter is *H*. Continue to see what is next. You ask, "What box?" He answers:

Figure 6–15.

You ask, "What position?" He needs only one movement to answer.

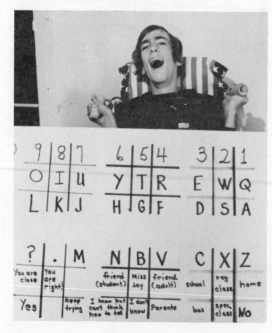

Figure 6–16.

Now you know the second letter is _____. He has just greeted you with: "_____!"

Content

There are many options for choice and complexity of content to be put in the cells: pictures, words, phrases, simple alphabet letters, Bliss symbols, and combinations of these. The choice of content depends upon the individual for whom it is designed.

A *set* of boards allowed one student even more flexibility. On five boards of 81 cells each he used sight vocabulary as a communication tool. Sight vocabulary words were arranged by function. The student first was taught to combine words functioning as nouns and words functioning as verbs and as descriptors. In addition, he had two other matrices of 81 cells each. One contained alphabet letters and frequently used words. The other was covered with clear contact paper. This plastic-covered board provided flexibility as words corresponding to current lessons could be quickly written. Information could easily be erased to allow room for another set of information for another lesson.

Other Uses

This basic communication system has many other uses. A classroom teacher may be having a discussion with the rest of the class and wish to involve the severely disabled individual in the discussion. The teacher could quickly draw one tic-tac-toe grid on the chalk board and write several pieces of information in the various positions of the grid. The child could then be asked to indicate which of the spaces relays his idea or his answer.

Another example is a grid on which the information is changed; it is similar to a communication board. Different sheets providing either 9 or 81 items of information are used, depending on the topic of discussion at the moment. For instance, during a math period, a grid of 9 or more items of math information might be used (see Figure 6–17).

3	+	5
2	=	4
7	Answer Not Here	1

Math Options Are Endless

Figure 6–17. Insert needed numerals and signs for operations.

Then, during social studies period, the page may be flipped to include 9 or 81 items of information relating to the social studies unit.

Communication in a Group

Many times, nonoral individuals who cannot write need to be able to communicate to a group. While the previous suggestions may be appropriate, other ideas may help.

As mentioned before, 9 or 81 cell grids can be printed in reverse formats on two sides of a placard. Placards can be set between the disabled sender and a receiver or group of receivers.

A person cannot only focus the beam of a headlight to indicate a message on a communication board placed within an arm's reach, but she can also project the light to distant places. These headlights can be used to communicate to groups and/or to leaders of groups. In a teaching session involving a group of learners, the disabled person could be sitting with other students facing a chalkboard. She could guide the beam of light attached to her head to illuminate any of several choices or answers spaced apart on a blackboard which is several yards away.

Recording of Messages for Later Retrieval by Others

Many times communications and other types of interpersonal interactions have taken place between a nonvocal individual and other persons, and the nonvocal person wishes to share those interactions with a third party at some later time. For an individual without intelligible speech, this may be difficult or even impossible. For instance, it is very difficult for many disabled children to share with their parents the details of what happened at school or tell teachers what happened at home. A backpack designed to fit the back of a wheelchair is often the answer (see Figure 6–18).

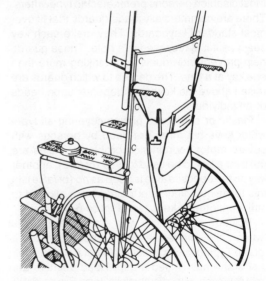

Figure 6–18. Check book pouch (and read my teacher's note about what I did after lunch!).

One pocket would carry books. A clip would hold notes and a second pocket would carry the communication board. A child, having something in mind, needs to first relay a message telling people in which part of the pack to look. Dymotape labels (raised lettering on plastic tape) on the wheelchair arms solve this problem. Two labels can be attached on each wheelchair arm so that they face away from a child and toward the persons to whom she is communicating. Labels say *check book pouch, check clip, check bottom pouch* and *thanks*. A child's eye or head movements could indicate which label a person should read.

Uses of Typewriters and Other Writing Machines

A typewriter is a very useful tool for a nonvocal individual. Many individuals who have severe coordination problems use typewriters with adaptations which enable them to type either with their hands or with a wand. Individuals whose disabilities include extreme weakness prefer to use a typewriter rather than attempt to write by hand. Typewriters are used by some disabled persons not only for writing tasks but also as aids to conversation. The use of a typewriter may be somewhat limited, however, because of the problem of transporting it into all situations.

Adaptations for Typewriters

Most disabled persons prefer electric typewriters. There are commercially made guards that fit over most standard keyboards. They make each key seem as if it is recessed in a hole. These guards help prevent individuals from striking more than one key at a time. The degree to which guards are raised above the keyboard depends upon needs of an individual.

Plastic or cardboard pieces covering all typewriter keys but three are used by persons with severe motor coordination problems. Holes are put over a key to be used for *yes* (or *true*), another key on the opposite side is used as *no* (or *false*). In this technique, fingers or pointers are allowed to strike only these keys (see Figure 6–19).

Pointers and pencils with erasers are helpful when child's fingers are weak but her grasp is good. Typing sticks attached to her hand will help her if she has limited grasp. Head pointers and mouthpieces with mouthsticks (see Figure 6–20) are helpful for persons with poor hand use but good head control.

Positioning of the typewriter is a very important consideration. For individuals whose movements are involuntary and flailing or extremely weak, it is very important to have the typewriter recessed so that the person can rest her arms from the elbow to the wrist on a table top and drop her wrists when

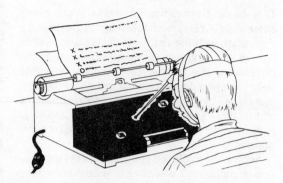

Figure 6–19. Plastic covering all but two keys and the space bar or carriage return.

her fingers strike the keys. For those individuals with flailing movements, sandbags over the arms or weights on the arms are sometimes helpful.

Other Writing Machines

VISTA [7] is a commercially available, electronic device which attaches to a standard-size electric typewriter. The alphabet is displayed in columns and rows on the attachment. The speed of the operation mechanism can be custom designed to fit an individual's motor capability. A light moves along a grid, illuminating the letters of the alphabet. The light moves down the first column of alphabet until the typist hits a specially designed lever. At that moment, the direction of the light movement changes and moves horizontally. This horizontal movement across the letters in the row continues at the programmed speed until the typist again hits the lever. Simultaneously this final letter is typed onto the paper in the typewriter. (See Fig. 6–21.) A major disadvantage of the *VISTA* machine lies in its expense and lack of portability. Most established typewriter companies have information about the *VISTA* machine. Descriptions of machines for similar purposes are included in the annotated bibliographies by Luster and Vanderheiden (1974).

The MCM/D Communication System [8] is an example of the importance of matching prerequisite skills, knowledge, and needs of individuals to features of communication systems. The MCM/D is like a miniature typewriter with a cradle for a telephone receiver and a visual display of what is typed. It is quite portable and practically indestruc-

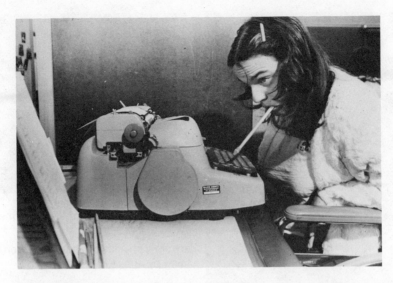

Figure 6–20. Merry's mouthstick is inserted into a plastic mouthpiece molded to accommodate her bite comfortably.

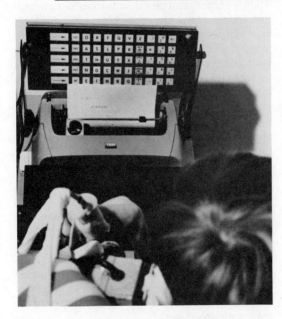

Figure 6–21. Chris controls the direction of light movement and printing of letters by pressing an activator with his head.

Figure 6–22. A nonvocal person can 'talk' on the phone.

Visual displays of typed material can be transmitted over the phone between two MCM's. Any individual who does not talk but who has enough coordination to type (with even one finger) can communicate over the phone.

This machine used in Figure 6–23 by a young nonvocal student is a portable communication device. Rather than having her teacher speak for her, she wheels herself to the office with the MCM on her lap and proceeds to type a *very important message* to the secretary.

Goals for this child include use of this machine at home and in the community.

Still another feature of the machine is its capability of interfacing with a cassette tape recorder.

tible (see Figure 6–22). It is designed so a deaf person can exchange typed messages on the phone to anyone else who has an MCM machine. Teachers of physically disabled students can find many ways to use it.

Persons do not need to be present to read the messages or school exercises as they are typed; messages can be stored on a tape recorder and played back on the display at a later time.

Several volunteers have designed apparatus for handicapped persons. Since communication systems are expensive to produce, and patents are difficult to obtain, substantial problems of dissemination are common. One of the most interesting machines has been developed with the use of free and inexpensive materials by a San Francisco State University student, Mike Davis. The machine is called, simply, the *Writing Machine*. It may be considered crude by some, but to the disabled student, his parents, and concerned professionals, it is ingeniously designed! Chris, who is pictured in Figure 6–24 using this electric machine, could write words to convey ideas by literally "using his head." He could also mark exercise papers and multiple-choice study sheets taken home from the high school where he attended regular classes. For leisure, he creates artistic line drawings. For upholding part of his responsibility of the household, he created personalized invitations to his high school graduation party (Figure 6–24). Never before could this very

Figure 6–23. "Call my Mom; I'm sick."

severely physically disabled person create something by himself.

Adaptive Uses of Tape Recorders

Tape recorders can be valuable tools for nonvocal individuals. Many physically disabled individuals with high academic ability are being increasingly integrated into regular schools. Many plan to go on to college but do not use conventional systems for communication. Lectures can be taped by individuals who cannot take notes. Teachers can program very simple to very complex lessons on tape recorders. Commercial tapes can be purchased for teaching various skills. Tapes can also be used for recreational listening.

Adaptations of Tape Recorders

Various devices have been developed so that switches on a cassette tape recorder can be turned on and off by persons with poor hand control. Small switches and switches for remote control can be covered with large surfaces. Then pressure can be applied to a larger surface, which in turn activates the switch underneath. A slat of wood or small panel can be placed on a hinge over a mounted switch.

Individuals with extremely poor hand use can be encouraged to use tape recorders by extending the *on* and *off* buttons. Place a piece of cardboard over all the buttons except the *play* and *reverse*. The cardboard prevents accidental activation of buttons other than *play* and *reverse* by random movements of the hands and feet. Long narrow boards (pieces of tongue blades) can then be attached to the *play* and *reverse* buttons so that they extend farther and have larger, wider-

spaced surfaces to contact.[9] (See Figure 6–25.) If this approach is used, the tape recorder probably will need to be stabilized.

Figure 6–25. "Finally! I can listen to what *I* want."

Other Uses

A tape recorder can be synchronized with a carousel projector. Usually a teacher must be present to help students with unknown words and to turn pages. The disabled student can be provided a carousel projector for viewing slides of each page of her reader. A tape on a tape recorder

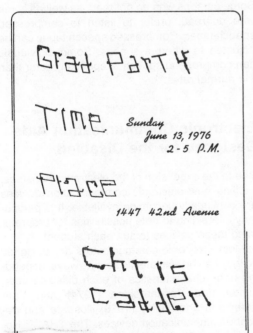

Figure 6–24. Pressing the bar on the right with the copper head stick on the helmet moves the far-away marking pen to the right on the paper. Pressing the lower bar moves the pen downward and starts to form the *a* in *grad*.

can be synchronized to the carousel so the student can hear what she is reading. She can then practice reading later by activating only the carousel projector.[10]

Other innovative techniques may be used to increase a student's use of tape recorders. We may (a) encourage nonvocal persons to initiate conversations with strangers, (b) promote independence in school work, and (c) encourage speed in study by practice in listening to compressed speech.

Initiate Conversations with Strangers

Sometimes strangers do not realize that the nonvocal person is intelligent, can understand, and has signals which permit conversation. One way to help a person initiate a conversation with a stranger is to use a cassette tape which continually repeats one message: "My name is _____ and I am _____ (years old). I say yes by looking at the right arm of my wheelchair and no by looking at the left. If I don't know, I'll look up. I like to talk about anything." This tape, placed in a battery-operated, cassette recorder, can be carried with a person in a wheelchair. The relay box can be placed so the disabled person can press it with her head, arm, or thigh. She can press until the entire message has been given, and she knows a repeat of the message is always ready on the tape recorder. Opening a conversation with this tool enables severely disabled individuals to encourage strangers to converse.

Promote Independence in School Work

A teacher can make taped lessons and special work sheets. The student can listen to the instructions and perhaps use one of the following ways of communicating her response as described by Leaning (1958):

Possible Taped Questions

1. How many _____ did you hear? (whistle blows, squeaks of a toy animal, hand claps)
2. What time is it when the big hand is on _____?
3. How much change is left from a dollar when the item purchased was 59¢?

Possible Means of Response

1. Using paste kept in a weighted paste container, paste teacher-prepared correct responses after the number of the question.

2. Responses may be printed on wood block scraps for easier grasping; the wood blocks can either be pushed or dropped into a predesignated spot on a table or wheelchair tray.

Another variation of the question-and-answer technique employs two tape recorders. The first tape recorder gives the question and leaves adequate space for the student to respond. The student can respond by kicking her foot on the wheelchair a given number of kicks. If the problem involves numbers, she could kick the correct number of times on the wheelchair. If the response involves multiple choice, A can be one kick; B, two kicks; C, three kicks; and D, four kicks. The second tape recorder records the number of times the listener kicks in response the the questions on the first tape recorder. It would be necessary, of course, to use the same kind of tape recorders and start them at the same time so that the counters indicate where the answers appear. In this way the teacher does not have to listen to the entire tape on which answers are recorded.

Compressed Speech

Some persons who do not read, as well as some who do read, prefer to listen to compressed speech tapes. Compressed speech tapes can be adjusted to different speeds. Some individuals can comprehend speech at speeds greater than the normal rates.[11]

Electronic Communication Aids Designed for the Disabled

Due to the expansion of the electronic industries, exciting new electronic communication devices are continually becoming available. It is particularly interesting to note possibilities for programming these devices to suit each student.

Most electronic communicators are designed so they can be activated in several ways, depending upon characteristics of each disabled user. Luster and Vanderheiden (1974) and Vanderheiden and Grilley (1976) illustrate and describe communication devices. The TRACE Research and Development Center for the Severely Communicatively Impaired [12] can be contacted for information on the most recent developments in communication devices. Most electronic devices are designed in a matrix format with a light behind each square. Pictures, symbols, alphabets, words, and messages can be displayed in each square of the matrix. Content of some matrices is permanent; content of some can be changed. Some matrices, like Figure 6–26,[13] contain only a few squares and some matrices contain as many as one hundred (Figure 6–27).[14]

Figure 6–26. Simple matrix with light (on no. 2) controlled by pushing switches. This boy uses his fingers and elbow.

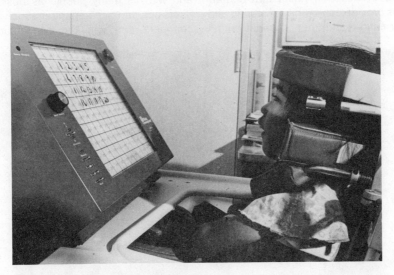

Figure 6–27. Matrix with possibility of learning to use up to 100 symbols or words. Up to 8 can be chosen for storage in "memory," and later replayed by lighting the chosen sequence when the "recall" button is pushed.

Some electronic communication devices are activated by direct selection. A student can touch the matrix cell desired and the information will be recorded. Auto-Coms (Vanderheiden and Grilley, 1976) and typewriters are two examples. For those children who have more problems controlling their motion, joysticks and other kinds of switches are used. These interfaces control the electric light bulbs to scan up, down, or horizontal and finally light or activate the desired cell on a matrix. Joysticks, headsticks, and mouth sticks can be moved in different directions to control directions of the scanning process. Pressure sensitive pads can be used which, when pressed, also move a light.

Most communicators can be adapted so they can be operated by elbows, jaws, tongue, hands, feet, and thighs. Some can be activated by eye movements or electrical charges in the skin surface.

It is important to select which features of output devices are best for individual students. *Visual outputs*, such as pointing to a message with a finger, a moving light, or a powered arrow, are not retrievable. *Printed output* on an electric typewriter or a strip printer can be retrieved. *Speech output* communication devices are in the process of development.

According to Le Blanc (1976), *visual* output devices are good for communicating on a person-to-person basis. He notes that *printed* output devices provide opportunity of storing and sending information and that *speech* output devices provide the opportunity for participating in the classroom, conversing on the telephone, and giving students the psychological boost of being able to "talk."

The MINI-COMM [15] is an example of a *miniature* portable unit providing visual output with a self-contained printer for retaining long messages. (See Fig. 6–28.) The possible message complexity ranges from *yes-no* signals to sentences and paragraphs. Speech output communication devices are in process of development in the MINI-COMM. The complexity of an electronic communication device depends on both the complexity of the message transmission desired, the needed output mode, and the severity of the physical handicap being circumvented.

Summary

A disabled individual may be nonspeaking and nonwriting but far from noncommunicating if given a chance. A disabled individual can be helped to make the necessary movements to point to particular pieces of information on the various communication systems. Much poetry has been dictated by way of communication boards as have several long stories and jokes at summer camps. It is important that the individual use her communication system in as many places and with as many people as possible. Simple directions can accompany the individual so that strangers can join the conversations. Other

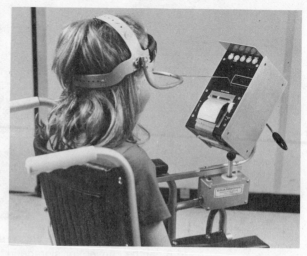

Figure 6–28. Mini-Comm.

systems do not require the person to be accompanied by someone able to receive the information as it is communicated. These systems allow disabled persons to preserve their communications when they work alone. Electronic communication aids allow the much desired independence.

Providing communication often depends upon collaborative efforts of speech therapists, occupational therapists, physical therapists, parents, rehabilitation engineering specialists, and nonvocal persons, if they can be helpful. There is no single way to help nonvocal individuals develop and use communication skills. There is a need, however, to be creative and try anything that may help.

Notes

1. Record of a conversation between Mary Ellen Rodda (teacher) and a student with severe communication problems (student).

2. SI/COMM head-mounted wand designed by Carmelita Heiner, 7545 Whitlock Ave. Playa Del Rey, Calif. 90291. SI/COMM, Inc.

3. Direct Focusing Headlight, Welch Allyn #6783–46000 in *Gentec Hospital Supplies and Equipment* (Catalogue), Gentec Hospital Supply Co., San Francisco, 1974, p. 269. One can also use bicycle lights designed to be worn on the head. Bicycle lights, however, often prove to be too diffused.

4. To provide consistency in teaching, we suggest you post large graphic illustrations of signs or manual language symbols used for particular individuals. Accompany the illustration with the word for which it stands. Pages in *Signs for Everyday* produced at the Elwyn Institute in Elwyn, Pennsylvania 19063, can serve as examples.

5. Ontario Crippled Children's Centre. Symbol Communication Programme (Brochure) 1975. (Available from Blissymbolics Communication Foundation, 862 Eglington Ave. East, Toronto, Ontario M4G 2L1.)

6. Helen Mansen, a teacher of orthopedically handicapped children in Visalia, California, has designed a variation of the communication board that is based upon the use of a tic-tac-toe format.

7. VISTA, Bush Electric Company, 1245 Folsom Street, San Francisco, California.

8. MCM/D Communication System, Micon Industries, 252 Oak Street, Oakland, Calif. 94607.

9. Tape recorder adapted by Aleene Yacoub.

10. Mary Ellen Rodda made slides of reading material and used synchronization of a tape recorder and a carousel projector to teach reading to physically disabled individuals.

11. See "compressed speech" in the portion of the chapter "Accompanying Disabilities" which discusses visual disabilities.

12. Papers, books, brochures and reports on communication systems can be obtained from: The TRACE Research and Development Center for the Severely Communicatively Impaired (Formerly the Cerebral Palsy Communication Group), University of Wisconsin, Madison, Wisc. 53706.

13. Communication Board, Zygo Industries, Box 1008 Portland, Oregon 97207.

14. Matrix Communicator, DUFCO, 901 Iva Court, Cambria, Calif. 93428.

15. MINI-COMM, COMM-AIDS, 5775 Cohasset Way, San Jose, Calif. 95123.

References

Bliss, C. K. *Ontario Crippled Children's Centre symbol communication research project: Teaching guideline.* Ontario: Crippled Children's Centre, September 1974. (Available from: 350 Ramsey Road, Toronto, Ont. M4G 1R8.)

Bliss, C. K. *Semantography—Blissymbolics.* Sydney: Semantography Publications, 1965. (Available from the Canadian distributor: Mrs. A. Fraser, 195 Newton Drive, Ontario M2M 2N8.)

Bliss, C. K., & McNaughton, S. *The book to the film "Mr. Symbol Man."* Sydney: Semantography Publications, 1975. (Available from the Canadian distributor: Mrs. A. Fraser, 195 Newton Drive, Willowdale, Ontario M2M 2N8.)

Kafafian, H. *Study of man-machine communication systems for the handicapped.* Washington, D.C.: Cybernetics Research Institute, February 19, 1970.

Leaning, P. A. *The challenge of cerebral palsy, A short study of its implications for teachers and parents.* Auckland, New Zealand: New Zealand Crippled Childrens Society, 1958.

Le Blanc, M. A. What do you do if you can't talk with your voice or hands? In B. L. Lund (Ed.), *Conference on systems and devices for the disabled: The Proceedings.* Boston: June 1976. (Available from the Biomedical Engineering Center, Tufts New England Medical Center, 171 Harrison Ave., Boston, Mass. 02111.)

Luster, M. J. *Preliminary selected bibliography of articles, brochures and books related to communication techniques and aids for the severely handicapped.* Madison, Wisc.: Cerebral Palsy Communication Group, 1974. (*a*)

Luster, M. J. & Vanderheiden, G. C. *Preliminary annotated bibliography of communication aids.* Madison, Wisc.: Cerebral Palsy Communication Group, 1974. (*b*)

Luster, M. J., and Vanderheiden, G. C. *Preliminary annotated bibliography of researchers and institutions.* Madison, Wisc.: Cerebral Palsy Communication Group, 1974. (*c*)

McDonald, E. T., & Schultz, A. R. Communication boards for cerebral-palsied children. *Journal of Speech and Hearing Disorders,* 1973, *XXXVIII* (1), 73–88.

McNaughton, S. Visual symbols: A system of communication for the non-verbal physically-handicapped child. In the *American Academy of Cerebral Palsy Regional Course on Cerebral Palsy.* Palo Alto, Calif.: Children's Hospital at Stanford, May 1975.

McNaughton, S. *Symbol secrets.* Toronto, Ontario: Toronto Press, 1975. (Available from Blissymbolics Communication Foundation, 862 Eglinton Avenue East, Toronto, Ont. M4G 2L1.)

Ontario Crippled Children's Centre. *1974 Year end report.* (Available from Blissymbolics Communication Foundation, 862 Eglinton Ave. East, Toronto, Ont. M4G 2L1.)

Ontario Crippled Children's Centre. Symbol communication programme (Brochure), 1975. (Available from above address.)

Signs for everyday. A special education program. (Available from Elwin Institute, Elwin, Pa. 19063.)

Schlesinger, H.S. Bimodal communication for cerebral palsied children. In the *Syllabus of regional course in cerebral palsy.* Children's Hospital at Stanford, Calif.: American Academy for Cerebral Palsy, May 8–10, 1975.

Vanderheiden, G. C., & Grilley, K. (Eds.). *Non-vocal communication techniques and aids for the severely physically handicapped.* Baltimore: University Park, 1976.

Vicker, B. (Ed.). *Nonoral communication system project: 1964/1973.* Iowa City: University Hospital School, University of Iowa, 1974.

Resources

Bliss, C. K. *Mr. Symbol Man* (Film). 1974. (Information available from Blissymbolics Communication Foundation, 862 Eglinton Ave. East, Toronto, Ont. M4G2L1.)

Brereton, B. L. G., & Ironside, M. *Cerebral palsy: Interaction games for severely handicapped children without speech.* New South Wales, Australia: Spastic Center of New South Wales, 1972. (Available from 6 Queen St., Mosman, New South Wales, Australia 2088.)

Copeland, K. (Ed.). *Aids for the Severely Handicapped.* New York: Grune and Stratton, 1974.

Cottam, N. Typewriting for the motor handicapped student. *American Journal of Occupational Therapy,* 1975, *XXI,* 56–59.

Feallock, B. Communication for the non-verbal individual. *American Journal of Occupational Therapy,* 1958, 60–63.

Goldberg, H. R., & Fenton, J. (Eds.). *Aphonic communication for those with cerebral palsy.* (Available from United Cerebral Palsy Associations of New York State, 220 W. 42nd St., N. Y.)

Gore, B., & Stoddard, J. *Teaching the cerebral palsied child.* Sacramento, Calif.: California State Department of Education, 1954.

Hagen, C., Porter, W., & Brink, J. Nonverbal communication: An alternate mode of communication for the child with severe cerebral palsy. *Journal of Speech and Hearing Disorders,* 1973, *38* (4), 448–455.

Jones, M. L. Electrical communication devices. *American Journal of Occupational Therapy* 1961, *15,* 110–111.

Laurentana, M. Head device for the severely handicapped cerebral palsied child. *Cerebral Palsy Review,* 1960, *21,* 6–8.

Lloyd, L. (Ed.). *Communication assessments and intervention strategies.* Baltimore, Md.: University Park, 1976.

Lorett, L. M. A method of communication for nonspeaking severely subnormal children. *British Journal of Disorders of Communication,* 1969, *4,* 64–66.

Richardson, N. K. *Type with one hand.* New Rochelle, N.Y.: Southwest, 1959.

Remberg, J., Guess, D., & Sailor, W. Training generalized functional acquisition of "yes" and "no" in three retarded children. *Review of the American Association for Education of the Severely/Profoundly Handicapped,* 1976, *1*(3), 8–39.

Sayre, J. M. Communication for the non-verbal cerebral palsied. *Cerebral Palsy Review* 1963, pp. 3–8.

7

SELF-CARE

June Bigge.

The necessity for teaching self-care to individuals with physical disabilities cannot be stressed enough. If we do not teach them self-help skills when they are children, they will become unnecessarily dependent adults. By teaching disabled children self-help skills, we are providing them an opportunity not only to survive in society but also to contribute to it. Equally important to preparing disabled individuals for future independence, of course, is preparing them for their present day-to-day experiences.

Because of the complexity, and often uniqueness, of physical conditions and limitations, specific goals cannot be the same for all disabled persons. While one child may be expected to become self-reliant, another may not be able to do more than master the most elementary self-help skills. In this chapter we will make several suggestions for helping physically disabled individuals with the following everyday activities:

1. eating
2. toileting
3. dressing
4. managing a home

Eating

Eating problems of some individuals with physical disabilities are related to problems of the total body. Those persons with coordination problems must have trunk and head control before they have ability to use arm, hand, and mouth muscles. Eating problems of other persons are directly related to problems of the shoulder, arm, hand or mouth. Persons using artificial arms or shortened arms may depend upon special appliances.

Many times, physically disabled children encounter *very* complicated eating problems. For help with these, mothers and teachers should be encouraged to seek help from infant specialists and therapists who can be located through state and local agencies serving the handicapped.

Physically disabled individuals are often not provided sufficient opportunities for learning to feed themselves. Many teachers feel they are helping physically disabled individuals if they wait on them. In fact, teachers may be helping only themselves. They often feel they must be *doing something* in order to help the child. They may also feel rushed and not allow the child time to help himself.

This section includes discussion of ways dependent disabled persons can be helped to eat more independently. Some guidelines will be presented for teachers and resource materials will be provided at the conclusion of the chapter.

Helping Dependent Disabled Persons to Eat

Some children with disabilities may need only minor assistance to acquire independence. Others may need considerable help in order to overcome the problems caused by their disabilities. The following are guidelines which teachers and parents might use to help these children:

1. Analyze eating problems.
2. Select appropriate eating positions.
3. Facilitate functions of eating and speech organs.
4. Provide training in eating and drinking.

Analyze Eating Problems

In order to help a child solve eating problems, the teacher must be able to analyze and specify the problem. Bowman, Calkin, and Grant (1975) wrote a simple manual for feeding handicapped children. In their book, *Eating With A Spoon: How to Teach Your Multihandicapped Child,* they suggest some key tasks which can become problems for children. They provide a helpful framework for finding eating subtasks that are problems. Perhaps an individual:

does not *"open his mouth* for a food-filled spoon"
does not *"swallow* food spooned into his mouth"
does not *"remove food from the spoon* with his lips"
does not *"chew* food spooned into his mouth"
does not *"pick up the utensil* if his spoon is lying on the table"
does not *"return* his *spoon to* his *plate"*
does not *"carry* his food-filled *spoon to* his mouth"
does not *"carry* his *spoon to* the *food and* then *fill it"* (p. 59)

Once problems have been defined, related or causal factors are important to note. What about the position of the individual for eating? Is the child able to flex his head in relation to the rest of his body? Observe the functioning of organs needed in both eating and speaking. Does the person's mouth open and close properly? Note lip closure. Does the child have the ability to take food off the spoon with his lips? Does the child have either clenched or protruding teeth? Consider either tongue thrust or lack of control of tongue movements. Does the individual choke easily? What about drooling? What are the specific problems related to chewing, swallowing, or sucking? Does the individual swallow with the mouth closed? What eating or drinking training is needed?

Select Appropriate Eating Positions

Positioning of individuals during eating is of utmost importance. Proper positioning provides balance and body support and includes placing the body with as much symmetry as possible. Wherever a person sits for eating, it is usually important to keep his head and body aligned in relation to the midline of the body. Perhaps the most important consideration is that the head should be flexed in relation to the body. Extension of the head should be avoided. Such extension interrupts swallowing and often encourages tongue thrust. Attempts to place the individual in a position which is as nearly normal as possible, or in midposition, will discourage abnormal reflex patterns and encourage more normal movements.

Special feeding positions may be chosen to inhibit motor patterns resulting from abnormal reflexes. Patterns of hyperextension or hyperflexion of the body can be inhibited. Similarly, abnormal reflexes which allow body movements to be governed by head movements can be inhibited. While inhibiting abnormal body movements, it is important that body positions for eating encourage isolated movements of arms, head and speech organs.

Mueller (1972) and Mueller (1975) describe and illustrate feeding positions for three situations: feeding either a very young infant or a severely involved baby; feeding an older baby; and feeding a baby in a chair. One position for feeding an infant or very severely involved baby requires that the infant be sitting as upright as possible on a pillow facing the adult. The pillow and the mother's body help support the child in the best position. At the same time, the person feeding the child has face contact with the child and can watch for asymmetry of head, jaw, and tongue movements.

The feeding position for the older baby is basically an upright position. A child is placed in a sitting position across someone's lap with his hips bent at right angles and knees slightly apart. Here again, the person who is feeding the baby can use his body parts to guide the child's position. If the child's extension pattern is very strong, the person feeding the child may cock the child's hips by putting his own raised and propped leg under the baby's knees. This position causes the child's buttocks to be lowered and allows needed increase in flexion in the hips and knees.

The feeding position in a chair is essentially the same as a normal child's. It is important to avoid scissoring of the legs. If the seat of the highchair is too deep, a foam rubber cushion can be inserted in the back. To maintain added flexion of the hips needed to inhibit extension, a rolled towel may be placed under the child's knees. It may also be helpful to add groin straps to maintain this position. A double strap must come from the center back of the seat with the child placed on the seat with his hips well back; then the two ends of the strap are brought between the legs around the upper part of the child's legs and fastened low behind the back of the chair.

Extraneous movements of the head, arms, or feet might be reduced by the use of head supports or guides. In many instances, they can be reduced by a position in which the body of the person feeding is used to restrict nonproductive movements. Excess movements are sometimes caused if the disabled individual feels unbalanced and insecure in the seated position. Care should be taken to insure that the feet are always supported and that the body weight is distributed as evenly as possible.

Other postural adaptations may include chair seat wedges placed on one or two sides of the child; chair seat wedges placed in the seat to encourage flexion of the hips and reduce hyperextension of the body; and raised foot rests with straps over the feet to insure that the feet maintain a stable position. Cutouts so table top or wheelchair trays fit snugly around the waist of a child help support sitting and arm positions. Head slings are an example of adaptations which may be needed to help the child maintain optimum posture.

Observe Eating and Speech Organs

Since speech and feeding mechanisms are the same, abnormal functioning of organs used in eating usually hinders not only eating but also speech development. Abnormalities of the oral mechanism first become obvious in eating and should be counteracted whenever possible. For instance, in attempting to drink from a nipple or bottle, a cerebral palsied infant may not be able to adjust the lips to seal the sides for leaks. Perhaps a youngster cannot close the jaws and coordinate the tongue for proper swallowing.

Not only should the child's lips, jaws, and tongue be observed during drinking, but also his overall motor patterns: a child should be watched to determine if he can isolate individual movements or if he reacts in overall reflex patterns. A child should be observed carefully for rotary chewing movements, and tongue movements necessary for transference of food. Rotary movements should not be confused with biting, since biting consists of vertical movements only. Swallowing is a frequent problem for handicapped children. To swallow properly, the mouth must be closed. A cerebral palsied child may show vertical movements of biting only and lack the ability to close the jaw. A child with cerebral palsy might *suck* the food from the spoon and the liquid from the cup instead of using the desired process of using *lips* to take the food and *sip* the liquid. A closed jaw is prerequisite for swallowing. The closed jaw also inhibits the tongue from pushing the food back out.

The earlier abnormal functioning of the organs used in eating is detected, the greater will be the opportunities for correcting unwanted motor patterns.

Provide Eating and Drinking Training

Mueller (1975) describes specific techniques for teaching eating once the food has reached a child's mouth. The fingers of a teacher are used to help the child learn to use more productive oral movements. A teacher might sit in front of a child with his thumb under the child's lower lip, index finger on the child's cheek, and the middle finger under the child's chin. This control should gradually be removed to allow the child to take over and use active oral movements. There are very specific directions which accompany these feeding techniques. More specific suggestions by Mueller (1975), Finnie (1975), and others can be found in the references on eating at the end of this chapter. Whenever possible use help from therapists.

Feeding should take place in a relaxed atmosphere. Sometimes involuntary movements of the body make the child appear to reject the mother when she is trying to breast or bottle feed. At other times, excessive body movements might cause a child to knock a spoonful of food to the floor. The adult must appear relaxed and not allow the child to feel the adult's understandable frustration and anger.

Finally, it is helpful to talk to a child while he is eating even if he is physically unable to make communicative gestures or otherwise respond. It may also be helpful to provide the child with verbal cues as he is fed.

Eating Independently

Whenever possible, disabled individuals ought to be encouraged to take increasing responsibility for their own feeding. Attempts to pick up pieces of food with their hands should not be discouraged. In order to practice movement of the food from hand to mouth, applesauce or peanut butter can be placed on a child's finger. The child might be helped to place his elbows on the table to stabilize his arms. He might also be helped to guide his fingers to his mouth. He might be encouraged at each meal to practice finger feeding himself. When it is seen that adaptions in the utensils or seating arrangements may be necessary, a child should be taught how to use them. In helping disabled persons to eat independently, it is important to remember to:

1. Select appropriate foods.
2. Provide guidance only when necessary.
3. Use adaptions when helpful.

Appropriate Foods

Often we need to teach children to bring their hand to their mouth in order to feed themselves. In order to accomplish this, we can encourage them to lick their fingers. Fingers can be placed in a bowl of frosting, cake batter or whipped cream. Hot dogs, beef or chicken bones with small pieces of meat on them, bread sticks, or cheese strips encourage children to hold something in their hands and bring it to their mouths.

To encourage chewing, try using green beans or carrots not fully cooked. These foods can be held readily and are easy to chew. Initially this type of food should be guided to the side of the mouth so the child will *chew* and not mash the food against the roof of his mouth with his tongue. Toast is a good possibility since it will dissolve if swallowed before being chewed sufficiently.

Teaching children to use forks and spoons requires the selection of foods that will adhere to the utensil. Cooked cereals, mashed potatoes and pudding are examples. For spearing with a fork, one might use smooth peanut butter on bite-size chunks of bread or small slices of meat.

Guidance

If a disabled individual can learn to eat independently, he should be given the opportunity. Guidance may take two forms. First, guidance can be provided through demonstration. Showing the individual what to do is often the first step. Second, physical guidance may be helpful to give individuals the "feel" of what they should be doing. Teachers should be sensitive to the parts of the task the individual can do unaided and refrain from giving help unless needed. When help is given, teachers should be sensitive to ways that the level of help can be reduced. Training may include complete physical and verbal cues to complete a task or subtask. At a later stage a verbal clue and less physical guidance may be needed. Later, only a verbal cue may be needed. The ultimate objective for many children is to develop their ability to complete tasks independently.

The initial step in helping a child feed himself might include filling the spoon and then wrapping the child's fingers around the spoon with the teacher's or child's hands on top. The child's hand should be turned so that the spoon goes straight in the child's mouth and the palm faces the child (supination). The teacher might guide the spoon and help the child place the spoonful in his mouth. Verbal clues are given for each action. Assistance should be reduced systematically step by step. The teacher might begin by moving the helping hand from the child's hand to his wrist. Scooping is the hardest step in the task and may be the last kind of physical assistance to eliminate. Next the teacher might withdraw the helping hand altogether. Finally, a child may need only verbal reminders or may be able to complete the task with no assistance.

Adaptions

Several sources for adaptions which can help disabled children eat independently are listed in the resource material at the end of this chapter. In addition, we can suggest a few samples of postural adaptations, and adaptations of silverware, plates, bowls and drinking aids. Some of these are available commercially and nearly all can be made by hand.

There are many adaptions of silverware. When training a child to use a spoon, various sizes of spoons should be tried. The spoon should be small enough to fit between the teeth of the bottom jaw so the child won't suck food off it but will take it with his lips. If the bowl is shallow this task is easier for the child. Spoons are available with bowls and handles of different lengths, contours, and sizes. (See Figure 7–1.)

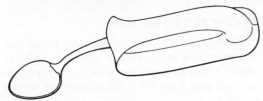

Figure 7–1. A spoon handle from a Clorox bottle.

When children can hold the spoon in a conventional manner but cannot maintain the grasp because of weakness or coordination problems, a clip can be added. Clips are customarily made of leather, metal, or plastic. They are attached to the handle of the spoon and are curved across the palm or back of the hand. This design helps in two ways. The spoon is held in a conventional manner and the clip prevents it from turning. The clip also prevents the spoon from being dropped. If the person has to use a palmar or total hand grasp instead of the conventional grasp, a similar clip is needed. In this case, one end of the clip would be on the spoon handle and the other end of the clip would go over the hand. Different curvatures of spoon handles may facilitate their use. A right angle in the middle of the handle helps an individual who must use a "baby grasp" because he cannot turn the hand enough when scooping the food. Spoons with swivel handles are often used

for individuals with poor coordination. The swiveling effect prevents food from spilling. Regardless of the position of the handles, the bowl swivels to the correct position. Contoured handles made of plaster of Paris, clay, or sponge rubber provide several additional options. The angle of the bowl of the spoon in relation to the angle of the handle provides still further options. Even if an individual cannot use his hands, he may still be able to feed himself. A head wand and a special spoon attachment on a plate allow self-feeding without hands. Such an apparatus, along with other adaptive devices, is described by Rosenberg (1968).

Knives and forks may be similarly adapted. A one-handed person might want to use a rocker knife. This knife is used by rocking a rounded blade back and forth like a rocking chair. One-handed persons might also learn to use a meat-cutting wheel, an instrument much like a pizza cutter.

There are several basic adaptions for dishes. Bowls are often used instead of plates. Bowls have the advantage of sides and rims which prevent food from spilling over. Bowls with bottoms wider than the circumference are not easily knocked over. Suction cups or rubber mats placed underneath the bowl or plate add stability. Materials such as soap suction holders and flour clay are further examples of stabilizers. Rubberized place mats may prevent plates or bowls from slipping. Feeding boards can be clamped to a wheelchair or table top. Holes in the feeding board keep cups, bowls, and plates from sliding and spilling. Plate guards (see Figure 7–2) are one of the most popular aids. A plate guard is a rim that can be attached to one side of the plate. Children can push food against it with their fork. The plate guard prevents this food from spilling and pushes the food on the utensil.

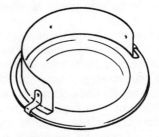

Figure 7–2. Food guards help those who have trouble picking up food with a spoon or fork.

Adapted drinking aids can be found in department stores. There are many styles of cups and glasses which were not designed for use by handicapped individuals but which can serve their needs very well. A soft plastic cup is good for a cup to teach drinking. The cup lip should be placed on the lower lip—not between teeth—with the child's mouth closed, head flexed, so that he sips liquid with *lips*. The cup may be cut out on one side so you can see the liquid and so that the child can drink to the bottom with his head flexed. (See Figure 7–3.) Cups and glasses with weighted bottoms might serve the needs of some individuals. Cups with double handles can be found. Some cups are styled with unusually wide bottoms and therefore are not easily tipped. Some glass holders with handle extensions can be used by the disabled.

Figure 7–3. Cut-out cup.

Drinking utensils may have to be designed or further adapted. It is possible to design a stand which holds a cup or glass above the table for a person unable to bend over. Flexible paper straws, straws slipped through holes in lids of glasses, and straws clipped to glass rims provide options for those who prefer to drink through straws.

Sandwiches may be held with various styles of sandwich holders. Tongs might be used which have velcro holding the handles together when a person is too weak or poorly coordinated to squeeze the handle and hold tension in the handles which in turn holds the sandwich. Sandwich holders constructed with pincher clothespins have been designed for amputees. If severely involved cerebral palsied individuals cannot hold sandwiches in their hands, it is possible to mount the sandwich holder at the end of the neck of a gooseneck lamp and base, or to a stick attached to a suction cup on the table. This raised holder allows a severely involved person to lean straight forward and take a bite whenever he desires. It may be necessary to put some sort of protective material on the sandwich holder so that, if the disabled individual accidentally bites the holder, he will not damage his teeth or mouth.

Please refer to the end of this chapter for elaboration of ideas presented and for additional aids.

Toileting

Toilet control is an integral part of the task of achieving physical independence. Of the many problems which face some disabled persons, loss of control is perhaps the most frustrating. For others, bowel and bladder control is physically possible but their inability to learn to control elimination is a source of frustration to parents, aides, and teachers.

Bladder and Bowel Care

For some physically disabled persons, bowel and bladder control is not entirely possible. Unfortunately, it may even be the reason younger children are kept from the most appropriate school program.

Bowel and bladder care are very important components of toileting. Some purposes of bowel and bladder training are to teach self-care, to provide maximum cleanliness and comfort for the child, to aid in preventing skin breakdown due to urinary or fecal irritation, and to alleviate emotional problems associated with incontinence. We describe, not recommend, some common procedures. Recommendations usually initiate with physicians. Training is usually the responsibility of parents, caretakers, school therapists, and perhaps enterostomal therapists. Teachers can help by aiding the students in becoming responsible for establishing routines for themselves to avoid accidents. Teachers can also be of more help in case of emergency leakages if they are informed about appliances worn and procedures used for bladder and bowel management. Parents of children with ostomies can help teachers by sending with the child the pamphlet called "My Child Has an Ostomy" (Hamilton, 1974). It answers fundamental questions a teacher might have about the ostomy itself. Space is provided for parents to describe to teachers the specifics about their child.

Management of Bladder Problems

The purpose of a bladder care plan is to attain the best possible method of emptying the bladder. Various methods are used for those who have partial or complete loss of bladder control. There have been a number of external urinary collection devices devised for the male. For the female, a diversion technique or catheter is more often used.

External urinary collection devices come in several styles. Usually a soft rubber tube, or condom, is placed over the penis and collects the urine in an external urinary collection bag (Swinyard, 1971). (See Figure 7–4.) The bag may be attached to a leg under clothing. Collection bags are suspended from a waistband; some have straps that encircle the hips for extra support. Collected urine is emptied from a conve-niently placed outlet. (See Figure 7–5.) Most bags are available commercially.

The most commonly performed *urinary diversions*, or ostomies, for children are the ileal conduit and the ureterostomy. An ostomy is a surgical opening through the abdomen into the bowel or another hollow organ, from which waste material is discharged when the normal function of the bowel or bladder is lost. The material is discharged from the bowel to a stoma (opening) and is collected into an appliance.

The *ileal conduit* is a surgery in which the ureters (hollow tubes carrying urine from the kidneys to the bladder) are implanted in an isolated segment of the small bowel which is brought out to the surface of the abdomen. It is sutured there to form the stoma through which the urine passes. A watertight collection appliance is then worn on the skin over the opening. (See Figure 7–6.)

The *ureterostomy* is a surgery in which the ureters are brought through the abdominal wall at

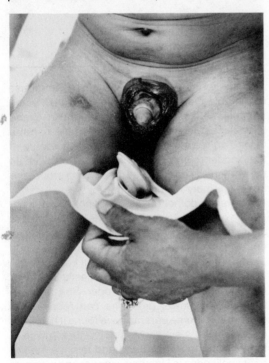

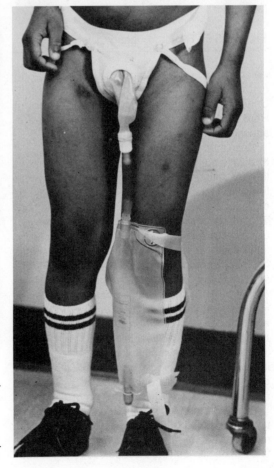

Figure 7–4. A condom.

Figure 7–5. External collection device with outlet at the bottom.

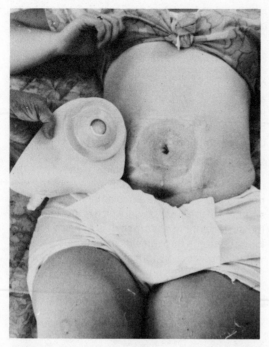

Figure 7–6. Result of urinary diversion.

and work in purses or in a small container. A patient may catheterize herself if she can stand or sit unassisted on a toilet. Catheterization procedure is carried out by inserting a small metal, glass, or rubber catheter into the bladder and draining urine every 2 to 4 hours. The child in Figure 7–7 *cannot* sit or stand alone. As a consequence, she will probably have to learn to catheterize herself from a reclined position.

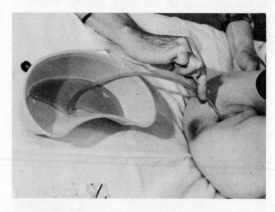

Figure 7–7. Intermittent catheterization.

waist level and sutured there. There may be one opening (unilateral) or two openings (bilateral). Urine is then discharged through the opening(s). Here again, an appliance to catch the urine is attached to the skin with adhesive.

One method of maintaining continence is through a *catheter,* or small rubber tube inserted through the urethra (hollow tube carrying urine from the bladder to the outside of the body) to drain urine from the bladder into a collection bag. These catheters can be changed by the individual or the caretaker. Both males and females can be fitted with catheters. Insertion of *indwelling* catheters should not be considered an automatic solution to loss of control (Bergstrom and Greendahl, 1968). The permanent presence of a catheter increases the likelihood of urinary infections and bladder stones. When a catheter is used, a high fluid intake is advisable for the person. Diluting the urine helps reduce the chance of urinary infection. Also, drinking cranberry juice is encouraged to help make the urine acidic, thereby reducing the possibility of infection or stones.

Another method of helping the female to maintain continence and keep bladder infections at a minimum is *intermittent catheterization*. Catheters can be carried very inconspicuously to school

Many females with partial urinary control use disposable diapers and protective pants. Some females with spina bifida are taught to Credé themselves. In this method, the whole hand is placed on the stomach on or above the dome of the bladder to give gentle pressure downward as the person sits on the toilet. This Credé procedure helps to empty residual urine.

If persons do not have urinary control, a major source of social discomfort is urine odor. The odor of the urine comes from bacterial growth. Alkaline urine generally has an odor. Acidic urine does not. Therefore keeping urine acidic will control odor. One drop of a deodorant on plastic pants or plaster casts helps eliminate odor. Specialists in bladder and bowel problems can recommend deodorants. Some parents have found it helpful to give the child a small glass of cranberry juice in the morning to acidify urine and to rinse his urinary appliances in Listerine, vinegar and water, or commercial cleanser deodorant. These children frequently take vitamin C daily to acidify urine.

Management of Bowel Problems

Since they have decreased sensation, many children with spina bifida and spinal cord injuries have not learned to recognize the signals that mean they need to go to the bathroom. The major objective of a bowel care plan then is to achieve planned defecation in order to avoid the embarrassment and inconvenience of involuntary evacuation. This calls for the establishment of a regular pattern of stimulation of peristalsis (wave-like muscular contractions that propel the contained matter along the alimentary canal) at the designated time.

Some individuals must have an ileostomy or a colostomy (Hamilton, 1974). Since an ostomy is a surgical opening in the abdomen through which waste is discharged, an *ileostomy* is an opening through the abdomen into the ileum, the terminal portion of the small intestine. The *colostomy* is an opening through the abdomen wall into the colon, the large intestine. Both discharge feces. Persons with an ileostomy or colostomy wear collection appliances. Teachers should be aware that these two ostomies require different types of appliances and care. A person with an ileostomy, for instance, may have difficulty after eating corn whereas a person with a colostomy may not. Physicians and parents can identify cautions related to individual children.

An important factor in bowel care planning is stool consistency. To achieve a stool which is fairly firm, such measures as timing, regulated diet, proper fluid intake, and laxatives can be used.

Another significant factor is regularity. Methods to facilitate bowel evacuation include manual removal, digital stimulation, and suppositories (Cheever and Elmer, 1975). To establish regularity, suppositories, laxatives, massage of the anal sphincter and enemas are used. Sometimes one or more of these measures is needed temporarily or permanently. Choice of these measures varies with the individual, the disability, and the physician.

Lowered skin sensation results in poor tissue nourishment. To prevent unnecessary irritation to the buttocks and area between the thighs, the areas should be cleaned with plain soap and water and patted dry at least twice a day. Exposing the perineum (area between the genitals and the rectum) to the air or to a heat lamp 15 or 20 minutes twice a day aids in preventing or eliminating irritation. (Some persons find that a hair dryer set on a cool setting works much faster!) A silicone pad placed under the buttocks is beneficial not only in preventing but also in healing pressure sores. A greaseless silicone cream can be used to prevent irritation. To avoid skin breakdown children should never sit in one position for long periods of time and every effort should be made to protect the skin from waste matter.

Ways to Help with Bathrooming

Persons who help with bathrooming of those children *without control* because of physiological reasons should be instructed in the special skin and apparatus care. This care is necessary to insure proper functioning and to prevent skin ulcerations. In case of emergency, they should know how to drain or temporarily stop a leak in a "leg bag" attached to a catheter or other collection device. Persons with catheters should be urged to have velcro or zippers inserted in their pants leg as demonstrated in the dressing section of this chapter. Zippers make the drainage of the leg bag easier. When transferring a person wearing a catheter, avoid any unnecessary pulling on the catheter. Pulling on the catheter can cause skin irritation which can lead to major complications. To help students *with control* to relax and void, adults may run water, give them something to drink, stroke the back of their necks or base of spines, or leave them alone in the bathroom for several minutes if they are safe by themselves. To simplify urination for males in wheelchairs, a portable metal or plastic urinal can be used. Most boys prefer to handle this task themselves, but advanced muscular dystrophy students may need assistance.

In some instances, lack of communication can be a source of frustration and anxiety. Children who cannot speak because of mental or physical disability may recognize the need to defecate or urinate but are unable to make it known in time. They need to be able to signal their needs by hitting a bell or making a sound or some other signal. Other children may not realize they are to indicate to someone that they have to "go to the bathroom." Some may eventually learn; others who are severely and profoundly disabled may never learn. Suggestions for toilet training are included in references in the chapter on such children.

Children's success in handling elimination problems may depend on how well parents, teachers, aides, nurses, and therapists work together. Everyone should be familiar with proper procedures and should know when and how much to help children. They should know where to obtain special equipment and how to care for the equipment. Children eventually should be trained to care for themselves if possible.

Transferring from Chair to Toilet

Three basic techniques are used to transfer from wheelchairs to commode: forward, sideways, and backward. Space limitations sometimes stipulate which transfers must be used. In a narrow bathroom, a forward transfer may be made by positioning the wheelchair facing the toilet with the front wheels against the base of the toilet, footrests up, feet on the floor with knees apart, brakes locked. A person then slides forward to sit on the toilet facing the back. To return, he slides backward, reaches back to take hold of both armrests and lifts his body into the seat.

Backward transfers may be made if the back of the wheelchair is detachable. The student should position the chair with the rear wheels against the toilet, brakes locked; he should then open back of wheelchair and slide backward onto the toilet seat. Legs remain on the wheelchair seat. To return, the individual slides forward.

For sideways transfer, teach the individual to position the wheelchair next to the toilet, lock brakes, remove the armrest on the side next to the toilet, place one hand on the toilet seat, the other hand on the wheelchair back and lift or swing his body onto seat. Reverse the order to get back into the wheelchair. A portable, raised toilet seat may be used if the toilet is too low for safe transfer.

Some disabilities stipulate precautions to take during transfers and toilet use. If a person has osteogenesis imperfecta, or brittle bones, special care must be taken in transfers. Transfers should be made very gently without jarring the individual. Special padding can be placed on the toilet seat. Constant attendance is usually recommended for the child who could easily injure himself. If the presence of people upsets him, a harness can be adapted to hold him on the toilet.

For individuals with cerebral palsy, relaxation is an important consideration in transferring. If a cerebral palsied child is wearing braces, it is sometimes more convenient to remove necessary clothing and lock the braces at the knees and perhaps the hips before the transfer. With an athetoid child, care has to be taken that uncoordinated movement does not cause the child to fall off the toilet. Each child must feel secure enough to relax. Again, constant attendance may be necessary or special chairs like the one in Figure 7–8 may be designed.

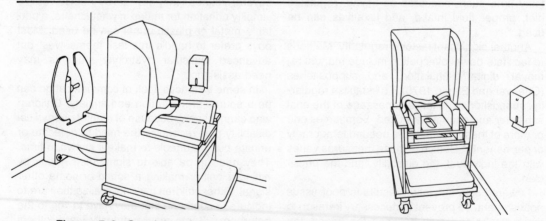

Figure 7–8. Special equipment provides physical security and privacy.

A majority of older students who are dependent upon help from others prefer to defecate at home. However, there will be times when students will have to defecate in school. If heavier students have to be transferred, two attendants or more usually are required. In the case of a student with advanced muscular dystrophy, a hydraulic lift is often used. When students have been lifted to the toilet or commode, they will have to be supported while the sling is removed and while they are sitting on the commode. This method takes a great deal of knowledge regarding management of physically weakened students. For home use, there is a special sling that has been designed with a hole in it. Students with advanced muscular dystrophy, however, may prefer using a bed pan when at home.

If children have use of upper extremities, they should learn to help themselves as much as possible. Special equipment such as hand rails have been designed to make the transfer safe and easy. They can learn to balance their weight on their feet and pivot themselves with their hands. Teachers should be familiar with all types of equipment and transfer techniques. They should particularly know ways to ask disabled persons for suggestions regarding appropriate help without embarrassing them. Most progress can occur when the teacher, student, and all others involved can communicate on this subject in an easy, relaxed manner.

Fostering Independence

Children often become overdependent upon parents and others who care for their bathrooming. In turn, parents become overprotective, thus hindering a child's chances of gaining individuality and independence. Persons should work together in planning a child's toilet training program in accord with his particular difficulties.

Toileting is a long series of skills that the individual needs to learn as one single task. The task begins when he feels the need to use the bathroom and ends when he dries his hands after washing them. To foster independence in this task we must teach each of the subskills of toileting and supply any equipment that enables the individual to complete these skills without help or with as little help as is necessary. The skills may not be necessarily learned in order, since some present more difficulty than others.

Dressing

Many options are available to help individuals dress themselves once their specific needs and abilities have been studied (Bare, Boettke and Waggoner, 1962; Lowman & Klinger, 1969; and May, Waggoner & Hotte, 1974). Specially designed garments that fit loosely can help camouflage a deformity and provide ease in dressing. If a person is confined to a wheelchair, the clothing can be fitted to the figure in a sitting position. For men, the trousers can be made a few inches longer to provide for the bend in the knees. Jackets can be made shorter to prevent bulking around the hips. Women's skirts are more comfortable if they are moderately full.

For some persons, front openings and easy fastenings facilitate dressing with a minimum amount of help. Roomy pockets set low in the garment provide secure places for commonly needed articles. Wrap-around garments, openings larger than usual, and tabs on the ends of zippers are all self-help features that simplify the task of dressing. These ideas and others are described further in this chapter and in the end-of-chapter references.

Self-Help in Dressing

Before clothing is purchased or made, the particular needs of each individual should be kept in mind: What will make dressing easier? What kinds of easy-to-fasten features are needed? What kinds of easy-to-adjust features are needed? What will help appearance? Will the clothes be comfortable? What kinds of clothes help prevent falling accidents? What kinds of clothing give protection for incontinence? Will the styles help to disguise a disability? Will the garments be easy to care for?

Mental readiness of disabled persons, their body balance, and their range of motion and strength often help determine if and how persons can be taught independence in dressing. For an indication of mental readiness, test whether the child can: 1) imitate a demonstration; 2) follow verbal directions; 3) relate clothing to appropriate part of the body, i.e., head into neck opening, arm into sleeve; and 4) keep clothes adjusted neatly on the body.

To determine if the child has adequate body balance for independent dressing, observe whether the child can:

1. sit alone in bed
2. lie on back or side, lie and lift body enough to pull on clothing
3. lean free from the back of a straight chair or wheelchair
4. sit alone on mat or stool
5. kneel with no help
6. stand, holding with one hand
7. stand with hands free while leaning
8. stand and use hands with no support

Information about motion and strength of individuals can be found by determining whether the child can:

1. grasp with one or both hands to pull on clothes and manipulate fastenings
2. place one or both hands to the back of neck, waist or feet
3. place both hands over top of head
4. manipulate fastenings

5. use strength to accomplish a task
6. use coordinated movements to accomplish a task

After this information is studied, individuals can be helped more readily to dress and undress.

Helping Disabled Persons Learn Self-Help in Dressing

To further help individuals learn self-help in dressing, follow these guidelines:

1. Analyze attempts in dressing tasks.
2. Provide assistance only when needed.
3. Teach individuals undressing skills prior to dressing skills.
4. Teach special techniques in dressing.
5. Teach what to wear and when.

Analyze Current Attempts

Care must be taken to observe individuals as they attempt particular dressing tasks and help only when necessary. Individuals should be encouraged to complete as much of the task as they are able. Observers should notice when a child faces a task that is difficult or impossible. Ellen, for example, had two physically involved arms and hands. She got stuck at the same point each time she took off her heavy winter coat with cuffs. She became discouraged and stopped trying. It was observed that, once she had slipped the coat or jacket off her shoulders with both arms still in the sleeves, she was unable then to free either elbow from the elbow of the sleeve. An observer noted that Ellen needed someone to push the armhole of the garment from the upper part of her arm to the lower part in order to free her elbow and allow her to pull the sleeve off. (See Figure 7–9.)

Attempts at dressing should be studied both at home and at school. Parents and teachers should notice the child's attempts to dress himself or help others dress him. Parents or teachers should analyze the different subtasks of dressing. Those helping the child at home and those helping in dressing activities during school activities should compare observations. A particular child may be able to undress himself at school when anticipating a swim or therapy. Sometimes, the same child is completely dependent on parental help at home; or the situation may be reversed. The parent may take time to insist that the child undress himself completely, whereas the teacher

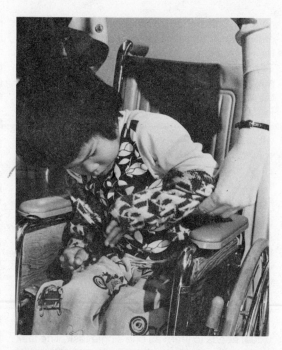

Figure 7–9. A little help at the elbow was all that was needed.

may feel rushed and provide assistance even when it is not needed.

At times it is not enough to know that the disabled individual can make the movements necessary to complete a dressing task. Teachers must notice other characteristics of the individual which influence his performance. The child may enjoy dependence and the attention gained from others. The individual may be unaware of what is expected. For instance, when he comes to school with a jacket on, he may not realize that his jacket should be taken off in the classroom. Perhaps the individual is not willing to ask for help or is unable to receive help graciously. Perhaps an individual does not show interest in learning new tasks. It is possible that the child has the motor skills for completing a task but is not able to plan the movements necessary for that particular task. And finally, an individual may not have had enough positive reinforcement when attempting new tasks, and, as a consequence, becomes easily frustrated and discouraged.

Provide Assistance Only When Needed

Sometimes disabled individuals are able to complete dressing tasks, but adults do not allow enough time for them to attempt the tasks. Individuals, therefore, do not try or become discouraged when they do because they are not allowed to complete the task by themselves. Some children are never given the opportunity to learn that they can complete some tasks unaided. This lack of awareness and experience frequently causes unnecessary dependence.

Undressing Skills

It is generally agreed that it is easier to take off clothing than it is to put clothing on. It is easier, for instance, for a child to pull a shoelace and untie a shoe than it is for the same individual to put a shoe on and tie the laces. Similarly, it is easier for most individuals to take off shorts and dresses than to put on the same garments. The task of removal of socks demonstrates steps of *un*dressing skills.

1. Cooperates passively when being undressed.
2. Moves limbs to aid in removal of clothing, holds out foot for shoe removal, pulls arm from last of sleeve, and withdraws foot from sock.
3. Pulls socks off over toes after adult removes sock to that point.
4. Pulls socks off over sole after socks are removed to that point.
5. Pulls socks off over heel after socks removed to that point.
6. Pulls socks off completely. (Adapted from Santa Cruz BCP Observation Chart, 1973, p. 10.)

When helping dress or undress a young child, hold him on your lap so that your arms are coming around the child's body in the same direction as his arms so that he will imitate your movements and learn to perform the same skills by copying the way you do it.

Teach Special Techniques in Dressing

Many techniques and special appliances are available to help disabled individuals learn dressing skills. For example, flipping a coat over one's head is a technique which is often used by children with either coordination or weakness problems. A child lays the garment flat on his lap, on the floor, or on a table. The collar should be near his body with the front of the coat on top and the lining showing. The child can then either push both arms into the sleeve, or push in the involved arm first and the lead arm second. (See Figure 7–10, p. 150.) Ducking the head forward while raising extended arms over the head is next. Finally the coat is slipped into place when the child

shrugs his shoulders and pulls down with the arms.

Special tools and buttons for moving buttons through the holes should be used whenever necessary and helpful. Other techniques are described in the resources section at the end of this chapter.

Teach What to Wear and When

While working with a child on dressing, the teacher should begin by teaching the child to become aware of appropriate ways to dress for different types of weather and different activities. These learning sessions can easily become a part of the daily curriculum. For example, a weather chart can be placed in the classroom with pictures pasted on the chart to represent different types of weather. This chart can be used for discussion of what, for example, they should wear on a rainy day. Oak tagboard serves as a good study chart on which to paste different cutouts of people. Children can dress the cutouts. Teachers should also help children become aware of suitable color combinations. Discussions between parents and child about appropriate selection of clothing are also helpful.

Clothing Features

Ideas from several sources (Bare, Boettke, & Waggoner, 1962; Loman & Klinger, 1969; and May, Waggoner & Hotte, 1974) are chosen for inclusion here because of their general applicability regardless of styles of the day. We will discuss:

1. beginning dressers
2. individuals with coordination problems and limited use of hands
3. individuals with braces
4. crutch users
5. wheelchair users
6. individuals with figure irregularities
7. individuals with prosthetic arms

Beginning Dressers

Full-length, center-front openings like those found on overalls, jumpsuits, some dresses, jumpers, shirts, blouses and pantsuit tops are helpful to persons just learning to dress themselves. Expandable neck openings of stretchable fabrics are also helpful.

Often fastenings either cause inconvenience or prevent independence of disabled persons. Type, size, and location of fasteners on the garment

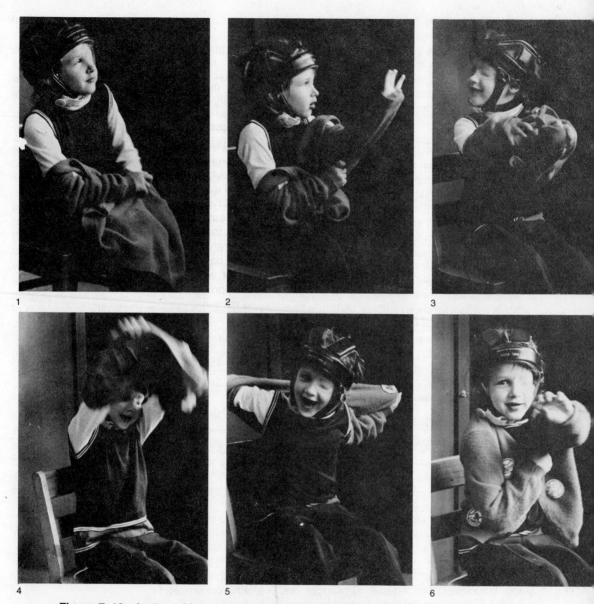

1   2   3

4   5   6

Figure 7–10. Analyze this process and teach it to someone for whom it will be helpful. (Sequence starts top, moves left to right.)

determine how easily they can be managed. *Zippers* are easy to pull up or down. Large zipper tabs are easy to grasp and may be made of a fabric loop or metal ring. Nylon coil zippers are pliable and less likely to snag. *Buttons* must be large enough to grasp and should not be sewn on tightly. A flat, smooth button slips through a buttonhole more easily than a fancy one. *Velcro*, a type of fastener material, requires a minimum amount of hand and finger dexterity to open or close. Velcro is two strips of nylon with rough surfaces that stick together. One side of the tape is made of tiny nylon hooks and the other side has a looped surface. When the two strips come in contact with one another, they lock and hold fast. They unlock by pulling the strips apart. *Hooks and eyes* are difficult to fasten unless they are large and sturdy. The type of metal hook and bar used on men's trousers is more manageable on skirts and slacks for those with hand limitations. *Grippers* are usually easier to unfasten than they are to fasten. They require considerable pressure to close. The location of fasteners has a great deal to do with ease in dressing. They should be easy to see, easy to reach, and easy to grasp. When located in the center front, they are usually easier to manipulate than on the side or back of the garment.

Because of the inconvenience of some fasteners, look for certain kinds of garments. Select boxer-style trousers or slacks with no fasteners, or boxer-style trousers with zipper fly and elasticized back waist. Knitted separates with elasticized waistbands and rib-knit expandable neck ties avoid the need for fasteners.

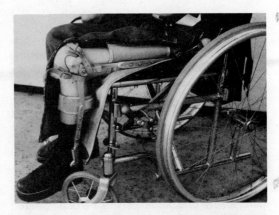

Figure 7–11. Dark strips of velcro down the side of trousers permit ease in dressing when braces are worn.

Coordination Problems and Limited Use of Hands

Most features helpful to persons learning to dress themselves are also recommended for persons with uncoordinated or insufficient hand use. Velcro is particularly helpful on openings in blouse and shirt fronts, jackets, fly fronts, skirt waists, and cuffs of long sleeves. If side openings are used, they should be on the side opposite a person's stronger hand.

Shur-lok, snap locks and zipper fasteners on shoes are much easier to manage than are laces. Velcro can replace buckles on shoes.

Individuals with Braces

Full-length crotch openings are helpful for some persons in braces, particularly for children who need to have diapers changed. The inseam is opened and Velcro or a zipper is inserted.

Wide pant legs are more comfortable for persons in braces. If trousers or slacks are too narrow to slip over braces, inseams of trouser legs can be replaced by a zipper or Velcro strips. (See Figure 7–11.)

Elastic bands on skirts, trousers or slacks add flexibility needed to accommodate braces. Knitted fabrics tend to catch on brace locks.

Undergarments should be selected either to fit snugly if fitted under braces or large enough to allow room for braces if worn over braces. Underwear which is reinforced in areas where braces may rub should be selected.

Crutch Users

Persons who use full-length crutches need garments which will not tear along underarm seams. Garments with double-stitched underarm seams are more durable. Certain fabrics, such as stretch-woven fabrics, tolerate more abuse than others. Reinforcements can always be inserted before using a garment. Garments should be chosen so underarm crutches fit comfortably under the arms without changing the lines of the clothing.

If Canadian or Loftstand crutches are used, coats which allow the crutches to fit over the sleeves should be selected.

Wheelchair Users

Pantsuits are popular selections for girls and women who use wheelchairs. Culottes also allow ample room for body movement and allow transfer to and from a wheelchair without embarrassment of exposure. Slim, straight skirts tend to ride up and full skirts tend either to bunch up as a person sits or get caught in the wheels. Wrap-around skirts are easy to put on and facilitate toileting. Skirts with some flare permit both wrinkle-free sitting and room for movement.

Long sleeves often get dirty when worn by wheelchair users. Therefore, short sleeves are commonly desired. Heavy belts in strong loops of trousers allow helpers to lift and support persons who cannot support themselves.

Individuals with Figure Irregularities

Overblouses and shirts designed to be worn outside help disguise figure irregularities. Balancing of hemlines helps disguise poor postures. Dress hemlines can be adjusted so they are balanced in spite of postural or other figure irregularities. Hemline imbalance with irregularities of the upper part of the body can be avoided by choosing two-piece dresses.

Individuals with Prosthetic Arms

Long-sleeve dresses and shirts are often desired by individuals with prosthetic arms.

Managing a Home

Increased self-respect frequently derives from being able to assume some responsibility for household tasks. The eventual goal may not be total independence but a greater degree of independence.

"Planning ahead" should be the motto for disabled persons who attempt household tasks. Many cannot carry out household tasks without substantial preplanning. For instance, menus must be planned well ahead. Individuals must learn what they are able to cook themselves and how to prepare a well-balanced meal. They should consider what they have on their shelves and what they need to purchase. They need to know where to go to buy food and how they will travel there. They need to consider the availability of various foods, particularly foods in season. They need to consider the value of their money and their purchasing power. They need to consider the time required to cook a specific food and the time that the foods will remain fresh. Finally, they need to plan the exact steps they will take to complete the meal. Will they need to allow extra time to cut the vegetables with one hand? Will they need any special appliances or any adaptions to expedite the task? It is important to realize that many disabled persons *can* do all the planning, though some may need help carrying out the plan.

This section will concentrate upon housecleaning and kitchen tasks since they often present the largest problems. Figure 7–12 clearly illustrates

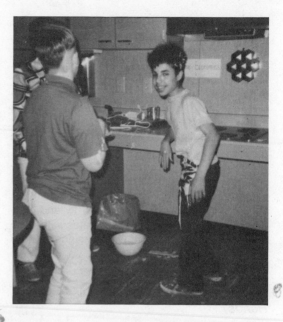

Figure 7–12. The beaters went wild!

one problem faced by two youngsters who were trying to make upside down cake!

Accomplishing Housecleaning

It is unrealistic to expect the person with extensive paralysis, limited energy, or severe coordination difficulty to do major housecleaning. Much energy is expended by a disabled person simply lifting body weight, using crutches, walking with braces, or propelling a wheelchair. Some persons, however, can find ways to do many household tasks. Homes adapted or designed to be barrier-free reduce inconvenience caused by the combination of a disability and a home full of physical barriers (Laurie & Laurie, 1976).

Heavy jobs can be scattered throughout the week rather than being undertaken all in one day. Long and complex tasks can be divided over several days so that work on each day will be as varied and interesting as possible. There will generally be some housekeeping tasks which disabled individuals will be unable to do.

Some tasks they will accomplish but only with extreme difficulty. Disabled persons should be able to ask others to help or assume leadership in establishing agreement among persons in the household about who will do what. This strategy will relieve anxiety of others regarding the appropriate kind and amount of intervention. A list of homemaking jobs which can be performed by disabled persons might include dusting, sweeping with a lightweight or electric broom, use of a canister vacuum cleaner that swivels easily in all directions, and use of various home-made and commercial reachers. Long-handled devices which extend a person's reach are very helpful tools. Long-handled brushes or sponges are helpful for bathtubs and sinks. "Home-made," custom-designed tools often are the most useful.

Shopping

Certain procedures are necessary whether shopping in the grocery, department store, pharmacy, or other kinds of stores. A first consideration is transportation to and from the store; the next consideration in importance would be recognition of architectural barriers enroute and within the store. Once in the store, the floorplan should be studied so that the person can go to desired areas with the least amount of unnecessary movement.

Problems involved in finding merchandise, reaching for it, carrying it, and finally paying for it should be anticipated.

Transportation

Sometimes we forget that walking or making the entire trip in a wheelchair are options if weather permits. For those persons living near shopping centers, these may be the most reliable means available. When these options are used, architectural barriers along the way and ways of carrying the merchandise once it has been purchased must be considered. Discussion of transportation is included in other sections of this book.

Anticipating Architectural Barriers

Shopping can be an adventure for those in wheelchairs willing to venture into different kinds of stores. Check by phone about any possible barriers before arriving at unfamiliar stores. Shop at slow times, if possible, since people milling around become barriers to disabled shoppers.

Each individual will have special kinds of problems depending on whether the individual uses crutches, canes, a walker, or a wheelchair.

Doors are a primary group of architectural barriers for disabled shoppers. Are the doors wide enough? Are they automatic or manually operated doors? Does one have to push or pull? Are there handles, door knobs, lever handles, or nothing to grab? Does it swing only one way or both? Does it swing freely, is it on a spring, or is it pressurized?

Turnstiles are another set of obstacles often found in grocery stores. These obstacles are impossible to overcome in a wheelchair and are very awkward for those with crutches. One should ask if there are other places for customer entrance.

Aisles should be checked. Are they wide enough? Do they take you to all parts of the store? Do the aisles connect smoothly or are they a maze? Are there racks or displays which project? Is merchandise stacked in the aisles in places where it can be knocked over easily? Shelves and counters often present problems. Can persons in wheelchairs see and reach the merchandise? Are some shelves so high that it is impossible to reach the items? Are the items stacked too high on shelves? Are the meat counters and deep-freezer sections too deep? Is the aisle leading to the checkout counter wide enough for someone in a wheelchair?

Before disabled individuals can begin to shop, they must plan. They need to decide how to shop. Persons may find it more efficient to go to certain sections of the store while continuously scanning the shopping list to see if any items they pass are on the list. If the person shops item-by-item from the list, he may "run" all over the store and may even retrace his steps. A disabled person should be encouraged to shop at the same stores and to be familiar with how the merchandise is categorized

Shoppers often need to use restrooms in the various stores. For persons with a physical disability, this need can be a nightmare. These persons need to learn how to use public restrooms. They may have to make adjustments such as making the wheelchair narrower while sitting in it when it is difficult for them to get into the restroom. They may have to ask strangers for assistance. Disabled shoppers may find problems at the door to the rest room. Is it wide enough for wheelchairs?

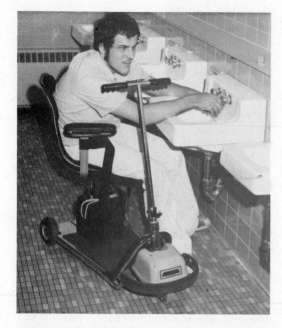

Figure 7–13. This logo tells disabled persons: Barrier free.

(Many wheelchairs are at least 28″ wide.) Does the door have to be pulled or pushed? (Pulling can be difficult for a person on crutches.) Does the door have handles, door knobs or a push plate? (Door knobs require superior fine motor control.) Is there a spring on the door causing it to close too rapidly for the person to pass through safely?

Similar kinds of questions can be raised about entrance hallways and passageways. Are there series of doors? Are the distances between the doors adequate for wheelchairs? Are the doors equipped with time delay or self-closing devices? Can the person in a wheelchair locate an empty stall once inside the restroom area, get to the stall, and maneuver to a toilet? Is one toilet free standing or are all in stalls? Are there privacy screens? Are there handrails in helpful places? Does the door to the stall provide clearance? Hopefully disabled shoppers and other citizens will encourage businessmen to place the barrier-free logo on the front of the store so that disabled persons will know that restrooms are accessible. (See Figure 7–13.)

Finding Merchandise

From early childhood, persons should be taught categorizations and groupings of merchandise. Whenever possible, parents should take children to stores with them and point out ways that store merchandise is grouped. Some groupings are

more obvious than others. At times, it may be necessary to teach individuals certain definitions that describe groupings. *Dairy,* for instance, is a word that is not self-descriptive. Dairy is the place one finds items such as milk, cream, and eggs. Shoppers who can read should be taught how to use the signs above aisles in grocery stores, store directories, and signs on counters in department stores. Knowing how merchandise is grouped, the location of groupings in a store, and the floor plan of the store will conserve time and effort for disabled shoppers.

Selecting Merchandise

Persons who cannot read need to know ways of finding items in the stores. Meat and cheese are easy to find in grocery stores because shoppers are able to see the product through glass on display cases or through plastic wrap on individual packages. Items in cans, such as vegetables and fruits, often have pictures on the labels. Shoppers can associate pictures with products. Items in cartons such as cottage cheese and yogurt may be difficult to identify since they lack picture representation on the outside of the carton. Nonreaders need to be taught which kinds of foods are found in which kinds of containers in which sections of stores.

Even though shoppers can identify items they wish to purchase, they may have difficulty reaching the items. They may wish to employ a neighborhood child as a "basket pusher and can reacher." In department stores, clerks can be asked to hold the merchandise so it can be seen.

Carrying Merchandise

In grocery stores, wheelchair occupants might use baskets placed on their laps for light articles. A low shopping cart on rubber swivel casters can be pulled easily by a wheelchair shopper. For a person who has difficulty walking, large shoulder bags are sometimes helpful. The shoulder bag shifts the weight from the hands and arms and distributes the weight over the trunk and shoulders. Shoulder bags are also useful for persons on canes or crutches since the bag allows the hands to be free to manipulate the canes and crutches. Wheelchair shoppers may prefer to have a large cloth bag attached to the back of the wheelchair.

Paying for Merchandise

Shoppers must be able to determine the price of items and the amount of merchandise their money will buy. Games such as Count Your Change (Milton Bradley) and Pay the Cashier (Dolch) and classroom lessons will provide practice in buying items and handling money. Shoppers often must keep track of purchases as they proceed to make sure they have enough money. The minicalculator is a helpful device. Students can practice in the classroom for problems anticipated in actually shopping. (See Figure 7–14.)

For a person with trouble in hand control or weakness problems, the calculator can be adapted to fit on the wrist like a watch or carried on a tray or lap.

Shoppers who are unsure of value of coins can learn to compensate for their lack of knowledge by paying with dollar bills only. They can be taught to read the number of dollars posted or registered and not worry about the number of cents on a given total. They then would learn to count out and give cashiers *one more* dollar than the number of dollars on a price placard or on the register. (See Figure 7–15, p. 156.) In this manner confidence is gained by the shopper because it never becomes obvious he does not know the collective value of coins.

Home-based Shopping Procedures

It is entirely possible for some disabled individuals to shop from their homes. Small local grocers often provide delivery service. Department stores

Figure 7–14. Calculators can contribute to increased independence in finances.

also provide delivery services for merchandise. Department stores, specialty stores, and mail-order companies encourage ordering by catalog. As a matter of fact, *Mail Order USA* is a consumer's guide that names 1,500 top mail-order catalogs in the USA and Canada. It evolved from a demand for alternative shopping sources by persons in rural areas, overseas, and the handicapped. *Mail Order USA* lists a variety of merchandise, including clothes for hard-to-fit people, crafts, and unusual gifts. Through such a guide, the homebound individual can obtain various catalogs and compare prices and variety. He can expand his purchasing ability by being able to "shop around." Shopping by telephone is a further alternative for some persons.

Kitchen Activities

Persons with severe coordination problems, weakness, or who use crutches or a wheelchair, may wish to use unbreakable dishes. (See Figure

Figure 7–15. The sign says *one dollar* plus some cents. The boy knows that *two dollars* will probably be sufficient.

Figure 7–16. We must find materials and procedures that encourage independence and responsibility from early ages.

7–16.) Sinks can be made shallow by placing a platform inside for easier use by persons in wheelchairs. Dishes and dishpans placed on the platform enables the person to reach items in the bottom of a dishpan or sink from a wheelchair. A front opening dishwasher makes accessibility easier for a wheelchair user provided there is sufficient space to position the wheelchair near the open door. Pullout cupboard shelves are desirable for reaching dishes, bowls, and pots. A broom closet may be converted into an easy-reach pantry.

Cooking must be done safely as well as efficiently. If stove burners are at the eye level of the wheelchair user, a mirror may be hung behind the burners with a forward tilt to permit viewing pot interiors. Knobs must be located safely. For instance, knobs should be placed on the front of the stove to prevent injury when reaching over burners. If a stove is unsuitable, cooking can be done with immersible fry pans, electric coffee pots, and table top broilers. All of these appliances can be placed on low counters or tables. Individuals lacking accurate sensation of hot or cold must protect all exposed parts of the body with padding. Aprons made with two layers of crib pads, or wheelchair lapboards can be used if hot pans are to be carried on the lap of a wheelchair user.

Selection of Menu

Menu selections may be limited somewhat if disabled cooks have limited reading ability and difficulty remembering recipes. Teachers and parents should begin teaching young disabled children how to cook so that they have acquired sufficient cooking skill by the time they wish to be independent. Several authors suggest ways that cooking can be taught. Ruth Friedman (1972) wrote a cookbook titled, *I Ate the Whole Thing*. Recipes were created so that even very young children could make their own portions. Children do not have to wait their turn to stir a pot or to wait until they can break an egg and contribute to a one recipe batch. Rather, they are able to measure their own ingredients and create their own dish. Steed (1974), Denslow (1972), and Yates (1972), have designed books for individuals with minimal reading skills. These books are also helpful for bilingual children. Disabled adults will want to obtain a very comprehensive manual designed and compiled by Klinger, Frieden, and Sullivan (1970) at the Institute of Rehabilitation Medicine, New York University Medical School. In addition to a comprehensive manual on equipment, this book includes sample menus and recipes.

Space, Storage, and Counters

Ample space is very important for wheelchair users. They should be able to maneuver their wheelchairs with ease within the kitchen. Persons who have trouble standing and walking may prefer to have a smaller floor space with items in easy reach.

Adequate storage of equipment and supplies may require a great deal of preplanning. It is generally recommended that equipment and supplies be placed at "point of first use." Cooking utensils should be stored near the stove. Baking utensils will be stored near the place where baking takes place. Items used frequently can be reached most easily if they are hung on the front of cupboards. Pegboards are handy for hanging utensils.

Ample counterspace is important to any cook. Disabled cooks particularly appreciate counter space which enables them to slide pans and other items instead of lifting. Persons in wheelchairs prefer counters low enough so they can rest their elbows and deep so that their legs can fit underneath. Counters should be designed so that wheelchair users can bring themselves close to the work area.

Utensils

Nearly every utensil a disabled cook needs is available commercially. The disabled person must only anticipate desired features of utensils before shopping. Funnels help prevent spilling when hand use is weak or unsteady. Large spoons with holes prevents spilling overflow of liquid while serving. Wedge-type jar openers prevent needless turning and twisting of jar lids. Screw-handled pans facilitate steadiness. Heavy pots and pans help counteract excess motion.

Special needs that cannot be met by commercial utensils and equipment can often be accommodated with simple home-made adaptions. Accidents like the one mentioned earlier in this chapter (see Figure 7–12) can be prevented with design and use of homemade adaptions (see Figure 7–17).

Two nails protruding from a board, for instance, can be used to keep food items from turning and rolling while they are being cut or sliced. A potato can be impaled on the two nails and managed easily by persons with weak or uncoordinated movements. Klinger, Frieden, and Sullivan (1970) demonstrate many home-made adaptions which streamline tedious jobs.

Figure 7–17. The beaters that "went wild" are now confined.

Appliances

Appliances are made with many different designs and weights. Electric appliances which have a plug to be pushed down into the socket are better for those for whom weakness is a problem. Some electric appliances, such as electric skillets, are heavier than others. Extra weight helps reduce excessive motion. Lightweight appliances may be preferred for those persons with weakness problems. An important feature in electrical appliances is the location and size of knobs and controls. It is often important to select electrical appliances on which knobs and controls are located away from the heated areas. If knobs are not long enough, they can be extended so that the person can operate them more easily.

Summary

Increased independence in self-care is a goal for every person with a physical disability. Eating, bathrooming, dressing, and managing a home are only a portion of those self-care tasks to be taught from early childhood. Persons with special problems can be taught to analyze their own problems and initiate some possible solutions. They may try shortcuts or special procedures. They may research available commercial aids which they can use to help themselves. They may make or design special tools and they may even find a helpful use for tools designed for purposes completely unrelated to rehabilitation! (See figures 7–18 and 7–19)

Figures 7–18, 7–19.

References

Eating

Bowman, M., Calkin, A., & Grant, P. *Eating with a spoon: How to teach your multi-handicapped child* (Rev. ed.). Columbus, Ohio: Ohio State University Press, 1975.

Finnie, N. R. *Handling the young cerebral palsied child at home.* New York: E.P. Dutton, 1975.

Friedmann, L. Bilateral upper extremity amputee sandwich holder. *The American Journal of Occupational Therapy,* 1974, *28*(6), 358.

Larson, C. B., & Gould, M. *Orthopedic nursing* (8th ed.). St. Louis: C.B. Mosley, 1974.

Lowman, E., & Klinger, J. L. *Self-help for the handicapped: Aids to independent living.* Institute of Rehabilitation Medicine, New York University Medical Center. New York: McGraw-Hill, 1969.

Mueller, H. Feeding. In N. Finnie, *Handling the young cerebral palsied child at home* (2nd ed.). New York: E. P. Dutton, 1975.

Mueller, H. A. Facilitation feeding and pre-speech. In P. Pearson & C. Williams (Eds.), *Physical therapy services in the developmental disabilities.* Springfield, Ill.: Charles C Thomas, 1972.

Robinault, I. (Ed.). *Functional aids for the multiply handicapped.* New York: Harper & Row, 1973.

Rosenberg, C. *Assistive devices for the handicapped.* American Rehabilitation Foundation (Minneapolis). Atlanta, Ga.: Stein Printing, 1968.

Souza, C. M. Meat cutting wheel for one-handed patients. *The American Journal of Occupational Therapy,* 1968, *22*(3), 211.

Toileting

Alter, V. Ostomy. *The Independent,* 1976, *3*(2), 11.

Bergstrom, D., & Grendahl, B. *Care of patients with bowel and bladder problems: A nursing guide.* Rehabilitation Publication No. 714. Minneapolis, Minn.: American Rehabilitation Foundation, 1968.

Cheever, R. C., & Elmer, C. D. (Eds.). *Bowel management programs: A manual of ideas and techniques.* Bloomington, Ill.: Accent Special Publications, Accent on Living, Inc. ,1975. (Available from P.O. Box 700, 61701.)

Forrest, D. Management of bladder and bowel in spina bifida. In G. Brocklehurst (Ed.), *Spina bifida for the clinician: Developmental medicine and child neurology.* Sup. No. 57. Philadelphia: J. B. Lippincott, 1976.

Hamilton, S. My child has an ostomy. Pamphlet, 1974. Los Angeles: United Ostomy Association, Inc. (Available from 1111 Wilshire Boulevard, Los Angeles, Calif. 90017.)

Hill, M., Shurtleff, D., Chapman, W., & Ansell, J. The myelodysplastic child: Bowel and bladder control. *American Journal of Nursing,* 1969, *69*(3), 545–550.

Ostomy Educational Folder. Largo, Florida 33540: Division of Howmedia, Inc., n.d.

Swinyard, C. A. *The child with spina bifida.* New York: Association for the Aid of Crippled Children, 1971.

Dressing

Bare, C., Boettke, E., & Waggoner, N. *Self-help clothing for handicapped children.* Chicago: National Society for Crippled Children and Adults, 1962.

Be O K self-help aids. Brookfield, Ill.: Fred Sammons, 1975.

Lowman, E., & Klinger, J. L. *Self-help for the handicapped: Aids to independent living.* Institute of Rehabilitation Medicine, New York University Medical Center. New York: McGraw-Hill, 1969.

May, E. E., Waggoner, N. R., & Hotte, E. B. *Independent living for the handicapped and the elderly*. Boston: Houghton Mifflin, 1974.

Santa Cruz BCP observation chart: Special education management system project document. (ESEA Title III Project #1328). Santa Cruz, Ca.: Santa Cruz County Office of Education, 1973.

Managing a Home

Denslow, E. *Happiness is good eating*. Mt. Pleasant, Mich.: Enterprise Printers, 1972.

Foott, S., Lane, M., & Mara, J. *Kitchen sense for disabled and elderly people*. London: Disabled Living Foundation, 1975.

Friedman, R. *I ate the whole thing*. Berkeley, Ca.: Author, 1973.

Gentil, Eric A. *A layperson's guide on building evaluation*. Lansing, Michigan: Office of Special Programs, Environmental Studies. Michigan State University, 1975.

Hossack, J. R. Home management for the disabled. *The American Journal of Occupational Therapy*, 1956, *10*(4), 143–46, 174.

Klinger, J. L., Frieden, F., & Sullivan, R. *Mealtime manual for the aged and handicapped*. New York: Simon and Schuster, 1970.

Lowman, E., & Klinger, J. L. *Self-help for the handicapped—Aids to independent living*. Institute of Rehabilitation Medicine, New York University Medical Center. New York: McGraw-Hill, 1969.

Laurie, G., & Laurie, J. *Housing and home services for the disabled*. New York: Harper & Row, 1976.

Mail order USA. P. O. Box 19083 Washington, D.C. 20036.

Rusk, H. A. Nutrition in the fourth place of medical care. *Nutrition Today*, Autumn 1970, pp. 24–31.

Steed, F. *A special picture cookbook*. Lawrence, Kans.: H & H Enterprises, 1974.

Yates, J. J. *Look and cook*. Seattle, Wash.: Special Child Publications, 1972.

Resources

Comprehensive

Connor, F. P., Williamson, G. G., & Siepp, J. M. (Eds.). *A program guide for infants and toddlers with neuromotor and other developmental disorders*. New York: Teachers College Press, 1976.

Ford, J. R., & Duckworth, B. *Physical management for the quadraplegic patient*. Philadelphia: F.A. Davis, 1974.

Galbreaith, P. *What you can do for yourself*. New York: Drake Publications, 1974.

Klinger, J. L. *Self-help manual for arthritis patients*. New York: The Arthritis Foundation (1212 Avenue of the Americas, 10036), 1974.

Project MORE Daily Living Skills Programs. *How to do MORE: A manual of basic teaching strategy*. Bellevue, Wash.: Edmark Associates, 1972–1975.

Washam, V. *The one-hander's book: A basic guide to activities of daily living*. New York: John Day, 1973.

Eating

Gratke, J. M. *Help them help themselves*. Dallas, Texas: Texas Society for Crippled Children, 1947.

Holser-Buehler, P. The Blanchard method of feeding the cerebral palsied. *The American Journal of Occupational Therapy*, 1966, *20*(1), 31–34.

National Foundation for Infantile Paralysis. *Self-help devices for rehabilitation*. Dubuque, Iowa: William C. Brown, 1975.

Rusk H., & Taylor, E. *Living with a disability*. Garden City, N.Y.: Blakiston, 1953.

Verhaaren, P. Nutritional needs of children with cerebral palsy: A review of literature. *Division of Physically Handicapped, Homebound, and Hospitalized Journal*, 1976, *2*(1), 6–10.

Toileting

Kamenetz, H. L. *The wheelchair book*. Springfield, Ill.: Charles C Thomas, 1969.
This book gives complete descriptions of all wheelchairs made, plus many other kinds of equipment and transfer techniques.

Kira, A. *The bathroom: Criteria for design*. Ithaca, N.Y.: Center for Housing and Environmental Studies, Cornell University, 1966.
This book gives many floor plans and ideas for convenient bathrooms for the disabled.

Lowman, E., & Klinger, J. L. *Aids to independent living: Self-help for the handicapped*. New York: McGraw-Hill, 1969.
This book gives many illustrations of adapted equipment.

Robinault, I. (Ed.). *Functional aids for the multiply handicapped*. New York: Harper & Row, 1973.

Rosenberg, C. *Assistive devices for the handicapped*. Minneapolis, Minn.: American Rehabilitation Foundation, 1968.
This book gives descriptions and instructions on adapting objects for the disabled.

Dressing

Cloth Research Development Foundation, One Rockefeller Plaza, Suite 1912, New York, N.Y. 10020. Information about Levi Strauss jeans adapted for handicapped and sources of other adapted clothes.

College university departments of home economics students may be interested in researching topics suggested to them, i.e., "Clothing for the Physically Handicapped."

Cookman, H., & Zimmerman, M. E. *Functional fashions for the physically handicapped*. New York: Institute of Physical Medicine and Rehabilitation, New York University Medical Center, 1961. (Pamphlet.)

Danzig, A. L. *Handbook for one handers.* New York: Federation of the Handicapped, 1957. (Pamphlet.)

Dressing techniques for the cerebral palsied child. *The American Journal of Occupational Therapy,* Jan.–Feb. 1954, *8*(1), Part I, 8–10; 37–38. Also March–April 1954, *8*(2), Part 2, 48–51; 69–70.

Fashion Able, Rocky Hill, New Jersey 08553.
Source of self-help items for independent living and easy on, easy off clothing.

Jay, P. E., et al. *Help yourselves: A handbook for hemiplegics and their families.* London: British Council for Rehabilitation of the Disabled, 1966.

Muscular Dystrophy Association of America. *Around the clock aids for the child with muscular dystrophy.* Pamphlet, n. d. New York: Muscular Dystrophy Association. (Available from 1970 Broadway, New York, N.Y.)

Shriner, M. *Growing up—Cerebral palsied children learn to help themselves.* Chicago: National Society for Crippled Children and Adults, 1961. (Pamphlet.)

A step by step guide to personal management for blind persons. New York: American Foundation for the Blind, Inc. (Available from 15 W. 16th Street.)
Helpful hints and explicit instructions on everything from hygiene to social graces.

Managing a Home

Gifford, L. *If you can't STAND to cook: Easy-to-fix recipes for the handicapped homemaker.* Grand Rapids, Mich.: Zondervan, 1973.

Gladestone, B. *New York Times complete manual of home repair.* New York: Macmillan, 1972.

Lawson, G. Everyday business. Newspaper reading. Sacramento, Ca.: Cal-Central Press, 1958. (Student workbooks.)

May, E. E., Waggoner, N. R., & Boethke, E. M. *Homemaking for the handicapped.* New York: Dodd, Mead, 1966.

Porter, J. P. (Ed.). *How things work in your home (and what to do when they don't).* New York: Time-Life Books, 1975.

Singerie, A. *How to fix it: An illustrated step-by-step guide to home repairs for the woman who wants to fix it now.* Garden City, N.Y.: Doubleday, 1974.

A step by step guide to personal mangement for blind persons. New York: American Foundation for the Blind, Inc., 1974. (Available from 15 W. 16th St.)

8

EDUCATION OF THE SEVERELY AND PROFOUNDLY HANDICAPPED

One of the more significant changes which has occurred in our society during the past half century is our response to the needs and problems of severely and profoundly handicapped children. The interests and welfare of these children and their families had been grossly ignored until recently. In few other instances have we witnessed such dramatic changes in attitudes; the handicapped have moved from a disenfranchised status to one of recognition and concern, if not total acceptance. From the institutional-custodial emphases during the first half of the century and from the closets and back rooms of homes across the country, we have gradually seen emerge a population of human beings who are finally being recognized as having all the rights and privileges

Robert Bradfield, *Ph.D., is a professor of special education at San Francisco State University, San Francisco, California.*

Jane Heifetz *is a coordinator of programs for the severely handicapped in the Department of Special Education, Government of American Samoa, Pago Pago, Samoa.*

which most of us in our society take for granted. Although there are still many thousands of "closet children" whose needs are unknown and unmet, and although great and frightening discrepancies in service still exist between geographical areas, a quiet revolution is in progress. Previously ignored as citizens, these children finally attain their rights to full and appropriate educational programs and services.

It is in education in particular that this change can be clearly documented. First there was the gradual and often reluctant acceptance of responsibility by state legislatures and boards of education for the provision of educational programs for more severely handicapped individuals. By 1975, all Americans between 3 and 21 years of age had obtained equal rights to an education. Out of the pioneer work of individuals such as Edgar Doll and Sidney Bijou and into the current work of Haring at the University of Washington, Lindsley in Kansas, Sailor first in Kansas and then in California, Brown in Wisconsin, and many others, we can follow the unfolding of an educational philosophy in which behavioral assessment, developmental change, and educatonal programming are intertwined into what may

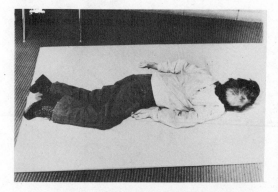

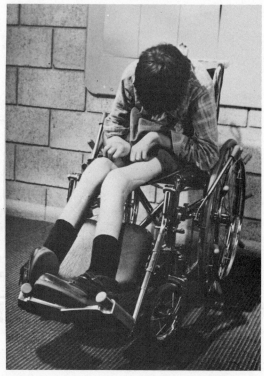

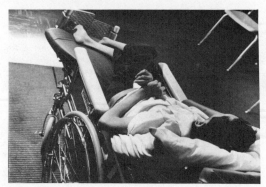

These children now have a right to an education . . .

eventually prove to be a model for all education. This includes such elements as (a) the recognition of the need for careful and precise sequencing of the most minute steps required for a change in behavior; (b) the development of continuous monitoring systems for assessment of that change; (c) respect for the complete uniqueness of each individual involved; and (d) the need of humans for highly unique stimuli and highly unique consequences. All of these elements are part of a rapidly developing educational philosophy where failure is the fault of the system rather than the child.

Assess

If ever a population of children were inappropriate for traditional types of measuring instruments common to educational practice, it is the severely and profoundly handicapped. Norm-referenced measurement is of little or no value in helping us improve the educational process for these children. Though developmental sequences are an extremely important part of the assessment process and provide a hierarchical arrangement of

skills to be learned, traditional measures of intelligence or performance which compare these chil-

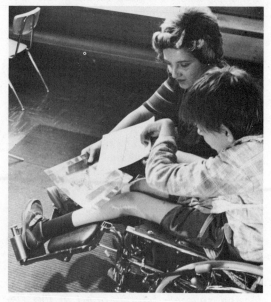

. . . and a chance to demonstrate they can learn.

dren to some mythical mean do little to enhance either assessment or the educational process. In fact, norm-referenced instruments may produce a negative effect as a result of the comparison process. The multiple impairments which characterize profoundly handicapped children make the use of instruments normed on populations without those impairments totally inappropriate. The most valid assessment data is that behavioral data which is obtained through a day-to-day, hour-to-hour, minute-to-minute, continuous monitoring system. The term *assessment* itself, when applied to the severely and profoundly handicapped, must be synonymous with terms such as *teaching, education,* and *programming.* It is not separate and apart. It is an ongoing, continuous measure of change and a source from which each new day's prescriptions spring. It is both the foundation and the evidence of behavioral change. Each of its parts is intricately woven to produce a fabric of successful educational intervention.

Observe—Don't Assume

Careful observation is not unique to special education. It is the foundation upon which all sound education rests. However, it may well be that in working with the severely and profoundly handicapped, the observation process reaches its most refined and precise level. The extremely small increments of behavior with which one must often work when involved with the severely and profoundly handicapped require that observational procedures appropriate to such small units of performance be developed. For too long persons in this field have made assumptions about the behavior of human beings that are not supported by careful, precise observational data. Errors can occur even in the most caring and loving environments dedicated to the children involved. Even those who devote their lives to such children can be misled by erroneous assumptions unless these careful, precise observational procedures are maintained. Essentially, there are two kinds of procedures: descriptive observation and precise observation.

Descriptive Observation

Descriptive observation as a process is continuous and free floating within the natural environment. It is an ongoing part of every teaching day

and every interaction with a handicapped child. It is not intrusive in that it attempts to provide a general description of the child through her behavior, her reaction to those around her, her response to the various stimuli to which she is exposed, and her behavioral repertoire, such as smiles, tears, and physical movement. Descriptive observation is both qualitative and quantitative in a very general way. It includes developmental landmarks which help to order the behaviors observed, but it is not necessarily limited simply to these landmarks. It provides a qualitative aspect by allowing those still hard-to-define behaviors, of which emotion is a part.

Precise Observation

Precise observation *must* grow out of descriptive observation. It is exactly what the term implies: highly precise, not only with regard to that which is being observed, but also to the conditions under which it is being observed and the changes which occur as a deliberate part of that observation. Unlike descriptive observation it is structured. It is often intrusive because it frequently involves deliberate attempts to record changes in behaviors and therefore requires deliberate manipulation of the environment as part of the procedure. It is also both qualitative and quantitative, as long as one can provide adequate description of the qualitative aspects. It is designed to document small units of behavior, such as a swallow, a blink, or a slight muscle movement. It is out of this observational procedure that all assessment, all educational planning, and all changes must be documented. Without continuous, precise observational procedures, the educational program for the severely and profoundly handicapped must surely fail.

Pinpoint Behaviors of Concern

Out of descriptive and precise observations should emerge a limited number of clearly defined, discrete behaviors upon which several observers can agree and the occurrence of which can be reliably monitored. In addition to the behaviors, you must identify antecedent events or conditions which precipitate or stimulate the behavior and subsequent events which provide either subtle or obvious consequences. It is this identification of specific behaviors and their unique antecedents and subsequent events which provide the subject matter for the severe and profoundly handicapped child's schoolwork. It is this process out of which prescriptions grow. Without it educational programs are haphazard at best.

An outstanding example of precise observation and a resulting prescriptive program is the case of Mary. Mary was 5 years of age, diagnosed as profoundly mentally retarded with severe physical disorder and cortical blindness. At the time of intervention she demonstrated an uncontrolled seizure pattern. Mary was observed for a period of 3 weeks and found to have a seizure everyday between 11:00 and 11:30 during an intensive feeding program involving the Mueller technique of jaw control to promote increased chewing (a precise observation; see Figure 8–1). It had previously been noted that Mary never had a seizure when being held and cuddled by a familiar adult and further that the feeding technique appeared to stimulate some anxiety in Mary (a descriptive observation). As a result of these observations, the following program was initiated:

First week: 20 minutes of individual attention while being held prior to

Name: Mary		Seizures
Date	*Time*	*Description; events surrounding; length; behavior following*
1/13/73	11:05	jack knifed forward—leaned more right than midline—on prone board with T.V. music box—volunteer helping—lasted 30–45 seconds—lethargic following
1/14/76	11:10	myoclonic seizure (chronic spasm, or twitching of a group of muscles)—sitting in chair—Patty (instructional aide) working with textures with her—lasted about 1–1/2 minutes—jerked several times following seizure—sleepy
1/15/76	11:03	myoclonic—on prone board with noodles and rice textures with volunteer—lasted 30 seconds—let out small scream following seizure
1/16/75	11:15	myoclonic—on wedge with toy mobile in front—one person working with her—lasted about 15 seconds—fell into dead sleep following seizure
1/17/76	11:13	myoclonic—on wedge with toy mobile—volunteer with her and two other students—lasted 45 seconds—lethargic following seizure

Figure 8–1. Courtesy of Mary Falvey, San Rafael, Calif.

lunch and having the reasons for jaw control explained to her. Decreasing her jaw control to 60% control.

Second week: 10 minutes of individual attention (being held); 70% jaw control.

Third week: 1 minute of individual attention; 80% jaw control.

Fourth week: 1 sentence reminder; 90% jaw control.

Fifth week: 100% jaw control only.

As can be seen in the data on her progress, Figure 8–2, p. 165, the program proved to be totally successful with the elimination of seizures during the time period designated. It should be noted that this procedure was later successfully extended to other periods of the day. All seizures were eliminated by the end of a 3 month period.

The pinpointing of behaviors should occur within the framework of a clearly defined developmental sequence. For many individuals who are severely and profoundly handicapped, we want to pinpoint specific performance levels in each of the following areas (p. 166).

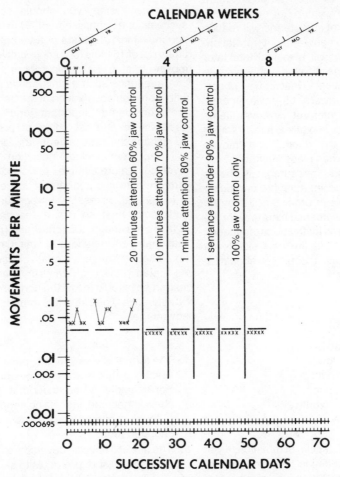

Figure 8–2. Elimination of Myoclonic seizures in a five-year-old multiply handicapped child. Courtesy of Mary Falvey, San Rafael, Calif.

1. motor
2. communication
3. self-help
4. interpersonal interaction
5. leisure

A number of excellent assessment instruments are available for this purpose. However, it is important to make certain that the instrument utilized has defined sufficiently small increments of developmental change at each level to provide a sensitive measure of each child's performance. Cohen, Gross, and Haring (1976) present an example of one such instrument.

Wherever possible, items on an assessment instrument should be written in measurable, behavioral terms. Use of such terms will reduce ambiguity of measurement and interpretation. Behavioral terminology will also facilitate later programming and specification of concrete objectives for instruction. Descriptive observations, such as "is aware of environment," may be very difficult to interpret. However, items such as "looks at people who talk to him," "smiles when touched around the mouth," and "moves finger around objects when placed in hands" are readily observed and measured. It bears repeating that each pinpoint must be as *precise* and specific as possible in order that it may be placed within this developmental hierarchy for the purpose of establishing an instructional sequence which allows movement to the next skill level. Instead of listing "eats with spoon," you should list discrete steps such as:

1. looks at spoon
2. grasps spoon
3. scoops with spoon
4. balances food on spoon
5. brings spoon to mouth
6. inserts spoon into mouth
7. removes food from spoon
8. removes spoon from mouth
9. places spoon in dish

Instead of *"accepts* tactile stimulation," you should redefine hard-to-define tasks in terms of behaviors that will be acceptable as *evidence* of progress toward task accomplishment. We cannot measure a child's acceptance. In this task, progress may take two forms. (*A*) Evidence of *increase* in number of different tactile stimulations accepted, such as:

1. adult blowing on
2. cool hair dryer
3. battery operated brush
4. towel rubbing
5. adults' hands rubbing
6. adult holding and rocking

and (*B*) Evidence of *decrease* in resistive behaviors, such as:

1. body jerking during tactile stimulation
2. crying during tactile stimulation
3. tensing of body during tactile stimulation

For each step, you should set criteria for success, or accomplishment. "Joe will look at his spoon within 1/2 minute of a verbal cue *look* ten times out of 15 trials for 3 consecutive days before moving to step #2 (grasp spoon)."

A sequence such as this one will provide you with a precise observation of the behaviors which are considered important and relevant for assessment and recording of progress. After completing the assessment (task analyses), you will also have a clear indication of the steps involved in more complex performances and the order of activities appropriate for remediation.

In general, assessment procedures should be sufficiently brief so that a teacher is able to obtain a maximum amount of information within reasonably short periods of time. One half to one hour of assessment is a relatively lengthy period. As stated previously, items in the assessment instrument should follow the normal developmental sequence. The use of this format yields several advantages:

1. The format allows you to bypass or skip items which the child is known to be able to perform. For example, if you know that the child can chew finger food, there is no need to assess all of those subitems which pertain to puree and chopped food.
2. The use of a specific developmental sequence provides a list of prerequisite skills which ensure that inappropriately high-level objectives are not established for a given individual.
3. The sequence also provides subsequent steps in sequences so that the teacher is aware of steps which usually follow when current objectives are met. In other words, the

assessment instrument can serve as an outline for curriculum development.

Choose Objectives for Instruction

Once the initial assessment has been completed and behaviors have been pinpointed in all areas, you choose which of the many skill difficulties you will focus on for the initial instructional period. In choosing objectives for instruction, the following factors must be considered.

Functional Activity

Activities built around self-help tasks are generally the most meaningful. For example, if a child needs instruction in "moving eyes toward stationary objects," instruction can be oriented to the eating program. Before the child is allowed to scoop the food, she must first look at the food. When working on palmar grasp as the first step in a fine motor program, you can use a spoon instead of a ring. Activities of this sort can often be incorporated in short snack periods.

Relationships Between Home and Curriculum

The goals and objectives of the curriculum should be established in such a way that they complement all facets of the child's life: Have the parents voiced any particular concerns or requests? What will make the parents' responsibilities for the severely handicapped child less difficult? What will improve the relationship between parent and child? Questions such as these must be asked if realistic goal setting is to occur.

Future Home Environment and Curriculum Objectives

In planning the curriculum for the severely handicapped child you must also consider where the child may be living in the future. Will she remain at home, in a group home, or eventually need to be institutionalized? What type of self-help skills are required in each of those settings? A well-planned and taught instructional program may help avoid the necessity for later institutionalization.

Time and the Curriculum

You need to be aware of the amount of time required to accomplish objectives. How many years will the child have in the school setting? In most cases, time may be limited for both you and child and therefore you must concentrate on the most essential self-help, domestic/vocational, and communication skills. Being able to feed one's self is a far more crucial objective than being able to complete a three-piece puzzle within a given period of time.

Out-of-School Activities

You must consider the nature and extent of the child's out-of-school activities. For most severely handicapped children, self-help, prevocational/vocational and communication skills are necessary for satisfactory use of both work and leisure time. The self-help skill of bathrooming becomes important to potential campers. Many summer camps required that campers be "toilet trained." The basic communication skill of indicating *yes* and *no* in some manner allows severely/profoundly handicapped persons to choose instead of having things forced upon them. They can choose food, clothing, and activities.

Objectives of Auxiliary Personnel

Coordination of programs between the classroom teacher, the occupational therapist, the physical therapist, and the speech therapist is essential. Many skill difficulties overlap other areas of performance. A severely handicapped child who fails to focus on stationary objects will encounter problems in gross motor development, fine motor development, self-help skills, communication, and pre-academic activities. Because the classroom teacher rarely is an expert in all of these areas, the related therapists must be utilized to ensure overall development of the child.

Opportunities for Human Interaction

Great care must be taken to maximize human interaction while working toward the attainment of specific skills. We have found that even in programs where the ratio of adults to children is very high, too often the severely/profoundly handicapped child spends a large portion of her day interacting with objects rather than people. Teevan (1973) made a study of the social interactions of children in normal kindergartens as compared to the interaction of chidren in programs for the multihandicapped. She found that multihandicapped children interacted only 70% as much with adults and 40% as much with peers as did normal kindergarten children. However, they interacted almost twice as much with objects and spent more than four times as much time not interacting with anything as did their normal kindergarten peers. It is important that schedules be established which reduce this discrepancy.

Select Appropriate Data Collection System

In order to maintain an effective educational management system with severely/ profoundly handicapped children, several types of records covering different kinds of data are necessary. Needless to say, it is important that this record keeping enhance rather than impede the instructional program by saving more time than it requires. Several basic rules should be followed in establishing your data system:

1. All information should be easy to understand and communicate to others.
2. Time requirements for recording should be minimal.
3. Records should reflect continuous monitoring of all important behaviors.

4. Records should provide feedback to both teachers and students whenever possible.

As indicated previously, use of appropriate data is necessary if effective monitoring is to occur. Data is usually recorded in relation to a series of steps or tasks for accomplishment. In addition to recording quantitative data, we suggest an additional step for communicating present levels of functioning and immediate objectives. As the initial assessment is completed and mastery levels[1] in each area are pinpointed on an assessment instrument, each of these mastery levels should be highlighted with a yellow felt pen to provide a quick visual record of what a child can already accomplish. Following this, each of those skills which form the immediate instructional objectives can be underlined in red with a date next to each item when instruction on that objective is initiated. A second date should be entered and the item highlighted with yellow over the red underline when attainment of the objective has been

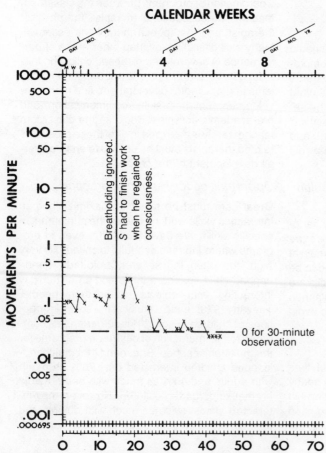

CALENDAR WEEKS

Figure 8–3.

Rate of breath-holding behaviors in a 5-year-old multiply handicapped child. *S* held breath until unconscious on an average of once every 10 minutes during 30-minute observation period. Teacher observed for 2 weeks, making certain child could not harm himself when unconsciousness occurred. Then (point *A*) she began ignoring breath-holding behavior and requiring completion of work when *S* regained consciousness. Breath-holding during this 30-minute period ceased by the end of next 4 weeks.

SOURCE:
Mary Falvey, teacher, San Rafael, Calif.

achieved. A record such as this one provides at a glance an overall picture of the child's skill level in several different areas and serves as both as assessment instrument and a list of objectives, complete with time estimates required for mastery of each subobjective.

The continuous monitoring of several kinds of performance data is essential if an efficient educational program is to be maintained. Each particular type of behavior and kind of information needed provides an important perspective for choice of type of data to best study pupil progress.

Rate Data

The basic performance data of any program should be rate data—that is, the frequency of occurrence of behavior over time. The attainment of a large percentage of the performance objectives which we set for severely/profoundly handicapped children can best be measured by changes in the rate at which the child is able to perform the task. Too often our failure to document rate change (or lack of rate change) results in the continuation of an inappropriate intervention for extensive periods of time. This failure means loss of valuable educational opportunity. Daily variations in performance, unless charted and anlyzed for gains over time, can often confuse and delay instructional planning. As an example, you might wish to work on "chews with lips closed." By establishing a behavior rate project with appropriate mastery levels for this behavior in terms of specific performance rates, i.e., "number of chews per minute," we can measure the increase in rate over several days or weeks, regardless of "good" or "bad" days. In this way we can observe the effect of instructional change by the variation in rate which results. Most important, this information is readily communicated to *anyone* working with the child.

An excellent example of a behavior rate project which focused on decreasing (decelerating) breath holding in a severely handicapped child is illustrated in Figure 8–3. We strongly recommend that anyone working with severely/profoundly handicapped children at least acquaint themselves with the literature on precision teaching for a more thorough discussion of behavior rate projects.

Percent

In some cases, recording data in terms of percent can provide an important perspective. For example, Figure 8–4 shows the pre- and posttest performance of a child on a four-part measure of the functional use of *yes* and *no*, while Figure 8–5 provides an example of a daily percent recording procedure. (See page 170 for 8–4 and 8–5.)

Duration

In a few cases we may wish to increase the duration of a specific behavior such as "lifts head when prone" and document the increased skill in terms of time. In this case we might maintain a chart similar to the one in Figure 8–6, p. 171, with time in minutes or seconds plotted along the vertical axis.

Total Length of Activity

You might be interested in decreasing or increasing the length of time that the child is involved in an activity, such as decreasing the time required to feed lunch to the child. In this case the total time consumed by feeding would be recorded. In other cases you may wish to increase time spent on an activity. In this case you might record the amount of time spent daily standing rather than sitting.

Trials Criterion

Finally, performance on some tasks requiring a predetermined number of responses to reach criterion level (i.e., "10 consecutive correct responses" or "does three out of four"), where rate is not an important consideration, can be charted to indicate the number of training sessions required to reach that criterion level. (See Figure 8–7, p. 171.) In cases such as this, however, daily recording should be maintained to provide a continuing record of response patterns.

We should emphasize once again, however, that the data-recording systems selected must be functional! The more complex the charting procedures become, the more difficult communication becomes. The more time which must be spent recording data, the less time will be available for teaching! By far the greatest amount of information will be obtained from daily rate data with other types of recording systems providing supplementary information.

Collect Daily Data

Time permitting, the accumulation of data each day is the most valuable indicator of pupil progress. Often, as little as a 1-minute sample of pupil behavior charted on the daily behavior chart provides relevant and informative data on such progress. If the classroom teacher does not have time to gather routine data, other staff members and aides can assist in the task. Parents, older children in the school, mildly handicapped children in other classes, university students, therapists, and others can be utilized to assist in this collection of data. If neither time nor staff resources permit the

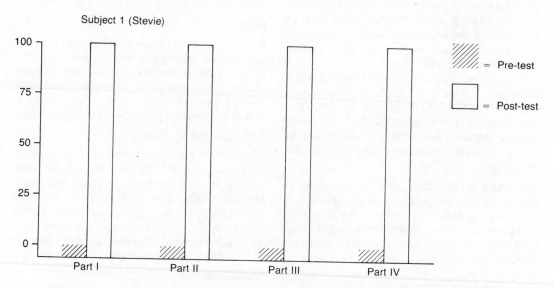

Figure 8–4. Pre- and posttest data may be plotted as indicated above. Here the percentage of correct responses on each part of the functional use of *yes* and *no* is shown for a 9-year-old retarded boy.

SOURCE: From "Training Generalized Functional Acquisition of 'Yes' and 'No' in Three Retarded Children" by J. Remberg, D. Guess, and W. Sailor, *Review,* 1976, *1*(3),33. Reprinted by permission of the American Association for the Education of the Severely and Profoundly Handicapped (AAESPH).

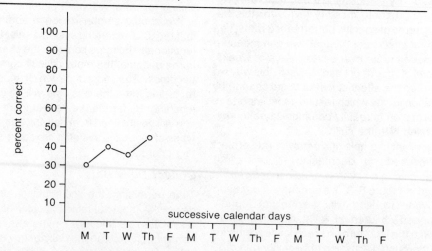

Figure 8–5. The percentage of responses correct may be recorded as shown above.

accumulation of data each day, the most frequent schedule possible should be established. It is better to obtain frequent data on a limited number of behaviors than to collect large quantities of data at any given time. The recording of evaluation data each day provides a number of significant advantages. Assuming that you have already established criteria for success or failure on a given

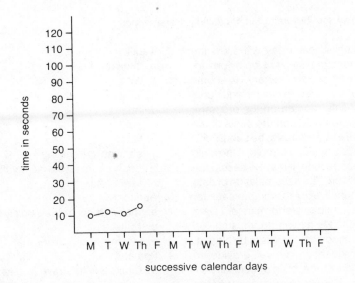

successive calendar days

Figure 8–6. A cumulative record of the amount of time during which behavior occurs.

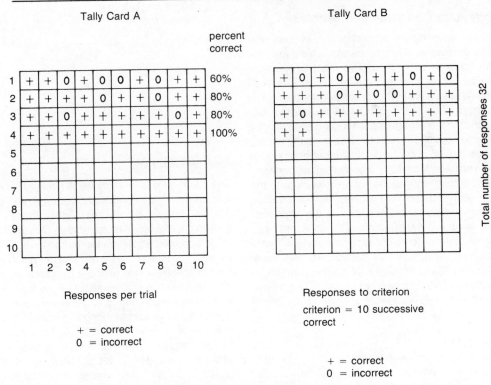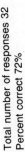

Figure 8–7. Two examples of daily response pattern recording.
   Note. Tally Card A can be used when a specific number of responses per lesson are required. In this example 10 responses per lesson are required and card can be used across several lessons, thus indicating a pattern of errors, attainment of criterion, and percent correct each lesson. Tally Card B can be used when a varying number of responses per lesson may be obtained. Or the lesson can be continued until criterion is reached.

task, the data gathered each day will allow the most rapid movement from step to step by providing immediate feedback on mastery. It should also indicate when the need exists for additional teaching on a particular portion on the program. You should be able to decide on the basis of the data accumulated if a task needs to be subdivided into still lower level skills. For example, if the child spits out finely chopped food, it may be necessary to return to pureed food. The accumulation of data on a daily basis tends also to compensate for fluctuations in a child's performance. Data gathered when a child is having an unusual "off day" or an unusual "good day" tends to be biased. Data gathered infrequently may well provide an inaccurate indication of the child's level of performance. Figure 8–8 provides an example of the Daily Behavior Chart.[2]

Conduct a Reinforcement Survey

Before beginning the instructional task itself, you must be aware of those things which may be reinforcing to each child. The most economical way to obtain this information may be to call parents or speak to other teachers and therapists or others who have regular sustained contact with the child. If the schedule permits, the child may be observed for short periods of time during recess or free time in order to determine what she does when unattended. Many times activities engaged in by the child while alone will provide clues to the most appropriate reinforcers. An alternative means of obtaining information is the *reinforcement survey*. Several minutes on different days may be planned to try out experimentally different categories and types of reinforcers. We must remember that a reinforcer is anything which increases the frequency of a behavior. The following listing suggests possible categories of reinforcers which may be systematically analyzed:

1. Movement
   a. rock in teacher's arms
   b. swing around
   c. bounce on teacher's knees
   d. hold up high in the air
   e. ride in wagon
   f. ride on rocking horse

2. Tactile
   a. blow on face
   b. kiss
   c. tickle
   d. hug
   e. sand
   f. water
   g. shaving cream
   h. nonhuman tactile stimulation (fan, brush, towel, etc.)
3. Auditory
   a. music (record, music box toy, human voice)
   b. rattle
   c. looking at magazines
4. Primary
   a. drinks—with straw; in glass
   b. crunchy foods
   c. soft foods
   d. finger foods
   e. spoon foods

Plan Instruction

The classroom is in many ways similar to a small laboratory. We continually attempt to blend unique stimuli and unique consequences with each "one of a kind" human being with whom we work and somehow come out with a product called "increased skill" or "learning." We are always involved in a process of discovery since we can never be certain about all the ingredients which we are combining and therefore must do a great deal of guessing along the way. In order to teach most effectively, it is essential that we establish an environment which allows us to examine, as carefully as possible, each of the variables in that environment to determine its effect on the learning of a given skill. We cannot afford to waste time with ineffective curricula or meaningless consequences. The children with whom we work are already far behind in the things

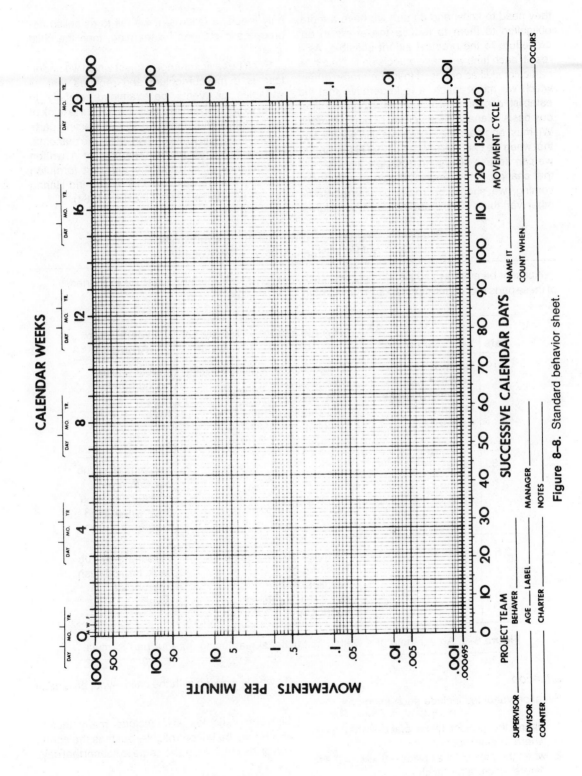

Figure 8–8. Standard behavior sheet.

they need to know and do and we have a moral obligation to them to reduce the errors in our procedure to the greatest extent possible. As a result, each time we make a decision to "teach" a particular skill as opposed to innumerable others which we might teach, it is imperative that we establish conditions which allow us on a continuous basis to analyze the validity of our judgment. We must engineer the environment in such a way that when we change any part of that environment we can assess almost immediately the effect of that change. If the desired effects are not forthcoming, we should be ready to change some other variables. There are no learning failures,

only teaching failures. If we fail to establish appropriate conditions for learning, then the child loses.

Each behavior change project which we undertake is a minicurriculum and requires that all variables, or events, be examined carefully. In order to accomplish this task it is helpful to think of each project as comprising four interacting parts where change in any part can affect the outcome. (Figure 8–9 provides an example of a written instructional plan using the four-part formula.) These parts are described by White and Haring (1976) as adapted from Lindsley (1964).

Situation	Events Before/Until	Movement Cycles	Events After/Arranged

It cannot be emphasized too strongly that each of these parts is of equal importance in the learning process and must be carefully examined.

Date	Situation	Events Before/Until	Movement Cycle	Events After/Arranged
1/19	Room 7 Teacher—Jones Working with aide—M. Green 9:00–9:15	Place child on wedge pillow with head, arms and shoulders hanging over edge.	Head raises.	Verbal praise, "good head raising"; rub back. 1:1
1/30	same	same	same	Verbal praise; rub back; turn on flashlight; turn off flash when head lowers.
2/5	same	Same as above plus turn on flashlight and say, "Raise your head, Mary."	same	Verbal praise; rub back; turn off flash when head lowers.

Figure 8–9. An example of a written instructional plan using the four-part formula.

Situation

Situation variables include such things as:

1. where the project takes place—what room, where in that room
2. when the project takes place—9 A.M. or 2 P.M., before lunch, after lunch

3. who is working with the child—you, an aide, a volunteer

Situation variables also include many factors which may be uncontrollable, such as the condition of the child when she came to school that day:

1. with breakfast

2. without breakfast
3. good night's sleep
4. poor night's sleep
5. family atmosphere

Events Before/Until

Events before/until include all those things which we deliberately design or manipulate to stimulate the behavior we wish to change; in other words, *curriculum materials* (food cut up into bite-sized pieces or placement of child on her stomach so that she can learn to raise her head.) They also include your procedures—what do you say or do ("look"; place spoon in bowl; set time clock).

Movement Cycles

Cycles should be a precise definition of the desired response stated in such a way that we know immediately whether the child has responded correctly (raises head off floor, looks at bowl) within 1/2 minute after verbal cue *look*.

Events After/Arranged

Events after/arranged are simply those things we select which we think will provide meaningful consequences for the child and which we can provide once the desired behavior has occurred. They may be primary reinforcement, such as food; physical contact, such as patting or rubbing; extrinsics, such as toys, sounds, light; or social reinforcement, such as smiles and verbal praise. A portion of this part of the formula simply explains the numerical ratio between the occurrence of the desired behavior and the occurrence of events after/arranged. For example, we might decide that each time the child raises her head off the floor that we will rub her neck and give verbal praise, which she seems to like. In this case, we have established a ratio of 1:1, or *one event after/arranged for each behavior occurrence*. In another case, we might want the child to show the behavior more than once before providing the event after/arranged. For example, the desired behavior might be *steps taken* with the event after/arranged being *hug and verbal praise*. We might require the child to take four steps before providing the event after/arranged. In this case, the ratio would be 4:1.

As the child is able to move quickly toward more independent functioning, the curriculum can become more practical and easier for you to plan and manage. As an example, a child who can eat independently, or semi-independently, will place fewer demands on you than the child who requires almost total teacher assistance. The long-range goal, short-term objective, and sequence of steps together provide a comprehensive perspective and rationale for a particular task. Hopefully, this perspective will help you focus on the most functional and practical methods and materials.

Effect Desired Learnings

One thing must be kept in mind with regard to each part of the learning environment formula—only the child's actions tell us *if a part is working*. We must never assume that the things we select as events before/until are stimulating or that the things we select as events after/arranged are rewarding; only the child can tell us if this is indeed the case! Perhaps we can change one part and positively effect the outcome. As such we must collect careful data and keep our projects consistent from day to day.

Although the initial commitment of time for written specification of teaching strategy is relatively great, substantial economy results when you begin to utilize the program. Generally, materials needed for a presentation will be available and convenient. You will not need to hesitate in determining appropriate behavior, since the specification of correct and incorrect responses has been completed. The standardization of procedures tends to eliminate confusion for both the child and for you.

Instructional Environment

The plans which follow are examples of the levels of specification required for an effective instructional program.

Since severely handicapped children require extensive dependence upon adults, activities must be carefully planned so that each interaction is maximized for all children in the program. It is impossible to plan any child's program in isolation. Scheduling should be such that the use of your time, your assistant's time, and the time of other auxiliary personnel adequately provides continuous involvement at some level for each child. In some instances volunteers, older nonhandicapped children and other handicapped children may provide important sources of additional help for teachers. Finally, therapists and other specialists can be incorporated into the work schedule in such a way that they provide an important segment of the continuous daily instructional plan. It is imperative in all instances that a clear, written plan for each child be available to minimize wasted time and maximize the pupil's progress.

Not all objectives for children need to be taught on a one-to-one ratio between you and the student. The student's time can be utilized for learning not only when given opportunity for direct instruction, but independently and in groups. There are a variety of *activities* which are appropriate with minimum supervision by auxiliary personnel and/or the classroom teacher. The following are some examples:

1. *Activities to promote interaction:* Position two or more children in standing boxes, bean bag chairs, sandboxes, etc., in such a way that they may make physical contact with one another to promote increased tactile discrimination, eye contact, grasping and other skills. Activities such as this are useful since they require only intermittant involvement of staff in order to reinforce any evidence of touching, holding, or other interactions.

2. *Activities to promote group sensory stimulation:* Several children may be placed in a sitting or prone position on a mat so that you may provide each child several turns with various stimulation devices: blowing on child with your mouth or a cool hair dryer or fan, brushing with small battery operated brush, rubbing her with a terry towel or hands, rubbing her hands and feet in warm water, hugging, holding and rocking, gently bouncing on knees or swinging around, lifting high in the air, or just touching her with your hands, electric vibrator, or different types of texture.

   Place several children in a seated or standing position so that they may either independently or with some assistance move their hands and fingers around in shaving cream, pudding, jello, finger paint, peanut butter, flour dough, etc.

3. *Activities to develop independent manipulation of objects:* Using masking tape, attach an object such as a spoon, a noise-making toy, a sponge ball, or a stuffed animal to the child's hands. The object should be positioned so that the child must hold the object. A method of reinforcing the movement of fingers around the object should be selected. As the child shows improvement, you may begin to fade out the degree of physical attachment to the object. For example, a possible fading sequence might be:

   a. well-attached thick paper tape
   b. loosely attached thick paper tape
   c. loosely attached thin paper tape
   d. loose piece of yarn
   e. loose piece of string
   f. intermittent physical prop by teacher
   g. independent holding

4. *Activities to increase communication* are described in the chapter, "Severe Communication Problems."

5. *Activities to improve general motor functioning* are described in the chapter, "Motor Development, Deviation, and Physical Rehabilitation."

6. *Activities to increase self-help skills* are suggested in the chapter, "Self-Care".

7. *Activities to increase independence in task completion without a teacher's presence* are described as thinking activities in the chapter, "Academics."

There are innumerable other program activities which you and your staff can initiate which place minimal demands on adult-time commitment. Some examples are:

1. *All-day eye contact.* Intermittently throughout the day approach the child and say her name. If the child turns toward or glances at you, she should be quickly reinforced. Record the number of adult initiations and the number of child responses using a double wrist counter or other convenient recording device.

2. *All-day spontaneous verbalization.* Identify those vocalizations which approximate verbal responses and reinforce at *any time* they are observed to occur during the day. Keep a daily record of spontaneous verbalizations.

3. *Other all-day projects.* Many behaviors can be initiated and reinforced on an intermittent basis throughout the day. Motor behavior, verbal communication, and concept development, require little change in classroom routine other than an adult-initiated stimulus. Reinforcement can be very effectively applied on this basis.

Whatever activity or whatever behavior is selected for modification, White (1971) lists four stages required in a successful project:

1. Pinpoint the behavior.
2. Record and chart its occurrence.
3. Change procedures on the basis of the data obtained.
4. Try, try again. Your change may not always be successful, so keep trying.

Summary

The development of a responsive environment which allows maximum growth for the severely/profoundly handicapped is a unique and challenging task, and one which provides great opportunity for the creative and innovative teacher. The potential for creation of individualized curricular intervention techniques is in many ways limited only by the imagination of those who work with these children if only they will follow one simple rule—"The child knows best." Until we recognize that each child has her own special "turn-ons"—that a stimulus for one may be meaningless to another and/or a reward for one may be aversive to another—our programs will be ineffective. Only the child can give us the information we need. It is through the careful observation of minute changes in a child's behavior over time and a willingness to change our intervention strategies on the basis of what that child tells us behaviorally that we can maximize the effectiveness of our teaching and respect the individual integrity of all children with whom we work.

Notes

1. *Mastery* is defined as the rate at which the teacher feels the child should achieve in order to demonstrate competence; similarly defined in White and Haring (1976), pp. 122 and 123.

2. "Standard Behavior Chart" from Norris G. Haring and Owen White. *Exceptional Teaching* Columbus, Ohio: Charles E. Merrill, 1976, p. 113 a. Reprinted with permission.

References

Alpern, C. D., & Ball, T. J. Education and care of moderately and severely retarded children—With a curriculum and activities guide. Seattle, Wash.: Special Child Publications, 1971.

Bradfield, R. H. Precision teaching—A useful technology for special education teachers. *Educational Technology,* 1970, *10*(8), 22–26.

Cohen, M., Gross, P., & Haring, N. Developmental pinpoints. In N. Haring and Brown (Eds.), *Teaching the severely handicapped* (Vol. 1). New York: Grune & Stratton, 1976, pp. 35–110.

Education for All Handicapped Children Act. PL. 94–142 November 29, 1975. (Available from the Federal Register, Washington, D.C. 20408.)

Kunzelmann, H. P. (Ed.). *Precision teaching: An initial training sequence.* Seattle, Wash.: Special Child Publications. 1970.

Lindsley, O. R. From Skinner to precision teaching: The child knows best. In J. B. Jordon & L. S. Robbins (Eds.), *Let's try doing something else kind of thing.* Council for Exceptional Children, 1972.

Lindsley, O. R. Direct measurement of prothesis of retarded children. *Journal of Education,* 1964, *47,* pp. 62–81.

Teevan, C. A study to compare the classroom interactions of multihandicapped and non handicapped children Unpublished master's thesis, San Francisco State University, 1973.

White, O. R. *A glossary of behavioral terminology.* Champaign, Ill.: Research Press Company, 1971.

White, O. R. & Haring, N. G. *Exceptional teaching: A multimedia training package.* Columbus, Ohio: Charles E. Merrill, 1976.

Young, B. J. Imagine you're the parent of a deaf-blind child. In J. B. Jordon & L. S. Robbins (Eds.), *Lets try doing something else kind of thing.* Council for Exceptional Children, 1972.

Resources

The American Association for the Education of the Severely/Profoundly Handicapped (AAESPH) P.O. Box 15287, Seattle, Washington 98115.

Air VOTAP News (Vocational Training & Placement of the Severely Handicapped). Free. (Available from P.O. Box 1113, Palo Alto, Calif. 94302.)

Haring, N. G., & Schiefelbusch, R. L. *Teaching special children.* New York: McGraw-Hill Co., 1976.

Haring, N. G., & Brown, L. J. (Eds.). *Teaching the severely handicapped* (Vol 1). New York: Grune & Stratton, 1976.

Larsen, L. A. & Bricker, W. A. A manual for parents and teachers of severely and moderately retarded children. 1968, *5*(22). (Available from the Institute on Mental Retardation in Infant Development, George Peabody College for Teachers, Nashville, Tennessee.)

Krumboltz, J. D., & Krumboltz, H. B. *Changing children's behavior.* Englewood Cliffs, N.J.: Prentice-Hall, 1972.

Myers, D. G., Sinco, M. E., & Stalma, E. S. *The right-to-education-child.* Springfield, Ill.: Charles C Thomas, 1973.

Sailor, W., Guess, D. & Baer, D. M. Functional Language for verbally deficient children: An experimental program. *Mental Retardation,* 1973, *11*(3)27–35.

Sailor, W. & Mix, B. J. *The TARC assessment system.* Lawrence, Kan.: H. & H. Enterprises, 1975.

Stainback, S., Stainback, W., & Maurer, S. Training teachers for the severely and profoundly handicapped: A new frontier. *Exceptional Children,* 1976, *42*(4), 203–210.

Stephens, B. (Ed.). *Training the developmentally young.* New York: John Day, 1971.

9

LIFE EXPERIENCE PROGRAMMING

Probably everyone involved with instruction of individuals with disabilities has experienced uncertainty about appropriate goals for these individuals. Until recently, little data was available to validate long-range needs. Now, however, we have an opportunity to respond to an in-depth analysis of the needs of the physically handicapped as reported by Bachmann (1971). She suggests some unmet needs and primary goals.

Bachmann (1971) reported on a survey of 167 physically handicapped young adults, most of whom had graduated from "special" schools during the years 1964–1965. The subjects ranged in age from 18–22 years. The purpose of the study was to determine the degree to which these subjects were experiencing success or failure in relation to certain variables: employment, recreation, social activities, friendships, self-care, leisure time, independence, and self-concept.

The findings of this study were disheartening. All but a very few of the students surveyed experienced failure in most or all of the areas listed

above. As an example, most of those surveyed were unemployed; nine were competitively employed; few had any friends at all; most were without social-recreational activities; most were almost completely dependent upon their parents or attendants for their daily care and activities; all but one had a poor self-concept. Television was the most frequent contact with the "outside" world.

Program Implementation

We assume that the variables Bachmann selected for study are high-priority needs of the physically handicapped. Until other data indicating a different ordering of needs are forthcoming, these variables can be the basis for establishing educational goals for physically disabled persons. Disabled persons and others involved in their training have a responsibility to work toward these goals:

1. Ability to obtain meaningful employment (whether it be homebound, sheltered workshop, or competitive).
2. Capacity for independent living appropriate to each one's physical and mental capabilities.

Ron Howard *is a doctoral fellow and graduate teaching assistant at Georgia State University in Atlanta.*

June Bigge.

3. Capacity for community involvement (including a variety of daily living skills).
4. Skills for participation in meaningful leisure-time activities (a well defined free time management system).
   a. recreational experiences
   b. meeting and retaining friends
5. Development of reliable transportation.
6. Mastery of self-care skills.
7. Ability to maintain residence away from parents, convalescent hospitals, or state institutions.
8. Development of a healthy self-concept.

Instruction based on the needs of the physically handicapped child was suggested by the Bachmann study. The recommendations formed the core of a project in Santa Clara County, California. Two teachers, Ron Howard and Mary Frances Strathairn (with cooperation of many others), designed and taught the *Life Experience Program* (1976) in response to Bachmann's findings. They developed a comprehensive program to teach daily living skills to individuals with physical disabilities. Program components were written to provide these students with skills, attitudes, and behaviors crucial for effective functioning in the nonhandicapped world.

How to use public transportation, how to use public telephones and public restrooms, how to order food in a restaurant, how to shop for groceries, how to purchase articles of clothing, how to use the bank, post office, and library, and how to ask directions from a stranger are samples of functional, or independent, skills for daily living.

A task analysis can be conducted on each of these daily living skills in order to identify the underlying basic skills or subskills required. Once skills have been identified and recorded on a rating scale like the *Functional Skills Evaluation Rating Scale* (*Life Experience Program:* 1976, 70), a systematic sequence of instruction may then begin (see Figure 9–1.)

Figure 9–1. Sample of a functional skills evaluation rating scale.

Student's name_____
Recorder's name_____
Take a city bus and return to start

FUNCTIONAL SKILL	RATING (record by month and year)									
	1		2		3		4		5	
	Pre	Post	Pre	Post	Pre	Post	Pre	Post	Pre	Post
1. Find the phone no. in phonebook.										
2. Call bus co. for information. a. Tell where & when & what time you want to go & return.										
b. Make note of where & what time to catch bus; ask if you need to transfer.										

	1		2		3		4		5	
	Pre	Post	Pre	Post	Pre	Post	Pre	Post	Pre	Post
3. Walk/have someone drop you off at/near bus stop.										
4. Wait at bus stop until bus comes.										
a. Check the sign on bus to see if it is correct bus no. & title.										
b. Quickly get in line or step up to door.										
5. Get on bus quickly.										
6.										

Figure 9–1, continued.

SOURCE: Adapted from the *Functional Skills Evaluation Rating Scale, Life Experience Program,* 1976, p. 70.[1]

Teaching a Functional Skill

In order to demonstrate features of the Life Experience Program, (LEP), one complete sequence on teaching one functional skill will be illustrated. *Take a city bus and return to start* is a functional skill which is part of the group of functional skills needed to learn how to use public transportation.

For any skill, instruction involves the following actions on your part:

1. Select (often in collaboration with students and parents) an appropriate skill to be learned. Inform students regarding which skill they will be learning if students are not involved in selection.

2. Conduct "Classroom Programmed Instruction: CPI" (Life Experience Program, 1976) as discussed later in this chapter, page 181.

   a. Demonstrate the tape/slide learning packet demonstrating sequences of subtasks to perform the selected skill.

   b. Or, help students study subtasks to be demonstrated and make the necessary slides.

   c. Conduct realistic role playing of situations to heighten student awareness of what will be expected of each of them.

   d. Show videotape(s) of trials by previous groups of students (if available).

   e. Encourage discussions, questions, and repetition of any of the above steps.

3. Conduct "Practice In Community: PIC" (Life Experience Program, 1976), discussed later in this chapter, pages 181–183, in which students are taken from school to the community to practice the skill.

   a. Use a portable videorecorder to videotape student performance.

   b. Once back in the classroom, ask for student feedback and show videotape of student performance (if available).

A systematic program of classroom activities, "Classroom Programmed Instruction: CPI" is carried out for each skill. Look at the functional skill, "Take a City Bus and Return to Start," as practiced in "Classroom Programmed Instruction."

Classroom Programmed Instruction: CPI [2]

Functional skill: How to take a city bus and return to start.

Objective: To enable the student to independently use a city bus to get to a predetermined destination and return to start.

Classroom activity:

1. *Prerequisites* (can be taught in earlier CPI session and practiced in the community)
   a. The ability to ask directions from a stranger and follow those directions.
   b. The ability to say (or give written statement) name, address, and phone number.
   c. The ability to cross a busy intersection. (See Figure 9–2, p. 182.)
   d. The ability to use a public telephone or to ask another person to place a phone call for her.
   e. The ability to obtain help when lost.
   f. The ability to get on/off a public bus.
   g. The ability to read street signs and/or recognize the corner where bus stops to let passengers on or off.
   h. The ability to recognize coin denominations.
2. *Discussion*
   a. Determine just how much each student already knows about public buses and their past experience in using them.
   b. Using the Functional Skill Evaluation Rating Scale lead the students through the entire task verbally.
3. *Role Play*
   a. Set up chairs in classroom as if it were a bus.
   b. Teacher or aide play role of bus driver with box for money.
   c. Lead students step-by-step through the rating scale. (See Figure 9–3, p. 182.)
4. *Role Play*
   a. Arrange for bus to come to school so students can practice getting on and off, dropping coins in box, moving to the seats, pulling the cord.
   b. *Or,* take the students to the place the city buses are parked and practice there.
   c. Take students to a bus stop to observe signs, benches (if any), people getting on and off buses.
5. *Discussion*
   a. Have students tell the steps that must be done to accomplish the objective.
   b. Question *each* student about the individual actions that must be taken.

   c. Review the prerequisites with each student.
6. *Role Play*
   a. Repeat as role play under #5c above.
7. *Activity*
   a. Map out on blackboard the route the bus will take going and returning. Colored chalk is a help in direction change.
   b. Use masking tape on classroom floor to make a model of bus route and have students walk it.
   c. Use signs on chairs for street corners and landmarks.

Practice in Community: PIC[3]

Functional Skill: Take a city bus and return to start.

Objective: Student will be able to independently take a city bus to a predetermined spot and return to start.

Suggestions: It is important that some measure of success is achieved the first time so that self-confidence will be enhanced and so that this activity can become a building block for future skills. Provide as much adult supervision as possible while still allowing the student to be as independent as possible, the adult assisting only when absolutely necessary. You may find that this particular task is more frightening to the students than any previous skill.

1. *Classroom Activity: Field Activity*
   a. Take the students to the bus stop.
   b. Follow them through each step on the rating scale (see Figure 9–4, p. 183), giving assistance when needed.
2. *Discussion*
   a. Upon return to classroom, have each student evaluate himself upon his performance.
   b. Reinforce verbally the steps the students performed properly.

Suggestions: Repeat the PIC on same bus route until the student is confident—then switch the bus route. Add a transfer to another bus. Pick a time of day when the buses are not too crowded. Further functional skills (i.e., stopping at a drug store, department store, eating at a restaurant) can be added as the student becomes confident while riding the bus.

Figure 9–2. Tina and Steve demonstrate they have learned to cross a busy intersection.

Figure 9–3. Rehearse for reality through classroom programmed instruction (CPI).

3. *Future Activity*
   a. Have student perform task on own while adult follows bus in car.

Suggestions

While completing the previous procedures, certain guidelines are important to keep in mind while planning and teaching a series of lessons:

Use pre- and posttests.
Rank the order of skills to be taught.
Task-analyze student trials of tasks.
Use scales for evaluating student progress.
Use props in role play.
Videotape student trials and accomplishments.
Involve students with the community.
Encourage student sharing of their feelings and performances.
Watch for evidence of hard-to-define skills and attitudes.
Provide adequate supervision.
Plan for transportation.
Elicit active involvement of parents.
Maintain awareness of current laws and barriers affecting the handicapped.

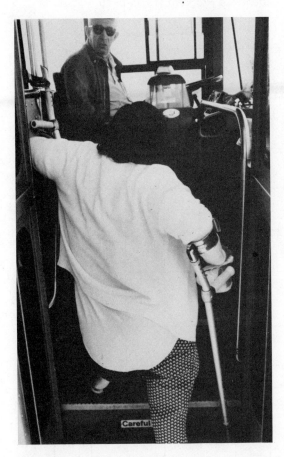

Figure 9–4. With practice Tina found a way to manage so no assistance is necessary.

Use an advisory board.

Include as goals a variety of life experience needs.

Coordinate academic curricula with life experience needs.

Use Pre- and Posttests

A series of pretests should first be administered so that you will know which skills need to be taught and on what level(s). A pretest provides information about where to start instruction, and it is also useful for comparison with a posttest administered at a point after completion of lessons.

Rank Order Skills to be Taught

A rank ordering of functional skills to be taught will be most useful for teachers. For example, you might decide to begin with "crossing a busy inter-

section," followed by "asking directions from a stranger," then "how to use a public telephone," and "how to use public transportation." Selection of a rank order may be an idiosyncratic decision. There may be no one best order.

Task-Analyze Student Trials of Tasks

All functional skills taught in a program must be analyzed; this is of the utmost importance because only then can teachers identify where a student experiences difficulty. For example, what parts or components of the skill is the student unable to accomplish? Once this is known, you may plan remedial instruction. Usually, having followed this procedure, you will experience a higher success rate with any given skill.

Use Scales for Evaluating Student Progress

Rating scales based upon results of task analyses show the variety of subskills needed to perform the task.

Refer to "Functional Skill Evaluation Rating Scale," Figure 9–5, pp. 184–86, developed as one component of the Santa Clara County Life Experience Program. Note the results of a task analysis in the listing of subskills needed to perform the functional skill, "Take a city bus and return to start." Note how the scale has been used as a pretest/posttest instrument providing a record of pupil trials and an overall evaluation, or rating, of student progress. The same scale can be used for follow-up evaluation one or more years later.

The Functional Skill Evaluation Rating Scale is a simple tool which serves the following purposes:

1. evaluates initial student performance
2. identifies "trouble spots"
3. assists teachers in planning future lessons (i.e., those components requiring further training)
4. identifies architectural barriers to be overcome and/or adaptive devices needed to successfully complete the task (a curb too low for boarding a bus; hard-to-use coin dispenser for athetoid students, etc.)
5. shows degree of progress between pretest and posttest
6. shows how much has been retained between the posttest and a review test conducted after a period of time has elapsed from the posttest

Figure 9–5. Sample of the functional skills evaluation rating scale.
SOURCE: From *Life Experience Program,* 1976, p. 70.

Student's Name _____

Recorder's Name _____

Take a city bus and return to start

FUNCTIONAL SKILL	1 Pre	1 Post	2 Pre	2 Post	3 Pre	3 Post	4 Pre	4 Post	5 Pre	5 Post
1. Find the phone no. in phonebook.					10/74					4/75
2. Call bus co. for information. a. tell where & when & what time you want to go & return.					10/74					4/75
b. make note of where & what time to catch bus; if you need transfer.					10/74			4/75		
3. Walk/have someone drop you off at/near bus stop.									10/74	4/75
4. Wait at bus stop until bus comes, as it approaches.										
a. check the sign on bus to see if it is correct bus no. & title.					10/74					4/75
b. quickly get in line or step up to door.			10/74							
5. Get on bus quickly.			10/74							4/75
6. Drop fare into box.			10/74							
7. Hold handrail to avoid falling.									10/74	4/75
8. Ask driver to let him know where to get off if not known.			10/74							4/75
9. Move quickly to nearest empty seat.					10/74					4/75
10. Listen for driver's announcement OR watch street signs/landmarks.			10/74							4/75
11. Pull cord to let driver know you want to get off at the next stop.			10/74					4/75		

RATING (record by month and year)

Take a city bus and return to start

FUNCTIONAL SKILL	RATING (record by month and year)									
	1 Pre	1 Post	2 Pre	2 Post	3 Pre	3 Post	4 Pre	4 Post	5 Pre	5 Post
12. Step off bus onto sidewalk/street whichever is safest.					10/74					4/75
13. Look for bus stop on opposite side of street for return trip.					10/74					4/75
14. Return to bus stop at appropriate time.			10/74							4/75
15. Wait at bus stop until it comes, as it approaches.										
a. check sign on bus to see if it is correct bus no. & title.							10/74			4/75
b. quickly get in line or step up to door.					10/74			4/75		
16. Get on bus quickly.					10/74			4/75		
17. Drop fare into box.					10/74					4/75
18. Hold onto handrail to avoid falling.										4/75
19. Ask driver to let him know where to get off if not known.					10/74					4/75
20. Move quickly to nearest empty seat.					10/74					4/75
21. Listen for driver's announcement OR watch street signs/landmarks.			10/74							4/75
22. Pull cord to let driver know you want to get off at the next stop.			10/74							4/5
23. Step off bus onto sidewalk/street whichever is safest.					10/74					4/75
24. Walk/ride car to home/school.									10/74	4/75

COMMENTS: (initial and date)

(Continue on p. 186.)

Take a city bus and return to start

Pretest Overall Rating _2_ Date _10/74_   Posttest Overall Rating _4_ Date _4/75_

5 Can do quickly with no assistance
4 Can do slowly with no assistance
3 Sometimes needs assistance
2 Always needs assistance
1 Unable to perform task

When determining the overall evaluation rating using the 1–5 scale, it is important to consider the low scores first. The overall rating is *not* simply an average of all scores. For example, referring to the ratings for "Take a city bus and return to start," there are more 5s than 4s. However, if the student consistently takes some time getting on and off the bus but does everything else quickly, he still must receive an overall rating of 4. The overall rating indicates the degree of proficiency the student achieves on the entire skill. To use another example, if a student performs quickly all of the components involved in "How to use a public telephone," but sometimes must have help depositing the coins, his overall rating would be 3. If, however, he can never deposit the coins, even by using an adaptive device, then his rating would be 2 regardless of how well he performed all of the other components.

Teachers may need an alternate rating scale for those students who are totally dependent on others. The following scale is suggested in the Life Experience Program (1976):

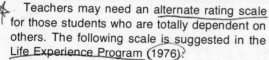

5. Answers or directs helper quickly and correctly, with confidence.
4. Answers or directs helper correctly but with hesitation.
3. Answers or directs helper correctly but with some prompting from helper.
2. Must be given constant prompting from helper in order to perform task.
1. Unable to answer or direct helper to perform task. (p. 3)

Use Props in Role Play

When setting up a role-play situation, you should make use of props. The students should bring to the class information and materials from the community. For example, most city bus lines will provide transfers, bus schedules, and bus routes for the entire class. Automobile clubs will furnish you with maps. Phone companies will provide a supply of phone books, and banks will often provide a bundle of assorted forms. Application blanks for establishing credit, for job interviews, and for a library card are also available. Teachers may duplicate copies of department store and grocery store directories for reading practice. Use *real* money when practicing counting and making change. Have students practice by asking other teachers for directions and then following through with the directions. It is most important to make the role playing as realistic as possible. Do not settle for substitute materials unless the "real thing" is impossible to obtain.

Videotape Student Trials and Accomplishments

Videotapes are a valuable evaluation tool. Students can see themselves in action and can evaluate their own performance. Often, self-evaluation is more effective than teacher critiques. In addition, videotapes can be a convincing method for soliciting parent support. Many times, parents will express doubt regarding their child's ability to perform a particular task. However, once they see a videotape of their child in classroom practice and in the community, they may be quickly convinced.

Involve Students with the Community

Community involvement is an important part of the program. It is impossible for you to replicate the community in the classroom. Role playing and discussions are helpful. However, it is actual practice in the community which trains students to interact in a meaningful way in the "outside" world.

CP1

When a skill is selected and the "Classroom Programmed Instruction" is completed, much time must be set aside for practice in the community. This practice is not simply a field trip. No more than four or five students should accompany you at any given time. Plan on returning many times to repeat the skill until every student is functioning at his capacity. For additional ideas, refer to a plan for Practice in the Community (PIC), mentioned earlier in this chapter.

For each new skill, you may repeat the programs, "Classroom Programmed Instruction" and "Practice in the Community." When several skills have been learned, you may combine skills, thus making a more complicated task. In the Life Experience Program, the combination of skills in more complicated tasks are called *independence skills*. For example, the teacher may combine the skill, "How to call and take a taxi," "eat in a sit-down restaurant," and "go to a movie."

Encourage Student Sharing of Their Feelings and Performances

Student feedback regarding experiences in the community is vitally important. A student may simply wish to share his relief at having completed the task. Another student may want to discuss his problem in being understood. Another might need some encouragement because he was unable to complete the task. It is important to discuss failure as well as success. Students need to dicuss their own failures and learn from them. They must learn to laugh at their mistakes. Usually, students are mutually supportive and can be more effective than the teacher in ameliorating fears and anxiety.

Some possible topics for student discussion are

1. having the courage to try again
2. using a simple communication device (i.e., pocket-size communication board)
3. use of pictures for those without speech
4. how to handle emergencies
5. what to do when someone offers money
6. how to tell a helpful soul, "I'd rather do it myself, thank you."
7. courtesy
8. grooming and appearance

One interesting outcome of the Santa Clara County program has been that, while educating handicapped students to relate to the nonhandicapped, the staff have inadvertently been educating the nonhandicapped to the needs of the handicapped.

Watch for Evidence of Hard-to-Define Skills and Attitudes

Some basic skills are difficult to define. Yet these same skills are necessary for successful mastery of more obvious functional skills. Teachers should watch for evidence of student ability to:

work on tasks independently
complete a task
demonstrate willingness to try new tasks
follow through on tasks already begun
share feelings
use appropriate manners and social behavior
demonstrate self-confidence
demonstrate self-motivation
demonstrate a sense of humor
accept failure
demonstrate good sportsmanship
demonstrate self-respect
demonstrate warmth, affection, and sensitivity
  toward classmates and others
demonstrate a healthy, competitive spirit
demonstrate realistic attitudes toward abilities
  and limitations
be flexible when change is necessary
be open-minded
demonstrate respect for others and for the property of others
demonstrate respect for authority
express realistic fears and realistic trust
accept responsibility
demonstrate dependability

Provide Adequate Supervision

Teacher supervision may become a problem. It is easier to conduct this type of program in a team-teaching situation. However, given the teacher's desire, adequate supervision can be arranged. Aides and volunteers can be indispensable as supervisors.

Plan for Transportation

Some form of transportation is usually necessary. Perhaps the school district will be willing to purchase a vehicle and allow the teacher to obtain a license as a district driver. Approach the parents' club and, if necessary, solicit a station wagon or other car from sources such as car dealers and service organizations.

Elicit Active Involvement of Parents

The program will not succeed without the parents' support. *Involvement* is a key element. Rather than tell parents what wonderful activities are being provided for their children, ask parents to participate in the planning. Ask parents to assist with evaluation in the community (pretests, post-tests, and review tests). When teachers and parents work as a team, more carry-over at home will be assured.

Use Advisory Board

When developing a Life Experience Program, it is helpful to organize an Advisory Board. The Advisory Board should be composed of select education staff (an administrator, teachers, and aides involved in the project), at least one therapist, a few parents, someone from the medical and social services professions, and several key persons from the community who can lend practical assistance to the program. Consider also representatives from the Department of Rehabilitation, sheltered workshops, vocational training centers, regional centers, United Cerebral Palsy Associations, and other service agencies. Social welfare and social security, Chamber of Commerce, department of transportation, and consumer groups also provide needed assistance.

Include as Goals a Variety of Life Experience Needs

Other life experiences requiring significant attention are

1. leisure time management
2. prevocational and vocational training
3. social-recreational programs (adaptive physical education)
5. therapy

It becomes the teacher's responsibility to coordinate all of these activities in a workable daily schedule. The contents of this book are designed to guide instruction in these areas.

Coordinate Academic Curricula with Life Experience Needs

Although much has been said regarding daily living skills, it is important to keep in mind that these skills are but one component of the educational program for the physically handicapped.

Academics (whether in a self-contained classroom or in the mainstream of regular education) must not be neglected. Hopefully, the academic program will, in part, incorporate practical experience (i.e., counting money and making change, reading survival words). For more intellectually capable persons, higher levels of academic instruction should be included in the academic program.

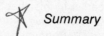 ### Summary

While using programs like the Santa Clara County Life Experience Program, teachers will find their roles infinitely more complex and challenging. However, the end results are proving to be worth the effort. Students are now graduating and progressing to sheltered workshops or to entry level, competitive employment. Many of these students were, a few years ago, considered unteachable and unemployable.

Notes

1. Adapted from the "Functional Skills Evaluation Rating Scale" *Life Experience Program: An alternative Approach in Special Education.* 1976, p. 70, with permission of the office of the Superintendent of Schools of Santa Clara County, 100 Skyport Drive, San Jose, California 95110.
2. The "Classroom Programmed Instruction (CPI)" example is adapted from the example on p. 89 of *Life Experience Program* (1976).
3. The "Practice In Community PIC" example is adapted from the example on p. 90 of *Life Experience Program* (1976).

References

Bachmann, W. *Influence of selected variables upon economic adaption of orthopedically handicapped and other health impaired.* Unpublished doctoral dissertation, University of the Pacific, 1971.

Life experience program: An alternative approach in special education. San Jose, Ca.: Office of the Santa Clara County Superintendent of Schools, 1976.

Resources

Gordon, S. *Living fully: A guide for young people with a handicap, their parents, their teachers, and professionals.* New York, N.Y.: John Day, 1975.

Katz, E. *The retarded adult in the community*. Springfield, Ill.: Charles C Thomas, 1972.

Park, L. Behaviors to normality for the handicapped adult in the United States. *Rehabilitation Literature*, 1975, *36*(4), 108–111.

Rehabilitation Gazette: International Journal & Information Service for the Disabled. (Available from 4502 Maryland Avenue, St. Louis, Missouri 63108.)

Rusalem, H. *Guiding the physically handicapped college student*. New York: Bureau of Publications, Teachers College, 1962.

ACADEMICS

The acquisition of basic academic skills is a difficult task for many school-aged children. Many books are available to help teachers instruct students with learning disabilities (check the end of this chapter for titles and other resources).

To provide additional help to teachers of students with physical disability, this chapter will share ideas about reading, spelling, handwriting and thinking skills. In discussing reading the focus will be on relating auditory and visual skills to reading; assessing perceptual skills through informal testing, error analysis, and diagnostic teaching; and determining reading and comprehension skills. Through these procedures, you can develop and implement the individualized programs which are necessary for each student to progress.

The section on spelling suggests ways of analyzing spelling errors. Simultaneously, teaching strategies are demonstrated for specific types of error.

Carolyn Compton, *Ph.D., is the education director of the Children's Health Council, Palo Alto, California.*
June Bigge.

Handwriting is a common tool through which youngsters demonstrate academic acomplishments. Teachers become unsure of what to do if a student has extreme difficulty in handwriting. This chapter will suggest ideas for students who do not write in the usual manner because they (a) cannot *hold* a writing utensil, (b) cannot coordinate movements to write, (c) are too weak to write, or (d) have missing arms or hands. The chapter "Severe Communication Problems" suggests other alternatives.

Finally, because of the authors' conviction that thinking skills should be taught with as much vigor as are the usual academic subjects, we propose methods for teaching these. Knowing that students who cannot write and those who do not talk have the most trouble practicing and demonstrating their thinking skills, specific suggestions are made for these children. Suggestions of course are readily adaptable to students with fewer physical problems.

To be sure, not all physically disabled individuals experience learning disabilities. Those with disorders not related to neurological functioning, such as amputations, degenerative muscle and joint diseases, and other limb deformities may learn normally with usual classroom instructional techniques. The percentage of learning disabilities in these students may be no higher than that found in the normal population. However, because many physically disabled students do have learning disorders, you must be familiar with the types of learning disabilities and the ways in which they affect the acquisition of academic skills.

Reading

Auditory Skills and Reading

Many of the current assessment tools and remedial programs for learning disabled students focus on the relationship between auditory perception and reading. To understand this relationship, it is important to remember that auditory perception is not the same process as auditory acuity or hearing. *Auditory perception* is the organization and interpretation of auditory stimuli—both speech sounds and environmental sounds—in the brain. It is the internal process of organizing things we hear and interpreting them on the basis of previous experience. It is discriminating, categorizing, and giving meaning to sounds. The process takes place in the brain and not in the ears.

Despite the tests and curriculum programs currently on the market for training auditory perception, there is conflicting evidence in the research regarding the concept that developing auditory perception skills is a prerequisite for reading. Hammill and Larsen (1974) summarized 33 correlational studies published between 1950 and 1973. They concluded that there was no validity to the assumptions that "particular auditory skills as measured are essential to the reading process" (p. 435). However, other longitudinal research indicates that auditory skills which deal with phonemic sounds such as sound blending (Chall, Roswell and Blumenthal, 1963) or speech sound discrimination (Bagford, 1968) have proven good predictors of reading success. In another longitudinal study, Hirshoren (1966) found a test of short-term auditory memory useful for predicting reading achievement.

Poor readers clearly exhibit certain behaviors which interfere with the reading process. Some of those behaviors which impede auditory skills are described below. Recognition of these behaviors when they occur will enable the classroom teacher to understand the student's errors.

1. *Poor Auditory Discrimination*—the inability to perceive the difference between two similar sounds; that is, the misperception of one word for another.

Examples: Mother asks Ann to bring her a *pin*; Ann brings mother a *pen*. The teacher dictates the word *grown* on a spelling test; Bill writes *Rome*.

2. *Auditory Figure-Ground Distractibility*—the inability to screen out irrelevant auditory stimuli and focus upon the primary auditory message.

Examples: Noise in the hallway makes it difficult for John to "hear" the speaker; the rest of the audience has no problem. Carol complains she can't "hear" the teacher because the student next to her is "too noisy"; that student is only cutting with scissors.

3. *Poor Auditory Analysis*—the inability to break down a spoken word into individual sounds and analyze their number and order.

Examples: Paul can spell *must* correctly but he does not understand that *must* and *muts* are the same sounds in a different order.

Tom cannot tell you how *shoe* and *push* are alike unless he sees the written words.

4. *Sound Blending Difficulty*—the inability to perceive a sequence of individual sounds and then blend them into a word; the opposite of auditory analysis, sound blending is also called *auditory synthesis*.

Examples: The teacher says "m–a–n"; Carol writes "and." David sounds out "im-por-tant" and says "impressed."

5. *Problems in Auditory Sequential Memory*—the inability to recall a series of auditory events *in order*; child cannot repeat a telephone number or a sentence, retell a story, or name the days of the week in order.

Examples: When mother asks Mary to hang up her clothes, make her bed, and empty the trash, Mary can only remember the first direction. Johnny carefully and slowly reads the sentence aloud *He takes good care of Spot*; when the teacher asks him to repeat it, John says *He takes care good of Spot*.

These examples illustrate behaviors related to auditory skills which interfere with the reading process. Aside from reading, they also interfere with a child's comprehension of spoken language; they make it difficult for her to comprehend and respond to the rapid flow of spoken language. One basis for reading is the receiving and expression of verbal language. Many students with reading problems have underlying language problems which have never been identified or remediated.

Visual Skills and Reading

As in the discussion of auditory skills, it is important to distinguish between visual acuity and visual perception. *Visual acuity* is related to the functioning of the eye; nearsightedness (myopia), farsightedness, and astigmatism are all problems of the eye mechanism related to the reception of visual stimuli. Perception is the transmission and organization of those stimuli by the neurological system and the brain. It is what we *make* of what we see and hear. (Bigge, 1976)

Hammill (1972) has also reviewed the correlational studies on the relationship of visual perception skills and reading comprehension. Of the 12 studies which satisfied his criteria, 8 reported no statistically significant relationship between visual perception skills and reading. In the same article, Hammill reports that 21 out of 25 intervention studies did not result in an improvement in reading through systematic visual-motor training.

It is clear, however, that reading, spelling, and writing do require the processing of visual symbols in the form of letters, numerals, and words. Many children display consistent behaviors which interfere with efficient visual processing. Understanding these behaviors will enable you to instruct the child more effectively.

1. *Poor Visual Discrimination*—the inability to perceive the difference between two similar visual symbols.

Examples: Bob confuses pairs of words such as:

nest	rest
came	come
went	want
when	then

Jane confuses operational signs in mathematics, $+$ and $\times$.

2. *Visual Figure-Ground Distractibility*—the inability to screen out irrelevant visual stimuli.

Examples: Alice complains that all the words run together as she reads. She frequently repeats words and phrases, includes words from other lines, or loses her place altogether.
Don cannot copy math problems correctly from the blackboard.

3. *Form-Constancy Problems*—the inability to perceive similarity in meaning in visual stimuli with slightly different forms; a generalization process.

Examples: Elizabeth becomes confused when the teacher writes "4" instead of "ч." Frank can read the words from the primer on flash cards with 100% accuracy; yet when he opens the book where the letter forms, size, and print are slightly different he does not recognize the words.

4. *Deficit in Visual-Sequential Memory*—the inability to process or recall a series of visual stimuli in sequential order.

Examples: Harry may read *stop* for *spot*; he often writes *gril* for *girl*.
Mr. Green has difficulty balancing his checkbook. $14.51 may be written down as $15.41.

5. *Difficulties in Spatial Relationships and Directionality*—the inability to organize visual stimuli in space; difficulty with left-to-right or top-to-bottom orientation.

Examples: John not only confuses *b-d-p-q*; he also has trouble with *n–u; m–w*; and *t–f*.
Susan cannot follow directions such as "Put your name in the upper, left-hand corner of the paper."
Jeff, at age ten, still writes Ɛ and ⌐ and cannot line up math problems correctly on a page.

Assessment of Perceptual Skills in the Physically Disabled

There are three procedures for the assessment of auditory and visual perceptual skills of the physically disabled:

1. informal testing
2. error analysis
3. diagnostic teaching

In this section, each procedure will be defined and examples of methods given.

Informal Testing Procedures

There are many formal and informal tests developed for the assessment of perceptual skills in children with learning disabilities. Unfortunately, these tests are often difficult to use with physically disabled children. The tests were developed for use with children who can respond in the usual ways—pointing to pictures, talking, drawing, and writing. Adaptations of the test format need to be made for the child with impaired expressive skills; the adaptations range from simply extending the time limits for children with slow speech and writing to major changes in the presentation format to allow a multiple-choice response rather than a verbal explanation.

The difference between formal and informal testing is that *formal tests* have standardized procedures for administration, timing, and scoring. They yield age-level and grade-level norms which allow you to compare the child with other children of similar age. Once the administration procedure or timing has been altered, the norms are no longer valid and fair comparisons cannot be made. *Informal testing,* or *diagnostic testing,* does not produce normed scores. The results enable the teacher to compare the child with others in the classroom but do not allow comparisons with others of the same age and grade. Because there are no norms, standardized administration procedures are not required and the examiner can modify both the format and the timing to allow the child the best opportunity to demonstrate her skills. In a sense, all diagnostic testing of severely involved, physically disabled students is informal because adaptations of formal tests are always required, and comparisons with nonphysically disabled students are risky.

There are many references available on testing physically disabled students, such as the ones at the end of this chapter, particularly Perlstein and Barnett, 1952, and Haeussermann, 1958. Formal testing is frequently done by psychologists trained in assessing the multidisabled. However, no matter how extensive the formal testing or skilled the psychologist, you will need more information. (Hammill, 1971) Following is a description of steps for classroom teachers to use in assessing the auditory and visual functioning of physically disabled students.

Step 1: Selecting the Response Mode. If a child has understandable speech or the ability to write, selecting a response mode presents no problems. The task is much more difficult when the child cannot speak or write. Although signing may be a possibility for some children, many physically disabled youngsters do not have adequate motor control for such refined gestural communication. For such children, the teacher must first determine the child's differential response to *yes* and *no*. Can he point to the words widely-spaced on a conversation board? Can he nod consistently for *yes* and shake his head for *no*? Can eye blinks be used for one or the other? Work together with the child to determine the communication system. Then assess whether a consistent pointing response can be obtained permitting multiple choice questions as a possible format. If the student can use a communication board and spell, then he can expand his responses if provided sufficient time. (See chapter on communication systems for further information.)

Step 2: Determining the Perceptual Process. Selection of the perceptual process to assess is based upon the educational question you are attempting to answer. The more specifically the educational question can be asked, the more appropriately the informal task can be designed, and the more useful will be the information obtained.

The figures 10–1 through 10–6, on pp. 194–5, are some examples of teacher-made, informal diagnostic tasks which assess specific perceptual processes. With informal testing procedures such as those described in these figures, the relationship between assessment and teaching is clearly seen. Too often the diagnostician does the testing and the teacher does the teaching or remediation. Optimally the two should proceed simultaneously in order that the educational plan for the child be continuously revised (Hammill, 1971). The assessment tasks described here could also be called *diagnostic teaching techniques* since many of them can be used as teaching activities.

Figures 10–1 through 10–6.

Educational Question: Can the student discriminate between similar phonic elements?

Task   I—Pronounce a series of word pairs which differ only in one phoneme.

       back–pack   initial consonant
       pet–pep   final consonant
       hem–ham   vowel

Have child indicate whether word pairs are *same* or *different*. Caution: Be sure child understands meaning of *same* and *different*. Include at least 30 word pairs.

Task   II—Pronounce series of single sounds and have child identify number of sounds heard and whether all sounds were same or different.

       p–p–p   3 sounds all same
       t–d   2 sounds different
       s–s–sh   3 sounds: two same/one different

Figure 10–1.

Educational Question: Can the student analyze the location and sequence of phonic elements?

Task   I—Read a list of words and ask child to indicate where he hears a given sound—at the beginning, middle, or end.

     m milk   *th* think
       summer   feather
       swim   breath

Task   II—Ask child to build or choose block design which represents the following sound pattern:

teacher says: child arranges colored blocks:
s p s | red | yellow | | red |

s s p | red | red | | yellow |

Caution: Be sure child progresses from left to right so results are not confused by directionality problems.

Figure 10–2.

Educational Question: Can the student blend isolated sounds and syllables into words?

Task   I—Give child a series of pictures and have him point to the one you say.

               c–u–p
               sh–oe
               dr–i–v–er

Caution: Keep blends, suffixes, and prefixes together. Be sure child knows names of pictures before you start.

Task   II—Have child listen to you say word broken into parts and then repeat it as a whole word.

pine–apple
Tues–day
an–i–mal
ca–ter–pill–ar

Figure 10–3.

Educational Question: Can the student discriminate similar looking words and letters?

Task   I—Present child with a series of words and have him indicate the one which is the same as the first word.

> *bed* bud dib bad dab *bed*
> *spot* stop *spot* pots past tops

Task   II—Utilize same procedure with single letters and numerals.

Caution: This procedure taps problems in discrimination, sequencing and directionality and requires careful analysis of errors.

Figure 10–4.

Educational Question: Can the student keep focused on the critical parts of a visual task?

Task   I—Present child with "hidden figure" pictures where he must find all the squares, shoes, toys, etc. in a complex background.

Task   II—Have child take a page from a book or of teacher's printing and locate all the *m*'s, or all the words beginning with *s*.

Figure 10–5.

Educational Question: Can the student generalize from one visual form to another with the same meaning?

Task   I—Prepare deck of alphabet cards with several forms of each letter.

A ɑ a   G g **g**

Shuffle deck thoroughly and have child name each one rapidly as presented. If naming is not possible select 5 or 6 letters with several forms and have child indicate how to sort the letters into groups, all A's together, etc.

Figure 10–6.

Examples of Error Analysis Techniques

Word (Stimulus)	Student (Response)	Error Type
cat	ɔat	letter reversal; directionality
boy	doy	letter reversal; directionality
will	well	auditory discrimination of vowel
make	mack	silent e rule; visual memory
say	sae	over generalization of silent e rule; visual memory
grown explain	grone explane	visual memory
enter advice	inter edvice	auditory discrimination of initial vowel
surprise	suprise	poor pronunciation
cook cut	kook kut	visual memory
light dress watch	lite dres woch	visual memory

Figure 10–7. Analysis of spelling errors.

Student Choices	Error Type
lite	visual memory
light	* * *
lihgt	visual sequencing
lit	visual memory; silent e rule
dress	* * *
bress	letter directionality
dres	visual memory
drest	auditory discrimination of final consonant
groan	homonym
grone	visual memory
grown	* * *
gron	visual memory; silent e rule
yaw	word directionality;
wah	letter directionality (inversion: y/h)
way	* * *
may	letter directionality (inversion: m/w)

Figure 10–8. Spelling error analysis using multiple-choice format.

Error Analysis Techniques

Analysis of a student's error pattern on a particular academic task can reveal the student's level of perceptual skills. Classroom teachers have daily examples of student's work readily available so new tasks do not have to be designed as in the informal testing procedure.

Written spelling is perhaps the easiest task for utilizing error analysis to determine perceptual skills. While the examples in Figure 10–7 are taken from student errors on the *Wide Range Achievement Test* (WRAT), (Jastak, Bijou, and Jastak, 1965) any spelling test can be used. The WRAT is used with children who can write responses. For the physically disabled student who cannot write, a multiple-choice format can be used.

Procedure

1. Give the student four spellings of a word and ask her to indicate the correct spelling. Present the words on cards or paper arranged in such a way as to facilitate the student's gesture or pointing response.
2. Analyze errors. The examples in Figure 10–8 illustrate the multiple-choice procedure and analysis of errors.

The use of error analysis is an efficient way to determine any student's spelling deficiencies. The pattern of poor visual recall and reliance upon auditory skills becomes immediately apparent. Also the opposite pattern may become obvious—good sight recall for words in a student's sight word vocabulary, and poor attack for new words due to weakness in auditory discrimination and analysis.

Diagnostic Teaching Techniques

The third method of assessing perceptual skills is through diagnostic teaching. When using diagnostic teaching, the teacher systematically experiments with several types of teaching materials to determine the most effective method for an individual student. In reading, for example, you would select two or three sets of materials emphasizing different approaches and try each of them with the student for a specified period of time and assess their effectiveness. Daily notes are taken describing the child's performance, and the rate of learning is documented. With diagnostic teaching, you should also ask the question, "How must this material be modified for the use of this student?"

Informal testing, error analysis, and diagnostic teaching are all ways in which the classroom teacher can obtain important information about the academic skills of the students. The use of this information in developing individual instructional programs will be discussed later in the chapter.

Assessment of Reading Level and Comprehension Skills

In order to plan an appropriate reading program for any student, assessment of perceptual skills should be accompanied by evaluation of the student's reading level and comprehension skills.

Assessing the Reading Level of a New Student

Reading *level* is assessed by asking a student to perform several tasks. These include:

1. Reading a graded list of single words to determine a recognition level.
2. Reading a series of graded paragraphs aloud and answering questions about the content to determine level of oral reading in contextual material.
3. Reading a series of graded paragraphs silently and answering questions about the content to determine level of silent reading in contextual material.

Commercial informal inventories are available. Standardized reading tests can also be used modifying print size and format when necessary. A multiple-choice format as described earlier can be devised. Many teachers prefer to construct their own reading level assessment, using the basal text available in their classroom. The following materials are needed:

1. A graded word list with at least 10 words from each reading level.
2. Two paragraphs at each reading level on separate cards or sheets. (Note the number of words in each paragraph.)
3. A scoring sheet for each student with the complete word list, all of the paragraphs, and five questions for each paragraph.

Procedure

1. Ask student to read a list of words corresponding to grade levels. Calculate percentage of words read correctly as sight words.
2. Select oral reading paragraphs for grade level at which students read the word list with 80% accuracy. Make a copy of the paragraphs on which to record student responses. Record student's errors as read. (See p. 198.)

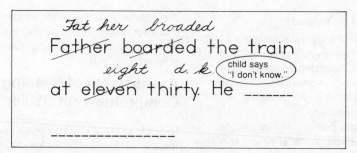

3. Ask five questions orally and record student's answers.

4. Discontinue *oral* reading when student makes 10 word errors in one paragraph or cannot correctly answer three questions.

5. Have student *silently* read another paragraph at the same level and ask five questions. Record the answers.

6. Discontinue silent reading assessment when student is unable to answer three questions about a paragraph.

The following guidelines are useful in analyzing each student's reading levels.

1. *Word recognition level* is that level at which the student can read the word list quickly and easily with 80% accuracy.

2. *Independent reading* (library, recreational) *level* is that level at which a student can read paragraphs orally with at least 90% accuracy and comprehension.

3. *Instructional level* (challenging but easily managed with your guidance) is that level at which the student can read orally with at least 80% accuracy and at least 80% comprehension.

4. *Frustration level* occurs at less than 80% accuracy and 80% comprehension. Learning is very inefficient when the student is in material at frustration level.

5. *Silent reading level* of 90% comprehension is required for independent assignments.

Informal inventories can usually be administered in less than 20 minutes per student. They yield a wealth of information about a child's ability to perform the basic reading tasks—sight word recognition, word analysis, fluency, and comprehension. A comprehensive review of informal inventories was completed by Johnson and Kress (1964).

Assessing Listening Comprehension in the Physically Disabled

Comprehension is, by definition, a receptive process. However, like all receptive processes, it is assessed through the expressive skills of speaking, gesturing, or writing. The physically disabled student with either receptive or expressive problems may appear to have comprehension difficulties.

Listening comprehension is a crucial skill for the physically disabled person since much of her information about the world will come from people talking to her and around her. The child with limited speech rarely gets the opportunity to question the speaker and clarify what she is hearing; thus misinformation can be obtained. Often, we say to someone, "Is this what you mean?" or "I thought you said . . . " to check the meaning. The child with limited speech does not have the same opportunity to clarify the meaning of the speaker.

Many tests for assessing listening comprehension have been developed for use with young aphasic children or others with severe receptive language deficits, such as *Assessment of Children's Language Comprehension* (Foster, Giddan, & Stark, 1972) and *Northwestern Syntax Screening Test* (Lee, 1969). With only minor modifications, such tests can be used with physically disabled students. These tests answer questions such as:

1. What is the level of the child's single word vocabulary? Does she know words such as *soldier, binoculars,* etc.?

2. How many critical elements can a child process efficiently? Can she follow the meaning of *little gray kitten under the chair* or only *kitten under chair.*

3. What parts of speech and syntactical constructions does she understand? Does she know the meaning of *behind, slowly, but, or*?

The answers to such questions are not only essential for the speech therapist working with the student in language development but also to the teacher and the parent. Very often, simply reducing the length of the sentence spoken to the student ("Bring chair here" instead of "Bring your chair over here to the table") increases comprehension dramatically.

Listening comprehension also encompasses material read to the student. For the physically disabled, listening is a major source of information about the world outside of school and home. To assess a student's level of listening comprehension for academic material, use the following procedure:

1. Select a series of paragraphs in a given subject area across at least a five-grade span, such as paragraphs from first through fifth grade science texts or third through eighth grade materials on Indians.
2. Determine the most efficient and consistent response mode.
   a. speech
   b. writing
   c. pointing (*yes–no* or multiple-choice questions)
   d. pointing (spelling on a conversation board)
   e. answering *yes* or *no* to multiple-choice items
3. Read the paragraph aloud to the student at normal reading speed. Ask her at least six questions about each paragraph. Include these question types:
   a. Immediate recall for specific fact—In what year did the French and Indian War begin?
   b. Immediate recall of general idea—Why were the French and Indians fighting the English?
   c. Vocabulary—What does the word *immense* mean?
   d. Inference—What difference would it have made if the battle had been fought in the winter?
4. *Instructional level* is determined by that paragraph which the student understands with 80% accuracy. Older students may have different levels of comprehension for different subject areas depending on experiences and interests. Also note the types of questions the student misses and utilize that information in designing lessons for a given student.
5. After instructional level is determined, experiment with the next highest level to see what modifications need to be made to increase comprehension. Variations to try:
   a. reading more slowly
   b. telling the child first what the story will be about, and reviewing some vocabulary words
   c. accompanying text with picture cues

Assessing Reading Comprehension in the Physically Disabled

An adequate assessment of reading comprehension requires more than the determination of the level at which a student can comprehend the material she is reading.

Reading comprehension requires the student to translate the individual visual symbols into meaningful words, phrases, and sentences. There are several types of reading comprehension problems:

1. decoding errors
2. poor language concepts
3. lack of experiential background
4. poor memory skills
5. poor expressive skills
6. lack of specific comprehension skills

For the large majority of students with average intellectual ability, the major cause of reading comprehension problems is poor decoding skills. The student with perceptual learning problems is often forced to read material too difficult for her. As she struggles with decoding, she cannot interpret meaning. The solution for this problem is simple—lower the level of material the student is reading to a point where she can read with 80% accuracy.

For other students, poor reading comprehension is due to poor language skills. If prepositions, conjunctions, and compound sentences are not comprehended in spoken English, they are unlikely to be comprehended in reading. If a student can decode the material, her level of reading comprehension is usually commensurate with her listening comprehension skills.

For many physically disabled students, the problem in reading comprehension is lack of experiential background. It is not that they cannot understand the verb form *wading*, they cannot appreciate how it would feel on a warm summer afternoon or on a cold, blustery winter day. All materials presented to students with "deprived" experiential backgrounds need to be accompanied by pictures, discussions, and other activities which convey the feeling tone of an experience. Many physically disabled students are "deprived," not for economic reasons, but because of experiential restrictions created by their disabilities.

Reading comprehension requires memory. Some students read the words, have the necessary concepts, but cannot recall the specific facts. Such students need memory prompts to improve comprehension:

1. Tell them ahead of time what the material is about and specific things to look for. This

strategy gives them a "pocket" to put information in as they read.
2. Have them read the questions they will have to answer before they read the paragraph.
3. Put key words and phrases on the board to aid recall.

Some students comprehend much better than we know but are unable to express their ideas. When the student cannot speak or write, we limit the questions we ask to specific facts and short answers. The result is that the student gets no opportunity to clarify her misconceptions and the teacher gains little information on the depth of the student's understanding of the topic. For such students, take time to develop a communication system such as that described in an earlier chapter.

Reading comprehension may be poor because a child lacks specific comprehension skills, such as:

1. recall of details
2. reading for the main idea
3. order of events
4. drawing conclusions

Many commercial materials ["Specific Skills Series," Boning (1974), and "New Practice Readers," Stone (1974)] designed for students with learning disabilities are available. Most can be used with physically disabled students with little modification in format.

Use of Assessment Data in the Teaching of Reading

The purpose of assessing perceptual skills, reading level, and comprehension is to determine for each student the most effective instructional program. The student with good perception, association, and memory skills will learn to decode in spite of the teacher. She can learn in spite of inefficient materials. She adapts to them with ease and teaches herself the skills not presented. The student with learning disabilities cannot learn from inappropriate and inefficient materials and teaching. She needs to be taught every subskill and will be able to manage only a slower rate of learning. Efficient materials and methods to meet her needs are essential.

The research data on the matching of perceptual strengths and weaknesses to reading methodology are mixed. Waugh (1973), Ringler and Smith (1973), Bateman (1968), and Robinson (1972) reported no interaction between a student's performance on perceptual tasks and success in a reading method presumably selected to match the learning profile. Lilly and Kelleher (1973) did find that when auditory and visual tests were reliable and related to reading there was a positive interaction between perceptual strengths and presentation of context material for recall.

Since the classroom teacher selects the materials for instruction, she should know the salient characteristics of common types of reading materials and the skills they require of children. Chall's book (1967) provides an excellent discussion of this subject.

Types of Beginning Reading Materials

A. Sight Word
   1. Contain controlled sight vocabulary with frequent repetitions.
   2. Introduce phonic elements separately and gradually integrate them into vocabulary.
   3. Use picture and context cues to aid comprehension.
   4. Require of the student   strong skills in:
      a. visual discrimination
      b. visual memory

B. Phonic Approaches
   1. Introduce sound-symbol association through systematic phonics; each sound introduced individually.
   2. Reduce sight vocabulary to a minimum.
   3. Emphasize phonic skills rather than "stories."
   4. Require of the student strong skills in:
      a. auditory discrimination
      b. sound blending
      c. auditory-visual integration

C. Linguistic Materials
   1. Teach basic word patterns rather than single letter sound; at pattern rather than a – t.
   2. Reduce nonregular words to a minimum.
   3. Emphasize linguistic patterns rather than "stories."
   4. Require of the student:
      a. auditory-visual integration

    b. Materials can be "slanted" in presentation to emphasize either auditory or visual skills.

D. Multisensory Teaching Approaches
  1. Teach sound-symbol association through simultaneous visual-auditory-kinesthetic (V-A-K) presentation.
  2. Emphasize different parts of the V-A-K presentation.
  3. Require of the student:
    a. consistent motor feedback
    b. V-A-K integration

The selection of reading materials for a student based entirely upon her scores on perceptual tests seems unwarranted by recent research. However, by studying test results and diagnostic teaching data some decisions can be made about materials for the beginning reader.

If a student has good visual discrimination and memory, the basic sight word basal reader may be the most efficient beginning reading method. It will allow her to get started in the exciting process of reading and to utilize the picture and context cues provided for story comprehension. Most "natural" readers—children who teach themselves to read before school—usually do so by acquiring a sight word vocabulary from signs and cereal boxes. The beginning reader with good visual memory can progress through the pre-primer, primer, and first reader materials and learn the phonics skills through the supplementary workbook activities.

For the student with poor visual recall, this method may be unwise. As demand for visual memory increases, the student becomes more and more frustrated and resorts to guessing wildly or attempting to "read" from the pictures alone. If this student has good auditory discrimination skills or generally stronger auditory processes, she should be placed in a systematic phonics approach which emphasizes the learning of sound-symbol associations through auditory-visual integration. Students with poor visual recall read slowly in any approach. The acquisition of a stable vocabulary is slow. However in a systematic phonics approach students do not develop the feeling that the reading act is a total mystery. They develop a basic word attack strategy which can be used in other academic areas such as spelling.

Linguistic materials also reduce the need for visual memory and allow students to develop a systematic word attack strategy. The mastery of sound patterns enables the student to progress more rapidly into "story" reading.

Multisensory approaches were developed for children who need motor or kinesthetic feedback to enhance poor auditory and visual perception skills. Only a small number of students in regular classrooms require the rigors of a multisensory approach. Conversely, for some students with physical and learning disabilities, the systematic multisensory approach builds an integrated V-A-K system which allows the children to learn reading, spelling, and writing effectively.

Prediction of Readiness

Given the complexities of the reading process, there is no absolute set of criteria which can be applied to a group of children which will sort out those who are "ready" from those who are "not ready" for formal reading. There are, however, certain guidelines which enable prediction of which students will have a successful experience in formal reading instruction. Two things should be kept in mind during the following discussion on guidelines. First of all, disabled students do not get "ready" for anything by themselves; the maturation process alone rarely improves prerequisite skills. Secondly, the term *formal reading instruction* implies a commitment on the part of the teacher; a commitment to select and utilize appropriate materials to help a student develop systematic word attack skills daily.

Guidelines

1. Normal students typically begin to read between 5 and 7 years of age; a mental age of 6 or 7 seems to be necessary to have developed the underlying language and perceptual skills necessary for reading. Mentally retarded students usually begin to master the reading process when their mental age reaches that of a first or second grader, even though their chronological age may be older.

Question: Do test results yield mental age scores indicating that the student is functioning at a 6–7-year-old level?

2. Reading is based on language. According to Myklebust (1960), the usual order of acquisition of language skills is a progression from inner language to receptive language (listening) to expressive language (speaking) to

reading and then to writing. A student who is ready for formal reading should have adequate receptive vocabulary and concept development.

Question: Do tests of receptive vocabulary indicate a functioning level of 6–7 years of age? Can the student demonstrate knowledge of basic concepts of size, shape, color, quantity, time and space? Sameness and difference?

3. We have discussed at length the perceptual processes and their relationship to reading. In order for a student to experience success in reading she must demonstrate some basic perceptual skills.

Question: Can the student learn fairly easily new tasks requiring basic auditory and visual discrimination? Can she remember spoken sentences and printed words such as her name?

4. The student who is ready for formal instruction exhibits attention for and interest in activities related to reading.

Question: Does the student like to be read to? Does the student like and understand the process of experience stories? Does the student select activities with letters and numbers when given free choice?

Spelling

Spelling is the academic subject which most clearly demonstrates the integration of auditory, visual, and kinesthetic skills. It is a process of translating oral words into graphic symbols using visual memory, phonetic, and motor skills. Hildreth (1947) points out the integration of the three major modalities needed for the spelling process. The essence of spelling is sequencing, a skill frequently deficient in the learning disabled child.

There are many ways to learn to spell. The efficient speller has strong visual memory; she can recall how a word looks. Good spellers also use phonics. The child with efficient phonic skills learns to sound out the "regular" words, then she memorizes the nonphonetic words.

As mentioned earlier in this chapter, it is possible to analyze spelling errors. Teaching strategies can then be developed such as in the chart below, pp. 202–3.

---

1. If the student demonstrates consistent weaknesses in visual memory:
   a. Emphasize the visual features of the word—color-code the silent letters.

 red

Increase the size of the silent letters.

Focus on the shape of the word.

fight

   b. Reinforce poor visual recall with tracing and writing activities, such as

   writing in the air
   tracing
   dictation
   eye tracing
   writing in clay

2. If the student demonstrates consistent weaknesses in auditory skills:
   a. Train auditory discrimination by emphasizing articulation by having the student:

   1. Watch you say the word.
   2. Feel your articulators.
   3. Say the word himself.
   4. Feel his articulators.

Most students learn reading and spelling in similar ways. Sight word readers often become sight word spellers and the phonics-oriented student utilizes these skills as her basic spelling attack. For this reason, reading and spelling are most efficiently taught as one unit. Analysis of spelling errors together with a reading level assessment can often lead to selection of an appropriate reading method.

Handwriting

The objective in teaching handwriting to the physically disabled is the same goal as for nondisabled: legible communication. While the goal may be the same, the means to this goal may differ significantly. Adaptations must be considered to enable some physically disabled persons to master handwriting. After describing some critical features of printing and cursive handwriting, this section will illustrate adapted and modified approaches which aid physically disabled children.

Florence and Mullins (1970) discuss features of printing and cursive writing. Children are usually taught to print before they learn cursive writing because printed letters are easier to form and more closely resemble book print. But printing is not the easiest form for some children to write. Printing which is made up of separate letters may cause problems for children who tend to transpose letters vertically or horizontally. Printed letters are not connected to each other, nor do they indicate spatial relationship or proper sequence. They are not slanted, so they do not indicate the direction of writing. Cursive writing may be easier for some disabled children to write because of its connective lines. These lines indicate the order, position, and grouping of letters. The slant of cursive writing indicates the left-right direction of words. But, learning cursive writing means learning a form of writing which is dissimilar to book print.

Students often have handwriting problems because they cannot hold a pencil, pen, chalk, or crayon. (See Figure 10–9, p. 204.) They may also have problems because they cannot coordinate movements needed to write on paper. (See Figure 10–10, p. 206.) These individuals may not be capable of performing fine motor movements and therefore may be unable to confine their writing to small spaces and to write without involuntarily moving the writing paper. Others may have prob-

---

    5. Emphasize often slurred syllables

       lit*er*ature

       lib*ra*ry

       sepa*ra*te

  b. Reinforce auditory discrimination with visual cues—use consistent lingusitic patterns

    cat

    rat

    sat

    Color-cue difficult auditory discriminations

          blue   *red*

    h**e**m   h**i**m

  c. Reinforce weak auditory skills with writing

    dictation

    tracing

    writing in the air

  3. If the student consistently makes writing errors such as reversals:

    a. Train letter formation through

       tracing

       writing in the air

       writing in clay

       sandpaper letters

    b. Reinforce letter formation with visual cues

       color-coding

    c. Reinforce the letter formation with auditory cues

       "a line and a ball makes a *b* "

Figures 10–9. *a–f.* Devices to aid those

(Pages 204–6) persons who cannot hold handwriting tools.

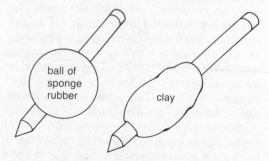

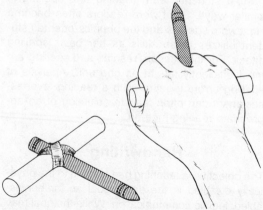

Figure 10–9. *a.* Pencil pushed through a ball of sponge rubber or other bulky material cut to fit child's grasp.

(Above)

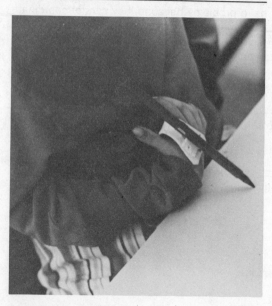

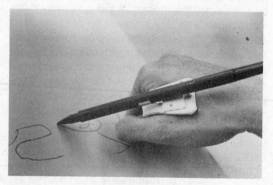

Figure 10–9. *b.* Pencil holders to
(Above and left) accommodate grasp and angle of hand.

lems because they are too weak to write normally. (See Figure 10–11, p. 209.) Still others have missing arms and need to learn to write with a prosthesis. (See Figure 10–12, p. 210.)

Care must be taken to equip persons with the best adaptations to fit specific functional problems. Many can be handmade while others can be adapted or purchased to accommodate each particular student's needs. Adaptations illustrated following represent only a portion of the possibilities. Typing and other means of expressing ideas are explained in the chapter on communications.

Thinking Skills

This final section of the chapter is written to suggest ways disabled individuals can practice and use thinking skills. The goal is to help the child assume responsibility for her own thinking. You should draw attention to the thinking process and provide guidance and reinforcement as the child learns the various skills. Objectives are based on increasing the number and complexity of children's thinking skills and increasing their ability to see relationships and solve problems. Sometimes learning occurs with classroom assignments and sometimes it occurs in "real-life situations."

Children are constantly faced with problems. Some are found in workbooks or on worksheets and require predetermined answers. Some problems are faced in social interactions and in other

Figure 10–9. *c.* Utensil attached to hand to prevent dropping; Large crayon made from melted crayons.

(Above)

Figure 10–9. *d.* Typewriter with or without guard.

(Above)

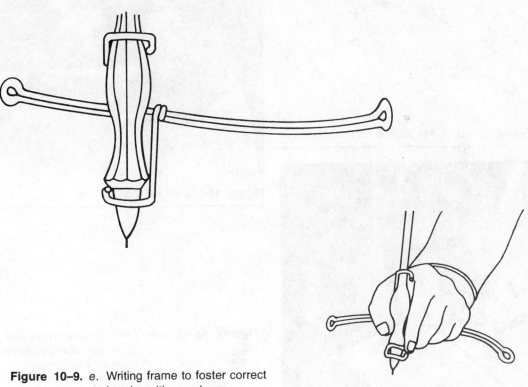

Figure 10–9. *e.* Writing frame to foster correct hand position and arm movement.[1]

interactions with the child's environment. Some kinds of problems take the form of problem-solving practice tasks suggested by classroom teachers. Finding and supporting an answer may be a goal for some problems. Other problems are open ended and provide opportunity for originality. All of these situations provide opportunity for the child to practice problem-solving strategies.

Those who work with physically disabled individuals will at some time experience the challenge

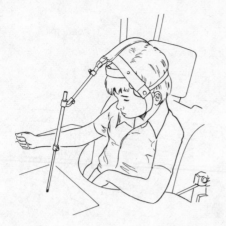

Figure 10–9. *f*. Use of other body parts.[2]

Figure 10–10. *b*. Script-writing guide.[4]

Figure 10–10. *a*. Magnetic wrist hold-down.[3]

Figure 10–10. *d*. Ink stamps.

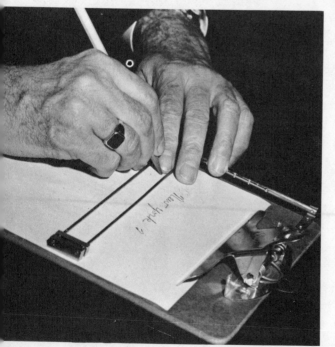

Figure 10–10. *c*. APH signature guide.[5]

Figures 10–10. *a–h*. Devices to aid those persons who have problems in motor coordination.
(Pages 206–8)

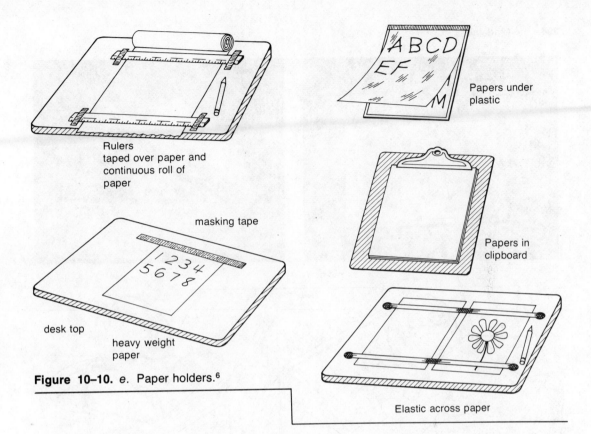

Rulers
taped over paper and
continuous roll of
paper

masking tape

desk top

heavy weight
paper

Figure 10–10. *e*. Paper holders.[6]

Papers under
plastic

Papers in
clipboard

Elastic across paper

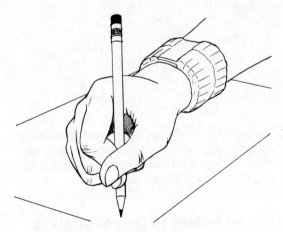

Figure 10–10. *f*. Wrist weights.

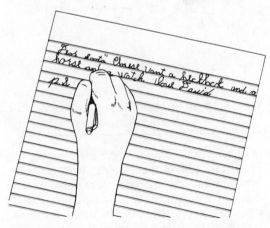

Figure 10–10. *g*. Raised lines as guides.[7]

Figure 10–10h, next page.

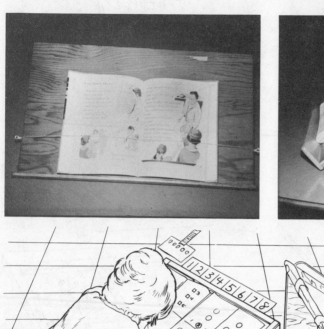

Figure 10–10. *h.* Slant boards providing correctly-angled writing surface.

of working with individuals who are unable to talk intelligibly, control their hands, type, or write. What are ways these individuals can demonstrate their use of thinking skills? How may they practice if they can't talk or write? We must find ways these individuals can gain the emotional and psychological satisfaction which results from the ability to make decisions and solve problems.

Activities can be planned so that even though children do not talk or write, they can work independently and demonstrate their use of thinking skills in problem solving. Almost any problem solving activity can be planned so children can respond in polar responses; sorting, matching, classifying, and making comparisons responses; and multiple choice, or sequencing responses. Activities can be designed to elicit thinking patterns which parallel those undertaken by nondisabled or mildly motor disabled.

Use of Polars in Demonstrating Thinking Skills

Many problems can be answered or solved with one or another of two polar responses. Pairs of polar responses might include *yes–no, true–false, high value–low value, agree–disagree,* and *same–different.* Accompanying each of the polars above is the possibility of a third option indicating an inability to answer or *I don't know* when confronted with *yes–no* problems. Ideally, three distinctive motor movements would be used, one for

Figures 10–11. *a–d*. Ways to aid persons who
are weak.

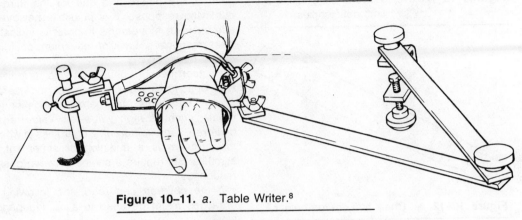

Figure 10–11. *a*. Table Writer.[8]

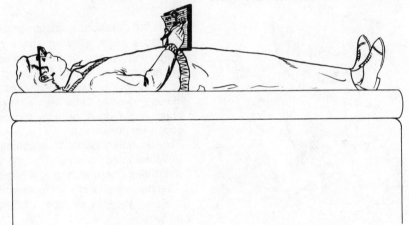

Figure 10–11. *b*. Prism glasses allow persons
to write when lying on back.

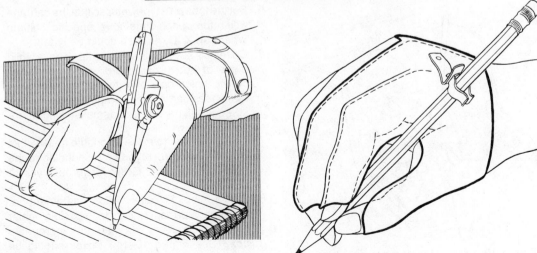

Figure 10–11. *c*. Splint and cuffs.

Figures 10–12. *a–c*. Ways to aid persons with limb deficiencies.

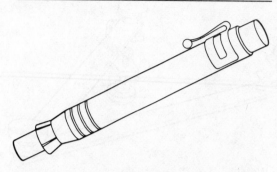

Figure 10–12. *a*. Chalk and crayon holder.[9]

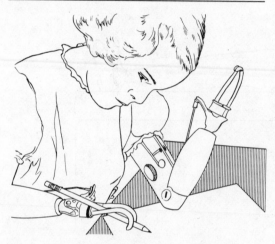

Figure 10–12. *b*. Use of the prosthesis.

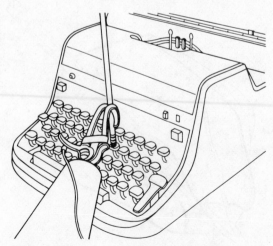

Figure 10–12. *c*. Use of a pencil to type.

each of the polars and one for the third and qualifying response. It is possible, however, to use only two movements in order to indicate all three responses. Lack of movement could indicate a response.

Factual questions usually provide the individual with options to respond *yes–no* or *true–false*. Some statements may permit ratings or judgments, such as *high value–low value, agree–disagree, same–different*. Regardless of whether the problem is a question or statement, the stimulus can require a choice between possible responses.

If the children can read, the following approaches might be used to allow independent work.

1. Write the questions or statements horizontally across a page, allowing ample room at the beginning or end of the statements for response marks. A *plus* (+) or an X may be used for the positive response; a *blank* or *minus* (−) or an O for the negative response; and a circle, dash, or blank for the neutral or qualifying statement.
2. Provide heavy paper to accommodate large uncoordinated strokes. The marking instrument might be attached to a hand splint.
3. Attach a large handle to blocks which will print a +, −, *yes–no*, or other desired response options.
4. Hang large paper on an easel with widely spaced answers to be marked with a paint brush or crayon attached to a long head pointer. (See Figure 10–13.)
5. Set the tabs on a typewriter so that the carriage will return each time to a specific column where an *X,* O, or dash could be typed.
6. Cover all keys of the typewriter with a solid piece of heavy cardboard, wood or plastic, cutting holes only over two or three needed responses and the carriage return. This strategy will prevent accidental striking of undesired keys.
7. Teach children to make a scribble mark with a different colored crayon corresponding to the different responses. Green for *agree*, black for *disagree*.
8. Provide boxes after each statement or question corresponding to possible polar answers. Students can mark the appropriate box. (See Figure 10–14.) Boxes should be spaced so students with poor motor control can mark one without the other.

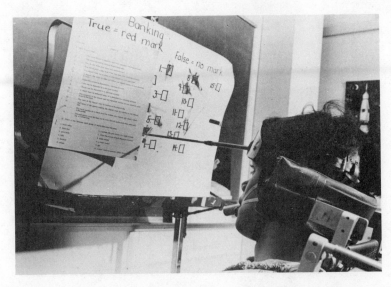

Figure 10–13. Students may be able to mark widely spaced answers.

(Statement)	Agree	Disagree	No Opinion
1. _____	☐	☐	☐
2. _____	☐	☐	☐

Figure 10–14. Any kind of mark on a box will designate the student's response.

9. Make holders for sentence strips which can be pushed or dropped into containers marked according to the options: i.e., *agree, disagree*. (See Figure 10–15.) Sentence strip can be inserted as needed.

For *children who cannot read,* the following approaches might be used:

1. Tape-record questions or statements. The recording must state the number of each statement or question. To each statement or question that is positive, students mark the corresponding number on a list of consecutive numbers. Numbers not marked designate the negative responses. For those with severe coordination problems, numbers should be placed far apart on a stiff piece of paper taped to a desk so the student can scribble over the number which corresponds to the *true*, or positive, statements.
2. If questions are written and children cannot

read, a second option includes using headphones and listening to a tape recording of the written material. Students then record answers in the same manner as students who can read the items.
3. If a teacher aide is available, or if children are participating in a small group, they can respond by (*a*) using any of several signals for *yes-no* and *I don't know*, (*b*) look at *yes* and *no* placed to the far right and far left of the blackboard, (*c*) use a head light [10] to point to response options written on the blackboard, or (*d*) hit a bell once for a positive response, twice for the negative, and not at all for a third response.

Sorting, Matching, Classifying, and Making Comparison Responses

Matching, sorting, classifying and similar ac-

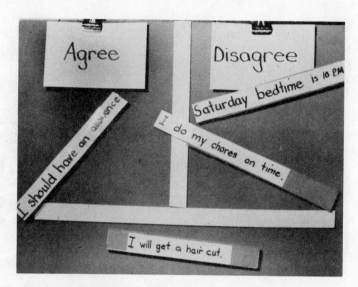

Figure 10–15. Sentence strips can be inserted into holders as needed.

tivities can be provided if materials and equipment are appropriate and are placed properly. Children may be able to *sort* sentence strips or other objects containing other kinds of information for sorting. For greater ease in handling, moving, or "knocking", strips would therefore need to be mounted on cardboard or inserted into teacher-made holders. Letters, words, or sentences may also be mounted under clear plastic, on stiff cardborad, on blocks of wood, or on a sponge. In this way, the same blocks can be used over and over again for different activities. Rubber balls cut in half can be moved from place to place and will not roll. Choice options can be pinned to the rounded halves of the balls. Words or numbers attached to magnets can be used on a cookie sheet.

Space for sorting of responses can be designated in many ways. Places designated to receive the objects may include desk tops or tray toys with strips of masking tape forming separate areas.

Four corners of a wheelchair tray with sides which prevent objects from being knocked to the floor can be designated as areas for choices. For the severely profoundly disabled, you could designate a lap or large floorspace to which selected objects may be knocked from a table top.

A child could use different kinds of containers to receive objects or sorting trays. (See Figure 10–16, p. 212–13.)

Basket and tray.

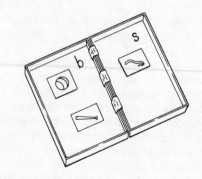

Attached lid and bottom of hosiery box.

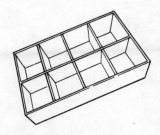

Box with dividers.

Jars.

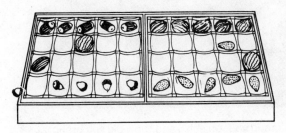

Candy or nut boxes.

Figure 10–16. Places for sorting.
(Pages 212–13, above and left)

For each activity, a sample object or sign may be displayed as a reference point. Other materials are sorted, matched, or compared with reference to the sample object or the sign. Attributes can be defined as the basis for sorting, matching, or comparing. There is an option for the individual herself to designate the category or the attribute for classfication or comparison. The child can then match or make comparisons according to her own criteria. The criteria should become obvious to an observer as the material is arranged. In Figure 10–17, p. 214, Laura completes a problem-solving exercise designed to parallel the written lesson of her 31 classmates.

Materials and problems for children *who cannot* use their hands at all will be similar to those described in the previous section. Someone, however, must point or move objects for these children. A child can be approached with prob-

lems such as: "We're looking for something that goes here" or "We're looking for something that goes with this," followed by questions all asked in the *same tone of voice:* "This one? This one?" or "Shall I put it here? Here? Here?" The disabled individual then would kick her foot, raise her eyes, or use some other signal when a teacher or someone else points to the one representing her choice.

Multiple Choice or Sequencing Responses

Content for choices in *multiple choice* activities and for sequences in *sequencing* activities may be provided by the teacher or may be generated by the child. A few ideas will be given for those individuals for whom the activities must be adapted. The choices can be numbered so that an individual could record the number instead of the whole word or sentence. For instance, a student indicates a letter or number which indicates her answer to the teacher's question. "Which *sentence* best tells about the fun at the beach?" "*B.*" "Which *word* tells how the children will move on the beach?" "*3.*"

	1	2	3	4	5	6
A	The	sun	shines	on	the	shed.

	1	2	3	4	5	6
B	We	will	rush	to	find	shells.

Numbers and letters can be used in many other ways. Numbering the problems and coding the possible solutions by numbers or letters allows a student to write only one digit to represent the problem and another digit or symbol to represent

Figure 10–17. Third graders are asked "group your objects" and "how did *you* group *your* objects?" (What attributes?) By using one fist to stabilize the other, Laura forms her groups.

the solution. For instance, if Problem 1 has four choices, *a, b, c, d,* or *1, 2, 3, 4,* the student would respond with some indication of the problem number and then some indication of the response letters or number. These responses could vary from writing the numbers to representing each of the numbers by the appropriate number of strokes with a paint brush. Likewise the first in a sequence could be marked with one stroke and the second with two strokes.

These activities can be varied for *nonreaders* by using several alternate strategies. The Language Master (Bell-Howell) card color-coded in red could represent "the problem card." It could be replayed as many times as necessary. Solution cards giving the choices are also run through the Language Master. In this way, the child is able to place one or more chosen solution cards with the appropriate problem card.

The tape recorder can again be used for nonreaders. Questions or situations can be recorded two times consecutively on the tape to assure the listener's comprehension. Answer possibilities can be coded with a number, letter, or color and can be recorded twice. The student would then

respond by marking the appropriate letter or number or by putting the appropriate colored block to represent her choice in a place designated for each problem. Some films and tapes also provide opportunity for more complex and lengthy problems. Audio and visual media may be viewed several times. The viewer can then request that the media be stopped at the portion(s) that indicate her hypothesis or answer.

Cubes, like those used to display photographs, can be used in many ways. Choices of pictures, representations of situations, or representations of attributes, can be lined up on cubes and the proper choice knocked out of line from the others by the child. Cubes can be used for sequencing, with one cube added which does not belong. The child can find that cube and knock it out of position. For instance, if the child was to spell the word *ate,* the first cube could say *a,* the second cube could say *o,* the third *t,* and the fourth *e.* The object would be to knock out the *o* cube. A paragraph of a story which contains inaccurate information may be knocked from the group. (See Figure 10–18.)

The individual could knock the cube over and over until the side indicates her choice of

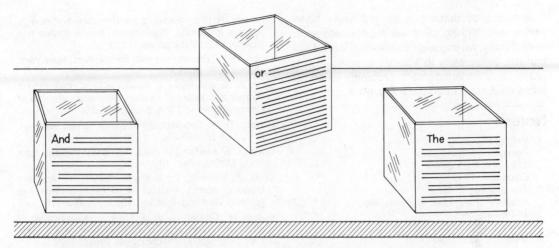

Figure 10–18. Knock away the one that does *not* belong.

alternatives. If she has several cubes, even more alternatives are presented and the task becomes more complex.

Other uses of multiple-choice format in which student can work with a tape recorder, typewriter, the tic-tac-toe, or other means suggested for multiple-choice format are in the chapter, "Severe Communication Problems."

Formulating and Testing Hypotheses

Situations that are truly problematic do not have predetermined or universally accepted answers. To attempt to solve these the problem-solving strategy is helpful. Individuals must increase their abilities to recognize a problematic situation, to *select* best alternatives or hunches, to *solve* by specifying a solution based upon the best information available, and to *summarize* and evaluate results. If only one person is involved in problem solving, these conclusions result from evidence gathered to support one of several hypotheses or answers that seems most tenable to one person. If more than one individual is involved in solving a problem, each may gather or interpret her own evidence to support differing hypotheses. If evidence differs, consensus should be sought. In these cases each person should state her own conclusions based upon her best evidence. The resulting consequences of decisions resulting from problem solving can be evaluated later.

Applying Problem Solving to Life-Management Problems

Thinking skills and problem solving abilities are needed for a variety of life-management problems: *sorting* and *matching* clothing, *sequencing* cooking procedures, *classifying* foods to comply with medically prescribed diets, and *comparing* features of wheelchairs when considering a new purchase. *Formulating and testing hypotheses* are more formal processes which might be used, for example, to research which of several strategies would seem most likely to result in action to get curb cuts installed in a downtown area.

For every action such as sorting laundry or planning a day's menu, individuals must learn to review their actions and evaluate consequences of each of their decisions. Use of thinking skills and problem solving strategies leads to increased awareness of their own strengths and limitations and helps to monitor their progress toward greater independence.

Summary

A core of the school program is the teaching of basic academic skills. This chapter focused on the physically disabled student with learning problems. Techniques for assessing each student's skills in perceptual tasks, reading, and spelling were presented, as well as ways to utilize the assessment data in the implementation of an individualized instructional program.

Special procedures can suggest ways handwriting and thinking skills will support academic work. Finally, we suggest that disabled individuals can use these skills to attempt to solve a wide realm of life-management problems such as those discussed throughout this book.

Notes

1. Writing Frame
   Zaner-Bloser (pamphlet)
   612 North Park Street
   Columbus, Ohio
2. The Enabler
   Adaptive Therapeutic Systems, Inc.
   36 Howe Street
   New Haven, Conn. 06511
3. Magnetic Wrist Hold-Down
   Preston Catalog #1095 Equipment for Health Care and Rehabilitation
   J. A. Preston
   71 Fifth Avenue
   New York, N.Y. 10003
4. Script Writing Guide
   American Foundation for the Blind
   15 W. 16th St.
   New York, N.Y. 10011
5. APH Signature Guide
   American Printing House for the Blind
   1839 Frankfort Ave.
   P.O. Box 6085
   Louisville, Kentucky 40206
6. Bigge, June. Project S.P.O.T., *Systems of Precise Observations for Teachers*. Printed Guidelines produced under contract for Bureau of Education for the Handicapped, U.S. Office of Education, 1970.
7. Raised-Line Paper
   Modern Education Corporation
   P.O. Box 721
   Tulsa, Oklahoma 74101
8. The Table Writer
   Adaptive Therapeutic Systems, Inc.
   36 Howe St.
   New Haven, Conn. 06511
9. Chalk & Crayon Holders
   Blakeslee, Berton. *The Limb-deficient Child.* Berkeley: University of California, 1963, pp. 306–307.
10. "Sharp Focus Headlight" is described in the chapter, "Severe Communication Problems."

References

Reading

Bagford, J. Reading readiness scores and success in reading. *Reading Teacher*, 1968, *21*, 324–328.

Bateman, B. The efficacy of an auditory and a visual method of first grade reading instruction with auditory and visual learners. In H. Smith (Ed.), *Perception and reading*. Newark: International Reading Association, 1968.

Bateman, B. (Ed.). *Reading performance and how to achieve it*. Seattle, Washington: Bernie Straub and Special Child Publications, 1973.

Bigge, M. L. *Learning theories for teachers*. New York: Harper & Row, 1976.

Birch, A. G., & Belmont, L. Auditory-visual integration in normal and retarded readers. *American Journal of Orthopsychiatry*, 1964, *34*(5), 852–860.

Boning, R. A. *Specific skill reading series*. Baldwin, N.Y.: Loft B., 1974.

Chall, J. S. *Learning to read: The great debate*. New York: McGraw-Hill, 1967.

Chall, J., Roswell, F., & Blumenthal, S. H. Auditory blending ability: A factor in success in beginning reading. *Reading Teacher*, 1963, *17*, 113–118.

Foster, R., Giddan, J. J., & Stark, J. *Assessment of children's language comprehension*. Palo Alto, Calif.: Consulting Psychologists Press, 1972.

Haeussermann, E. *Developmental potential of preschool children*. New York: Grune & Stratton, 1958.

Hammill, D. Evaluating children for instructional purposes. *Academic Therapy*, 1971, *6* (4), 341–353.

Hammill, D. Training visual perceptual processes. *Journal of Learning Disabilities*, 1972, *5*, 552–559.

Hammill, D., & Larsen, S. The relationship of selected auditory perceptual skills and reading ability. *Journal of Learning Disabilities*, 1974, *7*, 429–435.

Hertzig, M. E., & Birch, H. G. Neurologic organization in psychiatrically disturbed adolescent girls. *Archives of General Psychiatry*, 1966, *15*, 590–598.

Hirshoren, A. A comparison of the predictive ability of the revised Stanford Binet Intelligence Scale and I.T.P.A. *Exceptional Child*, 1966, *32*, 533–539.

Jastak, J. F., Bijou, S. W., & Jastak, S. R. *Wide Range Achievement Test Manual*. Wilmington, Delaware: Guidance Associates of Delaware, 1965.

Johnson, M., & Kress, R. *Individual reading inventories: Sociological and psychological factors in reading*. Proceedings of the 21st Annual Reading Institute, International Reading Association, Temple University, 1964.

Lee, L. *Northwestern Syntax Screening Test*. Evanston, Illinois: Northwestern University, 1969.

Lilly, M.S., & Kelleher, J. Modality strengths and aptitude treatment interaction. *Journal of Special Education*, 1973, *7*, 5–13.

Myklebust, H. R. *Language and language development*. In *The psychology of deafness*. New York: Grune & Stratton, 1960.

Perlstein, M. D., & Barnett, H. E. Natural history and recognition of cerebral palsy in infancy. *Journal of American Medical Association*, 1952, *148*, 1389–1397.

Ringler, L. H., & Smith, I. L. Learning modality and word recognition of first grade children. *Journal of Learning Disabilities*, 1973, *6*, 307–312.

Robinson, H. M. Visual and auditory modalities related to methods for beginning reading. *Reading Research Quarterly*, 1972, *8*, 7–39.

Stone, C. R. *New practice readers*. Novato, Calif.: McGraw-Hill Webster Division, 1974.

Waugh, R. P. Relationship between modality preference and performance. *Exceptional children*, 1973, *6*, 465–469.

Spelling

Hildreth, G. *Learning the three R's*. Minneapolis, Minn.: Educational Publishers, 1947.

Writing

Florence, J., & Mullins, J. A script to supplant cursive writing or printing. *Teaching Exceptional Children*, 1970, *3*, (1), 23–32.

Comprehensive

Bateman, B. (Ed.). *Reading performance and how to achieve it*. Seattle, Washington: Bernie Straub and Special Child Publications, 1973.

Bateman, B. *The essentials of teaching*. San Rafael, Calif.: Dimensions, 1971.

Becker, W. C., Engelmann, S., & Thomas, D. R. *Teaching 1: Classroom management* (2nd ed.). Chicago, Ill.: Science Research Associates, 1975.

Becker, W. C., Engelmann, S., & Thomas, D. R. *Teaching 2: Cognitive learning and instruction* (2nd ed.). Chicago, Ill.: Science Research Associates, 1975.

Becker, W. C., & Engelmann, S. *Teaching 3: Evaluation*. Chicago, Ill.: Science Research Associates, forthcoming.

Bereiter, C., & Engelmann, S. *Teaching disadvantaged children in the preschool*. Englewood Cliffs, N.J.: Prentice-Hall, 1966.

Bigge, J. The consultant in programs for the physically handicapped. In Kenneth Blessing (Ed.), *The role of the resource consultant in special education*. Washington, D.C.: Council for Exceptional Children, 1968.

Connor, F. P. The education of children with crippling and chronic medical conditions. In Cruickshank, W. M., and Johnson (Eds.), *Education of Exceptional Children and Youth* (3rd ed.). Englewood Cliffs, N.J.: Prentice-Hall, 1975.

Connor, F., & Cohen, M. *Leadership preparation for educators of crippled and other health impaired-multiply handicapped populations*. New York: Teachers College, Columbia University, 1973.

Connor, F., Rusalem, H., & Baker, J. W. (Eds.). *Professional preparation for educators of crippled children: Competency-based programming*. New York: Teachers College, Columbia University, 1971.

Connor, F. P., Wald, J. R., & Cohen, M. J. *Professional preparation for educators of crippled children: Report of a special study institute*. New York: Teachers College, Columbia University, 1971.

Connor, F. P., Williamson, G. G., & Siepp, J. M. (Eds.). *A program guide for infants and toddlers with neuromotor and other developmental disorders*. New York: Teachers College, Columbia University, 1976.

Cruickshank, W. M., Bentzen F. A., Ratzeburg, F. H., &

Tannhauser, M. T. *A teaching method for brain-injured and hyperactive children*. Syracuse: Syracuse University, 1961.

Cruickshank, W. M. *Cerebral palsy: Its individual and community problems*. Syracuse, N.Y.: Syracuse University, 1966.

Cruickshank, W. M. (Ed.). *Cerebral palsy: A developmental disability*. Syracuse, N.Y.: Syracuse University, 1976.

Denhoff, E. *Cerebral palsy: The preschool years: Diagnosis, treatment and planning*. Springfield, Ill.: Charles C Thomas, 1967.

Denhoff, E., & Robinault, I. *Cerebral palsy and related disorders: A developmental approach to dysfunction*. New York: McGraw-Hill, 1960.

Engelmann, Z. *Preventing failure in the primary grades*. Chicago, Ill.: Science Research Associates, 1969.

Exceptional Children. Official journal of the Council for Exceptional Children, 1220 Association Drive, Reston, Va. 22091.

Focus on exceptional children. Monthly. (Available from Love Publishing, 6635 East Villanova Place, Denver, Colo. 80222.)

Gallagher, J. J. (Ed.). *Application of child development research to exceptional children*. Reston, Virginia: Council for Exceptional Children, 1975.

Gallagher, J. J. *Teaching the gifted child* (2nd ed.). Boston: Allyn & Bacon, 1975.

Hart, V. *Beginning with the handicapped*. Springfield, Ill.: Charles C Thomas, 1974.

Haeussermann, E. *Developmental potential of preschool children*. New York: Grune & Stratton, 1958.

Jones, R., & MacMillan, D. L. *Special education in transition*. Boston: Allyn and Bacon, 1974.

Kauffman, J. M., & Payne, J. S. (Eds.). *Mental retardation: Introduction and personal perspectives*. Columbus, Ohio: Charles E. Merrill, 1975.

Krumboltz, J. D., & Krumboltz, H. *Changing children's behavior*. Englewood Cliffs, N.J.: Prentice-Hall, 1972.

Le Gay Brereton, B., and Ironside, M. *Cerebral palsy: Basic abilities: A plan for training the preschool child*. New South Wales, Australia: Spastic Center of New South Wales, 1975.

Lerner, J. W. *Children with learning disabilities: Theories, diagnosis and teaching strategies*. Boston: Houghton-Mifflin, 1976.

Markoff, A. *Teaching low achieving children reading, spelling and writing*. Springfield, Ill.: Charles C Thomas, 1976.

Marks, N. C. *Cerebral palsy and learning disabled children: A handbook guide to treatment, rehabilitation and education*. Chicago, Ill.: Charles C Thomas, 1974.

Myers, P. I., & Hammill, Donald D. Methods for learning disorders. New York: John Wiley & Sons, 1969.

McDonald, E., & Chance, B. *Cerebral palsy*. Englewood Cliffs, N.J.: Prentice-Hall, 1964.

Prehm, H. J., & Prehm, A. R. *Improving instruction for the retarded*. New York: McGraw-Hill, 1974.

Prehm, H. J., & Prehm, A. R. *Improving instruction through classroom research*. Denver, Colorado: Love, 1976.

Wallace, G., & Kauffman, J. M. *Teaching children with learning problems*. Columbus, Ohio: Charles E. Merrill, 1973.

Wallace, G., & McLaughlin, J. A. *Learning disabilities concepts and characteristics*. Columbus, Ohio: Charles E. Merrill, 1975.

Whitehead, M. B. Classroom methods for the physically handicapped. *Teachers encyclopedia*. Englewood Cliffs, N.J.: Prentice-Hall, 1966, pp. 877–900.

Writing

Robinault, I. (Ed.). *Functional aids for the multiply handicapped*. New York: Harper & Row, 1973.

Sharp, R. Teaching writing to trainable children: The Edwards Method. *The Pointer*, 1973, *18*(1), 60–61.

Slaff, N. Handwriting at the Frostig Center. *The Marianne Frostig Center of Educational Therapy Newletter*, 1975, *16* (3), 1–9.

Wallace, G., & Kauffman, James. *Teaching children with learning problems*. Columbus, Ohio: Charles E. Merrill, 1973.

Thinking

Bereiter, C., & Engelman, S. *Teaching disadvantaged children in the preschool*. Englewood Cliffs, N.J.: Prentice-Hall, 1966.

Beyer, B. *Inquiry in the social studies classroom: A strategy for teaching*. Columbus, Ohio: Charles E. Merrill, 1971.

Bigge, M. L. *Learning theories for teachers*. New York: Harper & Row, 1976.

Carin, A., & Sund, R. *Developing questioning techniques: A self-concept approach*. Columbus, Ohio: Charles E. Merrill, 1971.

Hunkins, F. P. *Involving students in questioning*. Boston: Allyn and Bacon, 1976.

Lavatelli, C. D. *Piaget's theory applied to an early childhood curriculum*. Cambridge: Center for Media Development, 1970.

Raths, L. E., Jonas, A., Rothstein, A., & Wasserman, S. *Teaching for thinking: Theory and application*. Columbus, Ohio: Charles E. Merrill, 1967.

Sharp, E. *Thinking is child's play*. New York: Avon, 1969.

Taba, A., Durkin, M. C., Fraenkel, J. R., & McNaughton, A. H. *Teachers handbook for social studies* (2nd ed.). Reading, Mass.: Addison-Wesley, 1971.

LEISURE

Everyone needs rewarding and enjoyable leisure-time activities. According to Brannan: "Our educational system must re-orient itself to include nonvocational goals as [among those] paramount in importance for preparing individuals for meaningful participation in society." (1975, p. 41) Students must be helped to plan, select and enjoy participation activities, spectator activities and appreciation activities during their free time.

Ingenuity is needed to help students with physical limitations find and enjoy leisure activities. Typically, many disabled persons encounter many problems when they try to use community resources. Transportation is a major problem that must be solved when one looks to community resources for recreation. Finding available and interested adults to help provide recreation or leisure-time activities for the disabled is also a problem. Many parents recognize the need for leisure-time activities, but daily problems of caring for the disabled children leave little time or energy.

Teachers can help children develop interests which provide pleasure and satisfaction during

June Bigge.

leisure hours. Teachers can increase awareness of capabilities and interests of the students. They can guide student exploration of leisure activities from childhood by helping to develop existing interests and creating new interests.

Many of the activities that are presented suggest *kinds* of projects which help disabled children and adults make productive use of leisure time.

1. *Guinea pig raising* is a sample of a realm of possibilities of leisure activities centered around care of pets and other animals.
2. *Music appreciation* demonstrates and suggests the many different kinds of knowledge that lead to appreciation during leisure time.
3. *Photography* demonstrates that adaptations can be made so disabled persons can be taught to use tools and appliances required by some leisure activities.
4. *Horseback riding* should not be overlooked; some sports may be *erroneously* perceived as impossible or dangerous.
5. *Card games* and other games can be adapted so physically disabled persons can participate.

6. *Nature study* reminds us of the opportunities to study the outdoors.
7. *T.V.* suggests exploration of leisure possibilities with media.

The bibliography and resources section of this chapter suggest more alternatives for recreation and leisure activities. Use these references as tools for study of ways to improve the life-long leisure needs of physically disabled individuals using school, home, and community resources.

Raising Guinea Pigs

Guinea pigs are often chosen as pets because they are easy to keep. They are attractive, lovable, and relatively clean. If properly cared for, they should live from 6 to 8 years. Guinea pigs do not have to be walked (like dogs) and can be left with food and water for weekends. Breeding guinea pigs is a hobby persons of all ages can enjoy.

Why Guinea Pigs?

Raising guinea pigs is an example of a potentially rewarding leisure activity for disabled persons. These animals provide opportunities for severely disabled persons to spend time watching and playing with the animals. The care of guinea pigs is relatively simple, and opportunities for observation and experimentation can productively occupy a disabled person's time. The animals provide opportunities for disabled persons to develop habits of responsibility. Cost factors and simplicity contribute to the desirability of this activity for such persons.

These animals are among the least expensive pets to purchase. There may be opportunities for profit by breeding and selling the guinea pigs. Space requirements are relatively minimal, and odor and noise are not a major problem as long as cages are kept clean. Guinea pigs thrive at normal house temperatures so special heating for the cages is unnecessary. Of all rodents, guinea pigs make the most satisfactory pets for the disabled. They do not move fast and they rarely bite. Rats can be more vicious and may need "gentling," a potential problem for an athetoid; mice are too small and therefore hard to catch.

What is Needed for a Project?

For a breeding colony, one would want one male and four to six females. A cage capable of holding six guinea pigs can be purchased or can be made with wire screening and wood. The minimum space requirement is 1 square foot of cage space per animal. A nesting box with a ramp leading to the top should be placed in the cage. A food trough and water bottle must also be purchased. Bedding material, such as straw or wood shavings, is needed. The staple in a guinea pig's diet is rabbit pellets supplemented by lettuce, carrots, and other raw vegetables.

What Care is Required?

Feedings may not be required daily, but persons should be sure the animals always have food. Water should be changed daily. The bedding should be changed several times a week and the cage should be scrubbed thoroughly at that time. Placing animals in cages and removing them from cages at certain times is necessary when breeding animals. The cage should be kept away from drafts, and must be covered each night in cold weather.

How Can Guinea Pigs Be Raised for Profit?

Breeding guinea pigs enables a person to earn money. Before breeding for profit, it is important to find potential customers. While breeding, there should never be more than one mature male in a cage. If guinea pigs fight, the culprit can be identified by the fur in his mouth. A female is mature enough to breed at 3 months and continues to breed for 3 years. The gestation period is 68 days and the litter size is three to four babies. Males do not eat babies and need not be removed from the cage. However, if the male is in the cage, the female will breed again ten hours after delivering a litter. Weaning takes place at 3 weeks, at which time the babies can be sexed and the males separated. Interbreeding for at least two generations is usually safe.

Skills for Raising Guinea Pigs
Feeding the Guinea Pigs

Feeding begins by teaching the child to open the cage. Care should be taken in choosing a latch. A latch to which a draw string and handle can be attached is most satisfactory for individuals with poor hand use. With any latch, allow sufficient time for practice. For homemade cages, a sliding door with an extended bar to push up and down is easiest to manipulate.

Removing the food tray from the cage is the next task. The food tray should be significantly smaller than the door so that precise hand movements are not required. The food tray must be attached to the cage to prevent tipping by the animals. One solution is to fit the tray in a track directly opposite the door.

Disposing of old food is followed by filling the tray with fresh food. These animals love trimmings from vegetable bins. The child can pour the food pellets into the tray with minimal spilling if he uses a plastic pitcher. Reopening the cage and replacing the food tray is the final step in feeding.

Changing the Water

Changing water begins with the subtask of removing the water bottle from the side of the cage. A plastic water bottle will eliminate the problem of breakage. A strap is the easiest method of holding the bottle in place. Once the strap is undone, the tube leading from the bottle must be removed from the screening. For the more severely disabled, a bottle holder can easily be made. (See Figure 11–1.)

Removing the cork from the bottle may be a task for which assistance is necessary. The bottle

Figure 11–1. A handmade bottle holder makes the task possible.

must be air tight, so the cork or screw lid must be firmly secured. Other subtasks include emptying the stale water, rinsing the bottle, returning the cork to the bottle, and returning the bottle to the cage.

Cage Cleaning

Before the cage can be cleaned, remove the animals. Removing the dirty bedding of shredded paper or tissues should be done outside if this is possible. Scrubbing is accomplished by adding a few drops of disinfectant to the cleaning water. The student should be furnished a brush which is easy to hold. A most important step in cage cleaning is washing and disinfecting the water bottle and food tray. These should be removed, washed in soapy water, rinsed thoroughly, refilled, and returned to cage.

How Can Projects be Extended?

Little has been done about observing guinea pigs in their "native environment." A cage or enclosure can duplicate a more natural habitat so animals can be observed. The many different varieties of color and hair length of guinea pigs also facilitate genetics experiments. You and the child should be able to find many other ways to extend a guinea pig project.

Music Appreciation

Listening to music can be a great pleasure for individuals of all ages. For individuals with physical disabilities, music appreciation and individual expression through music can be a dynamic and growing process, giving lifetime satisfaction.

Foundations of music as a leisure-time activity begin with the young child in the home and at school. The importance of a good music program cannot be overemphasized. Music *can* become a source of real pleasure, both in listening and participation. Children can learn to listen, create, and appreciate music in many ways. Learning within the classroom can be extended at home for continued enrichment and satisfaction. No music program can be considered successful unless it affects the total child, both inside and outside of the classroom.

The information provided in this section is designed to be particularly helpful to those teachers who have a limited background in music. This section will suggest ways to teach music concepts and activities to make music an enriching and enjoyable activity. We will also suggest procedures to accommodate physical limitations.

Introducing Music to Young Children

Music for young children should be simple and direct. It should have a strongly marked rhythm and a melody that is easily remembered. If a child has heard music frequently before he begins to talk or walk, he may be ready to participate in music activities as soon as he enters these stages. He will be able to learn to sing the songs with which he is already familiar and he will be able to keep time to the rhythmic tunes.

Where does learning about music begin? Natural rhythmic movements, such as walking and running, are the basis for discovering rhythm. The child experiments with his voice, making high and low sounds (pitch) and loud and soft sounds (volume).

People learn that sound can be produced in many ways. A beginning activity would involve having children listen to the variety of sounds around them. The bark of a dog, the wind blowing through the trees, and thunder are familiar sounds for children. In class, children may be asked to be very quiet and listen to sounds they hear. They can also listen for rhythmic patterns of sounds. A discussion of what they have heard will help everyone become conscious of certain dimensions and qualities of sounds, such as high, low, soft, loud, squeaky, full, and hollow.

Once individuals are conscious of rhythm and sound, they may begin to experiment. It is your responsibility to *select* experiences and materials that will enable children to discover, explore, and then form their own musical concepts. While the music activities should include the traditional activities of singing, moving, listening, and playing, the emphasis is on the *music* itself.

Teaching Musical Concepts

Rex (1972) suggests many music concepts and activities.[1] Readers can refer to her book for more ideas including additional ways to teach each concept. She also provides a list of records, songs, and piano music which help people learn the music concepts.

Beat

In music there is usually a steady, recurring pulse called the *beat*.

1. Activities
   a. play rhythm instruments
   b. use the body "instrument," e.g., clapping hands, tapping toes, slapping thighs, snapping fingers, stamping feet.
   c. step around the room to piano music, recorded music, or singing.
2. Things to remember
   a. Choose music that has a definite feeling or pulse.
   b. Choose music that has a comfortable tempo (speed) for stepping.
   c. Select rhythm instruments that are appropriate (in sound) for the expressive quality of the music being played.
   d. Select activities (stepping, playing, tapping) that do not overshadow the music.

Accenting of Beats in Patterns

Accenting of certain beats results in the grouping of pulses into meters (rhythmic patterns) of two, three, and four beats to the measure.

1. Activities
   a. In listening to recorded music or music played on the piano, lead the children to discover that the first beat (one) is emphasized more (accented) than the other beats (unaccented).

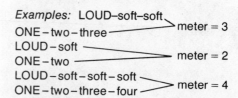

Examples: LOUD–soft–soft
ONE – two – three   meter = 3
LOUD – soft
ONE – two   meter = 2
LOUD – soft – soft – soft
ONE – two – three – four   meter = 4

   b. Play rhythm instruments on accented beat (one) and make a silent motion on unaccented beats.
   c. Clap hands on *one* and press hands together on unaccented beats.
   d. Clap hands on *one* (or kick foot) and nod head for counts two, three and four.
   e. Clap hands on accented beat and throw hands into the air on the rests (silence filling the beat).
   f. Divide the class so that one part plays clicking instruments on *one* and another part of the class plays ringing instruments on unaccented beats.
   g. Step around the room to music, stepping loudly on *one* and softly on unaccented beats.

2. Things to remember
    a. Choose music that has a definite feeling of meter.
    b. Choose music that has a comfortable tempo for the activity.
    c. Select rhythm instruments that sound appropriate for the expressive quality of the music being played.
    d. Allow the music to govern and dictate the activity helping children hear how beats are grouped.

Even and Uneven Rhythm Patterns

In music there may be rhythm patterns made up of sounds of equal duration (even rhythm) or sounds of unequal duration (uneven rhythm).

1. Activities
    a. Clap (or play rhythm instruments) rhythmic patterns of children's names.
    b. Clap (or play rhythm instruments) rhythmic patterns of the melody of familiar songs.
    c. Identify the relative duration of the sounds of the above patterns as "long" or "short" sounds.
    d. Discover that rhythm patterns formed by sounds of equal duration are *even* and suggest body movements such as nodding, swaying, tapping hands alternately, making a clucking sound, walking, running, trotting, jumping, and tiptoeing.

Rhythm of a Melody

In a song there is a rhythm of the melody (usually the same as the rhythm of the words of a song).

1. Activities
    a. Tap fingers to the rhythm of the melody of a familiar song.
    b. Play rhythm instruments to the rhythm of the melody of a familiar song.
    c. Clap rhythm of a familiar song to be identified by others.
    d. Step or nod to the rhythm of a melody of a familiar song.
    e. Chant words in rhythm while someone else provides a steady beat.
2. Things to remember
    a. Choose music with prominent patterns of rhythm in the melody.
    b. Select rhythm instruments that are appropriate for the expressive quality of the music.

c. Step to music that is in a comfortable tempo and that is rhythmically simple.
d. Step, play, or tap portions of the selection which contain prominent rhythmic patterns.

Tempo

Music may be fast or slow (tempo).

1. Activities
    a. When a child is able to clap successfully to a steady beat, ask him to clap a *fast* beat and then to a *slow* beat.
    b. Walk to fast music. Ask "How would you walk when you are in a hurry?"
    c. Walk to slow music. Ask "How would you walk when you are very tired?"
    d. Listen to the ticking (beats) of a metronome set at various speeds. (Being able to see the arm of the metronome move or a flashing light will add visual reinforcement.)

Pitch

Some tones sound high and some tones sound low (pitch).

1. Activities
    Explore the piano, autoharp, melody bells, resonator bells, or guitar.
    a. Find the highest pitch on an instrument; find the lowest pitch.
    b. Listen to sounds go up when you play to the right on the piano, listen to the sounds go down when you play to the left on the piano.
    c. Play a familiar song in the middle of the piano (range of the child's singing voice), then play the song 2 octaves higher. Ask, "What is different?" Use the same procedure for experiencing the lower range of the piano.
    d. Let the children improvise music on the instruments that suggests bird songs, rain, animals, thunder rumbling, elephants walking, mice scampering.

Compare the quality and pitch of voices and instruments; note that small instruments generally make higher sounds and large instruments make low sounds.
    a. children's and men's voices
    b. women's and men's voices
    c. finger cymbals and gong
    d. rhythm sticks and wooden block
    e. small drum and large drum [percussion family]

f. violin and string bass [string family]

g. flute and bassoon [woodwind family]

h. trumpet and tuba [brass family]

Have children arrange individual resonator bells or tuned water glasses according to pitch, low to high, or high to low.

Have children bring to class common articles or homemade instruments that make a sound; classify them as to high or low.

Sing and show the direction of the melody by hand movements.

```
                                  C
                                 high;
                   G
                   up
          E
         ing
    C
  reach
```

Reaching up high;
Bending down low.

b. Show the children a xylophone-type instrument, hold it vertically. Allow them to experiment by playing it, discovering that the larger the bar, the lower the tone. Let them play simple, short tonal patterns—ascending, descending, repeated tones.

Tones Combine to Make Harmony

Musical tones can be combined to form harmony.

1. Activities
   a. Play on an instrument middle C, E, G, and high C. Have children identify them as the

Tones Make Melodies

Tones in a melody may repeat or change (be higher, lower, or stay the same).

1. Activities
   a. Respond with body movements at appropriate ascending levels—touch toes, touch knees, touch waist, and touch top of the head and reverse for descending. Sing:

```
    C
  bend
          G
         ing
                   E
                  down
                            C
                           low
```

melody for "Reaching up high; Bending down low." Then play the tones simultaneously, forming the C major chord. Identify the new sound of three or more tones sounded at the same time as a chord.

   b. Play combinations of tones on the resonator bells.
   c. Experiment with playing chords on the autoharp.

Major and Minor Tonalities

Major and minor tonalities sound different.

1. Activities
   a. Sing or play the two scales below. Notice the minor tone in the second measure.

b. Sing many songs that are in the minor mode, contrasting them with songs in the major mode.

c. Listen to compositions or sing songs that change from major to minor within the song, and guide the children to discover where the changes take place.

Like and Unlike Phrases

Music contains phrases and sections that are alike (repetition) and unlike (contrast).

1. Activities
   a. Listen to phrases in "Twinkle Twinkle Little Star" and discover the like and unlike phrase(s).
   b. Walk to music, changing directions at each new phrase.
   c. Identify with one signal, all the like phrases, identify unlike phrases in a different way.
   d. Draw the phrase patterns on the chalkboard.
2. Things to remember
   a. Choose songs which have like or unlike melodic phrases and sections.
   b. Alike phrases include those phrases that are identical or almost alike.

Timbre of Sound

There is a difference in timbre (tone-color) of individual voices and instruments.

1. Activities
   a. Listen to the peculiar quality of tone produced by an oboe.
   b. Have children describe and compare the particular qualities of someone singing "middle C" and "middle C" played on an instrument.
   c. Have children discover, identify, and describe the difference in sound between percussion instruments that have a definite or an indefinite pitch.

definite	indefinite
autoharp	cymbals
melody bells	finger cymbals
resonator bells	gong
piano	triangle
	drum
	tambourine
	rhythm sticks
	wooden block

d. Let children select which rhythm instruments sound best for accompanying a selected song, recorded music, or composition played on the piano.

Intensity

Music can be loud or soft (intensity).

1. Activities
   a. Have children experiment with various rhythm instruments to discover which ones make loud and soft sounds.
   b. Let children decide whether a song they are about to sing should be loud or soft.

Studying Different Kinds of Music

Disabled students can be taught to listen for patterns and special features of different classifications of music and of different composers. We briefly illustrate how students may be taught to recognize music classified broadly as classical (including symphonic music and opera), jazz, contemporary, popular, and film theme music.

Assuming that further knowledge of music theory increases appreciation in music both as a listener and a participant, the final section in music appreciation teaches some basic music theory.

Classical

Classical music is the study of great composers and features of their music. Seligmann (1966) relates features of classical music to composers well known for their development or use of certain patterns: the fugue and Bach, the symphony and Haydn, the symphony and Beethoven, and the concerto and Mozart. Notice how these groupings of information from Seligmann and others provide a framework for teaching about classical music.

1. The fugue and Bach. Johann Sebastian Bach did not compose for the concert hall, but rather wrote music to be performed in the church by choral singers, a small orchestra, an organ, or music to be performed by solo musicians or small instrumental groups.

   Bach composed in many forms, but he is the best known composer of the fugue, which is a composition using a single melodic idea or theme. It is sung or played in parts called *voices*. The voices enter one after another to announce the theme of the fugue. A Bach fugue is rarely heard by itself. Usually a prelude, toccata, or fantasia is played before the fugue. These were originally written for keyboard instruments (organ, harpsichord).

2. The symphony and Haydn. Joseph Haydn is known as "the father of the symphony." Most symphonies are comparatively long and are divided into separate sections, called *movements*. To the listener, each movement of Haydn's symphonies resembles a piece in itself. Haydn's symphonies consist of four movements: the first movement is called *sonata form;* the second is called the *slow movement;* the third the *minuet and trio;* and the last movement may be in many different forms—often a *rondo*.

3. The symphony and Beethoven. Ludwig van Beethoven is known for his great symphonies. In using the sonata form, Beethoven expanded it and introduced several themes. He also called the third movement of the symphony a *scherzo* (vigorous movement with startling contrasts), instead of a minuet. In addition to changing the form of the symphony, Beethoven used instruments in bold new ways, using accompaniment instruments (tuba, double basses, etc.) to announce new themes or ideas.

4. The concerto and Mozart. Wolfgang Mozart made the concerto one of his most important contributions to music. A concerto is like a symphony for a solo instrument accompanied by an orchestra. Mozart composed concertos for piano, violin, flute, horn, bassoon. The concerto only has three movements: *the sonata form, slow movement,* and *rondo or presto*.

Opera

Opera is simply a drama sung instead of a drama spoken. Rarely is it a realistic picture of everyday life. Most operas are sung in Italian, German, French, or Russian; therefore the libretto (story) of the opera should be read beforehand if it is to be understood.

Most operas open with the overture, a short orchestral composition played before the curtain rises. There are also solo songs, called *arias,* giving the leading singers a chance to express their feelings.

Jazz

Jazz is a type of American music derived from various black cultures. Copland (1957) says it is characterized by melodious themes and a definite syncopated dance rhythm. In listening to a jazz band, it can be seen that certain instruments provide the rhythmic background (piano, banjo, double bass, percussion). Other instruments provide a harmonic texture, with usually one solo instrument playing the melody. Trumpet, clarinet, saxophone, and trombone are used as harmonic or melodic instruments.

Contemporary Music

In any type of art or literature, there have always been those who wanted to go beyond the language of their day, to say things in a new way; music is no exception.

When listening to modern music, the listener must have an open mind. It is also important to try to understand what the composer is trying to say. The more modern music is heard, the more meaningful the language of it becomes and the more enjoyment the listener receives. This type of music often seems to lack pattern and unity at first. With continued listening, however, its design becomes more apparent.

Some of the great contemporary composers include Aaron Copland, Charles Ives, Igor Stravinsky, and Bela Bartok.

Popular

In rock music, accents are often on the second and fourth beats rather than the first and third beats. Fox (1970) states that "these accents indicate when the body responses occur while dancing" (p. 53).

Lists of rock recordings listed in the "top forty" can be secured from local radio stations. Fox is one of the best guides for studying rock. He states that varieties of rock include pop rock, soul rock, rock-a-billy, raga rock, electronic rock, and church rock. He gives practical questions which allow students, with your guidance, to explore the music aurally. In addition he demonstrates ways to use earlier presented information about music structure and concepts to study the different types of rock as they relate to other music.

Billboard Magazine lists the "top 100" nationally. Bennett (1975) demonstrates a unit of study on pop-tune listening guides to develop listening awareness not only of pop tunes but other music.

Film Music

Film music constitutes a new musical medium that is a fascination of its own. It is amazing to see movie-goers who take the musical accompaniment entirely for granted. Copland (1957) contends that music serves the screen in a number of ways:

1. creates a more convincing atmosphere of time and place
2. implies the unspoken thoughts of a character or the unseen implications of a situation
3. serves as a neutral background filler
4. buildes a sense of continuity
5. underpins the buildup of a scene, rounding it off with a sense of finality

Good film music can have a tremendous effect on a picture. Many times it is the music that creates the entire mood of a movie. The listener should be aware of the music and decide if it is appropriate for the movie. Try to imagine a dramatic movie with the sound-track turned off.

A clef sign provides the key to the staff:

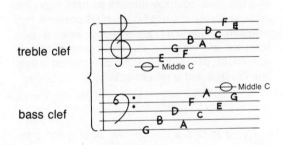

treble clef

bass clef

Music Theory Helps Formal Participation

In addition to knowledge of musical tones and patterns discussed previously, the participant may need skills in basic fundamentals of music. Brofsky and Bamberger (1969) and most state-adopted music texts outline the following aspects of basic music theory. Students should continue to read their state-adopted music guides and a programmed book which provide these fundamentals in greater depth.

Pitch and Movement

Seven letters are used to represent the 12 tones in our music. The letters *A* through *G*, with the aid of sharps (#) and flats (♭), provide the names for these 12 tones. The tones are arranged on the keyboard as follows:

Pitches are notated on a five-line staff:

The key in which a piece is to be played is indicated at the beginning by means of sharps (#) or flats (♭) which designate the *key signature.*

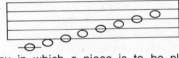   means that all *F* notes will be sharped.

Time and Movement

Durational values are indicated by notes and rests, the rests indicating silence.

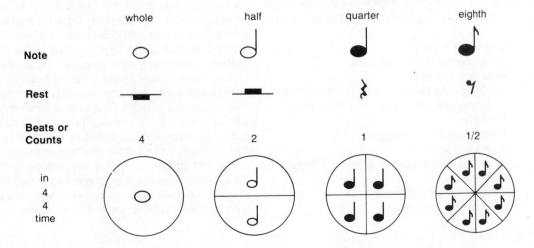

	whole	half	quarter	eighth
Note				
Rest				
Beats or Counts	4	2	1	1/2
in 4 4 time				

Depending on the time signature, these notes and rests are held for different lengths of time. The *time signature* is placed at the beginning of a piece; the top number designates how many beats there will be in each measure; the bottom number names the *kind* of note which receives one count (quarter, eighth). For example, In ¾ time there are 2 beats to each measure with the quarter note getting one count. In ⅔ time there are 2 beats to the measure with the half note getting one count.

Tempo

Tempo refers to how fast or slow a composition is played. Most pieces are preceded by a verbal designation of the tempo. Some of the most common designations in Italian are:

adagio = slow
largo = broad
andante = moderately slow
moderato = moderate
allegretto = moderately fast
allegro = fast (cheerful)
vivace = fast (lively)
presto = very fast

Dynamics and Expression

The dynamics (relative loudness or softness of musical tones) are indicated by markings also derived from Italian. The basic signs are:

p for *piano* = soft
f for *forte* = loud
m for *mezzo* = medium

Modifications of these markings serve as rough dynamic indications for the performer, as follows:

ppp = very, very soft
pp for *pianissimo* = very soft
p for *piano* = soft
mp for *mezzo piano* = less soft than piano
mf for *mezzo forte* = less loud than forte
f = forte
ff for *fortissimo* = very loud
fff = even louder
cresc for *crescendo* = gradual increase in loudness
dim for *decrescendo* or *diminuendo* = gradual decrease in loudness

Expression

Italian words indicate to the performer the manner of performance. Some common terms are:

animato = animated
cantabile = in a singing style
con moto = with movement
dolce = sweet (soft)
expressivo = expressive
legato = smoothly connected
sforzando (sf) = suddenly loud, a single note accented
tenuto = hold (the full value of the note or even beyond)

Once disabled children become interested and knowledgeable in music, they have the option of making it a part of their lives. They can enjoy music as individuals, and they can enjoy the growth of any group to which they contribute their musical skills.

Photography

In order to encourage readers to help even the most severely physically disabled persons find adaptive equipment to allow them to enjoy leisure time, we are including the main content of personal notes of a young teacher determined to help one student find a leisure activity.[2]

*   *   *   *   *

Trying to find a leisure-time activity for a severely involved, nonvocal individual with very little control over random movements of his body is not an easy task. The hardest part is getting started. The easiest way to get the ball rolling is to just spend time with the individual. Try to do a varied amount of activities to find out what he enjoys the most. This is a good time to learn about the person's intellectual and physical capabilities. Make sure you know what he can do in terms of seeing and hearing. Communication is another vital area which must be dealt with when working with severely involved people. In order to establish a good relationship between the individual and yourself, you must be able to communicate easily and effectively. Again, this is done in the initial contact period. If all preceding things are considered, it will be much easier to find leisure-time activities. These are the foundations of a good relationship which will enable the individual and yourself to grow.

After spending some leisure time with a teen-ager named Chris, I started to probe for some of the things he was interested in. (To communicate, Chris uses eye movements and a communication board.) We narrowed the list of interests to Boy Scouts, school, television, talking with people, looking at my 35 mm slides, watching me take pictures, and running his train sets. All of these things were great, but with the exception of watching, listening, or operating his train set, they did not allow for any individual independent participation by Chris.

I looked again at the list of his interests. I saw a pattern: "watching slides," and "watching me taking photographs." Why not let Chris take photographs, too?

I thought of myself. I love to photograph! It is a great means of expression and self-satisfaction for me. I feel I am not only documenting what I see when I photograph, but I am also putting a little of myself into every picture I take. If this hobby has helped me to grow, why shouldn't it do the same for Chris? When I told Chris about my idea, he became very excited. That's all I needed. I knew he would give me his fullest cooperation. I had found an activity which he would enjoy (if everything worked out).

The next thing I did was give a hard look at Chris's physical capabilities. The first thing that came to mind was his head control. At this stage I thought this was the only part of his body in which he had voluntary control. He operated a switch for his train set with his head, so maybe he could somehow control a camera with it. But I was starting to get ahead of myself. First, I had to realize what he could *not* do with a camera. He could not hold the camera, look through the view finder, focus, release the shutter without an extra device, or advance the film.

Now, what adaptations would I need to overcome these problems? Problem one—a tripod could hold the camera; two—the person who is attending could look through the view finder to line up the subject of Chris's choice; three—a long cable release with an air bulb could be operated with his head like the train switch.

The next step was to see what equipment I already had that we could use to experiment. I had a 35 mm camera, tripod, and a 20-feet bulb cable release. My plan was to have Chris depress the bulb release with the back of his head by pushing his head against the bulb. (I mounted the bulb behind his head on a board on the back top of his wheelchair.)

Unfortunately, to my surprise, this was not going to work. The bulb needed far too much pressure to activate the shutter on the camera. I could barely do it with my head. I knew it would not work with Chris. We tried anyway, but failed.

The next thing to do was to find a part of the body that not only was strong enough to activate the bulb but also had fairly good voluntary control. I remembered at school when Chris wanted to get somewhere on his own he would bang his feet against the floor to move his wheelchair. I would try to put the bulb under his feet somehow and he could squeeze it between his feet and the floor.

When I arrived at his house that night, I was disappointed to find that Chris's wheelchair at home was taller than the one at school. His feet were not firmly placed on the ground. He could not bang them on the floor as he did at school. It was fortunate that I discovered this problem in the beginning because the wheelchair he uses at home is the one which he would use for his leisure-time activities.

We could not use his feet so I thought we could take advantage of his scissoring leg pattern. I placed my hand between Chris's knees and told him to squeeze his knees together. There was a good amount of pressure. The bulb was then put into position, but it just slid out of place when Chris made an attempt to apply pressure. At this stage I started to get frustrated. The situation did not look good. I grabbed Chris by his thigh and said, "I hope we can figure out a way to get this thing to work!" At that moment it came to me. Why not try under his thigh; it was skinny enough to not be cushioned by fat. This would permit Chris to put greater pressure on the bulb.

First, we experimented. I had Chris lift his thigh as high as he could, then I put my hand under it so he could get the feel of something under him. Next he was asked to relax, then apply as much pressure on my hand as possible. After a few trials, I used the bulb release. It worked!

The next problem was to keep the bulb from moving after each trial. I thought we could use velcro tape, but his father suggested putting it under the pad on his wheelchair seat. This also worked. Chris was in business. He is now a photographer! (See next page.)

*   *   *   *   *

Figure 11–2. Cable release with air bubble that is pressed with the thigh and "zip"—a picture of Zip, a friend's dog.

Horseback Riding

We must not overlook horseback riding and other sports which involve an element of risk because we perceive them as impossible or dangerous for disabled persons. If properly conducted, they are no more dangerous for persons with disabilities than for those without physical problems. Reading about therapeutic horsemanship, for instance, convinces us it is not only possible but an exciting sport. It also reminds us that certain safety standards and procedures are important for success in any sport.

"The Outside of a Horse is Good for the Inside of a Person"

That the outside of a horse is good for the inside of a person is the basic premise upon which *therapeutic horsemanship* has been developed.

Horses are used to further rehabilitation of persons with physical and/or mental handicaps. Not all horseback riding programs for disabled persons must be structured as the discipline of *therapeutic horsemanship*. Neighborhood and local recreation park horseback riding programs are also beneficial leisure activities. Children with disabilities ranging from spinal cord injuries to autism can profit from a horse riding program. Riding can help improve total gross-motor functioning, such as increasing range of motion in the extremities and improving muscle tone and strength. It can also develop pleasurable use of leisure time and improved self-concept. For everyone, whether disabled or not, riding is a major accomplishment. Learning to control an animal which is four times one's size is a significant and rewarding achievement.

Therapeutic Horsemanship

The popularity of therapeutic horsemanship began in England in 1964 when the first riding school for the disabled was opened in Chigwell, England, under the directorship of John Davies. In 1967, the British Advisory Council on Riding for the Handicapped, later to become the National Riding for the Disabled Association, was formed. Now, many countries have their own National Association of Riding for the Handicapped.

The Program

Before students may receive equine therapy, they will receive a general information sheet and must fill out an information card. Then they must have a written referral from their physicians or the consulting physicians. Before the students begin their first lesson, they will be evaluated by a therapist who will discuss each of them with the riding instructor. During the first lesson, the instructor evaluates the student's riding abilities, i.e., position, recovering of balance, attitude, and intelligence. The instructor records this information on the pupil's progress cards. Before lessons begin, the instructor should remember that each student will progress at individual rates and that each lesson should be individualized according to student ability.

The Lessons

Procedures for the riding lessons have been elaborated by John Davies, foremost authority on therapeutic horsemanship. The English saddle is used because it offers greater opportunity for independent balance when compared with a western saddle. However, there are some students who require another type of saddle, such as a western, Portuguese, or side saddle. Students are first placed on a dummy horse (made out of an oil drum) in order to get the feel of the new position. Before mounting they are fitted with a safety helmet and safety harness (if their handicap requires this). They then meet their horse, pet him, and groom him.

Before mounting, students are taught to check the tack, i.e., make sure the bridle is on properly, all buckles are fastened, and the girth on the saddle is secure. The student is taught to mount, if able, in the proper, normal manner. Other methods of mounting are used according to their abilities.

After students are mounted, they are instructed in the correct position for riding. To achieve the "correct seat" takes a lot of hard work and concentration for nonhandicapped riders as well as disabled students. Students can be taught the methods of riding at the halt, walk, trot, canter, mount, dismount, and in the exercises. If students cannot extend their arms to hold the reins or cannot put their feet in the stirrups, volunteers are an absolute necessity. Some students, in their initial stages of riding, may require three volunteers—one to lead the horse and one on each side of the student to add support. The volunteers are trained by the instructor on correct procedures.

Adaptive Equipment

Adaptive equipment is another essential part of a therapeutic horsemanship program. Probably the most necessary and back-saving piece of equipment will be the mounting ramp. The following are descriptions of additional adaptive equipment:

Hand hold—a strap attached to d-rings on the saddle which helps in stabilizing riders so they do not have to rely on their balance.

Ladder reins—six- to eight-inch leather straps are stitched at intervals between the reins. They are used mainly by one-handed riders to allow control of both reins.

Safety helmets or *hunt hats*—these are used to protect the heads if a rider should happen to fall.

Safety or *body harness*—leather shoulder strap and leather hand hold.

Leading reins—used by the leader of the horse to help control the horse but not to interfere with a rider's control.

Safety stirrup—prevents a foot from falling through the stirrup and possibly getting caught in

a dangerous position should the horse shy at something.

Fleece saddle covers—go over the saddle to provide extra padding and a softer seat for those students with spina bifida or other losses of sensation below the waist who may be prone to getting pressure sores.

Bareback pad—a foam pad which is put on the horse and clinched up and used in place of a saddle for those students who have tight muscles causing a scissoring of the legs so the legs do not open far enough to sit on a saddle. The warmth from the horse will be felt through the horseback pad and will help to relax the tight muscles.

The previous examples of adaptive equipment should be used only as long as necessary. The goal is for the student to ride in as "normal" fashion as possible.

Horses

The most important part of a therapeutic horsemanship program is the hero of it all—the horse. Horses and ponies must be selected and trained very carefully. If a horse exhibits one bad habit (i.e., kicking or biting), he is not suitable for the

Figure 11–3. Mounting with a ramp.

program. He must always be patient, quiet, and willing to respond and move. The horses are trained to tolerate crutches, wheelchairs, chattering children, riders flailing around in the saddle, exercises being done all over them, being led by another horse on a trail ride, and standing by a mounting ramp. (See Figure 11–3.)

Often a stocky, Welsh pony, of 13–14 hands, is best for the program, as they are generally of good disposition, good size for the children, and easy to lead.

Each horse in a program should be schooled weekly by the instructor or an experienced rider in order to keep it alert, responsive, and well-mannered.

The objective for the students who participate in this program is the same as for any therapeutic or teaching program: to get the students to function at the point of their maximum ability. The goal is to get the students to ride with enough confidence, coordination, and strength to be able to participate and compete with their nonhandicapped peers.

Horseback riding is a great equalizer of people; when on a horse, a person with a physical handicap has just as much strength and power under his body as does a nonhandicapped rider.

Card Games

Games can be enjoyed by persons of wide ranges of ages and abilities. Card games provide opportunities for competition, problem solving, success, and failure. They provide ways for disabled persons to participate successfully with nondisabled persons.

Cognitive Skills Needed to Play Cards

Using task analysis we can study skills needed to play certain card games, abilities needed to preform cognitive tasks, and need for development of adaptions to accommodate physical needs. The process of analyzing what cognitive tasks a player must be able to perform in different games leads to definition of which tasks, if any, need to be taught.

Concentration, for instance, can be played if persons can only match numbers or pictures. On the other hand, rummy requires knowledge of at least (a) matching "same suits," (b) matching "same numbers," (c) identification of the number of a card in a group, (d) recognition of number of card groups in hand, (e) knowledge of how to place cards in consecutive order within suits, (f) value by face number, and (g) adding to accumulate points made in each hand.

Adaptions

The following are some suggestions for handling cards should players be unable to hold the cards

themselves or verbally indicate what manipulations they wish to make.

Cards

Various kinds of cards are available from toy or department stores. Cards with large numbers, magnetic cards, or crooked cards may be easier for some individuals to use. Jumbo cards with oversized symbols and numbers, and braille playing cards are available in pinochle and regular decks from the American Foundation for the Blind.

Use of Pointers

For a person who uses a pointer for communication, experiment with the tip of the pointer by surrounding the tip with masking tape or some other adhesive so that the point will adhere to cards. A sticky pointer may be used to lift cards from stock piles, designate cards to discard, or pass cards to someone else. A plain pointer can be used to point to cards players want to discard or pass to someone else. It can be used to hit something to signal *start, stop!,* or *I win!*

Management of Cards

For a child using a pointer, or for a child with poor coordination, a card holder may be advisable. *Aids to Independent Living: Self Help for the Handicapped,* by Lowman and Klinger (1969), has several good demonstrations of adaptions for games. If adapted equipment is not available to an individual, a fine card holder can be devised from a flat brush with bristles approximately 3″ high. (Patio brooms will do it.) Smaller brushes (See Figure 11–4) also work. The cards stand upright in the bristles when the back of the brush is placed on a flat surface.

For the nonvocal player who cannot handle cards, the tic-tac-toe communication system can be used. Use of this format is described in the chapter "Severe Communication Problems." One of each card of an extra deck of cards can be placed in each cell of a plastic photo holder. Instead of *asking* for a card, the nonvocal player can *signal* which card he wants. In the game of authors, for instance, a player can ask for a card by signaling the position corresponding to the desired author. Then he can signal the position of the letter which begins the name of the desired book by that author. (See Figure 11–5.)

If the cards in concentration are placed in the nine-cell tic-tac-toe format, a player can again signal the two positions he hopes will match. (See Figure 11–6.)

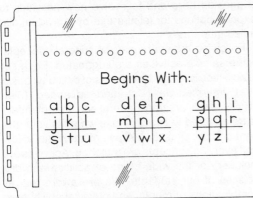

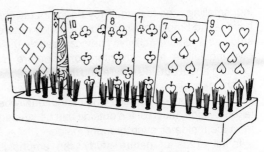

Figure 11–4. Try whatever works!

Figure 11–6. Signal *right* or *left box,* then to the position to tell cards that hopefully match in Concentration.

Signals

Special signals will be necessary for the following types of communication.

1. Request help arranging cards in desired order.
2. Signal which card(s) to pick up or put down.
3. Signal a win.
4. Signal when player wants to group cards and lay them facing up or down.
5. Signal a pass rather than a turn in which he will play.
6. Signal or point to a card in opponents' hand.

Players should help the disabled players find suitable signals. Because of the nature of some games, all players must use the same signals. In slapjack, for instance, all players must give the same signal (such as a kick on the floor) when the Jack is exposed. With ingenuity, each game can be adjusted to suit the needs of the players. Some means for communicating plays in the game must be devised for each disabled player.

Nature Study

The outdoors offers an environment where individuals use their senses of seeing, hearing, feel-

Figure 11–5. *a*) Twelve choices of authors! Child signals *right* or *left,* then the *position* of the card. *b*) Choice of book—child signals which *box* and then *position* for the beginning of a book title.

ing, smelling, and tasting. They need not always have refined motor skills in order to enjoy nature study as a leisure activity. They can satisfy their own inquisitive and adventuresome nature by learning about outside nature and the interactions which take place outdoors. For those severely physically disabled persons who cannot easily be taken outside, much of the outside can be studied from the inside or even brought inside.

In all areas of nature study, the emphasis should be on the *concepts* (interrelationships) relating to natural phenomena, rather than the scientific names and facts. Facts may change rapidly, but concepts remain more stable over many years. For some, it is more meaningful to understand concepts such as *how* and *why* than to memorize names.

Basically, a nature program should encourage the following in each student (*Child Ecology*, 1974 pp. 2, vi):

Awareness of a person's natural surroundings.
Appreciation and knowledge of living things that interrelate.
Respect for the environment by discovering how other creatures live, and how to preserve his surroundings, both for himself and other living things.
Knowledge that humans are a *part* of the environment, not just observers or manipulators.
Realization that the interrelationships of the environment are a necessary requisite to survival.

Nature study offers one of the best opportunities for the disabled to be involved in the *direct experience approach* to learning. In some instances, adaptations will still need to be made. As an example, for students who cannot participate in hiking activities, prepare another activity where the same concepts can be studied. If the class is studying animal locomotion, you can have these students study animals living near the classroom, home, yard, cabin, or campgrounds. Or, obtain graphic copies of different animal tracks, plaster of Paris castings, or models so that they can study animal travel. Students can then relate their new learnings to wildlife specials on T.V.

We find that the best approach for the study of nature is to place emphasis on the native plants and animals (species most commonly found nearby) of your particular community or section of the state. The plant and animal worlds are so extensive that one cannot possibly learn about them all. It would be most helpful to disabled persons to learn about those aspects of nature which they can readily see and examine first hand. Use books and other materials written specifically about their geographic area. Good resources for books, literature, and specimens are local libraries, education departments, museums, zoos, regional and national parks, and various agencies concerned with native studies (Sierra Club, Audubon, Friends of the Earth, and other local groups). For identifying specimens, use field guides designated for your particular section of the state or county. A particularly good reference which we have found helpful for activities with the disabled is Railton's (1972) *Teaching Science in an Outdoor Environment*. We suggest it because the activities can be used in any part of the country. It is also inexpensive and easy to use. The book contains the following imaginative and interesting ideas: the 100-inch hike (can be used in own yard or city street as well as in a park or designated nature areas); five senses hike (great for wheelchair bound who can use any or all of their senses); food chain activities (who eats who in the life cycle); and stream and pond experiences (like the child in Figure 11–7).

Study of animals, plants, climate/weather, earth science, conservation, and ecology can be a valuable introduction to sources of enjoyment for present and later use of leisure time. Use ingenuity to develop concepts such as those suggested here and to evolve new activities to expand options for leisure use by individual disabled students.

Following the statements of several concepts, some sample activities are suggested. Each set of activities is divided into levels of difficulty: *basic* (1's), *intermediate* (2's), and *advanced* (3's). (These levels are very general and are not meant to be adhered to exactly—use what fits your student and the situation.) Areas of study, activities, and evolving concepts are matched. Activities are included for the wide range of abilities and disabilities of our students. We are aware that all combinations of mental and physical ability exist in our disabled students and we have tried to account for this. Refer to the reference and resource sections at the end of this chapter for books providing details on things to make.

Figure 11–7. Discovering pond life.

Concepts and Activities Leading to Concepts

Animals (including micro-organisms)

A. **Concept**—*There are different kinds of animals; each has special characteristics.*

1. Expose the students to as many different animals as possible. (Traveling zoos will come to school—contact the local zoo. Some junior museums lend animals for periods of time to home and school.) Have "pet day" where everyone can bring and share pets. Gather animals from under boards, logs, rocks; provide them with an adequate "home," watch for a week, and return them to their original place. (Set a board down on the ground at school, and, after a week or two, look under to see who has adopted it as his home.)
2. Compare similarities and differences of animals. Study animal tracks from plaster castings or pictures. Find and observe as many different animals as you can in the lawn. (Se-

verely disabled can lie down, watch, and *feel*.) Cast animal tracks in plaster.
3. Observe the animals in the environment and establish a system of categorization (number of legs, mode of travel, size, body characteristics, etc.) to group the animals according to similarities. Start a compost heap. (It will soon be crawling with life.) Use a guide book "key" to identify and categorize animals found or seen. The purpose of this activity is not to name but to find out about the creature.

B. **Concept**—*Animals have essential survival needs: food, reproduction, and protection.*

1. Adopt animals as class pets (caterpillars, guinea pigs, snails, worms, ants, birds, chickens); feed and provide appropriate homes. Observe habits, including reproduction and protective adaptations.
2. Each student can choose an animal and study it first hand and to find out its specific needs; for example, gather foods a bird would eat (or find pictures of such food).
3. Study camouflage techniques through observation and use of audiovisual materials and equipment.

C. **Concept**—*The major characteristics of living animals include food, breathing, growth, reproduction, and adaptation.*

1. Observation and care of pets and class animals. Breed them if you have homes for babies.
2. "Adopt" an animal for a period of time in a local farm or animal protection center to witness first hand these major characteristics.
3. Compare the similarities and differences of characteristics of each animal in a sharing session as information is obtained. Show findings to rest of class. Trade animals.

D. **Concept**—*Animals live in an environment, or habitat, to which they are adapted.*

1. Watch a rotten log community. Visit various animal habitats (spider webs, ant hill, bird nest), or create them in class (build a bird nest, mouse nest). Make sun prints of organisms and objects representative of a particular habitat. (Use ozalid paper and develop in jar

with ammonia—directions are given in the *Outdoor Biology Instructional Strategies* [OBIS], 1975.)

2. Gather materials for (or pictures of) the home of an animal being studied. Compare animals found in a mowed lawn and a weedy patch.

3. Design models or shadow boxes of animal habitats, or invent an animal with coloring and markings which will camouflage it from predators. (Can describe verbally, with a typewriter, or with a communication device.)

E. **Concept**—*Animals can be classified as mollusks, arthropods, amphibians, reptiles, birds, mammals, fish, and insects.*

1. Keep examples simple. Observe lots of different animals. Use pictures or real animals (preferably) to point out examples of various classifications or characteristics of each.

2. Draw pictures or find photos in magazines or books. Collect names of animals that the students see at camp, zoos, museums, etc. Keep a classification chart and paste pictures or names under the appropriate column as you see and know the animal.

3. Give each student a list of characteristics and have him name the classification and specific animal. (A game possibility.)

F. **Concept**—*Different types of animals use different types of locomotion (fly, walk, swim, etc.)*

1. Have a "hopping circus"—various insects and animals which hop. Observe and examine travel modes of other animals in a similar manner.

2. List as many verbs as possible to describe how animals travel. List modes of travel and name as many animals as possible who use them.

3. Examine creatures who live in a pond or creek (bottom, surface, water's edge). Note modes of travel. (Can let water sit until various insects and other organisms develop there, and do experiments right at school.) Get close; you can have them look with a net or cup, or under a microscope projector, hand lens, or magnifying glass.

G. **Concept**—*Different types of animals make different sounds.*

1. Learn to identify sounds of things regularly heard about you (vacuum cleaner, phone's

ring, etc.). Change to sounds of common animals (dog, cat, bird). Students can use the tape recorder to record the sounds in their own home or room. (A game possibility.)

2. The students can study animals sounds through the use of record albums and tapes. Possibly the class can be divided into groups, each of which will study the sounds of an animal category (i.e., birds, small animals). Public libraries have such records.

3. Listen for bird calls; see how many birds can be identified. Listen for other sounds and try to determine the source. Ask them to record sounds around school. Explore why sounds are distinctive to each animal (communication, mating calls, warnings, greetings).

Plants

A. **Concept**—*There are different kinds of plants; each has special characteristics.*

1. "Walk" near school noting colors, shapes, textures of plants. Use senses to explore. (Color sections on paper plate while in class or give a cardboard shape to each; match colors and shapes to things found on nature walk.)

2. Guide student on "feely" hike with student's eyes covered with sleep-shades. Have the student change places and guide you. Make leaf and bark rubbings to identify various trees and plants. (Place a piece of paper on the specimen and rub the paper with a side of crayon or chalk—put the vein side of leaves up.) Make a collage or shadow box of plants, moss, cones, and seeds found in area. (A collage is a good souvenir from camp or a field trip.)

3. Key out various plants using a key for plants in your local area. Study leaf types and make a display of ones collected, labelled with the correct type name.

B. **Concept**—*The major characteristics of living plants include food, breathing, growth, and reproduction.*

1. Expose students to various types of plant life in class and around school (and wherever else they can experience it). Collect leaves and seeds and mount with glue on paper. Discuss how the listed characteristics are a part of all the plants that were seen.

2. Invent a plant, with its food, breathing, growth, and reproduction. Draw picture of it or describe it verbally or in writing. To study growth, stu-

dents can grow mold altering the following variables: dry or moist; very cold or warm or hot; light or dark location, and air supply covered or open. Discuss the age of trees and the procedure used to determine age of plants.

3. Discuss the life cycle of plants, emphasizing the various periods of growth. Students can record the stages of growth of a seed as a class project. Using a diagram, discuss how a tree grows.

C. **Concept**—*Plants need water, sunlight, soil, and the proper temperature.*

1. Let a portion of lawn go without maintenance. Note changes. Fertilize and begin to care for it and note further changes.
2. Conduct experiments by altering the amount and quality of water, sunlight, soil, and/or temperature in several different plants. Compare process of a plant kept in light as opposed to one in dark; given water versus no water; hot environment versus cold; soil versus water planting medium.
3. Observe location of eight different types of plant life around school. Record the types on a map of the area and decide why each is where it is.

D. **Concept**—*Plants can be classified as algae, fungi, mosses, ferns, seed plants, and conifers.*

1. Have available an example (real, dried, pressed, mounted, picture, casting) of each classification of plant for observation. Take walks and point them out as they are seen. Examine daily lunches for examples.
2. Adopt a tree. Each student chooses a tree which he will adopt and visit daily (whenever possible). Students are to find out everything possible about it. What kind of a tree is it? Make a tree scrapbook, including a drawing of the tree, leaves, bark, etc. What living things interact with the tree: birds (nest), rodents, insects, moss, fungus? What lives under the tree? In what type of climate does the tree live? Collect the names of plants that the students saw at camp, then classify them (algae, fungus).
3. Study flowers as a classification of plant. Identify the parts of a flower. Recognize similarities and differences between flowers. (Use of a hand lens is suggested.) Teach students how to use plant keys, so that they can identify and classify plants of interest to them.

E. **Concept**—*Plants have roots.*

1. Observe the growth of roots by growing plants in transparent containers (potatoes are fast and easy to see). Evaluate lunches daily to see who has a root. Look at pictures of root vegetables. Handle real root vegetables; prepare and cook them; eat them.
2. Make a game of identifying a plant by its root. Grow root vegetables in garden.
3. Study various types of roots, fibrous and tap. Discover why each exists by seeing where each grows (lawn, garden, lot). Discover functions of a root: anchors plant, absorbs water, stores food products.

F. **Concept**—*Different kinds of plants have different ways of reproducing.*

1. Collect and mount all kinds of seeds. Include ones we eat (sunflower seeds, peas). Grow a sunflower. Harvest its seeds and soak them overnight in salt water; let dry in sun or low oven. Grow and prepare popcorn.
2. Save seeds from vegetables from current garden to plant in next year's garden.
3. Talk about sprouts. Find out why not all seeds successfully produce plants. Relate the shape of the flower parts to its methods of fertilization. Observe and study seed dispersal. Identify ways by which plants disperse their seeds. Relate the pattern of seed dispersal with the place where seedlings grow.

Earth Science

A. **Concept**—*The movements of the earth in space cause day, night, and seasonal changes.*

1. Discuss, draw, paint, and paste characteristics of day and night. For example, at night it is dark, we sleep, it is quiet, colder, we need lights, etc.
2. Compare night with day (weather, animal life, sounds, etc.) Play recordings of sounds of day and night. Students can make recordings for the group to identify.
3. Study the effect of seasons on flora and fauna. Relate observed changes in the position of the sun and stars in the sky to the movement of the earth.

B. **Concept**—*All life and activity on the earth is dependent upon the energy of the sun.*

1. Dry fruit, make a fruit roll; discuss how the sun helps ripen fruits; how light and heat help plants grow. Experience each.
2. Compare sunny slopes with shady slopes. What are the differences and similarities? Make and use a solar heater for water. Dry clothes in the solar method.
3. Dehydrate food in solar dehydrator (they can make one). Locate east and west by the sun's movements. Estimate time using the sun and/or its shadow. Explain and show the process of photosynthesis. Work on developing class uses for sunlight and heat. Extend these ideas to their home and community.

C. **Concept**—*The movement of the earth affects the position of the stars.*

1. Make stars as an art project. Where do we see them? When? Discuss quantity, color, and size. View the stars at night; have them experience use of a telescope.
2. Look at the stars with the naked eye and with telescope. See a planetarium show. Make star maps on black paper with a star hole punch. Learn basic constellations.
3. Identify major constellations through class study and night observation. Point out the North Star. Why does it twinkle? Why are there different colors? Sizes? What distance away are the stars? Why do they exist? Which is the biggest star? Note that the sun is a star. What are the properties of a star's own light?

D. **Concept**—*The earth is but one member of the solar system.*

1. Make papier-mâché planets (imaginary ones too). Read and tell stories about them. Identify the earth and moon as a planet and satellite.
2. Look at the moon through binoculars or a telescope. Make models of planets; include convolutions. Learn the names of and interesting features about major planets.
3. Demonstrate size and distance relationships in the solar system. Record phases of the moon. Study photos of moon's surface.

E. **Concept**—*The surface of the earth is continually changing as a result of natural forces and human actions.*

1. Look around school and home to see how people have changed the earth. Make various model terrain types (dry and wet) in sand and mud in a ground box or sand table.
2. Observe the terrain—flat areas, slopes, gullies at home, school, nearby areas. Compare reasons for their differences. Discuss mountains, earthquakes, and volcanoes. Make papier-mâché volcano and blow it off with ammonium dichromate crystals obtainable from a chemical supply store or local high school chemistry department. Take great caution!
3. Students can be shown or can identify evidence of soil erosion and deposition. Discuss the types and causes of erosion, as well as the factors that accelerate erosion and those that slow it down. As a project, stop some erosion at or near school.

F. **Concept**—*Rocks can be classified as sedimentary, igneous, or metamorphic; minerals can be solid or liquid.*

1. Look at and handle various kinds of rocks and minerals. Use a hand lens. Make sand by crushing rocks.
2. Examine the composition of rocks. Break up a rock and study its properties under a microscope.
3. Test for hardness, cleavage, etc. Find rocks at home and near school and sort into the three categories.

G. **Concept**—*There are different types of soil.*

1. Play in dirt on ground or sand table. Make mudpies with various kinds of soil, clay, or sand. "Make" soil by starting a compost heap. Use in garden.
2. Discuss the origin and kinds of soil. Discuss and practice the uses of soil. Take samples and observe life in the soil.
3. The students can form groups to prepare presentations on different aspects of soil (as necessary for plants, kinds of life in soil, types of soil, etc.) Discuss the differences between top soil, subsoil, and bedrock.

Conservation/Ecology

A. **Concept**—*The study of ecology deals with the relationships between living things and their environment.*

1. Observe how living things around the school grounds are dependent upon their environment.
2. Take an ecological hike to observe the relationships between living things and their environment. Each student chooses a part of the environment (e.g., plant, animal, water). Students can then form groups to discuss how their part interrelates and is interdependent with the others.
3. Observe a bird nest and its immediate environment. Note the materials used in construction. Discover some relationships between the nest and other forms of life.

B. **Concept**—*All living things—human beings, animals, plants and the soil that supports them—are interdependent and interrelated with each other.*

1. Study the different levels of a tree and the animals that live there.
2. Read about, discuss, explore, and experiment with the interdependence of soil, water, and plant life. Plant a vegetable garden.
3. Study life cycles. Set one up to reflect one's present cycle.

C. **Concept**—*Conservation is the proper management of natural resources for the benefit of most people for the longest period of time.*

1. Have a guest speaker (for example, from the forest service) or visit with an agency which practices conservation.
2. Observe the conservation principles which are being practiced in the school and home. Decide what is missing. Identify "renewable" and "nonrenewable" resources. Work on alternatives to the use of nonrenewable materials.
3. Undertake projects directly related to conservation and current problems. Continue to practice conservation at home. List new inventions that have brought about changes in homes. Dams, lakes, and reservoirs help preserve water. Make a relief map of your state to show where dams have been built.

D. **Concept**—*The natural world tends to maintain a state of natural balance.*

1. Observe what happens when all snails are taken from fish bowl.

2. Explore the importance of nature in balance and what happens when people's actions cause imbalance. Do experiments.
3. Study various symbiotic relationships and discuss visible examples of interdependence.

E. **Concept**—*People are a part of the balance of nature and must stay in harmony with nature in order to preserve the balance.*

1. Walk. Observe that people in nature should not disturb the natural environment too much. Do not pick living plants—work with those that have fallen on the ground. Do not take small animals home. Observe them and then return them to their natural environment.
2. At home each student can carry out a major aspect of conservation towards fighting pollution. Find one aspect or more and stick with it. Discuss how people use plants, animals, and resources: food, clothing, shelter, pleasure, fuel, medicine, etc.
3. Practice in daily life ways that people can conserve (school supplies, food, clothing, public transportation, water, gas, electricity, etc.)

F. **Concept**—*People waste resources.*

1. Explore ways of reducing waste at home and school: turn off lights and water when not in use; use plastic cups, not paper, etc.
2. Set up a recycling center to cut down on waste at home and in school and put it to use. Crushing and recycling aluminum cans can be a money-making project.
3. Find *how* people waste resources in our school and at home. Decide and enact methods to reduce or eliminate waste.

G. **Concept**—*Pollution is the proliferation of waste products.*

1. Have a daily litter pick-up at school. Severely disabled in wheelchairs can spot it and point it out to more able students who can take it to its correct trash container.
2. Observe and record how pollution has affected the school and home. Work on eliminating it.
3. Analyze current problems that result from the growth of cities—overpopulation, smog, sewage disposal, etc. Make suggestions for solving them.

Summary

We have covered only a few areas in the vast subject of nature. Further areas of study are natural communities (interrelationships of plants and animals), weather, altitude, predator-prey relationships, native Americans (Indian uses of plants, animals and natural resources), astronomy, micro-organisms (ponds, creeks, puddles), food chains, and solar energy.

Ideas in this section can be strengthened by the use of additional resources. Many community resources can be very helpful, such as libraries, museums, botanical gardens, and park departments. Literature and materials from these agencies can be used in the classroom; some agencies may provide field trips or speakers. Some zoos operate an animal exhibit that can be brought to your school. Students should be encouraged to pursue their particular interest through the use of books or recordings. Many libraries can suggest appropriate books. Helpful titles also are included in this chapter's resource section.

A nature study program often provides new experiences for disabled students. It is hoped that this type of program will introduce the students to a new area of interest. In this way outdoor activities can be carried out with the hope that they will be enjoyed as life-time leisure activities.

Television

Each year statistics indicate that people spend large numbers of hours watching T.V. Perhaps statistics would be even more impressive if we gathered data only on that segment of the population who have disabilities. Physical handicaps often render individuals less mobile and consequently more confined to their living quarters. Physical inertia sometimes begets emotional and psychological inertia. Many disabled individuals, with other members of our society, have been taught or conditioned to be nondiscerning viewers.

It may be inevitable that disabled children will watch a lot of television. However, they should be encouraged to exercise their minds while doing so. We can teach them many ways to use thinking skills while watching and thus broaden their lives through T.V.

Make the Most of T.V. Viewing

In preparation for active utilization of television as a learning device, children can be taught to recognize kinds of shows:

news broadcasting, documentaries
children's programs
game shows
dramatic shows
variety shows
audience-participation shows
quiz shows
musicals
how-to-do shows
educational programs
public opinion shows
cartoons or animographs
seasonal shows
live-action adventure shows
police and detective stories
old films and classic theatre
sports broadcasting
serials or soap operas
series emphasizing social values
situation comedies
talk shows
specials

Within each category of programming there are, of course, variations. Children can be taught to distinguish between live drama, film, tape, and animated shows. They can learn to recognize morality lessons (bragging, cheating) and the difference between animated and live-action violence. They may be taught to distinguish features of sexism in which males or females are continually identified in stereotypic roles.

Recognize Features of Advertising

Children can be taught to notice details of commercials. They can analyze the production and make judgments about the messages. These skills foster a growing appreciation of T.V. production and help children become *discriminating* consumers of advertised products and programming.

Children can learn from studying commercials. They can study dimensions of commercials, such as frequency and content. Children can identify how many minutes of commercials per hour are allotted on children's programming compared to adult programming. Analysis of content of commercial messages develops thinking skills in children. They may be taught to note whether commercials direct children to ask parents to buy certain products for them, or if they are told that they will be superior to their peers if they use a certain product. They may notice words such as *only* and *just* which qualitatively influence concepts of prices. Children and adults can become aware of the choices of food and then research the *actual* attributes of foods advertised to find which are nutritious and which lack nutritional value.

While becoming discriminating viewers and discriminating consumers, viewers need to become aware of the necessity for commercials which support U.S. public service T.V. programming. Without advertisements, much programming for children would be impossible.

Analyze Production Procedures and Content

Broadcasting can be analyzed in many ways. Analysis of programming might be studied in terms of production and content. News broadcasting, for example, can be used to demonstrate kinds of production and content information which help viewers become more actively involved in the broadcasting process.

Production of News Broadcasts

Sophisticated learners may choose to study various methods for providing live, remote coverage of news stories; videotape, wire, and communications satellites are examples of techniques used. Procedures for transporting live news stories and recently filmed stories to national networks and local studios make fascinating study.

Uses of studio-made visual aids and visual fillers are particularly noticeable in newscasting. T.V. viewers can be taught to notice use of graphics to announce upcoming stories. Viewers can also be taught to note artists' illustrations when actual pictures cannot be obtained.

Persons needed to relay news to audiences can be another focus of study. News broadcasters, anchorpersons, commentators, producers, directors, film editors, news editors and reporters, of course, play a major role in production. Do these persons have the same roles and responsibilities? Are some shows produced which rely heavily on one anchorperson? Do shows have several broadcasters? These are interesting problems for investigation.

Choice of words used to relay news to audiences makes an interesting study. In some cases, the anchorperson studies news items selected by the director and the staff. These items must be edited so they relay news clearly to the most people in very brief announcements. To ensure the viewer's comprehension, newscasters may mention key points immediately before, or after any news item is presented or the filmed story or an interview is concluded. Viewers may be interested in time allotments for different news stories. They can analyze if relative length is correlated with the relative importance of stories. Planned news shows may be pre-empted with updated news of more significance. Viewers can learn how the broadcaster is informed of the changes and how he handles the situation. Viewers can also notice if newscasters look at a teleprompter above or next to the T.V. camera or read a script.

Content of News Broadcasts

Analysis of the content of news broadcasts may make more productive study than for some other kind of programming. Discriminating differences between *soft* news and *hard* news is a basic kind of information that aids in judging the nature and importance of news viewed. *Soft news* refers to events of less immediate importance, while *hard news* is news of a more urgent nature. Soft news can include minidocumentaries used on days when there is a shortage of hard news. Students can learn to identify news which could have been predicted in time to send a person with a camera to accompany a reporter and crew to cover the story (i.e., legislation to be passed, a union group planning a strike on a certain day). News that could not have been predicted and, therefore, presents more complex problems to the T.V. personnel, can be viewed from a different perspective than predicted news.

For those students wishing to study further the content of T.V. programming, a study of decision-making procedures regarding content can be helpful. In news broadcasting, for instance, how is the selection of network news determined? What news items were included, and more importantly, what items were deleted or neglected? Of those included, how are potential biases or actual biases managed? Are newscasting programs designed to include guests of various political points of view or is there a prevailing political attitude characteristic of a network?

References at the end of this chapter suggest ways teachers can help students learn about production procedures and different kinds of programming. Students can study about production personnel and their jobs, use of lighting and music for moods, special effects, approaches to staging, special camera techniques, and techniques to sensorially and emotionally exploit the viewer's imagination. Students can attempt to identify program adjustments for special audiences of persons who are deaf, blind, and who rely on a means of communication other than English. Students can watch for techniques such as the *chromakey effect* in which foreground figures are electronically cut into a background scene (such as a picture behind a newscaster).

Follow Specific Television Personalities and Shows

Many T.V. viewers do not note the identity of the actors and actresses, and they know little about interesting aspects of professional and personal lives of T.V. personalities. They may not be aware of the kinds of roles for which a specific personality is selected. Aspects of their personal lives, their hobbies, their childhoods, and their T.V. involvement need not be dramatic to be of interest to viewers. General interest in other people, including T.V. personalities, provides a healthy experience for individuals confined because of physical disability.

Enhance Academic Learning

T.V. can be used to supplement academic learning initiated at school. Phonics and reading can be practiced while watching T.V. Teachers can scan the *T.V. Guide* and, using flash cards, teach phonetic cues or sight words. Children can be taught to relate written symbols and corresponding sounds found in titles of programs and names of products advertised: *F* as in "Family Affair," *S* and *St* as in "Sesame Street," *D* as in "Disney." Sight words can be taught in this way as well. Names of most T.V. shows can be phonetically decoded. Writing letters in sequence from memory can be taught if children are asked to write or type as much of the title as they can after the title is flashed on the T.V. screen. The crossword puzzle in the *T.V. Guide* can provide spelling practice. These puzzles can also motivate students to find T.V. information. Older students with reading problems can practice reading by following T.V. scripts. Scripts for serials or soap operas can sometimes be obtained from T.V. stations. Once obtained, students can follow the script as the story unfolds.

Numerical skills and concepts can be practiced in different ways. *Time* can be practiced by relating the position of the hands on a clock and to printed notations of times in T.V. schedules. Scoring of sporting events requires addition, subtraction, decimals, and percentages. For those able to compute or estimate larger numbers, many game shows offer opportunities to read and hear larger numbers. Students can learn to determine whether one amount or combination of amounts is more or less than another.

Geography can be learned by identifying on a map locations where programs are filmed and locations where news and plays take place. Features of different climates, land masses, and flora and fauna can also be studied and programs checked for authenticity of impressions portrayed.

Critical thinking skills can be taught and practiced in many ways. Finding "bloopers" is one way to sharpen one's awareness in *finding inconsistencies*. One student caught a blooper. She noticed that *all* car windows were rolled *up* in a chase scene yet the hair of the driver was blowing as if the window were open. *Summarizing sequences* can be taught by asking students to flip from channel to channel and summarize the variety of shows being broadcast. They might be asked to *infer* (during the commercial) what might happen next in the story. They may be encouraged to improve *memory* skills by retelling stories or by recalling, in the appropriate order, the last three products shown during the commerical.

Students might compare their critical reviews of movies with those of professional critics who write in *T.V. Guide*. They can study and analyze views expressed in the "Free Speech Message." They can study the organization and content of the message so they can isolate the speaker's opinion from factual background information.

Summary

In conclusion, the opportunities for leisure-time activities for the handicapped are as broad as your imagination. With adaptations and practice there are few areas about which disabled persons cannot learn *something*. With guidance and encouragement beginning in preschool, future generations of disabled children and adults can develop and enjoy leisure activity and need not passively retreat to their television sets for solace.

Notes

1. Most ideas in the section "Teaching Musical Concepts" are quoted or paraphrased from Betty Rex's

Concepts of Music for the Young Child, 1972, pp. 4–41. The material is adapted with permission of the Pennsylvania State Department of Education. Some ideas for teaching the physically disabled are included.

2. This information was included in informal log and activities recorded by Bill Sciallo, a special education teacher in the San Francisco Unified School District, San Francisco, California.

References

Leisure & Recreation

Comprehensive

Brannan, S. Trends and issues in leisure education for the handicapped through community education. In E. Fairchild & L. N. Neal (Eds.), Common-unity in the community: A forward-looking program of recreation and leisure services for the handicapped. Eugene, Ore.: Center for Leisure Studies, University of Oregon, 1975.

Fairchild, E., & Neal, L. Common-unity in the community: A forward-looking program of recreation and leisure services for the handicapped. Eugene, Ore.: Center for Leisure Studies, University of Oregon, 1975.

Nesbitt, J., Neal, L., & Hillman, W. Recreation for exceptional children and youth. Focus on Exceptional Children, 1974, 6(3), 1–6.

Raising Guinea Pigs

Ashbrook, F. Raising small animals for fun and profit. New York: D. Van Nostrand, 1951.

De Rochemont, R. The pet's cookbook. New York: Alfred A. Knopf, 1964.

Music Appreciation

Bennett, M. O. Make the top 40 work for you. Music Educators Journal, 1975, 61(5), 33–37.

Brofsky, H., & Bamberger, J. S. The art of listening: Developing musical perception. New York: Harper & Row, 1969.

Copland, A. What to listen for in music. New York: McGraw-Hill, 1957.

Fox, S. From rock to Bach. Music Educators Journal, 1970, 56(9), 52–55.

McMillan, L. E. Guiding children's growth through music. Boston: Ginn, 1959.

Rex, B. Concepts of music for the young child. Harrisburg, Pa.: Pennsylvania Department of Education, 1972. (ERIC Document Reproduction Service No. ED 071 771).

Seligmann, J., & Danziger, J. The meaning of music: The young listener's guide. Cleveland: World, 1966.

Horseback Riding

Acorn Hill Equestrian Center. 10 S. 135 Book Road, Naperville, Ill. 60540.

Adams, R. C., Daniel, A. N., & Kullman, L. Games, sports, and exercises for the physically handicapped (2d ed.). Philadelphia: Lea & Febiger, 1975.

Davies, J. A. The reins of life. London: J. A. Allen, 1967.

Davies, J. A. Notes by S. Rafferty from Instructors Course. Acorn Hill Equestrian Center Naperville, Ill., June 1974.

McCowan, L. It is ability that counts: A training manual on therapeutic riding for the handicapped. Olivet, Mich.: Olivet, 1972.

Card Playing

Lowman, E., & Klinger, J. L. Self-help for the handicapped: Aids to independent living. Institute of Rehabilitation Medicine, New York University Medical Center. New York: McGraw-Hill, 1969.

Nature Study

Child ecology—A complete resource guide for the elementary school teacher. Los Altos, Calif.: Child Ecology Press, 1974.

Gross, P., & Railton, E. P. Teaching science in an outdoor environment: a natural history guide. Berkeley, Calif.: University of California, 1972.

Indoor-outdoor natural learning experiences. Pamphlet. (Available from Sacramento County Office of Education, Division of Educational Services, 6011 Folsom Blvd., Sacramento, Calif. 95819.)

Ken-A-Vision. Microscope projector. (Available from Ken-A-Vision Manufacturing Co., Inc., Raytown, Missouri.)

Outdoor biology instructional strategies. O.B.I.S., 1975. (Available from Lawrence Hall of Science, University of California, Berkeley, Calif. 94720.)

Ranger Rick's Nature Magazine. (Available from the National Wildlife Federation, 1412 16th St. NW, Washington, D. C. 20036.)

The outdoor world . . . of the Sacramento region. Pamphlet, (Available from Sacramento County Office of Education, Educational Services Division, 6011 Folsom Blvd., Sacramento, Calif. 95819.)

Vessel, M. F., & Harrington, E. J. Common native animals. California State Series Publication. Sacramento, Calif.: California State Department of Education, 1967.

TV

Bigge, J. L. Expected learning often comes through unexpected teaching. Exceptional Children, 1967, 34(1), 47–49.

Kaye, E. The family guide to children's television. New York: Pantheon, 1974.

Mayer, M. About television. New York: Harper & Row, 1972.

TV Guide. Radnor, Pa.: Triangle Publications.

Zettl, H. Sight, sound, motion: Applied media aesthetics. Belmont, Ca.: Wadsworth, 1973.

Resources

Leisure and Recreation

Comprehensive

American Alliance for Health, Physical Education and Recreation (AAHPER). 1201 16th Street N.W., Washington, D.C. 20036.

Avedon, E. *Therapeutic recreation*. Englewood Cliffs, N.J.: Prentice-Hall, 1974.

Brannan, S. A. *Our new challenge: Recreation for the deaf-blind*. Pamphlet, 1975. Seattle, Washington: Northwest Regional Center for Deaf-Blind Children. (Available from 3411 South Alaska, Seattle, Wash. 98118.)

Buell, C. E. *Physical education and recreation for the visually handicapped*. Washington, D.C.: American Association for Health, Physical Education and Recreation, 1973.

Carlson, B. W., & Ginglend, D. R. *Recreation for retarded teen-agers and young adults*. Nashville, Tenn.: Abingdon, 1968.

Chapman, F. *Recreation activities for the handicapped*. New York: Ronald, 1960.

Kraus, R. *Therapeutic recreation service*. Philadelphia: W. B. Saunders, 1973.

Kraus, R. G., & Bates, B. J. *Recreation leadership and supervision: Guideline for professional development*. Philadelphia: W. B. Saunders, 1975, pp. 219–234.

Overs, R. P., O'Connor, E., & Demarco, B. *Avocational activities for the handicapped*. Springfield, Ill.: Charles C Thomas, 1974.

Sessoms, H. D., & Stein, T. A. *Recreation for special populations: A plan for community action*. Boston: Holbrook, 1973.

Stein, J. (Ed.). *Physical education and recreation for impaired, disabled, and handicapped individuals: Past, present, future*. Washington, D.C.: American Alliance for Health, Physical Education, and Recreation Publication Sales, 1976.

Raising Guinea Pigs

Pet stores.

Libraries.

Roberts, M. F. *Guinea pigs for beginners*. Neptune City, N. J.: Tropical Fish Hobbyist Publishing, 1972.

Rosenblum, E. E. *Guinea pigs in color*. Neptune City, N.J.: Tropical Fish Hobbyist Publishing, n.d.

Schneider, E. (Ed.). *Enjoy your guinea pig*. Ontario, Canada: The Pet Library, Sernco Industries, n.d.

Music Appreciation

For Teachers

Alvin, J. *Music for the handicapped child*. London: Oxford University Press, 1965.
Discusses music listening and music appreciation as it relates to the overall maturation of the handicapped child. Covers music in relation to the child who is mentally retarded, maladjusted, autistic, cerebral palsied, physically handicapped (delicate), and deaf and blind.

Baldwin, L. *Music for young listeners*. New York: Silver Burdett, 1951.
For leisure music activities in the home. Easy reading. Baldwin's "Series for Listeners" aims at the development of the musically-oriented listerner who does not merely hear music, but thinks about what he hears. She divides her book by composers and relates their lives and their works. She examines a single bar of music and the whole piece of a composer's work. Baldwin's varied style keeps interest high.

Cheyette, I., & Cheyette, H. *Teaching music creatively in the elementary school*. New York: McGraw-Hill, 1969.
Curriculum objectives for each grade and many activities and songs to be used with children, ideas for accompaniment with simple instruments. Also includes some basic music fundamentals necessary to teach concepts.

Hawkinson, J., & Faulhaber, M. *Music and instruments for children to make*. Chicago: Whitman & Co., 1969.
Contains activities for involving children in becoming aware of sounds and rhythms around them. Also includes many ideas for constructing simple musical instruments from common materials and songs to be used for playing these instruments.

Libraries.
A source of books for children about music.

Nordoff, P., & Robbins, C. *Therapy in music for handicapped children*. London: Golancz, 1971.

Spaeth, S. *At home with music*. Freeport, New York: Books for Libraries Press, 1945.

State-adopted textbooks in music from state department of education.
Sources of information and instructional materials about music.

Records

Bowmar records. Catalog. (Available from 622 Rodier Drive, Glendale, Calif. 91201.)

Bowmar-materials for exceptional children. Catalog. (Available from 10515 Burbank Blvd., North Hollywood, Calif. 91601.)

Catalog of music publications. American Printing House for the Blind. (Available from 1839 Frankfort Avenue, Louisville, Kentucky 40206.)

Children's Music Center, Inc., 5273 West Pico Blvd., Los Angeles, Calif. 90019.
Distributor of records for disabled children.

Hap Palmer records. Educational Activities Inc., P.O. Box 392, Freeport, N.Y. 11520.
This series of records contains many songs that children like, while at the same time teaches them basic concepts such as colors, slow, fast, etc.

Recordings for recovery. 304 Sixth St., Oakmont, Pa. 15139.
A nonprofit organization which sends musical recordings out on loan to confined disabled persons.

Those persons requiring tapes or cassettes can hold them permanently by retaping.

Wampler, M. M. (Ed.). *Orff-Schulwerk: Design for creativity: A curriculum guide*. (A Report of the Curriculum Development in the ESEA Title III Research Project, Jan. 1966-June 1968). Bellflower, Ca.: Creative Practices Council, P.O. Box 1068, Bellflower, Calif. 90706.

Photography

Hillam, B. Shutterbugging again. *Rehabilitation Gazette*, 1975, *18*, 14.

Card Games

Morehead, A. H. (Ed.). *Official rules of card games*. Greenwich, Conn.: Fawcett, 1968. (Reprinted by arrangement with the U. S. Playing Card Co.)

Nature Study

A child's garden. 1972. (Available from Chevron Chemical Co., 200 Bush St., San Francisco, Calif. 94120.)

Buschbaum, R., & Buschbaum, M. *Basic ecology*. Pittsburgh, Pa.: Boxwood, 1957.

Golden Nature Guides. New York: Golden Press.

Hammerman, D. R., & Hammerman, W. *Teaching in the outdoors*. Minneapolis, Minn.: Burgess, 1964.

Life nature library series. New York: Time Incorporated, 1963.

Russell, H. R., *Ten-minute field trips*. New York: Doubleday, 1970.

S.C.I.S. Science Curriculum Improvement Study. (Available from the school department of Rand McNally and Co., Box 7600, Chicago, Ill. 60680.)

The how and why wonder book series. New York: Grosset & Dunlap.

Things of science. Individual topic science experiment kits. (Available from 231 W. Center Street, Marion, Ohio 43302.)

TV

Television Information Service, 745 Fifth Ave., New York, N.Y. 10022.
Free recommendations of coming children's TV programming—e.g., children's weekly shows, documentaries, specials, wildlife, sports, and music. Parents will also appreciate the free mailings.

Play

Hartley, R. E., Frank, L. K., & Goldersen, R. M. *Understanding children's play*. New York: Macmillan, 1957.

Arts and Crafts

Lindsay, L. *Art and the handicapped child*. New York: Taplinger, 1972.

McNeice, W., & Bensen, K. *Crafts for the retarded*. Bloomington, Ill.: McKnight, 1964.

Swimming

Newman, J. *Swimming for children with physical and sensory impairments*. Springfield, Ill.: Charles C Thomas, 1976.

Sports and Games

Adams, R. C., Daniel, A. N., & Rullman, L. *Games, sports, and exercises for the physically handicapped* (2d ed.). Philadelphia: Lea & Febiger, 1975.

Cratty, B. J., & Breen, J. E. *Educational games for physically handicapped children*. Denver: Love, 1972.

Fairchild, B., Croke, K., & Clay, S. *Recreation activities and games for physically handicapped children*. (Available from the Palo Alto United Schools Instructional Materials Center, 2850 Middlefield Road, Palo Alto, Calif. 94306.)

Pomeroy, J. *Recreation for the physically handicapped*. New York: Macmillan, 1969.

Robins, F., & Robins, J. *Educational rhythmics for mentally and physically handicapped children*. New York: Association, 1968.

Sosne, M. *Handbook of adapted physical education equipment and its use*. Springfield, Ill.: Charles C Thomas, 1973.

Special Olympics Inc., 1701 K Street N.W., Suite 203, Washington, D.C. 20006.

Sports 'n' spokes. 6043 N. Ninth Avenue., Phoenix, Arizona 85013.
Wheelchair sports and recreation.

Travel

American Automobile Association. 8111 Gatehouse Rd., Falls Church, Va. 22042.

Airline transportation for the handicapped. (Available from The National Easter Society for Crippled Children and Adults, 2023 W. Ogden Ave., Chicago, Ill. 60612.)

Avis and Hertz car rental agencies.
Specially adapted cars with hand controls for handicapped persons. Information available from local city offices.

Disabled International Visits and Exchanges, Youth and Community Services Department, The Central Bureau for Educational Visits and Exchanges. 43 Dorset Street, London WIH 3FN.

Evergreen Travel Service (Wings on Wheels), 19429-44th Street West, Lynnwood, Washington 98036.

Greyhound Lines Bus Service "Helping Hand Program." Local cities.

Rambling Tours, Inc., P.O. Box 1304, Hallandale, Florida 33009 or Handy-Cap Horizons, Inc., 3250 E. Loretta Drive, Indianapolis, Ind. 46227.

12

WORK

One of our most important responsibilities is to help disabled pupils prepare for present and future life situations, one of which may be the world of work. We refer to work as directing physical and/or mental effort toward the achievement of something productive. Work, in this sense, not only pertains to jobs where pay is received, but also to tasks related to daily living, personal growth, and leisure enjoyment.

Many questions and problems face disabled young adults leaving special education programs. Like nonhandicapped students, they face major decisions which may ultimately influence the future course of their entire lives. Surrounding those major decisions there are also unique questions. If they decide to pursue higher education, they may be confronted with very real concerns and specific questions, such as: Will further education help me obtain a job? Will I be able to keep up with the class work if I decide on college? Will I be able

Elaine Williams Gordon, *O. T. R., is the executive director of Goodwill Industries of San Francisco, California.*

June Bigge.

to record notes and take tests? Will there be architectural barriers that prevent my movement on the campus? Will I be able to live in a dormitory and care for myself? How will I get to and from school if I live at home? What colleges will accommodate physically disabled students needing special facilities and services? Will I be able to finance further education?

On the other hand, should the handicapped person decide against additional formal education and pursue a job, she is confronted with some very real but different questions: What jobs are available, and do I have or could I develop the requisite skills for these jobs? Where can I obtain training which will lead to a job? Will I be able to get to and from a job? Will I be able to function in the working environment? Will I want to do the particular kind of work in which I can function and which is available to me?

If the disabled individual concludes that immediate job placement in competitive employment is unrealistic, different questions are before her. Could I work and train in the environment of a sheltered workshop? Could I get to and from a workshop? Would the amount of money I could earn be sufficient for my own support? If not, what arrangement might be made for my support? Would I be eligible for supplemental income?

In order to prepare the disabled young adult and her family to deal with these impending alternatives, you can provide experiences toward that person becoming as socially competent, independent, and economically self-sufficient as possible. Appropriate preparation for vocational education should be initiated early in a child's life and should not be left to some future date. Inadvertent neglect of this preparation encourages dependent behavior which is incompatible with the self-reliance and determination needed to develop work readiness and work skills.

In the first section of this Chapter there will be a discussion on the desirability of preparing for work from early childhood. We will call attention to inadequate practices used with disabled youth which unintentionally create additional hurdles to be overcome. In the second section there will be ideas for curriculum planning and preparation for work in the classroom. Experiences are included which can help disabled youth make appropriate decisions concerning their involvement in present and future work-oriented tasks. Sample procedures demonstrate how such involvement may be done, starting with very young children. In the third section suggestions are included for students who, because of their disabilities, may not be involved in the job market but who will find an understanding of the world of work socially enriching. The final part concludes with recommendations for some basic work skills and adaptive behaviors which could be considered as life management tools for all persons. They are presented as tools for successful accomplishment in school, paid jobs, leisure, home responsibilities, interpersonal relationships, self-care and other life management skills.

Preparation from Early Childhood

In spite of numerous accomplishments and intermittently achieved goals by many disabled people, getting a job is still a primary rehabilitation goal. Working fits the social norms of this society. Many nondisabled individuals meet not only their economic needs but also their needs for social status and self-esteem through their roles as employees. It reasonably follows that in this society many people with handicaps have precisely the same need for economic stability, self-fulfillment

and self-identity through their roles as workers and through the social component provided by work.

To achieve equal status and acceptance as a worker, there are numerous hurdles to overcome. The more obvious hurdles may result from the mere presence of the disability. The more insidious ones may result from social prejudices which surround disability labels, or from the injurious hurdles presented by our society's preoccupation with health, youth, and beauty, and its fear and avoidance of sickness, aging, and disability. In addition to all of these possible obstacles, there is the myriad of problems caused by the lack of opportunities for interaction between persons with physical disabilities and those without. Isolation and lack of exposure to one another prohibits disabled and nondisabled children from forming natural peer relationships as well as mutual understanding and acceptance of one another. This isolation not only has negative effects on the children but it may also distort the perception of teachers and counselors working with these students. As a result, these "interested others" may fail the individuals they most want to help in four growth areas:

1. self-assessment
2. self-reliance
3. self-esteem
4. self-discipline

DEAR

To facilitate your awareness of behaviors that can influence these four qualities, the following are some personal experiences and observations. *If underdeveloped, these four qualities add to the intrinsic hurdles which must eventually be overcome if one is to gain status and acceptance as a self-reliant individual and worker.*

Self-Assessment

Appropriate self-assessment is more than merely repeating "I can do anything anyone else can do, I can do anything better than you." Self-assessment is a realistic self-evaluation of one's abilities, which can then be matched against the standards and/or demands of a given situation. When inaccurate self-assessment exists, it frequently appears to be due to a lack of experience imposed on the individual by the restrictions of her disability and/or by the lack of exposure to the capacities of nonhandicapped peers. In addition to these factors, exposure to inappropriate praise and well-intended comments on the part of parents, teachers, and therapists also nurtures inaccurate self-assessment. Verbal praise, for example, is not always placed in its proper perspective by the receiver. It may transmit meanings quite different from what was intended by the sender. Art work described by a sender as "marvelous," "beautiful," "fabulous," or "fantastic," does not necessarily mean genius quality. Is it any wonder that a 17-year-old, cerebral palsied quadraplegic suddenly feels the capacity to become another Michelangelo? An enthusiastic verbal reflection of the child's proud attitude toward her finished product would seem far less risky or deceiving. "You really feel good about this picture!" or "This must be your favorite!"

The payoff for inadvertently perpetuating inaccurate self-assessment or self-appraisal is eventual frustration in aspirations and goal attainment. The way she perceives her ability to function and how she is actually able to function may not match.

Self-Reliance

Self-reliance, in the sense we are using it, is depending upon one's own abilities and judgment. A deeper explanation might be demonstrated by recounting a personal experience. Several years ago a therapist was involved in a special research project working with very young, school-aged disabled children. These children were disabled by cerebral palsy and, in some cases, slow intellectual development.

A short time later this same therapist began to work in a sheltered workshop rehabilitation facility with disabled adults who were also limited by cerebral palsy as well as other types of disabilities. While working with these adults, the therapist reflected upon her past experiences with children and realized how she may have contributed to their lack of self-reliance as adults.

In the therapist's previous experiences, she viewed a patient's absence with relief and appreciation for the extra time provided to write progress notes, rehabilitation plans, or to prepare for the next day's work schedule. She did not confront the patient regarding the effects of her unannounced absences or discuss with her the responsibility for calling in and cancelling appointments. Thus she missed a "real live" opportunity to help the patient develop responsible self-reliant behaviors that eventually would be expected by employers. Inadvertently, this

therapist was contributing to the patient's lack of self-reliance.

She also allowed the parents to take full responsibility for cancellations. They either called in or wrote a note; any tardiness or absence that ensued was because "*They* didn't get the child up on time"; "*They* didn't get her dressed"; "*They* forgot to get her lunch ready"; "*They* didn't get her to the bus on time." It was sadly evident that the child was not expected to so much as set her own alarm or to remind someone else to help her do so if need be. No one normally expected any significant assistance or personal responsibility from the patient regarding her own daily schedule. This simple vignette depicts how early in life we inadvertently cheat a disabled youngster from experiencing the self-reliance which she will eventually need in her adult life.

Self-Esteem

Self-esteem, in the context we are using it, is self-respect, pride, and belief in one's own value and worth. Following are some behaviors sometimes seen in parents, teachers, and therapists that can produce a negative influence on the self-esteem and self-confidence of a disabled individual.

1. *Increasing the psychological size of one's self at the expense of another.* Teachers and other "significant adults" may behave toward children in the following ways: late for appointments, do not meet agreed upon commitments, converse away from the child, do not greet the child by name, avoid eye contact, and do not wait for the child's response. Sometimes such attitudes are inadvertently projected: big me, little you; important me, insignificant you; healthy me, sick you; smart me, dumb you.

2. *Perpetuating another's feeling of exclusion or difference.* Feelings of exceptionality may be perpetuated when disabled students notice that some students are always selected for field trips and they are not. Able-bodied students are reminded of their tardiness but nothing is said when the disabled student is late. Teachers and others tend to condescend, paternalize, and "talk down" to them.

3. *Making decisions which affect another without considering her view in the decision-making process.* Too often we design curriculum goals, change schedules, withdraw

privileges, reschedule assignment dates, change scoring procedures, and plan coming events without any input from the disabled persons involved.

Self-Discipline in Disappointment and Failure

Another personal observation demonstrates how over-protection from disappointment and failure may rob an individual of the experience needed for self-control in future disappointing or unsuccessful situations. For example, during classroom time, specific games were initiated on an individual basis to get a young child to use particular sets of muscles. While these games were highly successful in exercising physical muscles, they were often glaringly unsuccessful in exercising "psychological muscles." The child was rarely (if ever) allowed the "painful" experience of losing. To encourage his participation, "significant adults" almost always allowed the child to win. If it is true that a person's ability to deal with failure or disappointment is related to his previous experience or exposure, this child was deprived of some useful experiences he could later exercise to skillfully adjust to the realities and disappointments of the work world.

In summary, students can develop a "running jump" to many of the future hurdles in the work world if teachers collaborate with others in finding ways to help children develop self-assessment, self-reliance, self-esteem, and self-discipline from early childhood.

Preparation In the Classroom

Prerequisites needed in preparation for work cannot be taught suddenly when an intense desire for employment arises. Just as physical therapy started at the age of 18 does not make a crippled body stand up to its potential, neither does preparation for vocational job placement beginning at age 18 make a disabled person "stand up" to her job potential.

Teachers of young disabled individuals can contribute to the student's vocational exploration in the classroom. They can provide basic classroom experiences which help develop attitudes and behaviors which are prerequisites for employment. The sample program within this section offers ideas to:

1. foster student self-assessment
2. correlate current student responsibilities to future responsibilities
3. teach career awareness
4. provide transition from school to other community resources

Foster Student Self-Assessment

It would be practically impossible to estimate vocational goals for any one group of disabled children. The most important goal at this time is to encourage individuals to learn how to explore their capabilities and interests.

Prevocational work activities could be started with young students who, as a group, exhibit a combination of skills and limitations. For instance, some students may have not only motor disabilities but specific language problems. Some may have good hand use, while for others hand use may be uncoordinated or nonexistent. Some may be nonambulatory and the precise levels of mental abilities of others may be unknown.

You might begin by agreeing on classroom tasks such as running short errands, keeping one's desk orderly, keeping pencils sharpened, getting the school work completed on time, pushing a wheelchair for another child, and caring for the classroom pets.

Teachers and children together may then work out procedures for individuals or class members as a group to appraise task requirements in relation to individual capabilities. Individual performance on these classroom tasks can then be evaluated with the children. Records may be kept in many different ways from simple marks of __+__ for *does,* __O__ for *does not,* and __/__ for *needs help* to scales as in Figure 12–1. This figure demonstrates a formal, direct way children can evaluate themselves in relation to skills needed for various tasks. Informal, less direct methods are also beneficial. As with persons without physical disability, these pupils should eventually reach the conclusion that some children can do some things that others cannot do and encourage the children to combine their skills to accomplish tasks.

Of paramount importance is the realization by the pupil and teacher that every child be given turns at various tasks. Trying various tasks will provide some opportunity for pupils to improve their skills. For others it will provide the opportunity to find unique ways or adapted equipment to

Classroom Task	Subtasks	Functional Skill Evaluation	
		Spastic & in chair	Mild CP & blind
Feed parakeet	Move to cage between 9 & 10 a.m.	2	4
	Get food dish without letting bird out	1	4
	Shut & hook cage door	2	4
	Reach food box	2	4
	Pour food into dish using a funnel	1	3
	Put filled dish inside cage	2	3
	Remove water bottle	2	4
	Remove lid	2	2
	Fill bottle with water	2	4
	Replace lid	2	2
	Replace in bottle holder on the cage	2	3
	Put equipment away	2	5
	Check a chart when task is completed	2	2

Figure 12–1. Functional skill evaluation.

Note. Scale: 5—Can do quickly with no assistance.
4—Can do slowly with no assistance.
3—Sometimes needs assistance.
2—Always needs assistance.
1—Unable to perform.

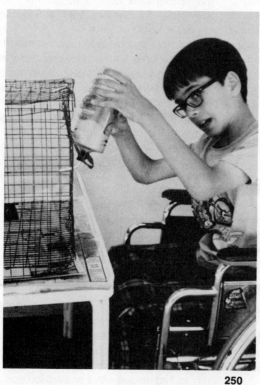 

help them perform the tasks. Still others will experience carrying out responsibilities even though they may always need assistance.

When assistance *is* needed, it should be recognized by the child and the helper. Care should be taken to avoid comments implying total accomplishment by the disabled person. "Look what Suzie did" (implying she acted on her own) or "Suzie did a good job of feeding the bird today." Be fair with these children by sensitively reflecting their accomplishments and at the same time allowing them to learn how to appraise their skills against those needed to do the task. Some comments might be: "Suzie really wants to see how much she can do by herself!" "Suzie wants you to see how she is improving!" or "See what Suzie and I did together."

Any processes of self-assessment must be tailored with caution so they do not become demeaning experiences. It is *vital* that these processes of self-assessment help children realize their assets and abilities as well as their possible limitations and restrictions.

Correlate Current Responsibilities to Future Responsibilities

Rather simple tasks such as caring for class pets provide opportunities for children to realize their capabilities and to practice behaviors and skills which are expected in later vocations.

Following through with study of the classroom task of feeding and caring for pets (see Figure 12–2, p. 252) helps teachers, parents, and children see one example of relationships of good classroom practices to preparedness for future occupational placements.

Teach Career Awareness

Activities in certain classrooms should be based upon the need to develop career awareness and to explore different kinds of careers. Students are able to assess task requirements in relation to work capabilities. (See Figure 12–3, p. 253.) Activities help students study concepts, skills, and adaptive behaviors common to many work situations. Furthermore, they are based upon a need to help pupils learn about and appreciate the work of others.

For children of all ages, we recommend teaching ideas presented by Kokaska (1974). He explains that career awareness includes development of concepts about work and one's relationship to it. Overlying concepts include:

1. Work has dignity.
2. Work means different things to different people.
3. Work has different rewards or satisfactions.
4. Education and work are interrelated.
5. All work can be classified into job families or clusters. (p. 2)

It is impossible to expose students to the 20,000 occupational categories which exist. Study the clusters such as the 13 described in the *Occupational Outlook Handbook.* These encompass jobs that range from entry level unskilled to those in skilled, technical, and professional categories. Career cluster groups based upon a concept of related activities are:

1. industrial production and related occupations
2. office occupations
3. *service occupations:* cleaning and related occupations, *food service occupations* (personal services occupations, cooks and chefs, meat cutters, waiters and waitresses)
4. education and related occupations
5. sales occupations
6. construction occupations
7. occupations in transportation activities
8. scientific and technical occupations
9. mechanics and repairers
10. health occupations
11. social science occupations
12. social service occupations
13. art, design, and communications occupations

We suggest that teachers and students explore clusters utilizing the following questions [1] (Kokaska, 1974) as guidelines to activities:

1. What are the occupations?
2. Who works in these occupations?
3. What is the life-style of the people?
4. Where are the jobs?
5. How do workers accomplish their jobs?

Figure 12–4, p. 253, and the following five questions show how activities centered around *food services*, one occupational area of the personal services cluster, lead toward student exploration of basic questions. Notice *basic* activities for young and/or less experienced students and *advanced* activities for older and/or more experienced students. (See p. 254.)

Classroom Task: Care for Pets

Current Classroom Practices	Future Occupational Practices
1. Feed pets daily at a specific time	Complete work tasks.
a. Move to cage between 9 & 10 a.m.	Follow daily schedule; get to work on time.
b. Open cage door.	Plan sequence of action.
c. Get food dish without letting pet escape.	Anticipate safety procedures.
d. Shut and hook cage door.	Complete tasks.
e.	
f.	
2. Reorder food.	Get materials ready for work; plan ahead to avoid running out of work supplies.
3. Put equipment away.	Put work equipment or materials in the proper place; clean up work station at end of day.
4. Become knowledgeable about pets, i.e., precautions to take & what to observe in order to keep pets in healthy condition.	Be aware of new developments which might arise and adjust to the new situation to the best of your ability.
a. Watch for signs of mites.	Identify possible problem.
1) Find something to help kill mites.	Search for possible solutions to problem.
2) Apply on bird according to directions.	Implement a solution.
3) Follow through to see if mites disappeared.	Follow up to check on effect of action taken.
5. Report to teacher and class the troubles encountered and how solved.	Develop a judgment of what to report to others.
6. Plan another way to put water bottle on cage so it is not dropped.	Discover unique adaptive ways to accommodate limitation caused by a disability.
7. Seek advice from others about other procedures for successfully securing water bottle to the cage.	Seek advice from others about creative suggestions and solutions to problems.
8. Review the steps of the job to be sure all were accomplished.	Seek suggestions for ways to improve.

Figure 12–2. Current classroom responsibilities prepare for future vocational responsibilities.

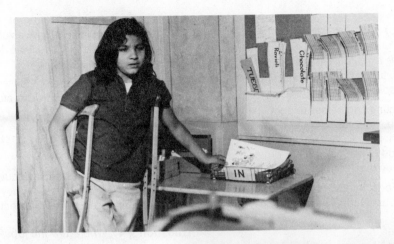

Figure 12–3. Students can be given opportunities to try different jobs while at school. (*Top*.) Janet reports for duty, picks up ditto master and *Work Order,* uses the duplicator and delivers work to her teacher. (*Center*.) Using their teacher's car, these students explore a work option of auto mechanics.

Figure 12–4. Activities to learn about food services. (Refer to p. 254.)

Question #1 *What are the occupations within food services?*

Activity. *Visit a restaurant and conduct other research to find the many different jobs people are doing.*

Basic. (For young and/or less experienced.) Find those who are:
    cooking (chef)
    bringing food (waitress)
    taking money (cashier)

Advanced. (For older and/or more experienced.) Define roles observed or perceived:
    waitress
    salad worker
    bus person
    dishwasher
    pot and pan washer
    assistant cook
    hostess
    cashier
    chef or cook
    maintenance person
    bookkeeper or accountant
    manager
    grounds keeper
    parking lot attendant
    legal counselor
    insurance broker

Compare kinds of jobs in different kinds of restaurants: i.e., 24-hour coffee shop, short order, family restaurant, cafeteria, and specialty restaurants. Explore vocabulary or jargon related to a job family.

Question #2 *Who works in these occupations (jobs)?*

Activity. Find what kinds of backgrounds and preparation workers in different jobs must have.

Basic.
Ask the workers how they learned to do their job.
Ask what they liked to do best in the job.
Ask what they liked to do least in the job.

Advanced.
Ask the workers to state what qualifications they perceive to be the most important for their job.
Compare qualifications of service personnel in different kinds of restaurants.

Question #3 *What is the life-style of food service personnel?*

Activity. Find how the type of job and job schedule affect the lives of the workers, or how their life-styles influence job selection.

Basic.
Compare the days of week the students go to school and the days waitress/waiter goes to work. Compare hours of work schedule and time student spends in school.

Advanced.
Interview one employee and ask questions about how their work affects the way they live.
Ask what influenced their job selection.

Question #4 *Where are the jobs?*

Activity. Study how to find jobs.

Basic.
Ask a working parent how he or she found his job.

Advanced.
Study employment application forms.
Study newspaper ads for jobs available.
Practice job seeking skills such as responding in interviews, defining capabilities, discussing disability openly, and setting nondisabled at ease.

Question #5 *How do workers accomplish their jobs?*

Activity. Describe or demonstrate what each person does as part of the job.

Basic.
Role play taking part as a customer, waitress or waiter, and cashier.

Advanced.
Watch any one restaurant worker and list all the activities and skills demonstrated.
List activities not seen but assumed to be part of the job.

After older students study what specific jobs entail, they are anxious to try some of the jobs. To further assess abilities and interests, students need opportunity to try simulated or actual jobs. Cooperation among school resources and other community agencies is necessary to arrange formal or informal on-the-job experience. Specific jobs are tried to obtain first-hand knowledge of job duties, the physical demands they impose, the physical capacities they require, the climate of the work situation, the emotional strains and stresses inherent in the job, the personality traits of the employer and the supervisory staff, the production standards, and the methods by which they have been established.

Provide Transition from School to Other Community Resources

It is important for you to provide transition from the students' use of school-sponsored resources to the students' use of other community resources. It is critical to locate and collaborate with community resources to insure job placement or continual vocational rehabilitation programming when appropriate. Collaboration of school and community agencies can begin while students are still in school. For more effective rehabilitation, initial stages of rehabilitation plans and practices can be developed and implemented as part of high school or college curriculum.

The State Department of Vocational Rehabilitation, state employment service, and sheltered workshops help accomplish goals of employment or vocational rehabilitation. These agencies specialize in the training and placing of the disabled. They help place some graduates in jobs in the competitive labor market. For those graduates not yet ready for unconditional competitive employment, there are special vocational rehabilitation programs.

There are five major programs of service provided in some comprehensive rehabilitation centers, hospital rehabilitation centers, sheltered workshops, and other such rehabilitative facilities. They are work evaluation, work adjustment, work experience, vocational skills training, and On-The-Job Training programs.[2] Students can become involved in these programs before or after graduation.

The *work evaluation* program is an exploratory evaluation process to provide reliable performance information which can help the counselor and client establish practical, mutually acceptable, realistic vocational goals. (See Figure 12–5.) The *work adjustment* programs are "treatment services" designed to help disabled individuals develop work readiness skills through understanding, accepting, and/or modifying attitudes and behaviors that interfere with securing and keeping a job. The *work experience* program is generally reserved for clients who have had work training or previous work exposure but need a temporary sheltered situation in which to 'brush up' on previously learned skills and to prepare for

Figure 12–5. Evaluators made a plastic jig to help Suzie. Her head swings constantly. She is deaf and can only control her little finger. Now she competes with others using her finger to count screws and to lift a piece of the jig to pour screws for packaging.

re-entry into the competitive labor market. They may need some time to work up to the stress and demands of a competitive work situation. *Vocational Skills Training* is a program for clients who want to develop specific, well-defined skills in a given trade, or on a specific job, which can be directly transferred to the competitive labor market in regular business or industry. If these vocational skills are learned on the job in the given industry where the individual will eventually be employed, it is referred to as *On-The-Job Training*.

Figure 12–6. Vocational skill training in truck dispatching leads to similar jobs in business and industry.

Once the primary responsibilities of vocational rehabilitation have been shifted from the schools to other community agencies, teachers can continue to be supportive and serve as a resource to those other community agencies. You can best help students by providing them with the opportunity to attain the fullest physical, mental, social, vocational and economic usefulness of which they are capable in their formative years.

Considerations for Those Unable to Work

Some individuals with physical disabilities do not have the option of deciding whether or not to prepare for a vocation. Their disabilities will probably prevent their entry into sheltered or competitive work situations (Bachman, 1971; Cohen and Kohn, 1974). What is in store for the people who may wish to work but are unable to do so?

Many disabled persons who are unable to find jobs find alternative ways to develop a satisfying life-style. They develop other resources which nurture feelings of self-worth. These resources may include becoming knowledgeable about the work world, political issues, developing meaningful interests, leisure activities, and finding avenues for interacting with people.

As with many working people, the social component of an activity means as much to them as the activity itself; i.e., looking forward to going to coffee break with a friend, having lunch with the "gang," and looking forward to interactions on the bus en route to work.

In contrast to mankind's past history, modern society has more time, energy and resources to pursue goals that are non-vocational in nature. Whereas major concerns have traditionally been related to job, income and survival, man's future now appears more related to expending time and energy towards solving problems dealing with structuring leisure and improving interhuman relationships. (Brannan, 1975, p. 41)

The Gray Panthers and other active groups of senior citizens in our society are delving into the question of what heretofore has been considered nonutilitarian endeavors. They are helping to pioneer a change in the social mythology that work is the only avenue through which a person can feel and be of value. We will need to stay in touch with their feelings and translate them into the lives of people with disabilities.

We should not exclude certain individuals from curriculum study suggested in this chapter when it becomes apparent that they will have extreme difficulty finding employment. The awareness of what people do in different careers gives them another area of appreciation as well as provides them genuine interests and involvement.

Tools Toward Life Management

There are certain skills and adaptive behaviors we consider as essential tools toward life management. They are tools not only for paid work but also for accomplishment of such endeavors as school work, leisure use, home responsibilities, self-care, and other life-management activities.

Readers are encouraged to adapt the tool list at the end of this chapter for its use with individual students. For each individual, a visual record may be kept by "highlighting" in color progress toward attainment of goals. Such "highlights" can indicate goals met; color in yellow unmet goals which are current objectives; blue over the yellow changing the original coding to green as unmet goals are accomplished.

Tools for Interpersonal Effectiveness

Finds ways to notify strangers how communication is accomplished (such as a card on the wheelchair or on a lapel which says, "I do not talk but I can think and I would like to visit with you. I say no by lowering my eyes, I say yes by looking up, I indicate *I don't know, sometimes,* and *maybe* by looking to the side.").

Expresses ideas using some communication system.

Informs others what they can do to help.

Uses assistance of other persons when needed; pays when appropriate.

Uses actions of others as social cues (choice of clothing, sitting with legs together when wearing a dress).

Changes behavior in accordance with the requirements of the situation.

Contributes to discussions and conversations.

Avoids making inappropriate interruptions.

Senses when not to prolong a discussion or conversation.

Realizes when it is appropriate to lead and when to follow.

Responds to needs and feelings of others.

Copes with stares of others.

Copes with people's attempts in interpersonal interactions.

Copes with rude questions about the disability.

Copes with persons who "talk down."

Helps people understand the disability.

Copes with overly kind and overly helpful, patronizing treatment from some nondisabled persons.

Avoids trying not to "bother" persons because of unique needs and as a consequence causes more "bother" (i.e., refusing to use a wheelchair on a tour and consequently slowing down the entire group).

Offers assistance when someone else needs help.

Takes only what belongs to her (credit for work done, property that belongs to others).

Deals with fact that people have unreal and discriminating concepts of physical disabilities.

Senses social relationships.

Listens and watches on cue.

Avoids excuses for trying tasks that seem difficult.

Uses tact in notifying uncertain observers that no help is needed.

Records own progress adequately.

Works with people of different ages.

Works with people using different languages.

Works with people she dislikes.

Avoids overreaction to unexpected change (excitement, disappointment, fright).

Finds ways to avoid loneliness and boredom.

Plans ways to avoid architectural barriers.

Copes with unavoidable structural barriers.

Acts to get architectural barriers removed.

Copes with prejudice (such as refused rental privileges).

Acts to get individual rights.

Tools for Self-Care and Personal Needs

Listed are tools for self-identification, self-care, health, hygiene and safety.

Self-Identification

Identifies self to strangers using communication devices such as speaking, writing, or showing an identification card.

Communicates name, phone number, address, and identity of parent or guardian.

Obtains identification card from the Department of Motor Vehicles.

Obtains Social Security Card, work permit, and birth certificate as needed.

Self-Care

Uses gestures, words, or some other communication system to make needs or wants known.

Eats by self or elicits help from others.

Bathes self or elicits help if needed.

Sets own alarm clock or takes responsibility for getting up on time.

Decides on appropriate dress and/or elicits help in dressing if needed.

Makes preparation for lunch needs (brown bag, purchase, etc.).

Carries "emergency fund" money.

Puts personal belongings such as medication and coats and lunches in designated places.

Removes and puts on wraps and work aprons.

Uses telephone.

Takes appropriate messages.

Demonstrates ability to write checks.

Demonstrates ability to balance bank account.

Demonstrates ability to calculate wages.

Deals with appropriate social advances.

Becomes registered voter.

Takes driving test.

Uses telephone directory and telephone operators.

Finds sources of financial support.

Understands reciprocal relationship between rights and responsibilities of disabled.

Educates others about disabled persons.

Demonstrates knowledge of citizenship.

Serves as her own advocate or finds someone who can be an advocate in her behalf.

Health

Maintains health.

Takes medication.

Wears Medic Alert bracelet if recommended.

Follows special diet.

Carries instructions as to what to do in case of emergency.

Identifies symptoms of general unhealthiness (unusual disinterest in eating, irregular bowels, etc.).

Obtains periodical medical checkups (teeth, eyes).

Treats colds.

Avoids exposing others to communicable sickness.

Dresses as weather dictates.

Develops habits of sanitation.

Practices good nutrition habits.

Hygiene

Uses tissues when necessary.

Covers mouth when coughing or sneezing.

Controls drool or absorbs it.

Keeps body, teeth, and nails clean.

Eliminates unpleasant body and breath odor.

Keeps hair neat and clean.

Keeps clothing neat and clean.

Safety

Avoids injury to self and others.

Regards rules and regulations.

Safely connects and disconnects electrical units and appliances.

Acts carefully around dangerous equipment and materials.

Reports injuries or emergencies to others.

Finds ways of carrying keys, identification card, and money to allow easy self-access and prevent loss.

Tools in Minimum Academic Knowledge

Academic knowledge includes language, reading, math, and writing skills.

Language

Answers *yes, no, I don't know, sometimes,* or *maybe.*

Knows all the simple verbal commands ("no," "stop," "start now," "do this").

Follows one verbal, written, gestural, or graphic instruction.

Discriminates "same" and "different".

Points to objects named.

Follows two written, verbal, gestural, or graphic directions.

Follows directions, *do this, right, left, up, down, front, back.*

Follows three or more verbal, written, gestural, or graphic instructions.

Reading

Learns at least by rote memory, reading needed for designated tasks [*insert, push, pull, top, bottom, L* (eft), *R* (ight)].

Turns dials and knobs to appropriate locations.

Recognizes important words in one's environment—*Exit, Men, Women, Out, In.*

Math

Makes items the same length/width/volume as a model.

Counts out or matches amounts demonstrated by a model.

Recognizes or matches color.

Recognizes or matches shape.

Recognizes or matches items where properties are combined (long–red, short–blue).

Matches numbers or marks (number *3* written on one part indicates it fits where there is a *3* on another part).

Writing

Writes some identifying marks for a personal signature.

Marks tallies.

Copies identifying information on tags or slips (number and type of product).

Tools for Good Work Habits

Listens, watches, and follows instructions.

Indicates receipt of the message or instruction.

Imitates one process or one model that is being demonstrated.

Repeats newly taught tasks without directions.

Accepts suggestions and attempts to follow them.

Stops work when error is identified.

Corrects mistakes or asks for help.

Completes a task and checks for error, checking quality of work against a model.

Finishes one task and moves to the next.

Can work alone.

Can work next to others.

Can ignore distractions.

Can change from one activity to another when appropriate.

Follows a daily schedule.

Phones or otherwise notifies concerned persons of sickness or delay.

Reduces or eliminates mannerisms (rocking while sitting, frequent yawning, profanity).

Copes with frustration if task completion is difficult.

Tolerates changes (in routines, composition of the group, schedules, etc.).

Gets materials ready.

Puts materials away.

Uses equipment and tools appropriately.

Begins work task as scheduled.

Returns to work station promptly after breaks and lunch periods.

Finishes work task and cleans up as scheduled.

Resists excessive socializing during scheduled work periods.

Transfers previously learned skills to new tasks.

Works at steady pace.

Maintains quality of work under pressure.

Maintains equipment.

Assembles equipment and materials for task.

Tools for Self-Reliance in Transportation and Mobility

Travels to and from school, work, or recreation with no help, with a volunteer, or with paid help.

Pays for transportation when appropriate.

Finds way when lost (uses I.D. card).

Provides directions where to be taken.

Asks for help when needed.

Acquaints self with city map.

Finds information about routes, schedules, and fares.

Asks for geographic directions.

Uses names of street intersections as landmarks.

Locates buildings using odd and even sequences of numbers.

Reverses routes traveled.

Reads a sketched map.

Uses buildings and other landmarks.

Crosses the street both where traffic is controlled and where there is no traffic control.

Arrives on time.

Moves in pedestrian traffic.

Able to direct attendant.

Estimates distances and time.

Follows directions to other destinations.

Able to drive own car.

Transfers betwen seating arrangements if necessary (from wheelchair to chair at work station).

Transfers between transportation vehicles (from car to wheelchair, from walker to crutches).

Moves from place to place in large areas.

Moves from place to place in small or narrow area.

Transfers between standing and sitting if possible.

Moves forward and backwards.

Moves around corners.

Moves to needed areas of a building (restrooms, cafeteria, work area on the third floor).

Avoids bumping into objects (doors, furniture, etc.).

Leans at different angles if necessary.

Stands at different angles if necessary.

Uses safety rules while operating rehabilitation vehicles (sets brakes of wheelchair, hooks seat belt, moves at safe speeds).

Assists physically those who are helping whenever possible (bears some weight while attendants assist with bathrooming).

Provides descriptions of how persons can help.

Expresses appreciation.

Tools for Selecting Work

Matches interpersonal skills with those required for different work situations.

Participates in formal and informal screening of interests and skills.

Investigates and selects from alternatives those which are most feasible.

Seeks advice about realistic goals and objectives.

Determines what task components can be accomplished with little or no training, which can be learned and which might be accomplished with special adaptations, procedures, materials, or rehabilitation equipment.

Finds information about potential work (jobs, leisure-time activities, school tasks).

Finds a contact person and pursues the desired work.

Completes job applications and sets up interviews.

Describes own limitations and assets during interview.

Compares own competency to those needed by obtaining information about specific job demands during interview.

Finds information about job as appropriate, i.e., duties, hours, location, pay and pay period, benefits, tools required, type of dress, architectural barriers.

Speaks openly about disability and set nondisabled person at ease.

Tools to Adapt a Working Environment

Positioning to Accommodate a Disability

Attains most appropriate posture and position from which to work.

Attains positions to carry out body movements needed for task completion (needs to sit, stand, reach, lift, carry, grasp, pinch, pull, push, bend, turn).

Attains positions which accommodate limited range of motion.

Attains positions which reduce excessive movements and maximize hand, arm, shoulder, and head control.

Uses strategies to accommodate muscular weakness.

Specifies special requirements that are needed for physical comfort at work, i.e., measurements for places to:

    sit in (chair)
    sit under (desk)
    move through (door)
    hold onto (rail)
    move on top of (ramp)

Assistive Equipment and Materials

Supplies own special equipment and physical adaptations whenever possible.

Describes or helps define features for other assistive devices and other special equipment to help with work.

Conserves energy if necessary and initiates solutions to solve problems about adaptations needed.

Recommends architectural changes.

Maneuvers up and down inclines using rehabilitation equipment if it is necessary.

Maneuvers stairs and curbs using rehabilitation equipment if needed (i.e., wheelchair, crutches).

Summons elevators, enters, operates, and exits from elevators.

Working toward attainment of *at least* these life-management tools can make a positive difference when disabled individuals experience great varieties of work activities.

Summary

Successful implementation of the ideas and suggestions in this chapter is closely correlated with your competency in use of effective communication skills such as those described by Gordon [3] (1970, 1974). Degree of effectiveness depends upon degree of your ability to listen to the feelings of others and to send clear authentic messages concerning your own feelings; and your degree of effectiveness depends upon your ability and willingness to search for mutually acceptable solutions to problems and conflicts. It is sometimes perplexing to know how and when to best help those we most want to help. It takes sensitive caring and carefully developed communication skills for teachers and others to be able to remain helpful without imposing their own wills or projecting their own value systems onto the decisions of the disabled students.

Notes

1. Adapted from Kokaska, "Career Awareness for the Handicapped in the Elementary Schools." From a study supported by a grant from the California State University, Long Beach Foundation, and presented at the Leadership Training Institute on Career Education. Refer to The Special Student. Iowa Department of Public Instruction, Des Moines, September 26, 1974.

2. "The Magic of Goodwill." 1972–1973 Biennial Report. Goodwill Industries of Southern California, Los Angeles.

3. "Active Listening," "I Messages," and "Mutual Problem Solving" are communication techniques described in Gordon's *Parent Effectiveness Training* (1970) and *Teacher Effectiveness Training* (1974).

References

Bachmann, W. *Influence of selected variables upon economic adaption of orthopedically handicapped and other health impaired*. Unpublished doctoral dissertation, University of the Pacific, 1971.

Brannan, S. A. Trends and issues in leisure education for the handicapped through community education. In E. Fairchild & L. N. Neal (Eds.), *Common-unity in the community: A forward-looking program of recreation and leisure services for the handicapped*. Eugene, Ore.: Center for Leisure Studies, University of Oregon, 1975.

Cohen, P., & Kohn, J. G. Follow-up study of patients with cerebral palsy. Paper presented in part at the Annual Meeting of the Academy for Cerebral Palsy, Denver, Colorado, Nov. 20, 1974.

Goldhammer, K., & Taylor, R. E. *Career education perspective and promise*. Columbus, Ohio: Charles E. Merrill, 1972.

Gordon, Thomas, *Parent effectiveness training*. New York: Peter H. Wyden, 1970.

Gordon, Thomas. *Teacher effectiveness training*. New York: Peter H. Wyden, 1974.

Kokaska, C. Career awareness for the handicapped in the elementary schools. From a study supported by a grant from the California State University, Long Beach Foundation and presented at Leadership Training Institute on Career Education: The Special Student. Iowa Department of Public Instruction, Des Moines, September 26, 1974.

Laurie, G. A compendium of employment experiences of 101 quadriplegics. *Rehabilitation Gazette*, 1975, *18*, 2–23.

Life experience program: An alternative approach in special education. San Jose, Ca.: Office of the Santa Clara County Superintendent of Schools, 1976.

"The magic of Goodwill." 1972–1973 Biennial Report. Goodwill Industries of Southern California, Los Angeles.

Occupational outlook handbook (Bureau of Labor Statistics, U.S. Department of Labor Bulletin No. 1875). Washington, D.C.: U.S. Government Printing Office, 1976–77.

Occupational Outlook Quarterly, U.S. Department of Labor, Washington, D.C.

Payne, J., Mercer, C. D., & Epstein, M. H. *Education and rehabilitation techniques*. New York: Behavioral Publications, 1974.

Stivers, S. N. "Re-orienting the task of education." *The Professional Reviewer* (Idaho State University), 1969, *7*(3), 3–6.

U.S. Department of Labor, Bureau of Labor Statistics. "Career education: What's job clustering all about?" *Occupational Outlook Quarterly*, 1973, *17*(4), 16–19.

Resources

Angel, J. L. *Employment opportunities for the handicapped*. New York: Simon and Schuster, 1969.

Arthur, J. K. *Employment for the handicapped: A guide for the disabled, their families and their counselors*. Nashville, Tenn.: Abingdon, 1967.

Bond, F. W., Lash, E. R., & Reynolds, R., Jr. *Career education: Vocational-technical series: Automotive*.

Galien, Mich.: Allied Education Council Distribution Center, 1972.

Brayman, S. J., Kirby, T. F., Misenheimer, A. M., & Short, M. J. "Comprehensive occupational therapy evaluation scale." *The American Journal of Occupational Therapy,* 1976, *30*(2), 94–100.

Brolin, D. *Vocational preparation of retarded citizens.* Columbus, Ohio: Charles E. Merrill, 1976.

Browning, P. L. *Mental retardation rehabilitation and counseling.* Springfield, Ill.: Charles C Thomas, 1974.

Careers for the homebound. Free Pamphlet. (Available from The President's Commission on Employment of the Handicapped. Washington, D.C. 20210.)

Career Related Instruction (CRI). Capital Area Career Center, 611 Hagadorn Road, Mason, MI 48854.

Daniels, L. K. (Ed.). *Vocational rehabilitation of the mentally retarded.* Springfield, Ill.: Charles C Thomas, 1974.

Directory of Accredited Private Home Study Schools. National Home Study Council, 1601 Eighteenth St. N. W., Washington, D. C. 20009.

Freeland, K. *High school work study program for the retarded.* Springifeld, Ill.: Charles C Thomas, 1969.

Geist, H. *The Geist picture interest inventory.* Los Angeles, Ca.: Western Psychological Services, 1971.

Gibson, M. B. *The Family Circle book of careers at home.* Chicago: Cowles Book, 1971.

Gold, M. *Try another way. Task analysis. Content & process. Formats for single pieces of learning.* 1976. (Films) (Available from Film Productions of Indianapolis, 128 E. 36th St., Indianapolis, Ind. 46205.)

Goldstein, H. *Social learning curriculum.* Kit. Columbus, Ohio: Charles E. Merrill, 1974.

Governor's Committees on Employment of the Handicapped, local Governor's office.

Hardy, R., & Cull, J. *Severe disabilities: Social and rehabilitation approaches.* Springfield, Ill.: Charles C Thomas, 1974.

Hayt, K., Pinson, N., Laramoro, D., & Mangum, G. *Career education and the elementary school teacher.* Salt Lake City, Utah: Olympus, 1973.

International Rehabilitation Review. International Society for Rehabilitation, 122 East 23rd St., New York, N.Y. 10010.

Jastak, J., & Jastak, S. *Wide Range Interest Opinion Test* (Nonverbal). Wilmington, Del.: Guidance Association of Delaware, 1970–1972.

JEVS Work Sample System. Kit. Philadelphia, Pa.: Jewish Employment and Vocational Service.

Job seeking skills reference manual. Minneapolis Rehabilitation Center, 1900 Chicago Ave., Minneapolis, Minn.

Journal of Rehabilitation. National Rehabilitation Association, 1522 K St. N.W., Washington, D.C. 20005.

Kingsley, R. F., & Kokaska, C. Economic competency: Implications for programs for the educable mentally retarded. *Middle School Journal,* 1975, *6*(1), 17–20.

Kokaska, C. J., Lazar, A. L., & Schmidt, A. Vocational preparation at the elementary level. *Teaching Exceptional Children,* 1970, *2*(2) 63–66.

Lorton, M. B. *Workjobs: Activity-centered learning for early childhood education.* Menlo Park, Ca.: Addison-Wesley, 1972.

Lorton, M. B. *Workjobs—For parents.* Menlo Park, Ca.: Addison-Wesley, 1975.

Payne, J. S., Mercer, C. D., & Epstein, M. H. *Education and rehabilitation technique.* New York: Behavioral Publications, 1974.

Performance. The President's Committee on Employment of the Handicapped, Washington, D.C. 20210.

President's Committee on Employment of the Handicapped, Washington, D.C. 20210.

Rehabilitation Literature. National Easter Seal Society for Crippled Children and Adults, 2023 W. Ogden Ave., Chicago, Ill. 60612.

Rehabilitation Record. U.S. Government Printing Office, Washington, D.C.

Sax, A. Innovations in vocational evaluation and work adjustment. *Vocational Evaluation and Work Adjustment Bulletin,* 1975, *8*(2), 59–63.

SBA Business Loans. Pamphlet. (Available from U.S. Small Business Administration, Washington, D.C. 20416.)

SBA Publications. Pamphlet. (Available from U.S. Small Business Administration, Washington, D.C. 20416.)

Turkel, S. *Working: People talk about what they do all day and how they feel about what they do.* New York: Pantheon, 1974.

Viscardi, H., Jr. *Give us the tools.* New York: Paul S. Eriksson, 1963.

Wernick, W. *Teaching for career development in the elementary school: A life-centered approach.* Worthington, Ohio: Charles A. Jones, 1973.

13

Advocacy

Parents or other intercessors find themselves with the responsibility of "advocacy" from the time a child's disability is recognized. They find themselves searching for ways to protect the interests and welfare of individual, or groups of, disabled children. Some remain in this role throughout a child's life if a child needs life-long protective supervision. Some parents can eventually transfer some responsibility to their disabled children. Teachers can help by teaching responsibilities to disabled students for finding "representation, protection, assistance, and/or advice regarding (their) rights, interests, and service needs" (Addison 1976, p. 9). All citizens should learn to recognize inconveniences, discriminations, and needs experienced by disabled persons; and, as citizen advocates, join them in pursuit of their rights and interests.

The content of this chapter is intended to:

1. Generate ideas for actions by disabled persons or by citizen advocates.
2. Provide resources to suggest to parents and others so they can generate, locate, and use resources needed for pursuit of rights and interests of disabled students.
3. Encourage the teaching of advocacy to disabled students.

When persons with disabilities leave school, they encounter many more problems than anticipated. During the elementary and secondary school years, physically disabled students are the focus of a wide range of services and activities. They have been able to depend upon others for help with their physical needs. Sympathetic teachers, therapists, and fellow students have made an effort to understand and help if they have a communication problem. They have received physical and occupational therapy. The physical plant has been constructed for use by those on crutches and in wheelchairs. They have been transported to and from school.

Physically disabled *graduates* and their advocates face additional challenges like those caused by special transportation needs, architectural barriers, rehabilitation needs, and the need for personal care: How can I find transportation to go places? How can we get our town to put in curb cuts? How does a disabled person apply for social

June Bigge.

263

security benefits? How can I get someone to come into my home to help me? How do I pay for an apartment and an attendant? What laws exist about discrimination and the disabled? What can I do if I find discriminatory practices?

We must help disabled individuals and their advocates develop skills in finding and obtaining help. They need to learn ways to get help that is available and to generate help that is not yet available. This chapter suggests ways able-bodied citizens and those citizens with physical disabilities can act to obtain help with:

1. general procedures for citizen action
2. architectural barriers
3. housing
4. transportation
5. exemptions, benefits, and social services
6. education
7. vocational training and employment
8. long-term care
9. civil rights and legal action

Practices pertaining to any citizen action in behalf of persons with physical disability include:

1. Find state *rules and regulations* and *local ordinances*. Address requests to:
   State Capital
   Legislative Billroom
   Requests can include the number of the bill, the popular name title, or subject area description.
2. Find any existing federal laws that pertain to specific problems. Address requests for copies of federal laws to:
   a. House or Senate Document Room
      U.S. Capitol
      Washington, D.C. 20510
      Requests must be in writing and include the Public Law number, popular name title, or subject area description.
   b. Any U.S. representative's office.
   c. Any law library.
   d. President's Committee on Employment of the Handicapped
   e. President's Committee on Mental Retardation
3. Communicate views to Congressional senators or representatives:
   When You Write to Washington: A Guide for Citizen Action Including Congressional Directory (annual publication).
   League of Women Voters of the United States
   1730 M. Street, N.W.
   Washington, D.C. 20036
4. Write your own proposed legislation and submit it.
5. Find ways to initiate legal action. Find lawyers and organizations that will handle legal rights/problems of persons with handicaps.
6. Join with other disability advocacy groups to form coalitions for action (to pass new legislation or lobby for increased appropriations).
7. Refer to the resource list at the conclusion of this chapter.

8. Use the following suggestions and resources as guideline for citizen action.

Architectural Barriers

1. Find content of existing federal laws on accessibility of buildings constructed or leased with federal funds; discrepancies can be reported to:
    a. Attorney General's Office Washington, D.C.
    b. Sections 501 and 502 of the Rehabilitation Act of 1973.
    c. Office or agency specified in the enforcing provision of the specific law.
2. Find content of federal laws on curb cuts and ramps:
    Director, Office of Highway Safety
    Department of Transportation
    Federal Highway Administration
    Washington, D.C. 20590
3. Locate national specifications ensuring that buildings and facilities are accessible to and functional for persons with physical disabilities. Send requests to:
    President's Committee on Employment of the Handicapped
    Washington, D.C. 20210.
4. Find content of state laws on accessibility of buildings and facilities; look up the state Administrative Procedure Act and building codes.
5. Develop awareness of legislation or need for legislation requiring state architects to conform in areas of construction not covered by federal legislation.
6. Insure that builders and developers are aware of the national and state specifications for designing buildings and facilities which are accessible to and usable by the physically disabled.
7. Register complaints about lack of compliance with the architectural barrier acts:
    a. Architectural and Transportation Barriers Compliance Board
    Switzer Building
    Washington, D.C. 20201
    b. Local human rights agencies
    c. Civil rights councils
8. Find policy and procedures regarding accessibility of polling places and use of absentee ballots for disabled persons.
9. Find procedures which individuals and interest groups can use to identify and eliminate architectural barriers.
10. Join organizations, interested groups and individuals forming organizations dedicated to eliminating barriers.
11. Obtain information on uses of the "international symbol of access for the disabled." (See Figure 7–13 in the chapter on self-care.)

Housing

1. Find content of Federal laws on housing and the disabled:
    a. President's Committee on Employment of the Handicapped
    Washington, D.C. 20210
    b. National Center for Law and the Handicapped, Inc.
    1235 North Eddy Street
    South Bend, Indiana 46617
2. Find content of legislation enacted by Congress to provide builders of housing complexes with incentives for providing housing for disabled persons:
    Office of the Assistant to the Secretary of HUD
    Programs for the Elderly and Handicapped
    Washington, D.C. 20410
3. Find content of Federal legislation providing rent supplement payments to physically disabled:
    Office of the Assistant to the Secretary of HUD
    Programs for the Elderly & Handicapped
    Washington, D.C. 20410.
4. Investigate inclusion or lack of inclusion of persons with physical disabilities within the protection of the Fair Housing Law and practices in the state.
5. Locate forms for evaluating accessibility of buildings and learn how to compare their specifications to actual features of the buildings. (See Figure 13–1, p. 266.)
6. Explore a variety of sources of information on barrier-free interior and exterior systems in housing.
7. Explore with others the pooling of Supplemental Security Income (SSI) in order to finance housing.
8. Explore alternatives for housing for disabled, i.e., using mobile homes for wheelchair living, remodeling homes, or building new homes of barrier-free design. (See Laurie and Laurie [1976] for a complete summary.)

Building undergoing evaluation: _____

Evaluator: _____   Date of Evaluation: ____/____/_____

day   month   year

Elevators (in apartment houses)

Are the corridor call buttons 122 cm above the floor? _____ If not, how high? _____ cm.

Does the elevator door provide a clear opening of 85 cm? _____ If no, how wide? _____ cm.

Does the elevator door remain open at least 10 seconds?_____

Is/Are the elevator door(s) equipped with safety edge and electric eye? _____

Is/Are the cab floor area(s) 1.86M^2 or more? _____

Is the height of the highest cab control or emergency button or switch no more than 122 cm above the cab floor? _____ Are braille equivalents adjacent to each? _____

Is there audible *and* visual indication of cab position? _____ If no, what? _____

Is there a unique indication of cab arrival at a level which provides egress from the building for handicappers? _____

Are there handrails 90 cm above the cab floor on each cab wall that is w/o doors? _____

Are floor landing braille indicators on both outer door jambs 150 cm above floor? _____

Figure 13–1. Factors affecting ingress/egress. Adapted from A Layperson's Guide on Building Evaluation.[1]

Transportation

1. Find content of laws enacted by Congress concerning mobility of the disabled:
   a. Urban Mass Transportation Act of 1964 as amended in 1970.
   b. Highways Assistance Act of 1973
   c. Department of Transportation
2. Clarify which congressional laws involve policy only and which have mandatory provisions.
   a. Department of Transportation
      Office of Environmental Affairs
      Washington, D.C. 20590
   b. Rules and regulations
      Federal Register
      National Archives and Record Service
      General Services Administration
      Washington, D.C. 20408
3. Suggest to local authorities possible programs for adapting already established transportation systems to the needs of the disabled or provide a system that deals primarily with the disabled.
4. Obtain information about inter- and intrastate transportation systems, policies, and practices for serving physically disabled persons.
5. Obtain information about local transportation system policy on accessibility of public transportation for persons in wheelchairs, as well as those disabled who are ambulatory.
6. Obtain information about future plans for use of specially designed buses for the disabled, i.e., Transbus and Dial-a-Ride.
   Local Urban Mass Transit Authority
7. Determine taxi company willingness to accommodate persons needing different equipment and different degrees of help.
8. Obtain information on disabled driver's license plates from the State Department of Motor Vehicles.
9. Obtain information about hand-control devices and other adaptations which allow disabled persons to drive safely.
10. Obtain information about local and international travel. An example is the airlines Wings on Wheels programs. Check each resource in the "Transportation Resources" list at the end of this chapter.
11. Work to overcome discriminatory regulations (Federal Aviation Administration [FAA]).
12. Locate individuals and agencies which volunteer to transport disabled persons, such as local chapters of American National Red Cross and local leagues for the handicapped.

Exemptions, Benefits, and Social Services

Tax Benefits and Exemptions

1. Find kinds of income tax deductions allowable for the disabled; i.e., for an attendant, maintenance, and use of personal rehabilitation hardware.
2. Find information on exemption for blindness.
3. Exercise fully the medical deduction.

Business Benefits

1. Find ways disabled persons can be financially assisted in establishing, acquiring, or operating a small business.
2. Find ways employers are assisted when they employ disabled persons.
   Small Business Administration: Handicapped Assistance Loans
   The Washington District Office
   1030 15th Street, N.W.
   Washington, D.C. 20417

Social Security Benefits and Supplemental Security Income

1. Find information about all social security benefits (including titles 19 and 20) to handicapped children from your local Social Security Administration (SSA).
2. Find information about benefits to widowed or divorced parents of disabled children from SSA.
3. Find information about the supplemental security income (SSI) for disabled children from SSA.
4. Distinguish the differences between social security benefits, and supplemental security income from SSA.
5. Determine eligibility for services from the state vocational rehabilitation agency from SSA.
6. Determine eligibility for Medicare.
7. Find procedures for appeal for a redetermination of benefits:
   Bureau of Hearings and Appeals
   Social Security Administration
   Washington, D.C. 20203

Education

1. Analyze the Education of All Handicapped Children Act (PL 94–142, November 29, 1975) a major federal commitment to insure that all disabled children receive full and appropriate educational programs and services.
   a. For a copy of the law PL 94–142, write to:
      Superintendent of Documents
      U.S. Government Printing Office
      Washington, D.C. 20402
   b. For other information, write for:
      Your Rights Under the Education for All Handicapped Children Act, prepared by the Children's Defense Fund, 1520 New Hampshire Ave., N.W., Washington, D.C. 20036.
2. Help school districts develop plans to provide full and appropriate educational programs and services to all handicapped children and thus meet conditions for eligibility for financial assistance from PL 94–142.
3. Find what federal laws are already in existence and take advantage of them; i.e., Rehabilitation Act of 1973 (PL 93–112) Section 504; 1974 Education Amendments to the Elementary and Secondary Act (PL 93–380).
4. Obtain statement of state policy and practices regarding education of individuals with physical disabilities from:
   a. state superintendent of public instruction
   b. State Department of Education
5. Obtain statements from the local boards of education describing local comprehensive plans for education of individuals with exceptional needs.
6. Obtain statement from local boards of education describing due process procedures which insure that parents, and when appropriate, students, are involved in decisions about educational placement of their children.
7. Find educational options available for students with special needs such as private schools, and regular classes.
8. Obtain statement about student rights from local boards of education.
9. Determine the student's legal rights regarding transportation, placement in state institutions or other residential care facilities, and education.
10. Identify sources for legal advice and representation for *right to education* programs and check prior lawsuits.

Vocational Training and Employment

1. Find content, regulation, and implication of the Rehabilitation Act of 1973 and other fed-

eral legislation relating to employment of the handicapped.

   a. (Rehabilitation Act of 1973, Section 503)
      Office of Federal Contract
        Compliance Programs
      U.S. Department of Labor
      Third and Constitution Ave, N.W.
      Washington, D.C. 20210
   b. (Rehabilitation Act of 1973, Section 504)
      Office of Civil Rights
      Department of Health, Education, and Welfare
      Washington, D.C. 20201
   c. *Federal Register*

2. Find content of federal guidelines and programs regarding vocational rehabilitation services and training.
    Rehabilitation Services Administration
    Office of Human Development
    Department of Health, Education and Welfare
    Washington, D.C. 20201

3. Find criteria for eligibility for state vocational rehabilitative services from the state's Department of Vocational Rehabilitation.

4. Question whether a disabled person is receiving the maximum amount of services and optimum benefits from programs offered by state vocational rehabilitation agencies.
   a. local Vocational Rehabilitation Office
   b. state Developmental Disabilities Council

5. Insist upon a written reason for denial of state vocational rehabilitation services and an annual review.
    Rehabilitation Services Administration
    Office of Human Development
    Department of Health, Education, and Welfare
    Washington, D.C. 20201

6. Obtain description of state legislation prohibiting discrimination in hiring or promotion because of physical disability:
    State Fair Employment Commission

7. Identify sources of help when discriminatory practices in employment are experienced.

8. Obtain information about requirements for employers to alter premises in order to make them safe for physically disabled employees.

9. Obtain information about requirements for employers to modify or substitute examinations substantially equivalent to usual examinations.

10. Find how employers might be encouraged to hire and promote handicapped workers.

Refer to articles circulated by the President's Committee on Employment of the Handicapped.

11. Assure that disabled workers are not forced to accept exemptions from workmen's compensation and minimum wage laws.

12. Seek employment in sheltered workshops, self-employment, and other competitive employment.

13. Check required affirmative action programs for federal contractors.

Long-term Care

1. Find information about alternatives to home care for disabled individuals, i.e., foster homes, modified motels, low-cost housing for elderly and disabled, nursing homes, and other facilities.

2. Find information about ways to help families keep severely disabled individuals at home.

3. Identify alternative plans for life-long protective supervision of disabled persons who may need it.

4. Identify sources of daytime activities for persons needing long-term care.

5. Locate sources of information on daytime programming for severely disabled persons not in school.
   a. United Cerebral Palsy Association Affiliates (UCPA)
   b. Association for Retarded Citizens
   c. Day care and development centers
   d. Societies for crippled children and adults

Civil Rights and Legal Action

1. Find how barriers can be removed through civil rights and legal action.

2. Study ways civil rights are protected and procedures for securing individual rights.

3. Find what legal assistance projects, funded by the Office of Economic Opportunity, are available in your community.

4. Find procedures for obtaining other professional legal assistance.

5. Report evidences of discrimination against persons on the basis of disability—housing, insurance, entrance to public places.

6. Find legal alternatives to protect those disabled children who reach legal age but are not considered legally competent.
    Office of Civil Rights
    Department of Health, Education, and Welfare

Office of New Programs
Washington, D.C. 20201

7. Involve yourself with state committees who are responsible for planning and implementing the Developmentally Disabled Assistance and Bill of Rights Act (PL 94–103).

8. Seek all rights specified in all sections of the Rehabilitation Act of 1973 (PL 93–112 as amended by PL 93–516).

Summary

Like other young adults, those with physical disabilities need to be independent, make friends, to be as self-supportive as possible, to contribute to society, and to lead meaningful lives. The extent to which they will be able to achieve these goals from infancy may depend upon . . .

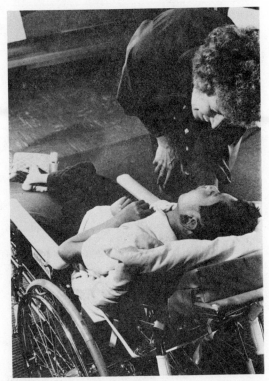

. . . intercessors who will serve as advocates in their behalf

. . . or their abilities to serve as their own advocates.

Notes

1. Slightly adapted from a portion of "A Layperson's Guide on Building Evaluation" furnished with permission of the compiler, Eric A. Gentil, Office of Special Program, Environmental Design Studies, Michigan State University, Lansing, Michigan, 1975.

References

General

Addison, M. R. Citizen advocacy. *Amicus,* 1976, *1*(4), 9–10.

A handbook on the legal rights of handicapped people. President's Committee on Employment of the Handicapped, Washington, D.C. 20210.

Biklen, D. *Let our children go: A organizing manual for advocates and parents.* Syracuse Human Policy Press, 1974.

When You Write to Washington. Pamphlet. (Available from 1730 M Street, N.W. Washington D.C. 20036.)

Architectural Barriers

Architectural and Transportation Barriers Compliance Board. Switzer Building, Washington, D.C. 20201.

Department of Transportation, Federal Highway Administration. Washington, D.C. 20590.

Gentil, E. A. A layperson's guide on building evaluation. Lansing, Michigan: Office of Special Programs, Environmental Studies, Michigan State University, 1975.

Housing

Fink, C.,Manus, M. & Manus, G. *Housing for disabled persons: Annotated bibliography.* New York: United Cerebral Palsy Association, 1975.

Frey, L. *Transportation and housing for the handicapped.* Washington D.C.: House Republican Research Committee Report, December 4, 1975.

Laurie, G. & Laurie, J. *Housing and home services for the disabled.* Hagerstown, Md.: Harper & Row, 1976.

State of Michigan. Building Evaluation Form. (Available from the Michigan State Department of Labor Construction Code Commission, Lansing, Michigan 48926.)

Transportation

A barrier-free environment for the elderly and the handicapped. United States Congress. Senate, Special Committee on Aging. Hearing, 92nd Congress, 1st session. Washington D.C.: U.S. Government Printing Office, 1972, 3 vol. in 1, p. 207.

California Paralyzed Veterans Association. Drawings of ramps, parking, telephones, rest room. (Available from M.N. Spencer, 6331 Reubens Drive, Huntington Beach, Calif. 92647.)

First Report of the Architectural and Transportation Barriers Compliance Board to the Congress of the United States, 1974. (Available from Architectural and Transportation Barriers Compliance Board, Room 1004 Switzer Building, 330 C Street S.W. Washington D.C. 20201.)

Frey, L. (Chairman.) House Republican Research Committee Report: Transportation and Housing for

the Handicapped. Washington D.C.: U.S. Government Printing Office, Dec. 4, 1975.

National League of Cities. Department of Urban Studies. Washington D.C. 20006.

The National Easter Seal Society for Crippled Children and Adults. Chicago, Illinois.

Raggio, J. J., Lipman, B. G. Gilhool, T. K., & Wolf, E. D. *The disabled & the elderly: Equal access to public transportation.* Washington,D.C. 20210. The President's Committee on Employment of the Handicapped, 1975.

Williams, R. A. L. *Barrier free design graphics.* Southfield, Mich.: Lawrence Institute of Technology.

Exemptions, Benefits, and Social Services

NWRO supplemental security income advocates handbook, 1975. Center on Social Welfare Policy and Law, 24 West 43rd St., New York, N.Y. 10036.

Education

How to look at your state's plan for educating handicapped children. (Available from The Children's Defense Fund, 1520 New Hampshire Ave. N.W., Washington, D.C. 20036.)

Public Law 94–142, Nov. 29, 1975. House Document Room, U.S. Capital Washington, D.C. 20510.

Vocational Training and Employment

Angel, J. L. *Employment Opportunities for the Handicapped.* New York: World Trade Academy Press, 1969.

Long-term Care

Helsel, E. Long term care services for the developmentally disabled. In R. Gettings (Ed.), *Synergism for the seventies.* Conference proceedings of the national conference for state planning and advisory councils on services and facilities for the developmentally disabled, 1972, pp. 343–361.

Civil Rights and Legal Actions

Abeson, A., Hass, N., Hass, J. *A primer on due process: Education decisions for handicapped children.* Reston, Va.: The Council for Exceptional Children, 1975.

Resources

General

Architectural and Transportation Barriers Compliance Board. Switzer Building, Washington, D.C. 20201.

Achtenberg, J. 'Crips' unite to enforce symbolic laws: Legal aid for the disabled: An overview. *University of San Fernando Valley Law Review,* 1975, 4(2) 161–213.

American Coalition of Citizens with Disabilities (ACCD). 346 Connecticut Ave N.W., Washington, D.C. 20036.

American Institute of Architects. Washington, D.C. 20006.

Child advocacy project: Rights handbook for physically handicapped children. Boston, Mass.: Easter Seal Society for Crippled Children and Adults of Mass. and National Easter Seal Society for Crippled Children and Adults, April 1974.

Congressional records of summaries of passage of public laws.

The Council for Exceptional Children Publications. 1920 Association Drive, Reston, Virginia 22091.

Department of Health, Education, and Welfare, Office for Handicapped Individuals, 330 Independence Avenue S.W. Washington, D.C. 20201.

Department of Transportation, Federal Highway Administration, Washington, D.C. 20590.

Department of Transportation. Directory of Organizations Interested in the Handicapped. (Available from Committee for the Handicapped, People and People Program. Connecticut Ave and L Street, Washington, D.C. 20036.)

Fact Sheets on Income Deductions & Others. (Available from Coordinating Council for Handicapped Children, Chicago, Illinois 60605.)

Gailes, A., & Susman, K. Abroad in the land: Legal strategies to effectuate the rights of the physically disabled. *The Georgetown Law Journal,* 1973, *61*(6), 1501–1523.

Governor's Committee on Employment of the Handicapped. State government of each state.

Lassen, P. L. *Barrier free design: A selected bibliography.* Washington, D.C.: Paralyzed Veterans of America, 1973.

Local offices of social services agencies.

National social services agencies such as Muscular Dystrophy Association and United Cerebral Palsy Association.

President's Committee on Employment of the Handicapped. Washington, D.C. 20210.

Publications of the Social and Rehabilitation Service. Office of Public Affairs, Social and Rehabilitation Service. Dept. of Health, Education and Welfare, Washington, D.C. 20201.

State senators and representatives. State House of appropriate state.

U.S. Government Printing Office, Washington, D.C. 20402.

Architectural Barriers

American Institute of Architects. Washington, D.C. 20006.

Attorney General's Office. Washington, D.C.

First report of the architectural and transportation barriers compliance board to the Congress of the United States. Washington, D.C.: Architectural and Transportation Barriers Compliance Board, 1974.

Lassen, P. L. *Barrier free design: A selected bibliography.* Washington, D.C.: Paralyzed Veterans of America, 1973.

National League of Cities. Department of Urban Studies, Washington, D.C. 20006.

National Easter Seal Society for Crippled Children and Adults. Chicago, Ill.

Housing

Department of Housing and Urban Development, 751 7th St. S.W., Washington, D.C. 20410.

National League of Cities, Department of Urban Studies, 1620 Eye St. N.W., Washington, D.C. 20006.

Office of the Assistant ot the Secretary of HUD Programs for the Elderly and Handicapped. Washington, D.C.

U.S. Department on Housing and Urban Development. *HUD Challenge.* 1975, *VI* (3). Special issue on the handicapped. (Available from Superintendent of Documents, Government Printing Office, Washington, D.C. 20402.)

Transportation

American Automobile Association

American National and Local Red Cross

Civil Aeronautics Board (CAB) in Washington, D.C.

Federal Aviation Administration, 800 Independence Ave. S.W., Washington, D.C.

Urban Mass Transportation Administration of the Department of Transportation, 400 7th St. S.W., Washington, D.C. 20590.

Exemptions, Benefits, and Social Services

Department of the Treasury

Internal Revenue Service

Social Security Administration, Washington, D.C.

Small Business Administration, The Washington District Office, 1030 15th St. N.W., Washington, D.C. 20417.

Education

Abeson, A., Bolick N., & Hass, J. *A primer on due process: Education decisions for handicapped children.* Reston, Va.: The Council for Exceptional Children, 1976.

County boards of education.

Department of Health, Education, and Welfare, Rehabilitation Services Administration, Office of Human Development. 330 Independence Ave. S.W., Washington, D.C. 20201.

Deputy Commissioner for Education of the Handicapped, Office of Education, Bureau of Education for the Handicapped, 400 Maryland Ave. S.W., Washington, D.C. 20201.

National and local rehabilitation association.

Rehabilitation Services Administration, Department of Health, Education, and Welfare, Office of Human

Development, 330 Independence Ave. S.W., Washington, D.C. 20201.

State boards of education.

The Governor's Committees on Employment of the Handicapped. Local governor's office.

The President's Committee on Employment of the Handicapped. Washington, D.C. 20210.

U.S. Department of Health, Education, and Welfare. Social and Rehabilitation Service. Washington, D.C. 20201.

Your school records: Questions and answers about a new set of rights for parents and students. 1975. (Available from The Children's Defense Fund, 1520 New Hampshire Ave. N.W. Washington D.C. 20036.)

Vocational Training and Employment

American Rehabilitation Foundation.

Angel, J. L. *Employment opportunities for the handicapped.* New York: World Trade Academy, 1969.

Audiovisual aids directory of the rehabilitation research and training centers. Washington, D.C. 20201.

Research directory of the rehabilitation research and training centers: Fiscal year 1974. (Available from Social and Rehabilitation Services, Rehabilitation Services Administration. Washington, D.C. 20201.)

Long-term Care

Local social services agencies. United Cerebral Palsy Association .

Civil Rights and Legal Actions

Amicus. Free publication. (Available from the National Center for Law and the Handicapped Inc., 1235 N. Eddy Street, South Bend, Indiana 46617.)

Closer look. (Available from the National Information Center for the Handicapped, Box 1492, Washington, D.C. 20013.)

Office of Civil Rights, Department of Health, Education and Welfare. Office of New Programs, Washington, D.C. 20201.

INDEX